D1409110

# REVIEW
# OF
# RESEARCH

**CONTRIBUTORS**

ALFREDO J. ARTILES
WILLIAM E. BLANTON
JACQUELYNNE S. ECCLES
CAROL SUE ENGLERT
KENNETH A. FRANK
JAMES PAUL GEE
JUDITH L. GREEN
GARY MOORMAN
M. C. O'CONNOR
DAVID N. PERKINS
DANIEL RODRIGUEZ
GAVRIEL SALOMON
TIMOTHY SHANAHAN
WOODROW TRATHEN
STANLEY C. TRENT
ALLAN WIGFIELD

# IN EDUCATION

# 23     1998

**P. DAVID PEARSON**
MICHIGAN STATE UNIVERSITY
**ASHGAR IRAN-NEJAD**
UNIVERSITY OF ALABAMA
EDITORS

PUBLISHED BY THE
AMERICAN EDUCATIONAL RESEARCH ASSOCATION
1230 Seventeenth Street, NW
Washington, DC 20036-3078

# Contents

# Introduction

When our advisory board met in September of 1996 to develop an outline and structure for the 1998 volume of the *Review of Research in Education*, we did what boards like this must have done over the years—we brainstormed topics and issues that deserved a place between the covers of the latest volume of *RRE*. We grounded our brainstorming activity in three ways. First we looked to the past by considering an analysis of topics covered in the first 20 odd volumes of *RRE* and the last 10 years of the *Review of Educational Research*, trying our best to uncover themes and issues that we had unintentionally obscured over the years. Second, we looked to the future: Mindful of the dawn of a new century, we asked ourselves which issues and questions our profession ought to be addressing as we move into that new century. Third, we looked to the present and asked ourselves which topics were so important at this point in our history that we could not help but give them voice. At the end of the first day of our meeting, we had filled up some 15–20 large sheets of chart paper with deserving topics and issues, enough literally for a decade's worth of *RRE* volumes. So much to know, so little space!

As we looked across the topics, however, some themes began to emerge. For example, we were sure that issues of special education had not been given full voice, but what was especially interesting about special education were competing views about how teaching and learning ought to be organized in our schools and classrooms. It was the social aspect of how the learning of special students was organized that intrigued us. And we knew it was time for technology to be re-examined, but again what we found interesting about technology were the explicit and implicit social relations that are involved in technology-centered learning, especially in asynchronous learning contexts. We knew that tutoring was gathering enough momentum, especially in early literacy programs, to deserve a full review, but what had not been adequately addressed was the social face of tutoring—the interactions between tutor and student. We also knew that motivation deserved to be covered again, but we wanted a reading of the literature that emphasized motivation in the contexts of schooling, where social aspects would be dominant. We had also committed ourselves to at least two chapters on methodology, one which would enhance our quantitative tools and a second which would enhance our qualitative tools. And we were excited as we persuaded ourselves that we would be able include methodological chapters related to the overall theme of the volume.

By this point in the conversation, on the morning of day two of our meeting, that theme was pretty clear to us. It would be the social organization of learning, and we would address several important topics through that broad lens. What remained was to sketch out the lead chapters, the chapters that would speak most directly to learning. We needed at least two. One, we thought, ought to place social accounts of learning within the broader sweep of general learning theories; among other things, it ought to speak to the tension and the synergy between individual and social views of learning. The second, we thought, ought to take a more critical view; it ought to address the question of whether our accounts of learning were any better, more thoughtful, more consistent, or more useful because we had adopted this social lens. At this point, near the end of our meeting, we felt as though we had the makings of a useful, thematically organized volume that would speak to a broad spectrum of the AERA membership. We spent the rest of the meeting considering who could write and who could serve as consulting editors for each chapter. And that is pretty much the story behind our volume. Although each chapter has taken on the character of its author(s), the basic theme and chapter organization have not changed much since its inception.

Our volume begins with a chapter by Gavriel Solomon and David Perkins on the "Social and Individual Aspects of Learning." Solomon and Perkins did just what we wanted them to do—they contextualized social views of learning within a broader context, they created an infrastructure for a range of social views, and they discussed how the social and the individual aspects of learning complement one another. Next comes a chapter by M. C. O'Connor that asks the question, "Can We Trace the Efficacy of Social Constructivism?" We had asked Cathy to examine the use of social constructivist views of learning as they had been applied in subject matter learning (e.g., math, science, social studies, or literacy) and to determine whether they had influenced how we think about those curricula, what students learn, or how students perform.

In Chapter 3, the lens shifts as Alan Wigfield, Jacquelynne Eccles, and Daniel Rodriguez offer us a detailed account of motivation in the social learning context we call school. In Chapters 4 and 5, we have our pair of methodological chapters. First, Jim Gee and Judith Green take us on a tour of the tools, grounded in rich examples, that are used by qualitative researchers (mainly discourse analysis and ethnography) to address learning in social contexts. Then, Ken Frank offers us two quantitative tools for consideration: (a) multilevel models that permits us to examine influences on curriculum, learning, and performance across social settings (e.g., district, school, classroom, and grouping), and (b) Social Network Analysis, a tool that allows us to examine how social networks of friendships, working relationships, and interaction evolve in settings such as classrooms, workplaces, and the like.

In Chapters 6–8, we address three more specific topics that differ from the previous topics in that they could have been addressed without the social lens. Nonetheless, we feel that the social lens provides us all with a particular, and we think eminently useful, reading of the literature in each of these domains. In Chapter 6, Tim Shanahan reviews the literature on tutoring, with a special focus on recent efforts to use tutoring to enhance the literacy skills of youngsters who are at risk of failure in our schools. In Chapter 7, William Blanton, Gary Moorman, and Woodrow Trathen examine the use of electronic tools to create social spaces for learning, with a special focus on their use in teacher learning networks. Finally, in

Chapter 8, Stanley Trent, Alfredo Artiles, and Carol Sue Englert take a critical look at our changing views of special education, both in theory and in practice, from the perspective of social learning theory.

In the final analysis, the value of this volume rests with you as readers. Those of us who were involved in this effort—conceptualizing it, writing it, reviewing it, editing it, and revising it—benefitted greatly from the experience. In many ways, because so many of us were involved in each and every chapter, it was a social learning activity! We hope that those who pick up this volume will enjoy and benefit from reading in the same measure as we have benefitted from creating it.

*P. David Pearson*
*Ashgar Iran-Nejad*
Editors

# Chapter 1

# Individual and Social Aspects of Learning

GAVRIEL SALOMON
Haifa University

DAVID N. PERKINS
Harvard Graduate School of Education

Social learning is in the air. Daily observations and experiences as well as recent scholarly traditions suggest that a certain amount of learning takes place beyond the confines of the individual mind. Learning appears to involve social aspects. Scenarios ranging from a group of children collaboratively trying to solve the question of how to construct a kite to a university professor writing a research paper with a colleague advance the case for a social side to learning.

But impressions do not make social learning an obvious category. Are there any theoretical and empirical grounds to justify social learning as a distinctive phenomenon? Is there anything qualitatively different in this kind of learning to distinguish it from the familiar individual conception of learning? Can one make the case that social learning is more than an epiphenomenon or individual learning multiplied, that the social aspects of learning are anything more than the kind of secondary help a learner might get from audiovisual displays, bookmarks, and road signs?

If we can raise the question of whether social learning is a valid and viable phenomenon, the opposite question might equally well be raised: Is it not possible that solo learning is simply a figment of the traditional laboratory-based psychology, on the one hand, and of a socially shared respect for the individual qua individual, on the other? The idea of social learning is not really new, having been an important part of early developments of the science of psychology ("folkspsychology," as formulated, for example, by Munsterberg [1914, cited in Cole & Engestrom, 1993]). This branch of psychology fell into neglect because of its Gestalt-like nature and thus its alleged lack of rigor, its central phenomena left to anthropology and sociology to handle. It was distinguished from the more rigorous laboratory-based, experimentally oriented, and far more prestigious psychology of Ebbinghouse. Social learning has thus continued to be largely ignored by psychologists over the years, relegated at best to the study of background context, not really on a par with the learning of the individual (Gardner, 1985).

This relative neglect now appears to have been corrected. With the growing interest in Vygotsky's theory, retrospective examinations of the role of social inter-

---

We wish to thank the reviewers of this chapter, Stellan Ohlsson and Orlando Lourenço, for their valuable comments and suggestions. Some of the ideas discussed herein were developed as part of a collaboration involving David N. Perkins and the Universidad Jorge Tadeo Lozano, Santa Fe de Bogota, Colombia, on the theme of organizational learning.

1

actions in Piaget's works (DeVries, 1997; Lourenço & Machado, 1996), Bandura's (1989) reformulation of the individual in reciprocal relations with the social environment, the conception of learning as a constructive (and, hence, socially and culturally situated) process (e.g., Lave & Wenger, 1991), and newly designed empirical work, the study of individuals' learning has come to be embedded in social and cultural contexts and interactions. A focus on the individual learning in social and cultural solitude is increasingly being seen as conceptually unsatisfying and ecologically deficient. As Bronfenbrenner (1977) has pointed out, "In ecological research, the principal main effects are likely to be interactions" (p. 518), and these interactions occur, to a large extent, among an individual, his or her social surroundings, and the artifacts culture provides.

Two conceptions of learning seem to be involved here, each with its own metaphor. On one hand, we have the conception of the individual learner, emphasizing the acquisition of knowledge and cognitive skill as transferable commodities (e.g., Anderson, Reder, & Simon, 1996). On the other hand, we have the sociocultural conception of learning as a collective participatory process of active knowledge construction emphasizing context, interaction, and situatedness (e.g., Cole & Engestrom, 1993). Thus, one can speak of the "cognitive, acquisition-oriented" conception of individual learning versus the "situative, participatory" conception (e.g., Greeno, 1997; Sfard, in press).

It is fruitful to view these conceptions as two levels of analysis, each of which sometimes neglects the other. One can make an analogy with two perspectives on the spread of a flu: cell biology and epidemiology (Ohlsson, S., personal communication, June 23, 1997; Sperber, 1984). Clearly, the two complement each other: Subverted cellular mechanisms figure in the invasion of individual cells by viruses, but the viruses have to arrive at individual cells to infect them. Although each process can be understood in its own right, understanding the interplay yields a richer and conceptually more satisfying picture.

Something similar might be said of learning: It takes place in individuals' minds, and, as we elaborate later, it takes place as a social, participatory process, offering two distinctively different perspectives on learning. While each of these perspectives is often treated independently of the other, our aim here is to examine their interrelationships, not as two separate logical categories but as two perspectives on the phenomena of learning. Thus, while children often practice arithmetic or climbing trees alone, "individual" learning is rarely truly individual; it almost always entails some social mediation, even if not immediately apparent. Likewise, the learning of social entities (e.g., teams) entails some learning on the part of participating individuals. It is such variations in kind and balance that we mean to examine.

Specifically, our goals in this chapter are as follows. First, we want to clarify the distinctive meanings of the notion of social learning vis-à-vis individual learning. Second, against that backdrop, we want to examine the possibility that social learning, in its various senses, is a distinctive and important way of looking at learning. Finally, with both the "acquisition" and the "participation" metaphors in view, we want to suggest ways in which individual and social aspects of learning interrelate and interact in synergistic ways.

## A MAP OF THE TERRITORY

Teasing the varied meanings of social learning apart and illuminating their nature is a daunting endeavor. To make the mission easier, we adopt a loose but unifying information-processing perspective on learning within which different views of learning can be described, compared, and contrasted. As used here, the idea of information processing includes no biasing presumptions about where those processes lie or what entity they serve (e.g., Hutchins, 1996; Perkins, 1993). The information processes in question might occur within the mind of an individual or within complex webs of social interaction. The entity learning might be an individual or a social entity such as a team, a corporation, a loose group of individuals, or even a society. In any case, information is being processed, and learning and forgetting occur in the sense that lasting changes resulting from the processing—whether "in" the individual or "in" a social entity—can be identified.

From the standpoint of information processing, learning for individuals or collectives is a considerable challenge. The learning entity in question, whether a person trying to skate better or a loose society of individuals trying to get along with one another, must be able to construct a repertoire of new representations or behaviors based on prior experience. It must have the opportunity to test and select among alternative representations or behaviors, or refine one or combine them. It will need feedback of some sort, from internal or external sources, about how well an alternative fares. It can benefit greatly from information sources—anything from a text to the incidental or deliberate modeling provided by another wiser agent performing the activity in question—as well as guidance through self-regulation or provided by others. To learn, it will need to face an approachable but manageable level of challenge, not too hard to cope with but not so easy as to yield completely to the existing repertoire. The learning entity will also need conditions that sustain motivation and energy. And so on.

In other words, learning by any entity in any setting has what might be called critical conditions. Such conditions figure not only in the logical story of how learning can come about but in the practical story of ensuring that it does come about. Often learning fails not for subtle reasons, such as the learner missing the point, but for gross reasons, such as the lack of a source to provide an important point.

With such general challenges in mind, it is useful to speak of a learning system as an information-processing system aimed at facilitating these critical conditions for the learning entity in question. Thus, simple trial-and-error learning of an individual organism through reinforcement is one kind of learning system, with certain ways of dealing with such critical conditions as generating alternatives (by accidentally varying behaviors) and selecting alternatives (through reinforcement). Learning that involves deeper understanding aided by peers in a collaborative setting is yet another kind of learning system, in which alternatives are provided by different team members and the selection of the best one is a matter of detailed deliberations and agreements.

The ideas of critical conditions for learning, on the one hand, and learning systems designed to facilitate those conditions, on the other, provide a backdrop for addressing the question posed earlier: What are the distinctive meanings of social learning? We distinguish six meanings for the sake of conceptual clarity. In later sections, we elaborate further on the first four as more concerned with the dynamics of learning.

1. *Active social mediation of individual learning.* In human society, one of the

most fundamentally social forms of learning is that in which a person or a team helps an individual to learn. A teacher teaches reading, writing, and arithmetic; parents correct a child's ungrammatical utterances or misuse of words on the fly; a master takes on apprentices and guides their development; children work together to master algebra problems, each learning from the other. In such cases, the facilitating agent and the primary learner form a joint learning system, the former helping the latter to achieve critical conditions of learning. For instance, the agent may provide information in the form of instruction or demonstrations, informative feedback about what is right or wrong and what to do instead, approachable but challenging tasks, encouragement, scaffolding of the learner's performance as it unfolds with tips and hints, and so on.

The exact forms taken by such learning systems vary, of course: A skilled individual tutor can tune the learning system much more finely to a particular individual than a classroom teacher can to a room full of individuals (Lepper, Aspinwall, Mumme, & Chabay, 1990; Lepper, Drake, & O'Donnell-Johnson, 1997). A team studying together can elaborate on a member's attempts to solve something the individual could not do on his or her own (Damon, 1984; Slavin, 1994). But such differences aside, the broad idea is the same: to create a better learning system for the primary learner by bringing in a facilitating social agent to help meet the critical conditions of learning.

Loosely speaking, socially mediated individual learning might be considered the same as instruction, and the point no more than that instruction inevitably involves a certain amount of social mediation. But far more is at stake than this. Instruction, in its prototypical forms (involving lecturing or question-and-answer sessions), may be considered a special case—albeit not a very interesting one—of social learning. However, as a learning system, it often does not meet the critical conditions of learning very well. And, when regular instruction is, in fact, effective, the processes involved may not be very socially mediated (as, for instance, when skilled students learn effectively from lectures because of their own autoregulation skills, but rarely from each other).

*2. Social mediation as participatory knowledge construction.* In the version of active social mediation sketched so far, there is a clear distinction between individuals and the learning products they carry away as their transferable cognitive possession, on the one hand, and the social agents facilitating that learning, on the other. But there is a second version of social mediation that deserves recognition: the sociocultural version, which sees learning less as the socially facilitated acquisition of knowledge and skill and more as a matter of participation in a social process of knowledge construction (e.g., Cole, 1995; Greeno, 1997). Although the illustrative phenomena are the same—individual tutoring, team problem solving, collaborative and cooperative learning, and so on—the way they are understood in this second version of active social mediation is very different. Social mediation of learning and the individual involved are seen as an integrated and highly situated system in which the interaction serves as the socially shared vehicles of thought. Accordingly, the learning products of this system, jointly constructed as they are, are distributed over the entire social system rather than possessed by the participating individual.

3. *Social mediation by cultural scaffolding*. Even when a learner does not receive direct help from another agent actively adjusting to the learner's needs—the first case of social mediation mentioned earlier—the learner may enter into some kind of intellectual partnership or at least be greatly helped by cultural artifacts in the form of tools and information sources. Such artifacts can range from books and videotapes that tacitly embody shared cultural understandings (Perkins, 1986) to statistical tools and socially shared symbol systems embodying, for instance, a "language of thinking" that includes such finely distinguished terms as *hypothesis, conjecture, theory,* and *guess* (e.g., Gigerenzer, 1991; Tishman & Perkins, 1997). Artifacts are themselves culturally and historically situated, carrying the wisdom and hidden assumptions that went into their design. Thus, they form a learning system with the learner, reorganizing action and determining what can be carried out (along with when, where, in what form, and for what purpose) (e.g., Cole, 1995).

4. *The social entity as a learning system*. Another very different meaning of social learning occurs when people speak of learning involving teams, organizations, cultures, or other collectives (e.g., Argyris, 1993; Argyris & Schon, 1996; Huber, 1989; Levitt & March, 1988; Senge, 1990). Here it is not necessarily the case that one agent is helping another to learn. Rather, the focus falls on a collective agency that, as a collective, acquires more knowledge, understanding, or skill, or a different climate or culture. A sports team attains patterns of coordination among the individuals that might be quite useless for any of the team members functioning alone. A business organization develops internal procedures, based on commonly held tacit assumptions, that meet customer demands more efficiently and more quickly. In such cases, the agreements need not be stated, and the procedures are not executed (and perhaps not even overseen) by any one individual, but they advance the performance of the organization. In summary, the group constitutes a collective learning system, a system that will function better or worse as a learner depending on how well its structures address critical conditions of learning.

5. *Learning to be a social learner*. Still another sense of social learning concerns a special case of learning: learning to learn. Contemporary cognitive science recognizes that learning to learn is a fundamental aspect of learning (e.g., Chipman, Segal, & Glaser, 1985; O'Neil & Spielberger, 1979; Perkins, 1995; Pressley & Brainerd, 1985; Segal, Chipman, & Glaser, 1985). Youngsters acquire knowledge, understanding, and skill not only in particular areas (e.g., language use, soccer, or algebra) but about learning itself. For instance, the field of "metamemory" concerns children's developing understanding of their own memories and how to manage memory (Pressley & Brainerd, 1985). Of course, all of this applies to the learner functioning individually. However, an important dimension of learning to learn involves learning to learn in ways that participate in and capitalize on the social milieu. One simple aspect is learning when and how to ask questions or to ask for help. Another is learning how to enter into reciprocal learning relationships ("I'll help you with this if you help me with that, or we will both help one another with this particularly difficult idea"). Here, the individual learner's learning system

extends its capacity to deal with the critical conditions of learning by acquiring new ways to capitalize on the social surroundings.

6. *Learning social content.* The foregoing categories all concern social factors in the service of learning. Attention to certain of these is the principal purpose of this chapter. Solely for the sake of logical completeness, another possible meaning of social learning needs to be acknowledged: the learning of social content. Social content includes such matters as how to get along with others, how to maintain reasonable assertiveness, how to collaborate in reaching decisions and taking collective actions, and so on. This sense of social learning is quite different from those considered previously. To speak of the learning of social content is not to introduce any new way of understanding learning systems, as the other perspectives have done. Here the learning system would be one of those already discussed, operating on social content.

With six meanings of social learning in view, the first four provide the natural focus for development. All four deal with what might be called the dynamics of learning, in contrast with the last two, which deal more with what is learned. The first, social mediation by an active agent (*social mediation* for short), reflects a range of major figures and lines of inquiry in such areas as cognitive development; tutoring; peer tutoring; collaborative, cooperative, and reciprocal learning; and more. The second involves a major stream of contemporary thinking that emphasizes participatory learning and "distributed, situated cognition." The third deals with the mediating role that tools and cultural artifacts, embodying accumulated social wisdom, play in the process of learning. And the fourth reflects a tide of interest in team and organizational learning sustained by practical interests in the worlds of business, government, and sports and by the inquiries of psychologists, sociologists, and anthropologists into the workings of collectives of various kinds and sizes.

## FOUR PERSPECTIVES

With these four perspectives and the ideas of critical conditions and learning systems at hand to organize the analysis, we take a close look at the social mediation of learning in the next section, followed by discussions of participatory learning, mediation through cultural tools, and, finally, the learning of collective entities.

### The Social Mediation of Individual Learning

The simplest and most familiar modes of social mediation are configurations of one to one (tutor, parent, or teacher to learner), one to many (teacher to a group), and many to one (a pair, trio, or other group of collaborative learners with the learner as a participant). In all of these cases, the interactions between the learner and the "other(s)" are expected, and often found, to enhance the individual's learning. Two distinguishable entities are involved in the learning system: the learner and the "other," entities sometimes in complementary relations (as, for example, when a knowledgeable adult tutors a remedial student) (Lepper et al., 1990, 1997) and sometimes in more symmetrical relations (as, for example, when classroom peers work well together, each facilitating the individual learning of the other) (Slavin, 1994).

How does this version of social mediation work, and what does it yield? When does the social context facilitate learning, and when does it fail to do so? The theoretical underpinnings of the socially mediated learning of the individual were greatly influenced by Vygotsky's conception of the zone of proximal development. According to this conception, external social processes become internalized to serve in a mental capacity, thereby raising the level of individuals' cognitive performance to one they could not have reached on their own (Vygotsky, 1978). Whether directly inspired by Vygotskian thinking or by more current constructivist sources, social "scaffolding" (Scardamalia, Bereiter, McLean, Swallow, & Woodruff, 1989) entails two critical processes: internalization and active construction of knowledge in the form of active solutions to problems or formulation of designs, with the help of explicit guidance, modeling, encouragement, mirroring, and feedback (e.g., Brown & Palincsar, 1989; Perkins, 1991; Slavin, 1994).

The importance of active, constructive participation is underscored by an interesting difference between tutoring and peer problem solving. Whereas adult tutors aim to facilitate the learning of their tutees, peers working together often aim simply to accomplish the task. Consequently, the individual learner often has more of a chance to participate actively in critical planning and decision making when interacting with an expert tutor than with peers (Rogoff, 1991). This highlights an important aspect of social mediation of individuals' learning: Mediation is effective not necessarily as a function of simple "internalization, with modeled information being transferred across a barrier from a social partner to the inside of a child, or with information being transmitted" (Rogoff, 1991, p. 362). Rather, mediation is effective through active participation whereby learners "transform their understanding and skill in solving the problem" (Rogoff, 1991, p. 362). Thus, according to this view, it is active construction that is so crucial to learning, not some social guidance going underground. It becomes clear why social learning and a constructivist approach to learning have become close allies (Resnick, 1991).

Lepper and his colleagues emphasize this theme in their analyses of expert tutors, who routinely attain impressive progress in mathematics with remedial, failure-prone, and math-phobic students within a single session (Lepper et al., 1990, 1997). Many of the features that distinguish such expert tutors from their less effective colleagues are those that characterize social facilitation of individuals' learning in general: intensive interaction, rapid feedback, highly personalized and situationally contingent guidance, encouragement, and the elicitation of responses from the student in the form of explanations, suggestions, reflections, and considerations rather than the provision of ready-made information, directions, error corrections, or answers. Effective social facilitation through teamwork, although it occurs less reliably, appears to share the same characteristics.

As these points make plain, this perspective on social learning involves the critical conditions for an effective learning system mentioned earlier. Most important, social mediation of learning by tutors or peers, when well conducted, can meet these conditions far more effectively than its solo learning alternative. In fact, some of the conditions we have mentioned are, by necessity, socially based and cannot be easily met by most learners without the facilitating social context: informative feedback, challenge, guidance, and encouragement.

There are further characteristics that distinguish socially mediated learning from relatively solitary learning to the advantage of the former. One such condition involves the "objectivization" of one's thoughts, still-to-be-formulated ideas, and considerations, which, when communicated and shared, can be discussed, examined, and elaborated upon as if they were external objects. Objectivization of this sort is quite impossible outside the social context. Slavin (1994) pointed to two additional conditions necessary for social mediation to be effective: shared group goals and personal accountability. In his review of the research literature, he found that, in their absence, no significant enhancement of learning takes place; members of the learning system may work in incongruent directions and may not expend the needed mental effort (for other factors that debilitate social facilitation, see O'Donnell & O'Kelly, 1994; Salomon & Globerson, 1987).

## Social Mediation as Participatory Knowledge Construction

The account of social mediation reviewed so far has two features that some would view with suspicion. First, the notion that cognitive processes can be socially mediated suggests that these same processes, under the right conditions, might proceed without such mediation. Second, by and large the focus has fallen on the learner's learning, without a recognition that the facilitating social agent also may learn.

These concerns have led to a different conceptualization of social mediation influenced by the more qualitative, holistic way of anthropological thinking; the neo-Vygotskian sociocultural school of thought; and a sharp critique of typical laboratory learning studies as too removed from the social context of real life. Especially motivating are systematic findings about the nonsystematicity of human performance, so highly dependent on particular cultural and social situations (e.g., Lave & Wenger, 1991). Such factors led to the development of a new paradigm for the study of learning in social contexts (e.g., Lave, 1988; Resnick, 1991; Wertsch, Del Rio, & Alvarez, 1995). According to Wertsch (1991), the basic assumption of this sociocultural paradigm is as follows:

Human mental functioning is inherently situated in social interactional, cultural, institutional, and historical context. Such a tenet contrasts with approaches that assume, implicitly or explicitly, that it is possible to examine mental processes such as thinking or memory independently of the sociocultural setting in which individuals and groups function. (p. 86)

Given the relative novelty of the sociocultural approach, much of its vocabulary and many of its basic constructs are still somewhat vague; it is not easy "to refer to them as a mature scientific paradigm with generally accepted theoretical foundations, a methodology, and a well-delineated set of prescriptions for relating theory to practice" (Cole, 1995, p. 187). Nevertheless, the basic ideas are relatively clear: It becomes unreasonable to separate cognition or motivation from the socially mediating context or, for that matter, to separate individuals from their activities and the contexts in which they take place. As stated by Resnick (1991): "We seem to be in the midst of multiple efforts to merge the social and cognitive, treating them as essential aspects of one another rather than as dimly sketched background or context" (p. 3).

Indeed, new composite units of analysis have emerged for study and design. Cognitive activity, goal, social interactions, and learning materials are seen as a merged unit uniquely situated in a particular context. The base paradigm is the historical event in which events and contexts are necessarily and inevitably interwoven (Hickey, 1997). The unit of analysis is the interpsychological functional system composed of interacting individuals, situations, activities, contents, and meanings (Newman, Griffin, & Cole, 1989). According to Sfard (in press), "the identity of an individual...is a function of her being (or becoming) a part of a greater entity. Thus, talk about stand-alone learner and decontextualized learning becomes as pointless as the attempts to define lungs and muscles without a reference to the living body within which they both exist and function."

Despite these contrasts with the social mediation of individual learning, the notion of learning systems as information-processing systems that must meet critical conditions of information provision, feedback, and so on still makes sense. However, the description of a learning system changes. Knowledge, rather than being transmitted or internalized, becomes jointly constructed ("appropriated") in the sense that it is neither handed down ready-made nor constructed by individuals on their own. Rather, knowledge, understandings, and meanings gradually emerge through interaction and become distributed among those interacting rather than individually constructed or possessed (Pea, 1993). And if knowledge is distributed among participants in a specific activity context, it is necessarily situated as well (Greeno, 1997), that is, intimately welded to the context and the activity in which and by means of which it is constructed. Therefore, participation becomes the key concept (as contrasted with acquisition and conceptual change) serving as both the process and the goal of learning (Sfard, in press).

Greeno (1997) asks whether we should "consider the major goals and outcomes of learning primarily as collections of sub-skills or as successful participation in socially organized activity and the development of students' identities as learners" (p. 9). The answer to this question from a sociocultural point of view clearly favors the latter: The name of the game is participation, and it stands in stark contrast to the decontextualizable cognitive attainments of the individual (Cole, 1991; Sfard, in press), as often—and, apparently, incorrectly—attributed to Piaget (Lourenço & Machado, 1996). Whereas accounts of learning offered from Piagetian or traditional information-processing perspectives emphasize individuals' (solo) knowledge construction, often facilitated by social scaffolding, the socioculturally inspired account emphasizes the socially based participatory construction of knowledge. And whereas the former views learning and knowledge as pertaining mainly to individuals' transferable cognitive attainments, the latter sees learning more as a highly situated activity of participation (cf. Anderson, Reder, & Simon, 1996; Greeno, 1997).

These differences between the situative and cognitive approaches can perhaps best be illustrated by the differences in the instructional design implications that follow from each. In the situative approach, social knowledge construction develops distributed knowledge, skills, and understandings around the target activity system. What is acquired is rather "holistic," and the hoped-for transfer is to other similar activity systems. In the cognitive approach, social knowledge construction serves individual knowledge construction. The aim is to equip the learner with portable chunks of knowledge, skill, and understandings that can serve in other contexts.

Emphasis on the situative approach raises serious questions about what in fact should be "taught" in school, the role the subject matter disciplines should play, and what criteria for evaluation should be used. After all, if effective participation is a major criterion, what would we consider the desired learning outcomes to be? But then, of course, such questions do not seem to be congruent with the main thrust of the sociocultural approach.

We thus have two versions of the basic idea concerning social mediation of learning. The more common one (the cognitive, acquisition-oriented version) views the social system enhancing the individual's learning as individual, striving to improve mastery of knowledge and skill. The more radical version (the situative, participation-oriented version) views the individual and the social agents as a unified learning system in which learning outcomes are both situated in the particular interactive context and distributed among the participants. In a later section, we attempt to interrelate the two.

## Social Mediation by Cultural Artifacts

The role of tools and symbol systems as both reflecting and affecting the human psyche has long been recognized. But scholarly attention has focused on tools as social mediators of learning mainly as a result of the Russian sociocultural tradition of Vygotsky (e.g., 1978), Luria (1981), and Leont'ev (1981), along with their Western interpreters (e.g., Cole & Wertsch, 1996). Here we use "tools" in a broad sense, including not only physical implements but technical procedures (e.g., the algorithms of arithmetic) and symbolic resources (e.g., those of natural languages and mathematical and musical notation).

A system formed by a person or persons using tools is not usually first and foremost a learning system. It is a system for doing something else, accomplishing some task like digging a ditch or having a conversation across an ocean. Nonetheless, any such system is secondarily a learning system, and at two levels. Hutchins (1996) points out how the conduct of an activity also characteristically involves development of the practitioners and development of the practice. The combination of persons and tools creates a new cognitive entity with an enriched cultural legacy and extended capabilities. The person may learn to use the tool more effectively, the tool and the objects to which it is applied thereby supplying information and feedback to that end, providing important conditions of learning, and helping to teach the user about a better way of accomplishing the task through the tool. Moreover, some tools mediate learning about a wide array of other matters. They may do so simply as information sources, as in the case of books or films, functioning as vehicles for symbolic communications. But more than that, they may do so as implements of information handling, as with a student's notebook and pencil (or, today, laptop computer), a flexible platform for organizing ideas expressed in the symbolic tools of text, formula, and diagram.

Tools characteristically play a double role: as means to act upon the world and as cognitive scaffolds that facilitate such action. Some tools not only enrich one's cognition but actually transform it. Memory is just not the same once certain language structures and writing have been acquired. The same applies to acquired ways of reasoning and to socially shared theories that constrain, color, and direct one's thinking and interpretation (e.g., Wertsch et al., 1995). For example, statistical tools are said to have become psychological models for the interpretation of human conduct (e.g., the analysis of variance model serving to explain human interaction) (Gigerenzer, 1991).

The cognitive transformations triggered by tools have two sides. One side is learning effects *with* the tool. This recognizes the changed functioning and expanded capability that takes place as the user uses and becomes accustomed to particular tools. Impact occurs through the redistribution of a task's cognitive load between persons and devices (e.g., Pea, 1993; Perkins, 1993), including symbol-handling devices (e.g., a spell check), or across persons, mediated by devices and symbol systems (telephones, fax machines). As these examples suggest, such tools are all around us, but their possibility also invites the design of special-purpose tools for supporting various cognitive functions. For instance, experiments have shown that a computerized "reading partner" that provides ongoing metacognitive-like guidance improves students' comprehension of texts while they read with the tool (Salomon, Globerson, & Guterman, 1989).

In addition to effects *with*, there are effects *of* the tool. This concerns the more lasting ripple effects of using the tool beyond actual occasions of use: the impact on one's cognitive arsenal of skills, perspectives, and ways of representing the world (Salomon, Perkins, & Globerson, 1991). Thus, for example, computer-based learning environments offer students "problem spaces" in which they can work through their understandings of challenging concepts (Perkins & Unger, 1994). Students who read texts with the reading partner just mentioned have been shown to become better readers of novel, print-based texts and also better essay writers, apparently as a result of having learned to be more self-regulating (following the tool's model).

The contrast between *of* and *with* effects parallels, in some ways, the contrast between a cognitive, acquisition-oriented view of learning and a situative, participatory view. The acquisition stance emphasizes how tools can affect cognition in a relatively lasting and generalizable way even when people function in their absence. Thus, for example, Scribner and Cole (1981) studied the cognitive effects of literacy without schooling in the African tribe of the Vai, and Salomon (1994) studied the way in which elements of media symbol systems can become cognitive tools. On the other hand, as Olson, Torrance, and Hildyard (1985) have argued with respect to literacy, "It is misleading to think of literacy in terms of consequences. What matters is what people do with literacy, not what literacy does to people" (p. 15).

Thus, the "lessons" taught by tools involve not just the immediacies of changed performances while the tools are available but aspects of a culture's accumulated wisdom and intellectual history (Vygotsky, 1978). One cannot wield a screwdriver or write down an equation in a historically blank and culturally neutral way. Rather, "the history of a culture—an inherently social history—is carried into each individual act of cognition" (Resnick, 1991, p. 7). As argued by Cole and Wertsch (1996):

Higher mental functions are, by definition, culturally mediated. They involve not a direct action on the world, but an indirect action, one that takes a bit of material matter used previously and incorporates it as an aspect of action. Insofar as that matter itself has been shaped by prior human practice (e.g., it is an artifact), current action incorporates the mental work that produced the particular form of that matter. (p. 252)

A case in point is the introduction of computers into schools. Whereas computers were initially used as electronic workbooks for drill-and-practice purposes, it became apparent that, in fact, they tend to carry with them an entire educational philosophy of knowledge construction, symbol manipulation, design, exploration, and discovery (e.g., Sheingold, 1987). Although often assimilated to business-as-usual, in trend they serve as subversive instruments, their introduction promoting the restructuring of classroom learning environments, changes in teachers' ways of functioning, redefinition of curricula, and new ways of assessment.

Widely adopted tools often send certain "messages" about priorities through their presence. For instance, the ubiquitous use of the typewriter, and today keyboards and printers, signals the priority of legibility and speed over the personal touch of calligraphic style. The Macintosh interface, in contrast with the pre-Windows IBM interface, has been said to express a more human and "analog" view of how one might relate to computers. The spread of pasta machines, spell check devices, hand calculators, and computer-aided design programs sends the message that now, unlike in the past, "Everybody can do it without much learning." Learning was once required for those skills, sometimes even within a privileged guild, but no more. Such circumstances create a tension between—and sometimes heated debates about—the risks and losses of "deskilling" a practice versus the gains of convenience and accessibility.

## The Social Entity as a Learner

The core notion of the social entity as a learner is that collective entities can learn. Such entities might include families (e.g., Moll, Tapia, & Whitmore, 1993), high-performance teams (e.g., Hutchins, 1996), health organizations (e.g., Cole & Engestrom, 1993), business organizations (e.g., Argyris, 1993; Argyris & Schon, 1996; Senge, 1990), and more. Close attention to the social entity as a learner might strike some as odd in this overview of social learning with educational issues and agendas in mind. After all, the principal learners in schools are not groups but individuals, even if team-learning techniques are sometimes used. However, such a reaction mistakes both the scope of learning and that of education as developed here. Not only does a great deal of individual learning and education occur outside of schools; just as families, teams, corporations, and other organizations can be said to learn, so one can speak of educating them. Family therapy sessions or prebirth child-care sessions educate families, not just the individuals involved. Coaches and trainers educate teams of athletes. Corporate consultants concerned with organizational learning might reasonably be said to educate the corporations whose practices they improve. It is within the compass of this broad view of learning and education that the inquiry proceeds.

With this said, it is also true that the learning of social entities takes a decisive step away from the literature of earlier sections. The scholars concerned with the learning of social entities constitute, by and large, a camp of their own. A number of other shifts are notable. The social entity typically, although not always, has to learn on its own, subject to its own autoregulation. When there is a "teacher," usually the relationship is not one to many, as in a classroom, but one to one, as with a coach and team or a consultant addressing the needs of an organization. Whereas a common problem with individual learning is its desituated character, most learning of social entities is well situated. Sports teams, for example, do not study and practice for years before starting true play. Corporations do not apprentice to other corporations for years before making a go on their own. Finally, at a conceptual level, concepts such as learning, memory, models and modeling, reinforcement, trial and error, and so on need to be reinterpreted in the context of social entities.

With such differences in mind, three questions are particularly apt for a brief analysis of the learning of social entities: What is learned? How is it learned? And how can it be learned better? For all three questions, it is also important to examine whether the answers involve any distinctively social characteristics or amount to straightforward extrapolations from the case of the individual learner.

As to what is learned, Huber (1989) suggests that learning consists in knowledge, in a broad sense, acquired by any unit of an organization and available for acting upon. Superior learning lies in knowledge more widely distributed across units, with common rather than disparate interpretations. Huber, following Morgan and Ramirez (1983), writes of such knowledge as "holographic," in that each unit carries at least a rough picture of the whole.

Levitt and March (1988) advanced organizational routines as the stuff of organizational learning, including policies and practices and their underlying belief systems. By definition, acquiring new routines represents a change in overt behavior, a requirement Huber does not make. Weick (1979) pointed to emerging agreements about standard operating procedures, what is right or wrong in the organizational conduct, and the meanings to be assigned to whatever the organization does. Trying to define an orchestra, he wrote:

If we then ask where [the] orchestra is, the answer is that the orchestra is in the minds of the musicians. It exists in the minds of the musicians in the form of the variables they routinely look for and the connections they routinely infer among these variables. (p. 141)

Similarly, Argyris and Schon (1996) focus on stable changes in organizational behavior. Cole and Engestrom (1993) offer an analysis of activity systems that specifies several loci within which organizational learning can occur, such as the prevailing rules, the division of labor, the mediating artifacts (both physical and conceptual), the aims of the enterprise, and, of course, individual learners.

While some differences are apparent among such views, they are, by and large, compatible. It is also clear that all entail distributions of knowledge only partly analogous to those in the mind of an individual. We do not ordinarily consider possession of an artifact knowledge, yet possession of a database constitutes a kind of organizational knowing. Patterns of division of labor within an organization are kinds of know-how that have no easy individual analog. As noted earlier, knowledge possessed by individuals or larger units about how to coordinate with other units in a particular organization is a distinctively social kind of knowledge.

A second question was how learning occurs. Here it is useful to turn back to the notion of a learning system. One function of a learning system is generation of new representations and behaviors. Within collectives, this can certainly occur through individuals or groups evaluating current practices and goals, reflecting, and devising new plans. It can also occur through "grafting," as an organization acquires new personnel or purchases data sets (Huber, 1989). Imitation of various kinds is a commonplace mechanism of learning in groups, as in individuals. In groups, collective patterns of behavior may be imitated, such as a new division of labor pattern (Levitt & March, 1988). Productive variation may be stimulated by "organizational slack" that makes room for accidental variations and casual experiments (Levitt & March, 1988).

Feedback on old or new structures and practices commonly takes the form of assessment of performance against such distal goals as bottom-line profit and such proximal goals as people's happiness or divisional efficiencies. Comparison with the performance of other departments within an organization or other organizations can generate feedback and almost inevitably does so in competitive situations. Levitt and March (1988) argue that an organization's history wields a much more powerful selective influence than speculative feedback based on exploration of conjectural scenarios. Another source of feedback derives from comparison of current structures and practices with conceptual models promulgated by the literature and consultants.

While other aspects of a learning system could be examined, these examples of generation of alternatives and of feedback suffice to point out some characteristics of organizational learning and make the case that it involves distinctive features. Grafting, for example, has no straightforward analog in the individual learner, nor do processes of the social distribution of knowledge across various units and individuals.

If organizations can learn, this does not mean that they learn very efficiently. A strong theme in the literature on organizational learning is the weakness of the learning system involved. The learning of the collective suffers from a startling range of limitations (Argyris, 1993; Argyris & Schon, 1996; Huber, 1989; Levitt & March, 1988). Some of these limitations are equally characteristic of individual and collective learning entities. For instance, rare high-stakes events (e.g., an individual's marriage decision or major shifts of direction in a business) are difficult learning targets because they do not occur often to disambiguate the lessons of experience and because by the time they occur again, circumstances may have changed substantially.

Other problems in terms of learning are exacerbated by the specifically organizational character of the learning. For example, different individuals and units within an organization may hold somewhat different criteria of success. Also, advocates of a policy are likely to interpret any difficulties with it as reflecting an insufficiently vigorous pursuit of the policy, while opponents interpret the same data as signifying a bad policy. Feedback about the results of organizational actions may be distorted or suppressed as people rush to protect their turf or to maintain a positive climate. Argyris and Schon (1996) argue that self-sealing systems of beliefs arise in organizations because individuals behave toward one another in ways that pursue agendas while concealing them and because individuals aim unilaterally to protect both themselves and others against the distress of negative feedback. Under such circumstances, "single-loop learning" can still occur (accomplishing refinements in conduct without change in the underlying belief systems), but not "double-loop learning" (which involves making explicit and reconsidering tacit theories-in-use).

One broad systemic characteristic amplifies many of these problems: Organizational learning systems tend to take the "low road" (Salomon & Perkins, 1989). Learning occurs without any "high road" mindfulness or reflective abstraction. One or another problem is identified and a plan adopted, one or another individual gains more influence, one or another practice is reinforced as much by accidental circumstances as by any reliable consequences. Hutchins (1996) characterizes a great deal of organizational learning as more like a blind evolutionary process than deliberate design. This low road rather than high road character of organizational learning should not come as a surprise. After all, first and foremost organizations are performance systems, not learning systems.

In consequence, much of the contemporary literature on organizational learning focuses on how to make such learning function better. Broadly speaking, the aim is to introduce more of a high road learning process in which learning becomes a conscious and deliberate agenda of the organization alongside other more traditionally identified organizational functions. For example, Argyris and Schon (1996) focus on helping organizations to solve problems and take opportunities in ways that yield double-loop rather than single-loop learning. This involves helping individuals to air and test tacit assumptions publicly, avoid unilateral protection of themselves or others, and come together in collective problem-solving processes that deal with large-scale tacit issues, not just surface technical issues.

Epistemology is a strong theme in such initiatives (Argyris & Schon, 1996; Senge, 1990). Both leaders and followers in organizations tend to harbor broad impressionistic beliefs about what has happened or how to get things done that thrive on mechanisms of self-fulfilling prophecy but have at best a limited foundation in reality. Accordingly, interventions commonly foreground varieties of belief testing that look to hard data or a finer grain of informal observation.

Still another theme is that people attempting to guide organizations commonly do not understand organizational dynamics and need better mental models. Thus, interventions often try to introduce new conceptions of organizational dynamics. Senge (1990) foregrounds systemic aspects of organizational dynamics, introducing a range of "system archetypes" that capture typical but neglected patterns of interaction, such as repairs that backfire in the long run or the tragedy of the commons. Stacey (1992) emphasizes the chaotic characteristics of organizational dynamics and urges anchoring thinking in the here and now, avoiding too uniform an organizational culture, and developing a constantly evolving agenda rather than a long-term, stable vision. Argyris and Schon (1996) aspire to raise awareness of self-sealing interactions and shift an organization's models of learning toward double-loop practices that allow regular reexamination of underlying concepts and commitments as a part of problem solving and opportunity taking.

In summary, organizations, like individuals, can learn. Many of the fundamental phenomena of learning are the same for organizations. Not only the general characteristics inherent to any learning system but particular phenomena such as the troublesomeness of high-stakes rare events are common to both. However, organizational learning also has distinctive characteristics with reference to what is learned, how it is learned, and the adjustments called for to enhance learning. These characteristics derive from the fact that any organization by definition is a collective, with individuals and larger units in different roles that involve different perspectives and values, passing information through their own filters, and with noisy and loss-prone information channels connecting them.

Under such circumstances, it is hardly surprising that organizational learning would have a number of characteristic emergent features. In contrast with the mixed character of individual learning discussed earlier, the learning of social entities tends strongly to be low road and situated. "Teaching" occurs much less frequently than in the individual case. The high road of autoregulation is often virtually absent. Finally, the social entity can often be divided against itself, with different tacit beliefs and concealed agendas harbored by different subgroups or individuals. Of course, none of these phenomena are entirely absent from the individual case. For instance, one of the great lessons from Freud was that an individual mind can be divided against itself. Nonetheless, a number of contrasts in trend are conspicuous.

## HOW INDIVIDUAL AND SOCIAL LEARNING RELATE

We began by asking whether social learning is a meaningful concept, sufficiently distinct from individual learning to warrant attention. Our answer is an emphatic yes. As elaborated earlier, there is ample evidence to show that individuals' learning is facilitated by others, that meaning is often socially constructed, that tools serve as mediators, and that social systems as organic entities can engage in learning much as individuals do.

With the reality of social learning acknowledged, it is tempting to say that the tables have been turned on the notion of individual learning. Far from social learning being a questionable appendix to individual learning, individual learning itself is a suspect phenomenon. Thus, as some would argue, there is in reality no individual learning to speak of. Virtually anything one learns, according to the sociocultural view, comes deeply embedded in a cultural context, involves culturally informed and laden tools, and figures as part of a range of highly social activity systems, however alone the learner may be at particular moments.

All of this may be true enough, but dismissing the notion of individual learning altogether would be to throw out the baby with the bath water by blurring important distinctions. Individual learning is most sensibly viewed not as learning utterly naked of social contexts, influences, and participations but as learning in which the factors discussed earlier have relatively lesser rather than greater presence. Matters of degree and level of analysis are involved. Thus, the anthropologist Sperber (1984), discussing the relationships between culture and cognition, compared them with the relationships between epidemiology and cell biology. One of his main points was that epidemiology cannot be reduced to cell biology, and vice versa. Rather, each needs to be considered as an entity or process in its own right. In Sperber's spirit, we need to ask how individual and social learning relate to one another. Our answer takes the form of three propositions.

*Relation 1: Individual learning can be less or more socially mediated learning.* While almost all individual learning is social in some sense, the degree of active social mediation may vary considerably from situation to situation. The young basketball player practicing foul shots for hours alone enjoys relatively little social mediation during that period, although, of course, the activity occurs within the larger context of a highly social endeavor. The same basketball player practicing with team members and a coach functions in a highly socially mediated setting. The same point can be expressed from the perspective of situated or participatory learning. The basketball player's activities are always situated within the larger activity system of basketball, even during solo practice. But during solo practice, that larger system impinges only through the player's memories and the physical structure of the court, not through the immediate words and actions of the other players and coach.

Moreover, if at the individual end of the spectrum social factors still figure, it is likewise so that at the social end of the spectrum, in contexts of active social mediation, the learner remains—and should remain—an individual learner in significant ways. Perkins (1993), while arguing generally for the distributed character of cognition, notes that regulative functions need to be managed by the learner to some extent, or else the learner will not develop autoregulative cognitions. Learners who are constantly scaffolded in the management of their learning are less likely to develop such capacities. Bereiter (1997; Bereiter & Scardamalia, 1989) argues that some learners take the opportunity to engage in more intentional and deeper learning, above and beyond the affordances of the social situation and what it calls for. As pointed out by Damon (1991):

Even when learning is fostered through processes of social communication, individual activity and reflection still play a critical role. Sometimes...individual activity may build on collective questions and insights. Other times, however, individual activity actually may need to resist the collective illusions created by a group.... Any paradigm that assumes a one-way, deterministic relation between the collective and individual knowledge construction is overly simplistic. (p. 392)

Finally, it is worth noting that while the social end of the continuum may have been neglected in many earlier developmental, cognitive, and behaviorist studies, and important phenomena passed over, those studies proved fruitful in other ways. Many valuable insights about cognition and learning have emerged from laboratory investigations of individuals learning as individuals. For some purposes, such as the focused examination of particular learning processes of self-regulation, the detailed study of misconceptions in science, or the analysis of basic neuropsychological processes of learning, this may be a better approach than a more socially oriented one.

*Relation 2: Individuals can participate in the learning of a collective, sometimes with what is learned distributed throughout the collective more than in the mind of any one individual.* A further sense of social learning is the learning of social entities. This sense generates another relationship between individual and social learning. To return to the case of the basketball player, the individual player, even during solo practice, is not only learning in his or her own behalf but acquiring skills that strengthen the team. At moments of practicing together or planning together, the team learns collective skills such as rapid coordination, many of which cannot be reduced to the skills of any one individual but have to do with the way they work together. By hiring a star player, the team may learn through "grafting" (Huber, 1989), in which no individual involved acquires new knowledge and skill, but the team does.

Note that the learning of a team or other collective entity, like the learning of an individual, can itself be more or less mediated by social factors outside the entity. In other words, the first continuum applies to both. In the case of the basketball team, a mediating "other" might be a coach or an opposing team.

*Relation 3: Individual and social aspects of learning in both senses (Relations 1 and 2) can interact over time to strengthen one another in what might be called a "reciprocal spiral relationship."* A third answer to the question of how individual and social learning interrelate suggests that the two complement each other in a spiraling dynamic of reciprocal influences. Individual and social causes became influenced by their own consequences and, sometimes, even defined by them (Bronfenbrenner, 1977; Weick, 1979). This notion extends Sfard's (in press) suggestion that individual and social conceptions of learning be considered side by side to exploit the advantages of each and as a protection against theoretical excesses.

To sharpen the idea, let us trace a couple of these spiral reciprocities. A student experiencing difficulties with mathematics may benefit from joint problem-solving sessions with a group of peers (active social mediation of learning), with student and peers reaching, through negotiations, several understandings concerning the way they want to proceed (the social entity learning to function), which leads to a certain division of labor concerning homework to be done by each member (but with mediation by cultural artifacts such as textbooks). The student then returns the next day to the group of peers to compare notes with his or her partners and to jointly solve new and more demanding problems (further active social mediation of a different sort, with the team members having progressed in their math understanding).

In other words, the student learns through different learning systems with varying degrees of social mediation and collectivity at different moments, with their characteristic ways of providing information, generating feedback, and so forth.

For the student—indeed, for all participants—these different learning systems are symbiotic. They benefit one another. Students may learn more efficiently and thus reach a deeper understanding of the subject matter at hand, an achievement they will walk away with as their own, while the team may learn to learn better as a team through participation in such spirals (e.g., Bereiter, 1997).

A further example turns from the world of schools to the world of business. A manufacturing company's sales slump raises a general readiness for changes in the company's business practices. With such a readiness "in the air," a member of a financial planning team for the company collaborates in discussions mapping probable sales changes for the upcoming year (learning as participation), accepts the assignment of investigating the projected cost of key materials and begins by consulting a range of sources in books and on the Internet (individual learning supported by cultural artifacts), discusses questions with a professional consultant (social mediation of individual learning), and returns to the group to meld the insights gained into the collective understanding of the group. The suggested changes, now shared by the management, filter down through the organizational grapevine, triggering excitement and gradually becoming a new kind of standard operating procedure (learning of a social entity). As in the case of the student, the different learning systems with their different ways of meeting the critical conditions of learning are symbiotic. The spiral through them benefits the individual and the collective alike.

A further large-scale characteristic of individual and social learning deserves note here. It is not just that learners learn better through the reciprocities between different learning systems. More than that, the patterns of reciprocity themselves evolve; the reciprocity itself "learns," so to speak. When individuals enter a social learning situation, they take away from it not only knowledge about the topic at hand but knowledge about how to manage such situations. Likewise, the team, group, classroom, teacher, or tutor changes as well, affected by the other members of the interaction. Or consider the example of a research team. While its members enter the team's planning meeting with their own knowledge, dispositions, preferences, attitudes, and preconceived notions about the research question and methodology, the team's deliberations might well result in an agreed-upon agenda, focused questions, division of labor, and even a team's uplifting spirit. Now each member goes home and ponders the deliberations, reconsidering his or her position and way of relating to the others. One of them might, for example, take notice of the fact that another member tends to dominate the discussions and, hence, decide to introduce turn-taking procedures. Each change taking place on one occasion colors the interactions on subsequent occasions, thus allowing for developmental continuity (Damon, 1991). Hence, the reciprocal relationship is all the more a spiral one (Salomon, 1993).

Spiral reciprocity is less evident in the sociocultural approach to social learning, in which the learning system is a social system without a clear demarcation between individual learner and social agent. The argument made is that cognitions, themselves socially distributed, are inseparable from the socially based activity and from the tools used. As stated by Cobb (1997), "There is no need to equip individuals with tools or to place them in social context for the simple reason that individuals do not act apart from tools and contexts" (p. 174). However, we still think that the argument made by Damon (1991) applies here as well. Although, according to the sociocultural, participatory view, the different components of the learning system may not exist without each other (Cobb, 1997), which is the essence of being a fully integrated social system, we believe that each still retains its separate identity and attributes as an individual, as a team, or as a tool.

## IMPLICATIONS FOR THE DESIGN OF INSTRUCTION

A great deal of learning occurs without instruction. The toddler struggling to climb onto a couch, the car shopper sizing up competing vehicles, the newly formed management team getting to know one another, are all in the midst of learning, but no teacher or instructional plan shapes their learning. Broadly speaking, instruction is designed learning, learning mediated not by fortunate circumstances but by intentional design. When a parent helps the toddler just barely enough, an article advises the car shopper, a book or workshop provides the members of the management team with good initial steps to follow, then we have instruction. When the design of instruction is guided by systematic and validated principles and theories, instruction becomes a design science (Perkins, 1992).

The present analysis of individual and social learning argues that this design science needs to be conceived on a wider scale. If collectives such as teams and corporations can learn, it makes sense to speak of instructing them, of establishing carefully designed conditions that favor their learning. Instruction involves collectives as well as individual learners. Moreover, the present analysis of social learning also informs the kinds of designs that would serve best.

Earlier we emphasized that effective learning of any scope involves not one learning system but several functioning together in spirals of reciprocity. Well-designed instruction therefore involves different learning systems at different moments in synergistic interaction. Admittedly, this formula is broad. Its concrete implications become plainer when one looks to the rather impoverished spirals characteristic of many school settings, for example, the routine seesaw system between the teacher interacting didactically with many students and the lone student in front of a textbook or worksheet. Innovative instruction of virtually any sort involves a dramatic enrichment of this seesaw model with more varied and intricate spirals of reciprocity.

Another implication of the discussion is that good learning, whether individual or collective, depends greatly on self-mediation or mediation by other agents; in other words, it depends on high road (intentional, conceptually oriented) rather than low road (practice and automaticity-oriented) learning (Salomon & Perkins, 1989). Typical school settings do not offer nearly the opportunities they might for the development of self-regulated, high road learning. If anything, the problem is even more acute for the learning of large collective entities such as corporations, which characteristically have little "metacognitive" awareness of their own learning. The collective that worries about mediating its own learning and the learning of individuals within it is far more likely to learn better and foster individual learning.

Relatedly, the development of autoregulation of learning in individuals and collectives needs to include attention to the social nature of learning. It is not enough to learn to direct one's own learning as an individual learner abetted by artifacts such as textbooks. Learning to learn in an expanded sense fundamentally involves learning to learn from others, learning to learn with others, learning to draw the most from cultural artifacts other than books, learning to mediate others' learning not only for their sake but for what that will teach oneself, and learning to contribute to the learning of a collective. If the reciprocal spiral described earlier has any validity, then an individual's contribution to the learning of the collective is likely to benefit the individual as well.

If all of this seems like a celebration of the potentials of social learning, it is—up to a point. However, the dark side of such interactions also has to be recognized. What is learned by an individual may upset or even subvert rather than abet collective ends, as with the student taking advantage of his or her team members' work or the corporate climber being more interested in personal advancement than in the overall success of the organization. What is learned by the collective does not necessarily benefit the individual learners, as when a teacher forms a tacit contract with students (e.g., "I won't ask too much if you do the little I ask") or a limited conception about learning takes sufficient hold in particular populations (e.g., a team of students reaches an agreement to pretend to work but, in fact, gangs up on the teacher to do as little as possible) (Salomon & Globerson, 1987). In such cases, the collective has "learned," but what it has learned happens to be profoundly limiting both for itself and for the participating individuals.

The remedy for such pitfalls lies in the concept of instruction as designed learning. Cautionary examples such as the foregoing occur along the "low road," where the goals and processes of learning receive no autoregulative attention from the agencies involved. While haphazard learning has served the human species and many others well enough, one of our most important achievements as a species must certainly be the many "high road" ways we design learning for one another, and indeed for ourselves, individually and collectively. Recognition of the social side of learning in one sense complicates the challenge of instruction by introducing more choices to be made. But it also enriches the instructional palette with which we attempt to paint our own future selves.

## REFERENCES

Anderson, J. R., Reder, L. M., & Simon, H. A. (1996). Situated learning and education. *Educational Researcher, 25*(4), 5–11.

Argyris, C. (1993). *On organizational learning.* Cambridge, MA: Blackwell.

Argyris, C., & Schon, D. A. (1996). *Organizational learning II: Theory, method, and practice.* New York: Addison-Wesley.

Bandura, A. (1989). Human agency in social cognitive theory. *American Psychologist, 44*, 1175–1184.

Bereiter, C. (1997). Situated cognition and how to overcome it. In D. Kishner & J. A. Whitson (Eds.), *Situated cognition: Social, semiotic, and psychological perspectives* (pp. 281–300). Hillsdale, NJ: Erlbaum.

Bereiter, C., & Scardamalia, M. (1989). Intentional learning as a goal of instruction. In L. B. Resnick (Ed.), *Knowing, learning, and instruction: Essays in honor of Robert Glaser* (pp. 361–392). Hillsdale, NJ: Erlbaum.

Bronfenbrenner, U. (1977). Toward an experimental ecology of human development. *American Psychologist, 32,* 513–531.

Brown, A. L., & Palincsar, A. S. (1989). Guided, cooperative learning and individual knowledge acquisition. In L. B. Resnick (Ed.), *Knowing, learning, and instruction: Essays in honor of Robert Glaser* (pp. 393–451). Hillsdale, NJ: Erlbaum.

Chipman, S. F., Segal, J. W., & Glaser, R. (Eds.). (1985). *Thinking and learning skills: Vol. 2. Research and open questions.* Hillsdale, NJ: Erlbaum.

Cobb, P. (1997). Learning from distributed theories of intelligence. In E. Pehkonen (Ed.), *Proceedings of the 21st Conference of the International Group for the Psychology of Mathematics Education* (Vol. 2, pp. 169–176). Lahti, Finland: University of Helsinki.

Cole, M. (1991). Conclusion. In L. B. Resnick, J. M. Levine, & S. D. Teasley (Eds.), *Perspectives on socially shared cognition* (pp. 398–417). Washington, DC: American Psychological Association.

Cole, M. (1995). Sociocultural settings: Design and intervention. In J. V. Wertsch, P. Del Rio, & A. Alvarez (Eds.), *Sociocultural studies of mind* (pp. 187–214). New York: Cambridge University Press.

Cole, M., & Engestrom, Y. (1993). A cultural-historical approach to distributed cognition. In G. Salomon (Ed.), *Distributed cognitions: Psychological and educational considerations* (pp. 1–46). New York: Cambridge University Press.

Cole, M., & Wertsch, J. V. (1996). Beyond the individual-social antinomy in discussions of Piaget and Vygotsky. *Human Development, 39,* 250–256.

Damon, W. (1984). Peer education: The untapped potential. *Journal of Applied Developmental Psychology, 5,* 331–343.

Damon, W. (1991). Problems of direction in socially shared cognition. In L. B. Resnick, J. M. Levine, & S. D. Teasley (Eds.), *Perspectives on socially shared cognition* (pp. 384–397). Washington, DC: American Psychological Association.

De Vries, R. (1997). Piaget's social theory. *Educational Researcher, 26*(2), 4–17.

Gardner, H. (1985). *The mind's new science: A history of the cognitive revolution.* New York: Basic Books.

Gigerenzer, G. (1991). From tools to theories: A heuristic discovery in cognitive psychology. *Psychological Review, 98,* 254–267.

Greeno, J. G. (1997). Response: On claims that answer the wrong question. *Educational Researcher, 20*(1), 5–17.

Hickey, D. T. (1997). Motivation and contemporary socio-constructivist instructional perspectives. *Educational Psychologist, 32,* 175–193.

Huber, G. P. (1989, March). *Organizational learning: An examination of the contributing processes and a review of the literature.* Paper presented at the Conference on Organizational Learning, Pittsburgh, PA.

Hutchins, E. (1996). *Cognition in the wild.* Cambridge, MA: MIT Press.

Lave, J. (1988). *Cognition in practice.* New York: Cambridge University Press.

Lave, J., & Wenger, E. (1991). *Situated learning: Legitimate peripheral participation.* New York: Cambridge University Press.

Leont'ev, A. N. (1981). *Problems in the development of mind.* Moscow: Progress.

Lepper, M., Aspinwall, L., Mumme, D., & Chabay, R. (1990). Self-perception and social perception processes in tutoring: Subtle social control strategies of expert tutors. In J. M. Olson & M. P. Zanna (Eds.), *Self-inference processes: The Ontario Symposium* (Vol. 6, pp. 217–237). Hillsdale, NJ: Erlbaum.

Lepper, M. R., Drake, M. F., & O'Donnell-Johnson, T. (1997). Scaffolding techniques of expert human tutors. In M. Pressley & K. Hogan (Eds.), *Advances in teaching and learning* (pp. 108–144). New York: Brookline Press.

Levitt, B., & March, J. G. (1988). Organizational learning. *Annual Review of Sociology, 14,* 319–340.

Lourenço, O., & Machado, A. (1996). In defense of Piaget's theory: A reply to 10 common criticisms. *Psychological Review, 103,* 143–164.

Luria, A. R. (1981). *Language and cognition.* Washington, DC: Winston.

Moll, L. C., Tapia, J., & Whitmore, K. P. (1993). Living knowledge: The social distribution of cultural resources for thinking. In G. Salomon (Ed.), *Distributed cognitions: Psychological and educational considerations* (pp. 139–163). New York: Cambridge University Press.

Morgan, G., & Ramirez, R. (1983). Action learning: A holographic metaphor for guiding social change. *Human Relations, 37,* 1–28.

Newman, D., Griffin, P., & Cole, M. (1989). *The construction zone: Working for cognitive change in school.* New York: Cambridge University Press.

O'Donnell, M., & O'Kelly, J. (1994). Learning from peers: Beyond the rhetoric of positive results. *Educational Psychology Review, 6*(4), 321–349.

Olson, D. R., Torrance, N., & Hildyard, A. (Eds.). (1985). *Literacy, language and learning.* New York: Cambridge University Press.

O'Neil, H. F., & Spielberger, C. D. (Eds.). (1979). *Cognitive and affective learning strategies.* New York: Academic Press.

Pea, R. D. (1993). Practices of distributed intelligence and designs for education. In G. Salomon (Ed.), *Distributed cognitions: Psychological and educational considerations* (pp. 47–87). New York: Cambridge University Press.

Perkins, D. N. (1986). *Knowledge as design.* Hillsdale, NJ: Erlbaum.

Perkins, D. N. (1991). Technology meets constructivism: Do they make a marriage? *Educational Technology, 31*(5), 18–23.

Perkins, D. N. (1992). *Smart schools: From training memories to educating minds.* New York: Free Press.

Perkins, D. N. (1993). Person plus: A distributed view of thinking and learning. In G. Salomon (Ed.), *Distributed cognitions: Psychological and educational considerations* (pp. 88–110). New York: Cambridge University Press.

Perkins, D. N. (1995). *Outsmarting IQ: The emerging science of learnable intelligence.* New York: Free Press.

Perkins, D. N., & Unger, C. (1994). A new look in representations for mathematics and science learning. *Instructional Science, 22,* 1–37.

Pressley, M., & Brainerd, C. J. (Eds.). (1985). *Cognitive learning and memory in children: Progress in cognitive development research.* New York: Springer-Verlag.

Resnick, L. B. (1991). Shared cognition: Thinking as social practice. In L. B. Resnick, J. M. Levine, & S. D. Teasley (Eds.), *Perspectives on socially shared cognition* (pp. 1–20). Washington, DC: American Psychological Association.

Rogoff, B. (1991). Social interaction as apprenticeship in thinking: Guided participation in spatial planning. In L. B. Resnick, J. M. Levine, & S. D. Teasley (Eds.), *Perspectives on socially shared cognition* (pp. 349–364). Washington, DC: American Psychological Association.

Salomon, G. (1993). No distribution without individuals' cognition: A dynamic interactional view. In G. Salomon (Ed.), *Distributed cognitions: Psychological and educational considerations* (pp. 111–138). New York: Cambridge University Press.

Salomon, G. (1994). *Interaction of media, cognition, and learning.* Hillsdale, NJ: Erlbaum.

Salomon, G., & Globerson, T. (1987). Skill is not enough: The role of mindfulness in learning and transfer. *International Journal of Educational Research, 11,* 623–637.

Salomon, G., Globerson, T., & Guterman, E. (1989). The computer as a zone of proximal development: Internalizing reading-related metacognitions from a reading partner. *Journal of Educational Psychology, 81,* 620–627.

Salomon, G., & Perkins, D. N. (1989). Rocky roads to transfer: Rethinking mechanisms of a neglected phenomenon. *Educational Psychologist, 24,* 113–142.

Salomon, G., Perkins, D. N., & Globerson, T. (1991). Partners in cognition: Extending human intelligence with intelligent technologies. *Educational Researcher, 20,* 2–9.

Scardamalia, K., Bereiter, C., McLean, R. S., Swallow, J., & Woodruff, E. (1989). Computer-supported intentional learning environments. *Journal of Educational Computing Research, 45,* 51–68.

Scribner, S., & Cole, M. (1981). *The psychology of literacy.* Cambridge, MA: Harvard University Press.

Segal, J. W., Chipman, S. F., & Glaser, R. (Eds.). (1985). *Thinking and learning skills: Vol. 1. Relating instruction to research.* Hillsdale, NJ: Erlbaum.

Senge, P. (1990). *The fifth discipline: The art and practice of the learning organization.* New York: Doubleday/Currency.

Sfard, A. (in press). On two metaphors for learning and the dangers of choosing just one. *Educational Researcher.*

Sheingold, K. (1987). The microcomputer as a symbolic medium. In R. D. Pea & K. Sheingold (Eds.), *Mirrors of minds: Patterns of experience in educational computing* (pp. 198-210). New York: Ablex.

Slavin, R. (1994). *Cooperative learning: Theory, research, and practice* (2nd ed.). Boston: Allyn & Bacon.

Sperber, D. (1984, April). *Anthropology and psychology: Toward an epidemiology of representations.* Mallinowski Memorial Lecture presented at University of Paris.

Stacey, R. (1992). *Managing the unknowable: Strategic boundaries between order and chaos in organizations.* San Francisco: Jossey-Bass.

Tishman, S., & Perkins, D. N. (1997). The language of thinking. *Phi Delta Kappan, 78,* 368–374.

Vygotsky, L. S. (1978). *Mind in society.* Cambridge, MA: Harvard University Press.

Weick, K. (1979). *The social psychology of organizing* (2nd ed.). Reading, MA: Addison-Wesley.

Wertsch, J. V. (1991). A sociocultural approach to socially shared cognition. In L. B. Resnick, J. M. Levine, & S. D. Teasley (Eds.), *Perspectives on socially shared cognition* (pp. 85–100). Washington, DC: American Psychological Association.

Wertsch, J. V., Del Rio, P., & Alvarez, A. (Eds.). (1995). *Sociocultural studies of mind.* New York: Cambridge University Press.

Manuscript received September 1, 1997
Accepted December 10, 1997

# Chapter 2

# Can We Trace the "Efficacy of Social Constructivism"?

M. C. O'CONNOR
Boston University

## INTRODUCTION

The board and editors of *Review of Research in Education* have posed the following questions, to be addressed in this chapter:

We now have a large corpus of work in which a social constructivist view has been used to design instruction (in math, science, literacy, social studies, etc.). What have we learned about the efficacy of the social constructivist approach to learning environments? Has "social constructivism" affected the flow of research and practice in education? What, if anything, has been its "effect" on the measurable outcomes of learning, on teaching, on curriculum, and on research about these things?

These questions, as posed, are not answerable for several reasons. First, the questions presuppose a single coherent and identifiable "view" (i.e., set of beliefs and assumptions) that goes by the name of social constructivism. This presupposition fails, as I discuss at length here. Second, even if there were a single theoretical entity conventionally called social constructivism, there would be large practical and philosophical difficulties with tracing its "effects" on outcomes of any kind, for reasons discussed in the final section of this chapter. Finally, the questions as posed assume particular relationships among theory and research and practice that might be characterized by the metaphor of an intrinsically ordered production line: Theory precedes research, and the output of research determines practice. If theory, research, and practice are not intrinsically ordered in this way, then another presupposition fails. In fact, a prior question might be posed: What relationships do exist among social constructivist theory, education research, and practice?[1]

Nevertheless, attempting to answer some form of the questions is worthwhile. The board's questions were probably motivated by the widely shared recognition that something has changed in education research and practice. There has been a shift in the last three decades toward considering the "social" (whatever that may mean) in studies of learning and teaching. For many people, the expression "social constructivist" seems to capture something important about social aspects of teaching and learning, although it is often not clear what that is. On the other hand, one also encounters attacks, in newspaper editorials and politicians' speeches, against "constructivist" and "social constructivist" educational research and practice. In

---

Many thanks are due to the following individuals, who provided detailed and thoughtful responses to various drafts of this chapter: Courtney Cazden, Paul Cobb, Russell Faux, Annabel Greenhill, Lee Indrisano, Ali Iran-Nejad, and David Pearson. All remaining omissions, errors, infelicities, misconstruals, and so on are, of course, my responsibility.

these cases also, the intended denotation is unclear. As struggles continue over education governance, accountability, and the allocation of resources at federal, state, and local levels, there are those who may find in the term *social construction* an easy target. Its two component parts, used together, evoke any number of engaging or objectionable images. Many who are unaware of theoretical works on the topic feel free nonetheless to use the expression as a nontechnical term. And as the term is more widely accepted as denoting some increasingly vague set of beliefs or practices, it will become progressively easier to tar many different research and practice efforts with a very wide and uninformative brush.

In this chapter, I attempt to address the spirit of the questions posed by the board by adjusting them in several ways. First I address the multifaceted entity known as social constructivism through an informal typology of several major theoretical trends that have come to be associated with the term *social construction*. The works chosen have all been brought to bear on education research of some sort or another.[2] This characterization is not intended to be exhaustive. Rather, its purpose is to determine a minimal set of distinctions useful for approaching the board's questions.

In the second part of the chapter, I try to trace these informal clusters of "social constructivist thought" to two different areas of educational research. The purpose here is to examine the other assumptions found in the questions by exploring a limited inventory of work on research and practice in (a) the teaching of K–12 writing and (b) the teaching of K–12 mathematics. Based on the small sample of work I present, a finding of sorts begins to emerge. When we attempt to trace the "efficacy" or even the presence of social constructivist ideas in "research and practice in education," we immediately find that a concern with social aspects of learning arises from numerous sources, not just theories that might be called social constructivist. Furthermore, research and practice in writing and mathematics education bear somewhat different relationships to the three clusters of social constructivism to be described in the second part of this chapter. Partly because of the nature of the content that defines the subject matter area and partly for historical reasons, the ideas of these three clusters are taken up differently in the two areas, making it difficult to generalize about social constructivism and education research. Finally, the use of theory in research and practice in these two domains is found to be inconsistent with the production line metaphor mentioned earlier. In the conclusion, I discuss why rendering a judgment on the "efficacy" of social constructivism and its "effect on the measurable outcomes of learning" is not yet possible outside of the most limited inquiry.

## AN INFORMAL TYPOLOGY OF SOCIAL CONSTRUCTIVISMS

An intensional starting point for this typology is hard to come by. While there are a number of writers who explicitly set out the tenets of "constructivism" (as discussed later), there are very few who claim to have distilled the criterial properties of social constructivism. If instead we explore the meaning of the term extensionally, looking at the set of published research that describes itself as "social constructionist" or "social constructivist" or that proclaims its concern with "the social construction of (fill in the blank)," we find a very heterogeneous collection indeed. What is more, some researchers who do not label themselves as social constructivists could nevertheless be construed as addressing the same concerns as those who do. An extensional account of the framework guided by self-identified social constructivists is therefore not ideal either.

Instead, I briefly review the work of a selection of writers who explicitly articulate and develop a theory that concerns aspects of the social world and the nature of knowledge or the nature of learning. They fall (or are pushed) into three clusters, each of which displays a different emphasis and set of concerns. This informal typology is in the nature of a heuristic; it will become immediately clear that I have not covered all possible ground and that I have simplified the positions held by many people. This simple typology should be seen as a tool with which to consider the questions posed by the board in terms of the works reviewed in the third part of this chapter.

## Social Constructivism₁: The Sociology of Knowledge and the Construction of "Reality"

This cluster is composed of several strands of recent work in the sociology of knowledge. The implications of this work for education are less obvious than those of the next two clusters; to many outside of education research, however, work in this cluster is the only proper denotation for the term *social constructivism*. Unlike some antecedent structuralists such as Talcott Parsons, these scholars were not concerned with how large-scale social factors (such as class, gender, and generation) impinge on the social institutions that preserve and transmit official knowledge. Instead, they explored and theorized about the actual creation (or construction) of everything that passes for "knowledge" in a particular society, whether it consists of "elite ideas" or "commonsense knowledge." The work described subsequently has in common an emphasis on the collective: Individual action is a central part of the analysis, but individuals act as part of a group. It also implies a contrast set for the word *construction*: The "construction" of knowledge and reality is to be taken in contrast with the "preexistence" or "natural origination" of knowledge and reality.

### Berger and Luckmann

In *The Social Construction of Reality*, Berger and Luckmann (1967) foreground a mysterious quality of social life, building on the work of Durkheim and Weber: "Objective facticity" and "subjective meanings" both characterize the social world and, furthermore, are in a dialectic relation.[3] Individuals invest situations and "social facts" with meaning and interpret them in relation to their own lives. Yet, these same situations and institutions, created through a collective investment of meaning, take on a given quality, a quality of autonomous reality that seems to persist and to be accepted by the very individuals who, acting collectively, created the meanings in the first place. Berger and Luckman are fascinated with how subjective meanings can become objective facticities. Ideas, institutions, and practices that come to seem natural and unquestionable are in fact conventions that are solidified by various means; investigation of those means is the task of the sociologist of knowledge.

The sociology of knowledge must concern itself with whatever passes for "knowledge" in a society, regardless of the ultimate validity or invalidity (by whatever criteria) of such "knowledge." And insofar as all human knowledge is developed, transmitted and maintained in social situations, the sociology of knowledge must seek to understand the processes by which this is done in such a way that a taken-for-granted "reality" congeals for the man in the street. In other words, we contend that *the sociology of knowledge is concerned with the analysis of the social construction of reality.* (Berger & Luckmann, 1967, p. 3)

There is a huge range of aspects of "reality" that might be subjected to this analysis, some more persuasive than others. Berger and Luckmann use examples such as psychotherapy to explore how institutional arrangements have purposes (here, the purpose of "controlling deviants"). They show that those purposes must in turn sustain adjunct bodies of knowledge and belief, made natural in theories:

Since therapy must concern itself with deviations from the "official" definitions of reality, it must develop a conceptual machinery to account for such deviations and to maintain the realities thus challenged. This requires a body of knowledge that includes a theory of deviance, a diagnostic apparatus, and a conceptual system for the "cure of souls." (p. 113)

In addition to culturally specific institutions such as psychotherapy, however, Berger and Luckmann also discuss more central and universal aspects of reality, such as death. They point out that a great deal of social construction exists around this unavoidable reality of nature: "Needless to elaborate, death also posits the most terrifying threat to the taken-for-granted realities of everyday life. The integration of death within the paramount reality of social existence is, therefore, of the greatest importance for any institutional order" (p. 101).

The charge is sometimes made that this viewpoint denies the independent reality of anything, that it implies that everything is socially constructed. Berger and Luckmann make no such implication. Throughout the work, phrases such as "regardless of the ultimate validity or invalidity (by whatever criteria) of such 'knowledge'" remind us that Berger and Luckmann are not asserting the equivalidity of the various knowledges they study; rather, they are principally concerned with the mechanisms that underlie what they see as the central tendency of social life: the construction and legitimation of symbolic universes. They remain well aware of the boundaries but are fascinated by the extent to which those boundaries remain in the background in everyday social life, veiled by the intricate constructions of the collective:

Man is biologically predestined to construct and to inhabit a world with others. This world becomes for him the dominant and definitive reality. Its limits are set by nature, but once constructed, this world acts back upon nature. In the dialectic between nature and the socially constructed world the human organism is itself transformed. In this same dialectic man produces reality and thereby produces himself. (Berger & Luckmann, 1967, p. 183)

While work of this type seems removed from educational concerns, there are education researchers who find it especially useful in framing their concerns. Jenny

Cook-Gumperz's *The Social Construction of Literacy* (1986) is a paradigmatic example. The book contains studies of classroom life that examine the mechanisms by which individuals reproduce the social order moment by moment. James Collins's chapter,[4] a microanalysis of grouping in first-grade reading classes, studies the subtle yet important differences in treatment among groups jointly constructed by students and teacher. The differences are seen by the teacher as natural, yet Collins shows they emerge from a complex array of socially constructed realities, not a straightforward and instrumental response to reading abilities. Donna Eder's chapter on a similar topic shows that assignment of students to ability groups within a first-grade classroom, supposedly based solely on student aptitude, was shown to be affected by time and size constraints. "However,...there is an attempt to maintain an illusion of harmony between positions and people by attributing discrepancies to lack of aptitude rather than to lack of opportunity. This attribution, in turn, leads individuals in lower positions to view themselves as failures, while the relative and restricted nature of the competition remains hidden" (Eder, 1986, p. 155). To understand literacy, according to Cook-Gumperz, we must look beyond standard measures of skill, because they too are socially constructed in Berger and Luckmann's sense.

When we ask how knowledge is transmitted, we are making assumptions about what constitutes valid knowledge. Valid knowledge is a creation of the society, its ideology of learning and of pedagogy.... The nature of the skills we refer to as literacy skills in present-day schooling can only be revealed by examining the implicit and explicit theories which guide instructional activities in classrooms and the interactional analysis of actual classroom practice. (Cook-Gumperz, 1986, p. 15)

## The Sociologists of Science

Berger and Luckmann's general sociological enterprise is also pursued by a small group of sociologists of science who examine the dialectic between seeming "objective facticity" and collective convention in scientific disciplines. They explore how scientific facts and principles, which seem to be "written in the book of nature" and "discovered" there by scientists, depend (to varying extents) on human agreements and ways of construing experience. Here I briefly discuss Bloor (1991 [first published in 1976]) as a central and early member of this tradition. Again, this work seems not to bear a direct relationship to education research, but later sections revisit these ideas in the form of questions about the social construction of content area knowledge in the classroom and in the discipline itself.

David Bloor is the originator of the "strong program" in this new sociology of science. Mainstream sociologists of science had traditionally investigated the extent to which social factors impinged upon scientific progress, for example, by altering access to scientific institutions for certain groups or by altering research strategies or acceptance of theories as a result of spurious social goals (e.g., rivalries, politically imposed "ideological correctness"). In general, social factors were considered only to be hindrances to the pure pursuit of science. Bloor held instead that the processes of science itself—and, even more dramatically, the "knowledge" that has accumulated in particular disciplines—are to some extent (still to be determined) the product of collective "construction."

> Theories and theoretical knowledge are not things which are given in our experience. They are what gives meaning to experience by offering a story about what underlies, connects and accounts for it. This does not mean that theory is unresponsive to experience. It is, but it is not given alone with the experience it explains, nor is it uniquely supported by it. Another agency apart from the physical world is required to guide and support this component of knowledge. The theoretical component of knowledge is a social component and it is a necessary part of truth, not a sign of mere error. (Bloor, 1991, pp. 12–13)

Bloor takes on the most difficult of disciplines to consider within the strong program: mathematics. He does not assume anything about the independent existence of mathematical structures and relations outside the realm of human experience. Instead, he explores the question of what aspects of mathematical knowledge can successfully be understood as the products of human collective construction. Some aspects yield easily to such an analysis: Proofs are negotiated and renegotiated in multiple ways, as the elements that compose them (e.g., terms and definitions) are renegotiated (Bloor, 1991, pp. 146–153). But these results are overshadowed by the difficult cases at the center of mathematical knowledge. How can one argue that the Pythagorean theorem is socially constructed in any interesting or convincing sense?

Not one to shrink from such difficult questions, Bloor presents the extreme views in this regard, one of which is J. S. Mill's empiricist and psychological account of mathematical knowledge. Mill sees mathematical knowledge as arising from humans' experiences with objects. In this view, "the wide applicability of arithmetical reasoning is due to the fact that we can, with more or less difficulty, assimilate many different situations to these models" (p. 88). Bloor goes on to report how this view was subjected to withering attack by Gottlob Frege. In Frege's view, numbers, for example, are "concepts" that partake of the pure realm of objectivity. To use psychological methods of argument in pursuit of understanding mathematical knowledge is to render "foggy and indefinite" what should be orderly and regular. Frege savaged empiricists who "betake themselves to the nursery or bury themselves in the remotest conceivable periods of human evolution, there to discover, like John Stuart Mill, some gingerbread or pebble arithmetic" (Bloor, 1991, p. 93).

Bloor himself argues for a view of mathematics that encompasses Mill's in some respects but that foregrounds and critically explicates a notion of the social. Even if we view the basis of mathematical knowledge as sorting objects, ordering them, and arranging them, that account is incomplete without the understanding that only certain ways of sorting, arranging, and so forth are specially valued. That valuing is "the work of institutionalization" (Bloor, 1991, p. 100). Bloor tries to use this concept of institutionalization to explain mathematical phenomena that Mill could not encompass in his experience-based theory. For example, Frege argued that neither zero nor very large numbers can be explained by Mill's experiential grounding, so Bloor locates these numbers in the realm of social conventionalization. For Bloor, zero is explicitly a social artifact or convention, and very large numbers are possible objects of manipulation only as derived from physical models of smaller numbers in combination with routines and techniques that can be extended indefinitely (p. 102). Although Bloor only begins the task of giving a sociological account of mathematics, his attempt challenges us to think more deeply about the nature of mathematical knowledge and its sources.

Bloor (1991) does not deny that there is a reality outside of our constructions, but he makes explicit his assumption that humans are unavoidably epistemologically challenged: "If knowledge does depend on a vantage point outside society and if truth does depend on stepping above the causal nexus of social relations, then we may give them up as lost" (p. 14). He goes on to examine the nature of objectivity itself, defining it not as a relation between an empirical effort and the "real" world of nature but as a relation between individuals committed to coming up with an account of what they experience, whether those individuals are U.S. physicists or Azande medicine men. "Does the sociology of knowledge say that objectivity is impossible?... Emphatically it does not.... Objectivity is real, not an illusion, but its nature is totally different from what may have been expected" (p. 143). Objectivity lies in shared conventions and shared belief in the repeatable, the empirically verifiable; it is "socially accomplished." The sociologist of science must ask how humans come to share a sense of what is repeatable, what is empirically verifiable, and, finally, how they come to share a sense of "objective facticity" about these things.

## Ethnomethodology

In this sociological framework, the impulse is the same as in the preceding two, but the grain size is different. Ethnomethodologists aim to systematically build up a theory of social reality from the most minute building blocks. An attempt is made to systematically discover and characterize the methods whereby humans as members of social groups accomplish the creation and maintenance of reality, second by second, moment by moment. Pretheorized categories of any kind (e.g., ethnicity, gender, motivation, narrative) are eschewed in favor of discovering members' own categories of social reality. Their microanalytic lens provides a view of the intricacy and order, the shared and conventional quality of mundane reality of all kinds. An early and famous example is Sacks and Schegloff's (1973) analysis of ways in which speakers "collude" in dealing with the "problem" of ending telephone conversations.[5] Although a great deal of later work in ethnomethodology concerns the analysis of conversational structure, the larger theoretical enterprise extended into areas such as the conduct of scientific inquiry (e.g., Lynch, 1985) and even idiosyncratic topics like the learning of jazz improvisation (Sudnow, 1978).

Ethnomethodological studies in the sociology of science appropriate the microanalytic lens of ethnomethodology to address some of the questions Bloor set out. They are driven by the insistent vision that the moment-to-moment details of everyday scientific work (e.g., the disposal of a dead laboratory rat [Lynch, 1985] or the decision to eliminate a subject from a neuropsychology experiment [Star, 1983]) reflect a process of sustained but completely tacit convention that is central to the conduct of science. These often unnamed practices reflect shared ways of seeing and thus sustaining reality. In this vision, there is wonder at the capacity of humans to create—through habitual interaction and tacit agreement—a set of shared "methods" that almost defy analysis in their complexity.

Ethnomethodological sociologists of science are not necessarily committed to any particular stance toward the objective reality of nature. Rather, they are fascinated with how the entire enterprise of science itself is coordinated and sustained. Nature may be the object, and nature's phenomena cannot be "wished away", but what is of chief interest is the extent to which scientists create a shared symbolic universe through interactional practices at the microscopic level: the way they talk about a complex graph together, the way they use metaphors together to think about the payload of bombs. Like Berger and Luckmann, ethnomethodological sociologists of science do not necessarily take a position on the ontological status of scientific truth. Rather, they are fascinated by human coordinated action against the background of what is perceived as real and inevitable. How does the facticity of science come to be out of the subjective experiences of different individuals?

While ethnomethodology is perhaps not obviously related to the concerns of education researchers, it has had an influence on education research through at least two writers. Erving Goffman influenced the course of ethnomethodology, and his unique ability to see humans managing every nuance of their interactions with others, constructing the self moment to moment, continues to influence researchers who look at face-to-face interaction both inside and outside of classrooms. Hugh Mehan's early work took up the ideas and analytic assumptions of ethnomethodology (Mehan & Wood, 1975). These ideas and assumptions probably influenced his well-known work on the structure of lessons (1979) and on the construction of learning disability in face-to-face individualized education plan (IEP) meetings (1996). Also, I review in the third part of this chapter two works that bring ethnomethodological assumptions and methods to research on writing and mathematics learning.

## Critical Social Constructivisms

Social constructivism$_1$, as elaborated so far, does not entail a particular stance toward the politics of anything. One may accept all that Berger and Luckmann propose and still favor conservative, liberal, reactionary, or revolutionary political positions. Yet, the sociological stance itself, the push for inquiry into what is taken by people to be true and natural and necessary and how it comes to be taken as such, is prerequisite for the development of what might be called a critical social constructivism.

Because they are the historical products of human activity, all socially constructed universes change, and the change is brought about by the concrete actions of human beings.... Reality is socially defined. But the definitions are always embodied, that is, concrete individuals and groups of individuals serve as definers of reality. To understand the state of the socially constructed universe at any given time...one must understand the social organization that permits the definers to do their defining. Put a little crudely, it is essential to keep pushing questions about the historically available conceptualizations of reality from the abstract "What?" to the sociologically concrete "Says who?" (Berger & Luckmann, 1967, p. 116)

Berger and Luckmann take care to distinguish their system, which has the potential to lead to political questions, from a relativistic system that would have no basis from which to pose any such inquiries. "Mannheim...coined the term 'relationism' (in contradistinction to 'relativism') to denote the epistemological perspective of his sociology of knowledge—not a capitulation of thought before the sociohistorical relativities, but a sober recognition that knowledge must always be knowledge from a certain position" (p. 9).

Although they may not refer to themselves as "social constructivists," a number of writers on education share the assumption that "knowledge" and "reality" in a particular time or place are at least partially the product of constructions by certain strata of the collective. These constructions, they would argue, justify and natural-ize hierarchies and stratifications that serve some segments of society at the ex-pense of others. Thus, some of the central assumptions of social constructivism$_1$ are found in work that seeks to uncover the relationship between the practices and institutions of education and the larger social order. Work on the reproduction of that social order through education (Bourdieu & Passeron, 1977; Willis, 1977), work on "critical pedagogy" (Apple, 1982; Ellsworth, 1989; Freire, 1970; Giroux, 1983), and critical studies of particular areas of education (e.g., Gee, 1990; Graff, 1979) all represent extensions of this cluster.[6]

## Summary

The writers cited in this section differ in their methods and in their ultimate goals, but all share an emphasis on the status of what is taken to be knowledge. (This contrasts with the next cluster, social constructivism$_2$, in which the emphasis is shown to be on the processes of learning.) Is the emphasis in this work on the individual or on the collectivity? In Berger and Luckmann's treatise, the two are portrayed as being in eternal dialectical tension. According to Berger and Luckmann:

It is possible, for example, to analyze the macroscopic social roots of a religious world view in certain collectivities (classes, say, or ethnic groups...), and also to analyze the manner in which this world view is manifested in the consciousness of an individual. The two analyses can be brought together only if one inquires into the ways in which the individual, in his total social activity, relates to the collectivity in question. (1967, p. 79)

Yet, in the terms of this chapter's informal typology, the emphasis in this cluster is on the collective, particularly when taken in contrast to social constructivism$_2$ and social constructivism$_3$ (described later). The individual's role is critical, and foregrounding it differentiates this sociology of knowledge from more traditional approaches. However, in the actual analyses, the focus is on the collective's beliefs and actions within a reality that the collective constructs through its individual members' beliefs and actions. It is at the level of the collective's construction of social reality that the primary implications for education research can be found, for example, in what is considered to be most important to teach, in what it means to have learned something, and in who are considered to be the important consumers of education. These issues are discussed further in the third section of this chapter.

## Social Constructivism$_2$: Expanding the Purview of Piagetian Constructivism

Quite a different background gives rise to the second cluster discussed here. Work in this cluster starts from consideration of the individual's cognitive growth, whether that growth is the result of development or the result of learning. The generic researcher in this cluster is a psychologist who started out as a constructivist, that is, someone who worked within a Piagetian framework, in which the child is theorized as an active learner, one who, through the processes of assimilation and accommodation, adapted to the world outside, forming and reforming categories and structures that "succeed" (i.e., that work to explain the phenomenal world and to allow the learner to interact with it effectively).

### The Ideas of Constructivism and Radical Constructivism

This beginning provides the base for the idea most widely associated with constructivism[7]: that learners are active creators of their knowledge, not passive receptacles into which preformed knowledge can be placed. In this theoretical domain, a "construction" has a special status. It is the building up, piece by piece, of an internal mental structure. This structure, made up of pieces that preexisted it (which were, in their turn, constructed), is relied on by the child in reorganizing her or his activity on the basis of further experience. It eventually yields to another construction that encompasses it. This, however, is the bare minimum on which those labeling themselves "constructivists" might agree. In fact, some have used the term *trivial constructivism* to designate the position that accepts the active role of the learner in building conceptual understanding (von Glasersfeld, cited in Steffe, 1988, p. 121).

Traditional Piagetian constructivism holds that the child is always assimilating data from the world and accommodating to the world by creating new knowledge structures; it is, in principle, impossible ever to "give" children preformed knowledge. Yet, even this basic implication is ignored in many education-related uses of constructivism. Instead, for example, the implication is turned into a desideratum of pedagogy: Children should construct their own knowledge, and therefore we should refrain from "giving them preformed knowledge." As Thompson (1995, p. 123) points out, this is a basic misunderstanding: We cannot give children preformed knowledge even if we want to; by the tenets of this theoretical framework, they have no way to receive it. They are invariably constructing their own understanding of everything in the environment at all times, including that information that we, as parents or teachers, may try to "give" them (see also Cobb, 1994b).

The term *radical constructivism* has been used to designate the position that gives primacy of place to this implication and that calls us in addition to reconsider the traditional concept of knowing. The foremost exponent of radical constructivism, Ernst von Glasersfeld, acknowledges Piaget and Vico and characterizes one of the concept's central tenets as follows: We must "give up the requirement that knowledge represent an independent world, and admit instead that knowledge represents something that is far more important to us, namely what we can *do* in our *experiential* world, the successful ways of dealing with the objects we call physical and the successful ways of thinking with abstract concepts" (von Glasersfeld, 1995, p. 7). Radical constructivists do not deny an absolute reality, but they do claim (along with many others in the history of philosophy) that it cannot be directly known (von Glasersfeld, 1995, p. 7).

Another implication that is highlighted in radical constructivist work is that children may manage to construct knowledge structures that allow them to act as if they "have" the same knowledge as someone else, but in fact we cannot know whether two children have the "same" knowledge. Given that knowledge is the result of idiosyncratic paths of experience and that it is highly unlikely that anyone will tread exactly the same path in learning something, then each child's collection of knowledge structures is effectively unique.[8] How then, the puzzle arises, do people ever communicate?

Radical constructivism, as presented so far, is a theory of learning, not a theory of teaching (Cobb, 1994b; von Glasersfeld, 1995). Yet, from the few principles and puzzles described earlier, several implications for teaching fairly naturally emerge. I mention just a few here. First, given that each child's constructions will be dependent on what has preceded them, and given that they are uniquely the product of experience, the pedagogical implication arises that one must start teaching from "where the child is." This requires that one first find out where the child is in order to teach effectively, and that furthermore one must find out where each child is. Just as important, one must have some idea of how the child is to get from where she or he is to the target state, as well as an idea of the nature of that target state. This requires a deep and detailed knowledge of what it means to understand or know the target.

Furthermore, two of the central tenets (the inaccessibility of any reality other than what we experience and the uniqueness of each individual's constructions) (von Glasersfeld, 1995), when taken together, lead to another question with ramifications for teaching and curriculum: How do we come to share understandings of anything? In some cases, the world outside will so constrain our constructions that we will usually end up with an understanding insignificantly different from that of others. It must be so, because we all live collectively and share workable understandings about many things. But what about cases in which the environmental constraints are not very strong and do not result in a convergence on the same "reality"? How, for example, might a classroom full of children come up with commensurable constructions of place value? And what is the relationship between those constructions and the "legitimated" understanding of mathematics educators? We are led to ask even further, What are the relationships among an individual child's construction, a teacher's construction, and the accumulated "knowledge" of the discipline itself?

## Where Does the Social Enter In?

As presented so far, (radical) constructivism is pulled in two directions: (a) toward the necessity of studying in detail how an individual learner proceeds to construct an understanding of some relation or object or phenomenon and (b) toward the necessity of studying how individuals within a group may achieve shared understandings. It is through attention to both directions that a concern for the social enters in.

Over the last 40 years, a large group of researchers have taken up central parts of the various forms of constructivism mentioned thus far. But much of the attention has focused on the individual learner and his or her intellectual expansion in the relatively narrow world of concrete experience. It was obvious to Piaget and his colleagues that the social was part of that world in several important ways; the learner often carries out the processes of assimilation and accommodation in the context of other humans. Does this have any appreciable role in the construction of knowledge? Social structures, relationships, and practices are themselves targets for learning. What is the nature of this kind of learning? Is it the same as that formulated for narrowly cognitive domains?

As the social world has expanded in importance for constructivists, several different perspectives on its importance have emerged.

*The social environment as catalyst for individual constructions.* Considerations of school-based learning inevitably confront something that is not part of infant cognitive development. School-based learning proceeds sporadically; results are uneven; something called "motivation" (and the lack thereof) rears its head; learners are involuntarily present in the learning environment. Developmental psychology considers mechanisms underlying learning and development. In educational psychology, the focus expands to include questions about what elements drive or block learning. What drives the learner to persist in constructing ever more complex and powerful models and representations? How can those forces be harnessed, implemented, built into instruction?

Often, the answers to these questions make reference to the world outside the individual's head: Social needs and affiliations can support, drive, or impede learning. The cognitive conflict or impasse that impels learning and development within the Piagetian paradigm can perhaps be created artificially, but how? Some researchers have voiced the hope that it will come naturally out of group interaction. Others observe that one will do things in collaboration that one would never attempt alone. In any case, the study of classroom learning brings with it an avalanche of ways that the social environment may affect learning. Constructivists in the classroom cannot avoid this any more than anyone else can.

*The social as generator of target structures and target milieus.* What kinds of learning require interaction with the social world? With respect to school learning, are there aspects of content area knowledge that are intrinsically social? Are there aspects of content area knowledge that can be learned only by interacting with other humans in certain kinds of activity settings? A recurrent emphasis in the history of curriculum studies is the importance of the activities of members of a discipline, proposed as the critical complement to the knowledge of those members (Bruner, 1960; Dewey, 1916). For example, in mathematics and science, the ability to make an argument or construct a proof is something that arises out of a general awareness and acceptance of the principles and purposes of a field. In history education, some have asked what "historical thinking" consists of and how historians come to engage in it. As discussed at length later, the activity of writers has come to be a concern of those who teach writing.

If we view the disciplines as multidimensional communities of practice, in possession not only of special knowledge but also of skills and complex understandings about what is valuable, what is sensible, and what is "not done," then we must ask some very different questions about the content areas in relation to their parent disciplines. For example, what forms of social practice characterize a particular discipline and must therefore be made available to early learners in order for them to acquire productive and powerful knowledge of the content area? And what kinds of social arrangements in the classroom are required to accomplish this?

## John Dewey

Of course, the individual's construction of knowledge within social realms is a longstanding concern of writers on education, not a recent discovery. A most thoroughgoing consideration of virtually every aspect of this topic resides in the writings of John Dewey (particularly Dewey, 1916). The scope and richness of Dewey's work and the pervasiveness of his influence may cause some to ask why Dewey is not more prominently featured in this chapter. While progressive education brought with it a focus on active learners constructing knowledge by engaging deeply with their environment in its fullest social embodiment, and while this vision of education captured the imagination of millions (resulting in misreadings and miscarriages that Dewey himself rejected), Dewey's influence is at this point too diffuse to yield to analysis in this chapter. It might be argued that he could be included in all three clusters of social constructivist thought. It is interesting to note, in this respect, that Steffe and Gale's 520-page edited volume on constructivism in education (1995) contains not a single reference to Dewey (however, see Prawat, 1995, for a convincing argument that this trend may be about to change).

## Summary

Obviously, this cluster spans a large territory. How does it differ from social constructivism$_1$? The Piagetian and radical constructivist underpinnings of social constructivism$_2$ ensure that the status of knowledge is never taken for granted; in the working world of research, however, the emphasis is on learning. What is most strikingly different from social constructivism$_1$ is that, in this cluster, there is a focus on the individual, with the collective as part of the learning context. This stems from the long roots of this cluster in developmental and learning psychology. Whereas the sociologist is, at the end of the day, traditionally concerned with aspects of collective life, the psychologist has traditionally been focused on the individual. In some social constructivist$_2$ research, we will see that the collective is taken very seriously as part of the research problem. However, comparatively speaking, in this cluster the collective is relatively backgrounded as part of the learning environment in which the individual functions and is studied.

## Social Constructivism$_3$: The Sociocultural-Historical Mind

Over the past two decades, Lev Vygotsky's work (and that of other Soviet psychologists such as Luria and Leont'ev) has been interpreted and extended by a range of leading scholars in a variety of fields.[9] I do not attempt a summary of this work here; instead, I highlight several features of it that have been particularly influential among researchers in education. Thus, in this cluster again there are inevitably a number of important theoretical issues that are not touched on.

Research in this framework is often referred to as sociocultural or sociohistorical analyses of mind and learning. The central emphasis is on the dynamic interaction between the collective and the individual. Whereas learning was considered primarily as an individual function in social constructivism$_2$, in this cluster the relation between the collective and the individual is theoretically central: It is in terms of both collective and individual that the sociocultural/historical psychologist theorizes learning. The nature of individual learning is explicitly problematized in terms of higher cognitive functions at the level of the collective, both macrogenetically and microgenetically. Here I cover several principal ideas in sociocultural-historical psychology, citing a few notable works in which these ideas are explored and extended.[10]

## The Intermental Genesis of Higher Cognitive Functions

The question behind many aspects of Vygotsky's work is how people come to be able to engage in certain kinds of higher order cognitive activities by virtue of their participation in the social world, or how "the individual response emerges from the forms of collective life" (Vygotsky, 1981, cited in Wertsch & Stone, 1985, p. 164). Among the most cited passages in Vygotsky is the following:

Any function in the child's cultural development appears twice, or on two planes. First it appears on the social plane, and then on the psychological plane. First it appears between people as an interpsychological category, and then within the child as an intrapsychological category. This is equally true with regard to voluntary attention, logical memory, the formation of concepts, and the development of volition. (Vygotsky, 1981, p. 163)

The mechanisms whereby this internalization comes about are the topic of a great deal of later theorizing (e.g., Wertsch 1985a, 1985b). A central part of the account concerns the role of speech/language, as externally used between interlocutors and as gradually internalized in an elliptical and idiosyncratic form ("inner speech") that unites with inchoate thought. A number of implications follow from this view of speech as progressively moving from outside the individual to inside, and again outward with the increasing elaboration required for forms of complex communication. For example, the language-mediated passages between the intermental and the intramental and back have been viewed as central to our understanding of the origins of self-regulation (Diaz, Neal, & Amaya-Williams, 1990) and as a critical piece in an account of the relationship between writing and thought.

Upon first reading, it is easy to interpret the preceding quotation as a claim only about the sources of individual learning. It is sometimes construed as a claim that social interaction is necessary for individual learning to occur. This interpretation, however, does not capture the extent of Vygotsky's theoretical proposals. Among the more radical is the proposal that higher cognitive functions such as logic, scientific reasoning, argument, and even aspects of memory are, in some sense (as yet to be fully articulated), truly collective functions: that the human species, through its unprecedentedly complex kinds of social interaction, gave rise to new levels of cognitive activity that are intrinsically collective. Whereas these are traditionally considered to be individual mental functions, Vygotsky eventually asserted that they were individual only as derived from collective mental functioning. That is, these functions truly exist and are fully realized between minds, or intermentally, and the individual "possesses" them only derivatively, or intramentally.

In some extensions of Vygotsky's work, we can see the foregrounding of the collective and attempts to redefine learning in terms of the collective. Michael Cole's work (Cole, 1996; Scribner & Cole, 1981) particularly stands out in its penetrating exploration of the collectively determined nature of cognition and the existence of higher order cognition at the *collective level.* In their influential work *The Psychology of Literacy* (1981), Scribner and Cole demonstrate the extent to which the cognitive consequences of reading and writing are a product of the larger sociocultural, historical, and institutional setting. Feature by feature, they debunked "great divide" accounts of literacy in which the acquisition of reading and writing were said to be followed ineluctably by gains in memory, logical reasoning ability, historical thinking, and even democratic impulses. What they showed is that the cognitive (and social) outcomes associated with reading and writing at the individual level are determined by the social practices within which reading and writing are embedded. In more recent work, Cole grapples with the institutional implications of Vygotskian thought (Cole, 1995). He studies student learning in an after-school program in terms of the relationship between the culture of the program itself and the culture of the institution within which it is embedded. In this work, Cole seeks a unit of analysis consistent with the study of learning as an intermental, collective accomplishment.

Finally, a recent work that should be included in social constructivism[3] is one that does not cite Vygotsky's work but clearly extends important ideas in the tradition. Lave and Wenger (1991) also place learning outside of the individual: It takes place in the participation framework, not in the individual's head. Since the learner does not learn isolated skills and acquire propositional knowledge but, rather, learns how to interact with an environment, both social and physical, the learning is, in part, embedded in the situation. One interesting aspect of this work is the light it brings to the larger question of the community reproducing itself, thus expanding the frame in which collective and individual are considered. How does the community maintain "certain modes of co-participation in which it [the community] is embedded" while incorporating newcomers? Furthermore, this work deepens the theorization of the social by calling attention to the changes in the social matrix, the community, wrought by the participation of the "learner." Lave and Wenger succeed in breaking away from the psychologist's ultimate focus on the individual and particularize both the novice and the expert in an expanded dance with each other. It is important to note that their studies of communities of practice do not include schools, and they see the extension of their theory to classrooms as important but problematic (Lave & Wenger, 1991, pp. 39–41).

## The Zone of Proximal Development (ZPD)

The other passage competing for most-cited status is the following:

The zone of proximal development is the distance between the actual developmental level as determined by independent problem solving and the level of potential development as determined through problem solving under adult guidance, or in collaboration with more capable peers. (Vygotsky, 1978, p. 86)

This has been interpreted in a number of ways (Moll, 1990), most commonly as either a purely local, individually based interpretation in which the ZPD is a property of individual minds (Brown, Campione, Webber, & McGilly, 1992) or a contextual property of situations that can elicit higher levels of performance from individuals (Brown et al., 1993).

Some research in education that labels itself as Vygotskian focuses only on the narrow situation of an individual learner in a scaffolding situation with an expert other. Usually, the ZPD is somehow incorporated in this scenario in one of its most local instantiations, as a property of an individual child that is maximized in face-to-face interaction between a more knowledgeable other and the child or as a property of the dyad itself (e.g., "The tutor creates a ZPD for the learner").

The concept of ZPD seems to invite multiple interpretations, and a study of the progression of Vygotsky's thought justifies more than one of these interpretations (Minick, 1987); within education research, however, it seems that there is a great deal to say within this local, face-to-face domain. In some sense, the entire literature on early socialization and enculturation can be given a natural interpretation within this "localist" Vygotskian framework. The development of abilities that are central to an individual's performance in school and in life can be well illuminated within such an approach (Diaz et al., 1990; Rogoff, 1995; Rogoff et al., 1993). Luis Moll, even while explicating the richness and diversity of Soviet sociohistorical psychology, nevertheless shows us why, in educational contexts, the ZPD is predominantly interpreted in terms of a local, face-to-face interaction. Dyadic and triadic interaction are an important ground for the genesis of school-based learning and the learning that precedes school (see Moll, 1990, and the papers therein).

Along with this interest in interaction comes a focus on discourse: the role of language in learning. Vygotsky's reinterpretation of Piaget's views on internal speech is only one source of inspiration in this area. Because work in this cluster foregrounds the interaction between individual and collective, a great deal of attention naturally focuses on different ways to conceptualize that interaction, and some of this attention centers on language. In this area, the ideas of Bakhtin have been influential (Bakhtin, 1986; Volosinov, 1971). Bakhtin studied the utterance: language embedded fully in an interactional context concurrent with both the utterance and the historical contexts out of which the utterance arose. Bakhtin's writings, contemporaneous with (although not inspired by) Vygotsky (Wertsch, 1990, p. 116), illuminate another aspect of the interaction between the collective and the individual, in their emphasis on the multiple voices heard in a single utterance and the multiplicity of minds that can be said to reside within and between two individuals.

Soviet work on face-to-face interaction often features evocative terms that denote the social configurations and relationships involved in joint intellectual activity and in socially situated human communication generally. In addition to *zone of proximal development*. These include terms such as *dialogicality, interanimation of voices, social languages*, and *ventriloquation*. All concern our conceptualization of that potentially liberatory (and potentially destructive) moment of contact between the individual and the collective. Yet, in many uses one finds in the recent literature, an intriguing penumbra of significance surrounds a very dimly lit center of meaning. Many scholars have commented on the large number of senses accumulating around the term ZPD, but the other terms have also accumulated a variety of variously legitimated senses. In recent education research, a use of these evocative terms is sometimes reminiscent of what one finds in the humanities. For example, in literary studies, one author's appropriation of an evocative term is viewed as an accomplishment if and only if a new sense is laminated in the process. The goal of insight, not an empiricist reproducibility, drives such uses. In education research, it sometimes appears that these terms, subtle and complex in their originators' works, are being used as tools to grapple with the slipperiness and complexity that is characteristic of human interaction in general and classrooms in particular and as tools to communicate about that complexity.

## Mediational Means

There is another aspect to sociocultural-historical work that has received perhaps less attention within education research, although it is no less fundamental. Vygotsky and his psychologist colleagues, of course, worked against a backdrop of Marxist thought that emphasized the determination of individual functioning and mind-set by historical circumstances. The Marxian notion of types of labor and relationship to capital as determining class membership—and, thus, orientations to the experienced world—influenced Soviet psychology. Vygotsky was specifically influenced by Engels's writing on tools and labor as the means whereby cognitive activity was effectuated and human life transformed (John-Steiner & Souberman, 1978, p. 132). This theme, developed further by Leont'ev and Luria, is generally referred to as the issue of mediation in human thought. Human activity in the world is characterized by pervasive use of tools, including both physical tools and symbolic tools such as language, and this observation led a number of theorists to explore the implications of this fact for cognition (as Cole, 1995, points out, this connection does not depend on Marxian theory but is found within American pragmatism and other philosophical traditions as well). This aspect of Soviet thought has been extended systematically by Cole (1995) and Wertsch (1991, 1995), among others.

## Summary

I have distinguished these three clusters of work in terms of two independent dimensions: relative interest in the characterization of knowledge versus learning and relative interest in the individual versus the collective. In the section on social constructivism$_1$, I showed that social constructivism in the sociological tradition features a focus on the nature of knowledge and "reality" and their origins in collective actions and attributions. What does this tradition have to offer education research? Perhaps the most immediate implication concerns society's beliefs and ideologies about the nature of education itself. This perspective prompts us to critically examine the basis for what we "know" about achievement, learning, educational institutions, and content area knowledge itself.

In the section on social constructivism$_2$, I showed that the constructivist tradition in psychology results in a type of social constructivism that centers on a consideration of learning at the level of the individual. While the nature of knowledge and reality is fodder for theoretical discussion and serves to distinguish different levels of commitment to constructivism, the principal focus of research is on the actual paths of individual learning within a variety of domains. Increasingly, the social contexts within which these individual learning paths are embedded have become an important consideration. The implications of this perspective for education are obvious and plentiful. Finally, in the preceding section, I indicated that work originating in a Vygotskian mold centers on the consideration of learning, with the central focus of interest on dynamic interaction between the collective and the individual. This is not simply a concern with points at which the individual contacts the collective; it is a concern with the ways in which individual functioning is derived from or seen in terms of collective levels of existence. This work provides a basis for reconsidering educational contexts as sites of learning and potentially could support a radical reconsideration of school-based learning.[11]

## AN INFORMAL EXAMINATION OF RESEARCH IN TWO CONTENT AREAS

### Reapproaching the Questions

The *RRE* editors and board asked what impact (if any) the ideas of social constructivism have had on educational research, pedagogy, curriculum, and learning outcomes. Let us replace the single entity "social constructivism" with the three clusters of social constructivist thought described in the previous part of this chapter. We now have a somewhat more precise handle on what ideas we need to trace, but we still face a number of problems. First, the questions imply that the current interest in the social contexts of learning is related in some way to the contents of (some variety of) social constructivist theory. Is this a reasonable assumption? And can we identify which aspects of research on social aspects of learning and teaching stem from theory and which do not? In what follows, I show that an abiding interest in the social contexts of learning and a thoroughgoing attention to social aspects of knowledge often spring from sources that have no relationship to the three clusters of social constructivism described earlier.

A related problem: The *RRE* questions presuppose that it is possible to trace the impact of social constructivism through the research literature. How might one do this? Let us take the most obvious approach: an examination of the words of researchers themselves. Is it fair to infer that research that actually cites work within the three versions of social constructivism described thus far was significantly guided in its conceptualization, plan, implementation, or interpretation by the ideas of those theoretical clusters? The selective review that follows shows that, at least in these cases, theory, research, and practice do not map easily onto the "production line" metaphor, with theory driving research. Instead, many researchers make use of ideas in the three clusters for a variety of important but post hoc purposes. Others use them heuristically. Most do not use them programmatically. I suggest here that this is a natural consequence of the fact that each of these researchers is attempting to investigate a multifaceted, extraordinarily complex phenomenon—classroom teaching and learning—and that the magnitude of its complexities calls for these seemingly contingent uses of theory.

The same question arises about pedagogy that appears to be influenced by social constructivist research of one sort or another: How can the influence be traced? Although this chapter does not take up pedagogy and curriculum to the same extent that research is examined, it is useful here to recall the critique offered by Cobb and others about self-identified constructivist pedagogy. The constructivist "mantra"— "Students construct their own knowledge"—is often taken to mean that pedagogy must sanctify the student's inventions and explorations at the expense of teacher instruction. In fact, however, constructivist learning theory implies absolutely nothing about pedagogy (Cobb, 1994b, p. 4). Self-labeled social constructivist approaches, analogously, often sanctify the student's interactions and group "collaboration" at the expense of any deep consideration of what is being learned (and how) or of the nature of the social interactions or larger social arrangements or institutions. What do the three versions of social constructivism imply about instruction, if anything? What are legitimate instructional interpretations of these three versions, if any?

In order to answer the question about impact on instruction, therefore, it is clear that we would have to look beyond the labels affixed by the designers of instruction. As David Cohen (1990) demonstrated in his bleak tale of mathematics reform in one classroom, deep programmatic changes in pedagogy, however well motivated and secured by research, do not easily find root in classrooms. The accoutrements of practice may change, and the terminology changes, but often teaching practices retain their prereform character, in spite of attestations by practitioners that they have changed. This disjunction between the labeling of research and instruction and its actual content is thus the source of another problem with the final part of the *RRE* editors' questions. Imagine that there has been a considerable effort to implement a defensible "social constructivist" pedagogical approach in some set of classrooms and that we agree on the validity of the approach. We want to discover whether the approach has caused student learning outcomes to change in those classrooms. We must first ensure that the implementation of the approach is consistent across classrooms. However, as the story of bilingual education inter alia makes clear, student learning outcomes (particularly the bad or indifferent ones, resulting in "no change" after massive intervention) are almost impossible to lay at the doorstep of any theory or approach, because the problems of implementation consistency across any two schools can almost always undercut any such claims.

Another related problem concerns the criteria for efficacy in learning outcomes. Imagine that we replace "social constructivism" in the questions with "behaviorism" and that we are looking back on these questions as posed in, say, a 1959 chapter. It would become apparent that "efficacy" can be evaluated only in terms that the paradigm itself accepts as valid. Even if social constructivist education researchers had compiled theoretically legitimated forms of assessment of learning (which they largely have not yet done), these forms of assessment would be framed in terms of the primitives of the theory (or theories). Two prior questions arise: What forms of outcomes would the social constructivist education community (if there were such) agree are legitimate and informative? and Does the nonsocial constructivist education community accept these outcomes? If we can find such a set, then we can go on to address the causal linkages.

In short, to draw conclusions about "effects," "efficacy," or "impact" is to assume that one can underwrite claims about cause: that the ideas of some variety of social constructivism did or did not cause change in research, teaching, curriculum, and/or learning outcomes. And there are problems in assuming causal linkages between a social constructivist theoretical framework and research programs, teaching practice, and learning outcomes. Nevertheless, doleful though my assessment seems, it is not a prelude to a nihilistic exit from the chapter; there is reason to continue to examine the editors' questions. Given the increased interest in the social contexts of learning, and given the general tendency of the society at large to alternately lionize, attack, or otherwise politicize education-related enterprises of any kind, there is reason to seek a clearer view about the basis for our beliefs and claims, our frameworks and "results."

In what follows, then, I examine writings on research and practice in two content areas. I have chosen to examine research in content areas such as writing and mathematics, instead of research in more general topics—such as "motivation" or "assessment"—because content area research is a nexus of conceptual, pedagogical, and curricular concerns. It is arguably the most central kind of education research in that it touches on the concerns of theoreticians, practitioners, learners, curriculum developers, content area specialists, and even politicians. Obviously, only a tiny subset of relevant papers can be discussed here. The work that I have included is important, but I have left out much work that is perhaps even more important. Nevertheless, the works reviewed here are sufficient to begin to address at least the two questions just posed.

## Writing in the Language Arts: Research and Practice

### The Writing Process and the Work of the Writer

One of the most important recent developments in research and practice on K–12 writing is dubbed "process writing." In general, the term denotes a pedagogical approach that foregrounds the practices of writing as engaged in by real writers. Theorists encourage teachers to honor the many purposes of authentic writing and the sources of writing within the writer's emotional and intellectual life. Imported into the classroom are conferences with both teachers and peers, in which a developing piece is discussed and readers respond to the writer; successive rethinkings and revisions that respond to those responses; and publication of finished pieces for local and sometimes nonlocal audiences.

Relative to the concerns of this chapter, process writing is of interest because it clearly reconsiders classroom writing as a social phenomenon at a number of levels. For the first time in the modern K–12 teaching of writing, the "skill" of writing is seriously theorized as an entire set of practices existing within a world of people and their individual and collective purposes. For example, the notion of "audience" implied by every rhetorician in history is explored in depth within process writing. It is made concrete and specific and considered in relation to the particular social world within which the writing takes place. So how did the researchers and writers who started this movement incorporate "the social" into their work, and can we see any signs of influence in their work from any of the three clusters of social constructivism?

*The Americans.* Janet Emig's influential work "The Composing Processes of Twelfth Grade Writers" (see Emig, 1983) was published in 1971, but the research was conducted during the 1960s. It is generally credited with beginning the new approach to writing instruction.[12] Emig first was moved to consider the writing process as such in a workshop in 1961 with Priscilla Tyler, and it seems that she was one of only a few who saw beyond the then widely held view that writing was not a worthy topic of inquiry (Emig, 1983, p. 62). Her unprecedented study shows the beginnings of concern with the social world (both interpersonal and institutional) within which the student composes:

Who the significant other in the composing process of secondary students is seems dependent upon whether the writing is school-sponsored or self-sponsored.... The most significant others in the private, and often the school-sponsored, writing of twelfth graders are peers, despite the overwhelming opportunity for domination teachers hold through their governance of all formal evaluation. American high schools and colleges must...consider that the teacher-centered presentation of composition...is pedagogically, developmentally, and politically an anachronism. (Emig, 1983, pp. 88–95)

In a later paper, "Writing as a Mode of Learning" (Emig, 1983 [originally published in 1977]), Emig considers writing as a "unique languaging process" that affords unique opportunities to learn. The essay is an attempt to provoke deep and practice-based inquiry into how writing brings about learning. While she cites Vygotsky's, Luria's, and Bruner's claims about the role of written language in supporting higher cognitive functions, these claims are introduced in an evocative way and support her point neither more nor less than the extended quotations she includes from Sartre and Robert Pirsig. The strongest voice we hear in this work is Emig herself, discussing her own insights about writing and learning based on her sustained consideration of them over decades.

In yet a later paper, "The Tacit Tradition," Emig's concern with the intellectual roots of her enterprise takes the shape of a discussion on what the field of writing process research has inherited from scholars such as Piaget, Dewey, George Miller, Suzanne Langer, Eric Lenneberg, and Luria and Vygotsky. In this short paper, she does not go on at length about what contributions in particular each of these scholars made to the tradition she celebrates, but she does peg them all as "transactionalists": "The learner/writer...is an active construer of meaning in her transactions with experience" (Emig, 1983, p. 153).

Emig's focus on the individual learner/writer encompasses both the internal processes of that writer and the contributions made by and taken from the "significant others" outside that individual. But the focus is unquestionably on the individual and on the process of learning. This focus is repeated in the enormously influential work of Donald Graves. Here I focus only on his book intended for teachers, certainly one of the most widely read and cited texts of its kind. *Writing: Teachers and Children at Work* (Graves, 1983) is an even stronger explication of the writing process than some of his more academic works. In this work, we see an integration of the view of writing as a process taking place within a social context with a thorough commitment to the real lives of teachers and students working together in classrooms.

The transformation of the "skill" of writing into a fully considered, purposive human activity is what characterizes the writing process "movement." Graves is one of its most widely known exponents.[13] In this view, in order to teach writing, one must be a writer, in the sense that one must fully and consistently engage in the many purposes of writing and their concomitant practices.

We don't find many teachers of oil painting, piano, ceramics, or drama who are not practitioners in their fields. Their students see them in action in the studio. They can't teach without showing what they mean. There is a process to follow. There is a process to learn. That's the way it is with a craft. (Graves, 1983, p. 6)

Only from the inside can one authentically teach the process of writing, Graves says. Revision is not simply a search for errors; it is an organic outgrowth of the writer's authentic attempt to rethink and reconfigure the piece as necessary, based on further thought and response from others. Also central is consideration of the full process of writing undergone by mature authors:

Young authors, who have their own work questioned, become more assertive in questioning the work of professionals.... At first six-year old children believe that professionals put their work together just as they do. But as the work of the professional is tested they gradually realize that the information is carefully chosen and filled with the facts needed for their understanding. (Graves, 1983, pp. 66–67)

In this volume, Graves provides for teachers many exemplars of this complex process, always showing that its particular character in any case grows out of the specific contexts of individual writers and responders in that classroom. But did this reconceptualization of the writing process—as individuals engaging in a social activity within a specific social setting—arise from any theoretical ancestors in psychology, sociology, or anthropology? In both Graves's and Emig's work, the social reconceptualization seems to stem almost entirely from the insights and experiences of the gifted writer and teacher, along with his or her colleagues.

*The British.* In 1975, James Britton and his colleagues published the results of a study carried out in the late 1960s on the development of adolescent writing abilities (Britton, Burgess, Martin, McLeod, & Rosen, 1975). While they share many of the influences cited by Emig, their emphasis is slightly different. The writing process, again, is primarily conceptualized as an individual's actions within a larger social context, but greater emphasis is placed on the role of spoken language as such: "Our classification presupposes what has been called an operational view of language—one, that is, which gives weight to the fact that language is something which is put to use...interpenetrating and continuous with consciousness" (Britton et al., 1975, p. 139). Britton et al. briefly review how Vygotsky's discussion of inner and outer speech has influenced their thinking about the composing processes of individuals: how the inchoate and inarticulate inner speech is a "bridge between external, communicative language on the one hand and thought on the other" (p. 39). The dialectic nature of the process described by Vygotsky evokes for them the essential character of the composition process. It also captures a theme central to their work: "the *developmental* role for writing in school...the talk by which children will govern their lives will require mental abilities that will best be developed by the practice of writing" (p. 201).

Just as important to the enterprise is their emphasis on reconceptualizing the various genres of writing engaged by students. In order to propose a developmental model, they argue, they must first thoroughly characterize what is to be attained. They develop a typology of mature writing genres by incorporating (in addition to two millennia of rhetoric theory) Roman Jakobson's, Dell Hymes's, and James Moffett's ideas about the relations between human communicative purposes and types of spoken and written expression. After constructing a typology of functions and a concomitant typology of audience types, they set out to relate to this model a diachronic sample of thousands of pieces of adolescent writing. Their ultimate purpose is to understand more about the development of writing abilities within different content areas and across ages.

In some ways, Britton et al. go much further in theorizing their model of writing development than the Americans. Their discussion of types of audience in terms of the relationships implied presages work by many later scholars. Their discussion of the relation between functions of writing and forms of thought is far more detailed than anything one finds in the original American process writing literature. On the other hand, although their discussions of Jakobson and Vygotsky inter alia are more substantively related to their own theorizing, in the end one is left with the sense that here, too, the most powerful insights in the work derive from the authors' profound appreciation of written communication and their very close connection to the teachers and students they study. One gets the sense that if Vygotsky had never been translated, these scholars might have arrived at essentially the same places. Nevertheless, his work obviously spoke to them in a powerful way, enough so that they saw it as worth integrating into what was already a powerful study about learning.

*Retrospective heuristics and labels.* What are we to make of discussions of Vygotsky and other "social constructivists" in the midst of work that seems principally motivated by sources outside of any social constructivist theory? Are these citations, ex post facto, mere window dressing? I see in them instead evidence of careful retrospection on the part of these writers. They have immersed themselves in a rich and complex world of practice: writing and the teaching of writing, both of which they know very well. Yet their intimate knowledge does not render trivial the task of analysis. They must isolate out of the complexity recurrent objects, properties, relations, and outcomes, and then they must make these recognizable to others. I see in Emig's and Britton's appeals to theoreticians an attempt to clarify what they have found through the retrospective use of theoretical constructs, both as heuristic devices to organize for themselves the complex world of the classroom and as labeling devices to collate their findings with constructs that may have familiarity or resonance for others outside of their field. This use of theoretical tools supports an effort to clarify the significance of what they have found and to make it recognizable to others.

## Process Writing in the Wider Society

In 1986, Lisa Delpit described process writing as an exemplar of progressive pedagogies that do not serve minority communities' needs; what she perceived as an abiding emphasis on "fluency" left minority children without access to the "skills" that White middle-class students could gain outside the classroom. Her critique is supported by her extensive teaching experience, as recounted in the article. It is thoroughly focused on the social world of formal education and the way its curricular ideologies mask the effects on children of some progressive pedagogies. In 1996, Keith Gilyard responded to her critique, challenging her description of process writing essentials and calling into question the basis of her conclusions about process writing in particular. Yet, he returns to her larger point about the meaning of curriculum and pedagogy within complex societies such as ours. He writes admiringly of Robert Brooke's writers' workshops for students, where, instead of taking on the identity of a student who is following the dictates of the instructor, students take on roles of "reflective thinker and community influencer," thus paralleling the kinds of personal commitments that "real writers" are driven by (Gilyard, 1996b, p. 26). Yet, Gilyard takes the process writing instructors to task for their politically neutral posture toward their students in the workshop. Citing Jim Gee, he points to the impossibility of an "agendaless" literacy. "The point is to truly model mature literacy, to show that literacy always means something in particular" (p. 26). "Writing and writing instruction are socially, not naturally, occurring phenomena. They are never heading nowhere" (p. 27).

Delpit does not cite research in her article; her position depends on her own interpretation of her experience. We can infer from Gilyard's discussion that he is familiar with both social constructivism[3] and some of the work in the first cluster, particularly that of what might be called the "critical social constructivists." Yet, as one reads through the essays that compose his 1996 volume, it seems that the insights and discoveries primarily emerge from his experience as a writer, a teacher, and a thinker, albeit a thinker who is very conversant with current theorizations. Although the larger social and political focus of Gilyard does not depend on any theorization, his uses of this work add a dimension to his own. Gilyard finds, in these theorists' work, counterparts to his own discoveries, framed differently, yet consonant with his own. By mentioning these counterparts, he induces the reader to consider his own findings twice, once from the unique perspective he constructs and once through the lingua franca that includes sociocultural/historical and critical theories.

## Other Large Studies of Writing

In continuing to explore the editors' questions, it is interesting to consider the theoretical framing of two studies that were obviously descendants of both British and American process writing. Langer and Applebee's (1987) and Freedman's (1988) studies are both research reports published by the National Council of Teachers of English. Langer and Applebee aimed to discover, at a detailed level, the kinds of learning and thinking that writing can foster by carrying out a close study of the teaching of 23 teachers and the writing of more than 500 students. Incorporating observation, experimental studies, and detailed case studies, their project resulted in conclusions about the kinds of writing that lead to more complex reasoning on the part of students. Their results led them to make the following comments about the nature of instruction in general:

Rather than providing information and evaluating what students have learned, effective writing instruction provides carefully structured support or scaffolding as students undertake new and more difficult tasks. In the process of completing those tasks, students internalize information and strategies relevant to the tasks, learning the concepts and skills they will need in order eventually to undertake similar tasks on their own.... The view that we have adopted grows out of a more general view of language learning, one that has been heavily influenced by the work of both Vygotsky and Bruner.... [Vygotsky] argues that higher level skills are the result of the child's learning of social-functional relationships; in becoming literate, children internalize the structures of socially meaningful literacy activities.... Thus approaches that are initially mediated socially are eventually internalized and become part of the repertoire of the individual. (Langer & Applebee, 1987, p. 139)

Langer and Applebee conclude the report with a brief discussion of the local, interactional facet of Vygotskian thought, but the report itself gives no indication that his theory shaped the study in the first place. The sociocultural references may add to the impact of the work by giving readers another analytical level on which to consider their results. Yet, once again, the work stands on its own, its real force deriving from Applebee and Langer's long-term immersion in research on the development of literacy.

Sarah Freedman presents an in-depth study of another aspect of process writing: the nature of response and how it supports learning. Her study is the first to involve a large-scale and detailed description of response that goes beyond rough "descriptions of formally structured peer groups, conferences, and written comments" (Freedman, 1987, p. 5). Freedman includes, in her report, a fairly lengthy introduction providing theoretical anchoring in which she discusses the importance of theories of how intellectual skills are learned in school (citing, for example, Anderson and Gagne) and theories of how oral language is acquired (citing, for example, Cazden, Clark and Clark, Ochs, and others) (p. 5). She also discusses the importance of Vygotsky. She considers response to be "both a social and a cognitive process—a point of view perhaps best articulated by Vygotsky" (p. 5). Freedman, like others concerned with classroom learning, finds the local, dyadic aspects of social constructivism$_3$ to be most useful and considers them primarily in terms of the individual learner. "Learning awakens a variety of internal developmental processes that are able to operate only when the child is interacting with people in his environment" (Freedman, 1987, p. 90).

Does Freedman rely on social constructivist thought in formulating her understanding of writing response? She states that her monograph "is based on the theory that the achievement of cognitive gain depends on the substance of social interactions...collaborative problem solving...as jointly accomplished teaching and learning" (Freedman, 1987, pp. 8–9). And "when Vygotsky's theoretical insights are applied to response to student writing, it becomes clear that response (1) should be collaborative between a writer and someone more expert on the issue being discussed, (2) should try to help developing writers solve writing problems or write in ways that they could not alone, and (3) should lead to independent problem solving" (p. 9). Yet, while the Vygotskian constructs help illuminate and clarify her findings, one can tell that she understands these constructs through another channel, through her close connection to teachers and student writers. Freedman's voice emerges most clearly in a final statement that reveals a deep concern with what one might label Vygotskian relationships: the dialectic interactions between teachers and their classrooms, students' vertical and horizontal interactions, and the larger institutional contexts within which they all work. Yet, the authoritative tone suggests that this knowledge about the social contexts of learning derives from her own work and is not a byproduct of reading Vygotsky or any other theoretician.

There are a number of difficulties that even the most successful teachers face when planning responses to students' writing. Although many successful teachers devise ways to provide individual, teacher-led conferences during the writing process, the organization of the typical school does not support individualized teaching of this type; and so even successful teachers do not always individualize instruction in this way.... In some cases teachers lean heavily on peer groups for elaborated response to writing...[but are] ambivalent about the success of peer groups. The ambivalence likely has at least two sources. First, students tend not to trust the opinions of their peers as equivalent to the opinion of the teacher and sometimes work to subvert peer response.... As long as students are trying to write for a grade and are anxious to relinquish responsibility of their writing to their teacher who awards the grade, conferences can easily become sessions in which students manipulate teachers to tell them "answers." Likewise peer groups can turn into group sessions in which students help each other get their writing "right" or can be devalued as useless by students. Radical reorganization of the classrooms will be needed in order to make *writing* and *learning* more important or even as important as *grading* from the students' points of view. (Freedman, 1987, p. 161)

Yet, there is a powerful compatibility between the Vygotskian view and Freedman's concerns. In work a decade later, Freedman's use of Vygotskian and Bakhtinian ideas has become much more integral to the work, indicating that this compatibility has been developed into a more instrumental relationship. Discussing her long-term collaborative study of American and British classrooms engaged in writing exchanges (1994), she makes explicit a very important point about the relation between the education researcher and the theory. She states that her work

situates theory in the specifics of everyday life inside classrooms, schools, school systems, communities and countries. In this way it aims to highlight *aspects of theory that need amplification* in order to be maximally useful pedagogically.... The *concepts of social interaction and of multivoiced dialogues are too general to account fully for the interactions in these classrooms.* (pp. 226–227) [italics added]

This statement clarifies a problem that emerges further in work discussed subsequently: The constructs of social constructivist theories are helpful in parsing the complexities of classroom learning and teaching, yet they are not tools ready-made for solving the range of problems these education researchers face; they are tools that must be adapted.

## (Micro)ethnography of Writing

Some writers use social constructivist concepts and labels to provide a set of frames that will aid readers in interpreting their work. Other researchers convey in their writings a sense that they are using those concepts as tools in the midst of their analytical work, to help them sharpen their own insights and intuitions, to bring clarity out of the chaos of classroom life. As is the case with any tool, however, some concepts may prove limited, unequal to the challenge offered by particularly complex data. Ann Dyson's (e.g., 1993, 1997) work on young children learning to write conveys this sense: When she cites Bakhtin or Vygotsky or some other sociocultural theorist, it is often as a tool to clarify her own thinking about what she is seeing in the complex worlds of the classrooms she observes so intensely and in the texts (verbal and written) produced by the children. She notes where the theorists' conceptualizations fortuitously shed light on a particularly multidimensional and confusing situation she has encountered.

> To help me make sense of the children's talk-filled worlds, I envisioned the complex landscape of discourse described by Bakhtin...(1993, p.5). Child authors, like adult ones, weave everyday voices into complex "fake worlds." They literally appropriate the utterances of others...to express their own attitudes.... The children's stories...looked quite different from the complex adult prose analyzed by Bakhtin...but they were still complex social undertakings. (Dyson, 1993, p. 19)

She also notes where her own conceptualizations diverge from the theorists' (e.g., Dyson, 1997, p. 211). Dyson uses the ideas of social constructivism[3] heuristically, while she conducts the work. She seems to be testing and clarifying her own intuitions in the process of research by using their concepts as interim guides, much as one might use a piano to work out ideas for a musical arrangement for guitar. The two instruments have very different constraints, and many properties disallow straightforward transfer from one to the other. Nevertheless, one can gain valuable insights from working on piano if the guitar is not yet available.

Dyson makes use of Bakhtin to think about the "unofficial worlds" created and enacted by children in the whirlwind of classroom life. Lensmire (1994) attempts an explicitly Bakhtinian characterization of the unofficial (even antiofficial) worlds that emerge in the practice of writing workshop in his fifth-grade class. By using Bakhtin's notion of "carnival," Lensmire provides for himself a way to critically examine writing workshop while enabling himself to "affirm what I take to be the core of workshop commitments—a vision of children writing themselves and their worlds on the page, within a classroom setting that liberates student intention and association" (p. 371). Here again we see a researcher faced with an inordinately complex topic: a group of children engaging in a multileveled blending of social and cognitive activity for a variety of purposes, within the ongoing official and unofficial social worlds of the classroom. Within this research site, Lensmire adapts theoretical tools in hopes of both understanding more powerfully and communicating more clearly about what he understands.

## Summary: The Theory-Research Interface and Process Writing

The field of process writing foregrounds many social aspects of learning, from the global to the very local, from those embedded in the notion of rhetorical purpose and audience to those entailed by classroom learning. Focus on these social aspects of learning to write is, by and large, not motivated by any social constructivist theory. Rather, it seems to originate in the experiences and insights of writers and writing teachers, in their deep knowledge of both the act of writing and the teaching and learning of writing. Of those who carry out research and pedagogy on K–12 writing, however, a number do make contact with social constructivist theories. Of the three clusters identified in the second section of this chapter, the one most frequently cited in the writing research seems to be the third: the sociocultural-historical variety.[14] This is not surprising given the focus of this cluster on the individual in constant contact with the collective, learning to participate in social practices by immersion in linguistically mediated social interaction. The nature of writing itself calls for a theorization that at least puts the collective on equal footing with the individual; yet, the pedagogical goals in the background of this research require that the individual learner remain at the center of the picture.[15]

Even in this small sample, we see a wide variety of relations between research questions and findings and the categories of theory. In those studies in which the cited theoretical works seem least determinative of the conduct or content of research, theoretical categories may still play an important role. Whereas the researcher may have come to his or her design and results based primarily on first-hand knowledge of the subject area domain (both its content and the teaching of it), nevertheless that researcher seeks to make the research more general in its implications by casting it twice: once in the original terms of the researcher and once in theorized terms known to a wider audience, in essence a descriptive lingua franca. In other cases, theoretical concepts are used heuristically in the midst of research, as tools to further the ongoing development of related theoretical constructs.[16] In both instances, it is important to recall that these researchers were not working in isolation. Even when their own insights about writing and classrooms were primary, they worked within a community of other researchers and teachers, colleagues who presumably also want to attain a deeper understanding and a more precise analytic purchase on the complex topics of concern. The use of theoretical constructs to label, describe, or analyze one's work must be understood as originating at least in part within the social milieu of research practice.

### Mathematics Education: Research and Practice

My goal in this section is again to explore sources of ideas about the social in mathematics education and to ask whether any of these ideas can be characterized as stemming from one of the three social constructivism clusters. In addition, I again take note of the ways researchers use the categories of theory.

### Concerns Underlying Mathematics Education Research and Practice

Before I review works that purport to focus on the social, however, I first describe several important influences that serve as background to any of the efforts that might be characterized as social constructivist. While there is no single move-ment in mathematics education parallel to process writing, it is important to sketch the unifying concerns that underlie much of the research in the field.

*"Problem solving," "inquiry," and the work of the mathematician.* Within K–12 mathematics education over the past 25 years, there is an important strand that, for want of a better term, I label "problem solving and inquiry." There have been several major influences driving this emphasis, including the burgeoning fields of cognitive science and information-processing psychology. Problem solving does not simply refer to students solving problems of the kind found in textbooks. Rather, it is shorthand for an entire set of revaluings and reconsiderations in which math-ematics educators attempted to shift the emphasis away from mastery of compu-tation and rote memorization of algorithms, along with the "brittle" performances that have been shown to result from these pedagogies. To what did they want to shift the emphasis instead? The answer: to mathematics as engaged in by real mathematicians (i.e., with a desire to explore the world in mathematically interest-ing and coherent ways and make sense out of complex situations, whether in the "real world" or in the world of mathematical structures).

Along the way, a number of mathematicians and mathematics educators, in try-ing to characterize what students should learn, have reflected on the authentic practices of working mathematicians through their own experiences and those of their colleagues, whether applied or theoretical, professional or hobbyist. Some of these works reflect on the personal qualities of intellectual courage and honesty required to create mathematics, as well as on the controversial and provisional nature of the actual creation. While such works have been around for some time (Polya, 1957), their influence began to coalesce in the 1980s. Davis and Hersh's (1981) and Alan Schoenfeld's (1985, 1987) volumes are exemplars of this empha-sis. Here I supply a more recent exemplar, one written without references to the education research literature but with a wealth of mathematical experience behind its observations:

For generations, high school students have studied something in school that has been called math-ematics, but has very little to do with the way mathematics is created or applied outside of school. One reason for this has been a view of curriculum in which mathematics courses are seen as mechanisms for communicating established results and methods.... Much more important than specific mathemati-cal results are the habits of mind used by the people who create those results.... We envision a curricu-lum [the goal of which is] to help high school students learn and adopt some of the ways that math-ematicians think about problems.... This includes learning to recognize when problems or statements that purport to be mathematical are, in truth, still quite ill-posed or fuzzy; becoming comfortable with and skilled at bringing mathematical meaning to problems and statements through definition, system-atization, abstraction or logical connection making; and seeking and developing new ways of describ-ing situations. (Cuoco, Goldenberg, & Mark, 1996, p. 376)

The most notable development in mathematics education from the view of the outside world has probably been the publication of the standards for instruction and curriculum by the National Council of Teachers of Mathematics (NCTM) (1989). These standards have been accompanied by other "consensus" documents such as *Everybody Counts*, constructed under the aegis of the National Research Council by mathematicians, educators, education psychologists, statisticians, scientists and engineers, teachers from elementary through graduate schools, state and local administrators and members of government, and leaders of groups representing parents, business, and industry (1989). The NCTM standards described the shifts in practice that reform classrooms should aim to accomplish: (a) toward classrooms as mathematical communities; (b) toward logic and mathematical evidence as verification and away from the teacher as sole authority; (c) toward mathematical reasoning and away from merely memorizing procedures; (d) toward conjecturing, inventing, and problem solving and away from an emphasis on mechanistic answer finding; and (e) toward connecting mathematics, its ideas, and its applications and away from treating mathematics as a body of isolated concepts and procedures (NCTM, 1989, p. 3). These standards grew out of prior research to some extent, but they have in turn influenced the research topics chosen subsequently.

*Analysis and presentation of content.* To this point, the similarities between the writing process movement and the problem-solving, inquiry mathematics community are obvious. Both are anchored in the personal experiential knowledge of educators who participate fully in the discipline that gave rise to their content area. However, within mathematics education, there is yet another major center of gravity that leads to a different trajectory for this movement. In mathematics education, there is an omnipresent and universal concern with the subject matter itself, both its underlying structure and its massive content. In spite of Cuoco et al.'s comments about habits of mind, it is undeniable that there is a huge range of specific knowledge and skills that must be acquired between kindergarten and 12th grade. The National Assessment of Educational Progress has identified five strands that cover what should be learned during these years: (a) number sense, properties, and operations; (b) measurement; (c) geometry and spatial sense; (d) data analysis, statistics, and probability; and (e) algebra and functions. The vastness and diversity of this content have led to at least two major bodies of work: research on conceptual underpinnings and research on effective instruction.

Research on conceptual underpinnings consists of explorations of content areas (e.g., proportional reasoning, multiplicative structures, fractions) carried out by mathematically sophisticated researchers who are seeking deeper and more illuminating ways to conceptualize these mathematical structures and relations so as to develop curricula that will ultimately provide more powerful springboards for students into mathematics and the mathematical sciences in general (good examples from the domain of middle school mathematics are contained in NCTM, 1988). However, perhaps the most pressing concern in the mathematics education research literature has been the search for effective forms of instruction, again often derived from the insights and discoveries of mathematics teachers with many years of experience. In the world of composition and writing studies, there is no analogue to the hosts of researchers concerned with ways of teaching the actual contents of mathematics. (Indeed, this is why, for so many years, writing was thought of as "merely a skill": It seemed not to have the content of a field like mathematics.)

*Analysis of individual learning.* Within mathematics education research, a large number of researchers evidence at least a loose affiliation with constructivism or radical constructivism. As briefly sketched in the second section of this chapter (as a precursor to social constructivism$_2$), Piagetian constructivism (in stark contrast to the behaviorist psychology that preceded it into the schools) has as its central focus processes by which the individual comes to build an understanding of the encountered world. It may be that Piaget's writings on the growth of mathematical and logical thinking laid the groundwork for this constructivist emphasis in mathematics education. The cognitive precursors to numerical cognition and to operations on numbers have received a great deal of attention in the developmental psychology literature. (There are also constructivists whose training is in information-processing psychology, not Piagetian psychology, but most of the characterizations given here are at least compatible with their concerns.) Ultimately, however, the constructivist focus on individuals negotiating their way into the world of mathematical objects and relations may stem from the irreducible components of mathematical learning: a single learner coming to know and understand a set of abstractions with complex relations to concrete embodiments of various kinds.

The implication of radical constructivism for education seems to be that "for the teacher, the mathematical realities of his or her students must be objects he or she comes to know through experimental encounters, and to know them is to construct a conceptual model of them using the construct of evolving schemes of action and operations" (Steffe, 1988, p. 122). In this literature, it is the radical constructivists who carry out extremely detailed and individually specified studies of how learners come to build an understanding of, say, number sequences and composite units (e.g., "one group of three"). While there are some mathematics education researchers who would not label themselves as constructivists, the basic constructivist assumptions sketched earlier have had a pervasive influence and, thus, determine part of the background against which we must consider specific research that foregrounds the social aspects of learning.

## Some Conceptualizations of the Social
## in Mathematics Education Research

These background influences have an influence on current conceptualizations of the social in mathematics education research. The standards themselves contain a great deal of intrinsically social conceptualizations of mathematical practices, although these conceptualizations have not been worked out within any theory of social interaction or social structure. There is a parallel here to process writing: No theory was necessary to reveal a deeply social aspect of the content area. The current emphasis on the pedagogical importance of social aspects of mathematics practice was driven at least in part by the insights of expert practitioners in the discipline into their own intellectual practices, which, they assert, are irreducibly social in at least some respects. In addition, constructivism itself is slowly moving toward an examination of the social aspects of learning, as described in the second section of this chapter.[17] For one thing, as educational researchers have sought ways to understand classroom learning, they have been forced to consider the many ways that social contexts and social phenomena play a role in the learning of individuals. These two influences are visible in different proportions in the few works reviewed subsequently.

*Lampert: The intellectual life of the mathematics classroom.* In Magdalena Lampert's work (e.g., 1990, 1991; Lampert, Rittenhouse, & Crumbaugh, 1996), the voice of a uniquely positioned teacher emerges, poses the research questions, and sustains the inquiry. Lampert's own classroom serves as the observational ground for her reflections on the complexities of the enterprise. Her expertise and reflections about teaching drive the inquiry at all points. Equally important, however, is her knowledge of mathematics: its practice and its history. These aspects of her identity combine to produce research papers characterized by an overarching concern with the connections to be established between the discipline as it exists in the wider world and the community established in the classroom (see also work by her colleague Deborah Ball [e.g., 1993]). One outgrowth of this concern is a close examination of group discussion. Lampert examines the discussions she orchestrates for anything they may reveal about students' changing conceptions of what it means to do mathematics in their classroom and in the larger world. She articulates in vivid detail how teachers in reform classrooms have responsibilities that are sometimes at cross purposes: They must support individual and collective inventions, yet they must always find ways to relate them to mathematical traditions.

A good example is Lampert's 1990 paper "Connecting Inventions With Conventions." Here Lampert describes how students develop notations for the activity of finding fractional parts of a population. As the episode develops, we see individual children proposing procedures by which to manipulate physical objects and then, by corresponding numerical representations, responding to each other's proposals and clarifying and changing their own. The interplay between the individual and group is striking, and Lampert's stated goal of developing a common culture of ideas about mathematics seems well served by what goes on in the class.

However, all is not always wonderful in this inquiry classroom. In a section titled "Despair, and a Mathematical Analysis of a Pedagogical Problem," we encounter reality: In spite of the meaningful discussions and the days of emphasis on making sense of the problem, students have begun to lose touch with the meaning of their procedures, seduced by the efficiency of the algorithms developed in the collective. They fail to make connections among the numerical algorithm, the drawings, and the original problem. Lampert reports how she was forced, at this point, to take a more directing role, consolidating the students around a common interpretation of the denominator of a fraction and relating it to the population problems she had been giving them (p. 262). Finally, she has the students make a public text that will contain directions sufficiently explicit and clear that outsiders could follow their procedures. This group assessment shows that Lampert's attempt to create a "community of discourse about mathematics" has had effects on individual student understanding and ability to externalize that understanding, as well as on the group's ability to collaboratively produce something more powerful than most individuals could have done on their own. This moment would be perfect fodder for an analysis using the second or third version of social constructivism, but Lampert does not use those tools. Her own conceptualization of the classroom culture carries the research text.

Lampert is fascinated with the role of talk within the collective, its power to alter ways of thinking and ways of doing, as well as its limits (Lampert et al., 1996). While Lampert cites a number of theoreticians in her various papers, including a few sociocultural-historical writers and Berger and Luckmann (1967) as well (Lampert, 1990), the most important sources of influence often seem to be those who write about the history of mathematics. She is concerned with actually finding in her students' stances correspondences with the historical trends of the past.[19] But in her published work, at least as important as any sources found in the bibliography are her own experiences as a teacher and as a mathematician. Using a sophisticated knowledge of teaching, of mathematics, and of mathematicians as historical communities, she reflects on her students' learning both individually and collectively. In Lampert's work, social constructivist theory rarely is used, even to label the phenomena. Instead, one gets a sense that she is indexing points of theoretical contact that readers may find of interest, given the nature of her enterprise. But if these works had never been written, her concerns and insights would be the same.

*Cobb et al.: The social dimensions of the learning experiment.* The work of Paul Cobb and his frequent collaborators Terry Wood and Erna Yackel spans a number of different kinds of projects and continues to appear in a wide range of publication forms. It is not possible to summarize all of this work here, but a few overarching characteristics emerge. First, to an extent not found in any of the other papers I have reviewed here, these authors make a point of explaining that their interest in Vygotsky (and other theoreticians discussed subsequently) followed their original theoretical impulses and arose out of what they learned as they pursued their study of constructivist teaching experiments in elementary school mathematics classrooms.

We must state at the outset that neither the theoretical nor the pragmatic aspects of our work were initially derived from neo-Vygotskian theory. Informed by an almost exclusively cognitive constructivist perspective, we initially intended to analyze individual children's learning as they participated in classroom mathematical activity. Our interest in symbolic interactionism and ethnomethodology developed in concert with our growing awareness of the insufficiency of this initial theoretical orientation. It subsequently became apparent that the way in which we were attempting to make sense of classroom life was, in many respects, compatible with certain of Vygotsky's theoretical notions. (Cobb, Wood, & Yackel, 1993, p. 91)

One of the most interesting aspects of this work is the rapidly changing trajectory of theoretical commitment. Early on, a departure from the individual-level focus that characterizes constructivism itself is apparent. "The emphasis on mathematical communication in both small-group and whole-class settings reflected our developing view that mathematics is a social activity—a community project...as well as an individual constructive activity" (p. 92). Cobb et al. put forth a deep consideration of the multiplicity of ways in which social context can shape individual learning, from their initial view that "social interaction was a catalyst for autonomous individual cognitive development" (p. 92) (essentially a Piagetian expectation) to the view that "mathematical activity can be viewed as intrinsically social in that what counts as a problem and as a resolution has normative aspects" (p. 93). In their year-long teaching experiment, the classroom embodied the kinds of interactional arrangements that Cobb et al. would expect to ensure group construction of mathematical knowledge; "the mathematical meanings and practices institutionalized in the classroom were not immutably decided in advance by the teacher, but, instead, emerged during the course of conversations characterized by...a genuine commitment to communicate" (p. 93).

Moreover, the research trajectory carries them into a consideration of the wider social community beyond the social aspects of classroom interaction. The project reported in this paper was originally conceived as something that would be carried out at the level of individual classrooms. However, it quickly became apparent that the participating teachers and researchers could not avoid conflict with the local school board, which apparently took a dim view of the approach that was being implemented. Yet, in the course of this conflict, teachers' views and views of community members changed; Cobb et al. observe that practices in the classroom change and are changed by the "social action system" at the level of school district and community. They find a resonance with Lave's (1988; Lave & Wenger 1991) work here, in the dialectical relation between the actions of the community and those of its members, as well as with Minick's discussions of activity theory: "An individual's psychological development is profoundly influenced by his or her participation in particular forms of social practice" (Cobb et al., 1993, p. 95).

What becomes obvious in reading this work is that Cobb et al. are grappling, through their experience itself and through their attempts to theorize it, with the tension between the collective and the individual within the content domain they are studying. Like Dyson, Freedman, and Lensmire, they are using these constructs heuristically to refine and clarify their own constructs, ones that will achieve a closer fit to the particular realities in which they are immersed. Faced with the reality of the classroom, they extricate themselves from the primarily individual focus that dominates constructivist research and turn toward the collective emphasis in the first and third clusters. But given their understanding of mathematical practices, still they refrain from going to the other pole, where the individual is

*embedded* or *included* in a social practice. Such metaphors tend to reify social practices, whereas we believe that they do not exist apart from and are interactively constituted by the actions of actively interpreting individuals.... By making this point, we are attempting to avoid any tendency that subordinates the individual to the social and loses sight of the reflexive relation between the two. (Cobb et al., 1993, p. 96)

This reflexive relation is central to their research situation. They go on to state that they will illustrate that the "reflexive relation between the individual and the social holds for students' mathematical development as well as for teachers' pedagogical development" (p. 96). But they do not subvert their vision to any subsuming theoretical categorization; rather, they stubbornly carve out a path that preserves the uniqueness of each classroom and their understanding of it. They reject (as does Confrey, 1995) Vygotsky's reification of social processes originating in the larger society, insisting that they "prefer to emphasize that a practice such as inquiry mathematics is interactively constituted in the classroom and does not exist apart from the activities of the individuals who participate in its constitution" (p. 100). (This insistence subsequently grows into an interest in ethnomethodological approaches, as discussed later.)

A major emphasis of their study of the year-long teaching experiment is on the way the teacher and students jointly negotiate mathematical meanings and, just as important, jointly accomplish the negotiation of discourse norms and "sociomathematical norms" (i.e., norms involved in jointly doing mathematics in the classroom). As the teacher attempts to induct students into "inquiry math," in which they are obligated to say "what they really thought mathematically," she has to find ways to guide students toward new discourse norms. Their detailed observations about this accomplishment include consideration of the ways in which the teacher manages emotion and affect. An incident in which the teacher attempts to bring students to see that an incorrect answer is not cause for embarrassment in her classroom is central to Cobb et al.'s work. Their conceptualization of individual cognition has broadened to include emotion, affect, goals, and motivation, as they see individuals in joint action in social settings.

The ideas of sociomathematical norms (e.g., What constitutes a "different solution"?) and discourse norms are of great interest with respect to the current chapter, because they are a collective accomplishment, yet each individual bears a dynamic and constitutive relationship to the norms throughout the school year. These are ideas that are forged out of a classroom reality fundamentally grounded in the practice of mathematics, and they hold the individual and the collective in tension. Along the way, Cobb et al. make reference to others' theorizations, but there is no preexisting category that encompasses both these discourse norms and sociomathematical norms.

In recent work by Cobb, it becomes evident that he is moving toward the construction of a theory that will extend various ideas in all three clusters of social constructivist thought (including ethnomethodology). Yet, he is adapting and testing these theoretical tools as he proceeds. For example, Cobb (in press) presents a microanalysis of four children using a hundreds board to learn place value. This analysis brings into apposition the ideas of social constructivism$_2$ and social constructivism$_3$ and presents a sort of test of them. A theoretical construct will be maintained in his framework only as long as it veridically represents and illuminates the complex amalgam of teaching and learning problems that mathematics reform education presents.

Simon and Blume (1996), following the lead of Cobb et al., carried out a study of the construction of new norms for justification among a class of prospective elementary school teachers. As teachers attempt to adopt the reforms summarized in the NCTM (1989) document, they find themselves engaging in very different kinds of activities, among them taking a whole new stance with respect to justification of a mathematical procedure or an answer to a problem. Following the novice teachers' immersion in problem solving in groups, Simon and Blume trace the teachers' progress from simply citing authority as justification for a particular solution (e.g., "In previous math classes you learned the formula for area is length times width") to actually sustaining inquiry in the face of two reasonable justifications, inquiring into the larger implications of one justification versus the other.

Many things emerge from this study; in stark contrast to a transmission model of teaching, Simon and Blume show that a logical justification of a problem persuades members of the class only if they share an understanding of the problem similar to like that of the justifier herself. At the level of commonsense experience, this is not surprising: Why should we accept what we don't understand? Yet, for a very long time, students in mathematics classes have been presented with proofs and justifications that they were expected to simply ingest and incorporate. In other words, the proof or justification itself was part of the "transmitted knowledge." In this microanalytic constructivist teaching experiment, Simon and Blume can see that, instead, individual understanding and collective understanding proceed in a dialectic, step-by-step fashion. "The development of classroom mathematical communities that identify their mission as collective sense-making seems to be a potentially attainable goal of current reforms" (Simon & Blume, 1996, p. 29). In this article, as in earlier papers by Cobb and collaborators, we see the constructivist background gradually expanding to social constructivism₂, encompassing social aspects of mathematical practice and social aspects of classroom learning.

Bauersfeld (1995) makes use of the ideas of social constructivism₁ in theorizing a pervasive yet invisible part of mathematics teaching and learning. An ethnomethodological approach allows him to point to work that constitutes the hidden part of the iceberg: the moment-by-moment construction of interpretations of pictures in a mathematics textbook. Bauersfeld's microanalysis involved the discourse surrounding first graders learning how to interpret a picture of four birds sitting on a telephone line, juxtaposed with three birds flying next to them. The canonical interpretation—although, of course, not the only one—is, in this context, $7 - 3 = 4$. But, Bauersfeld asks, how do we come to know that, and how do we come to see it as the only interpretation? What the discourse of the teacher and students accomplishes over time is the acquisition by the students of a "reduced way of interpreting" textbook conventions, in service of their becoming members of a sociocultural group that can participate in the social practice of "mathematizing." One gets the sense, in this paper, that the ethnomethodologists' dogged insistence on analyzing members' construction of moment-to-moment reality in terms of their own categories has allowed Bauersfeld to see aspects of teaching that are invisible, or at least very difficult to see, without those theoretical imperatives.

Nemirovsky (1994) also directs our attention to a social aspect of mathematics learning that is not always framed as social. He casts the activity of symbolizing, in this case learning the meaning of a velocity sign, as a sociocognitive practice rather than as the ability "to replicate a certain symbolic procedure.... Ways of symbolizing are not closed codes that one learns and, from that point on, one 'has'" (p. 393). He cites Bakhtin extensively to develop his idea that practicing a certain kind of symbol use "involves developing a point of view about the meanings of graphical shapes and about the situation represented by the graph, from which a style of symbol-use emerges as a natural, fruitful, and meaningful action in a specific context" (p. 393). Nemirovsky draws on work from all three clusters (including Lave, Lynch, and Confrey) to support his practice account of symbol use. Most striking is his inclusion, alongside this depiction, of a very detailed case study carried out with all of the attention to the microgenesis of content area knowledge that one would expect to find in a traditional Piagetian constructivist study.

## Mathematics Learning in the Wider Society

Recall that Delpit and Gilyard, in the field of writing pedagogy, raised a higher order concern about learning and social life: lack of access for all students and failure to acknowledge political ramifications of instructional and curricular decisions. Their concerns are echoed by a number of writers in mathematics education. Here, too, some express concerns about access and equity (Moses, 1994; Moses, Kamii, Swap, & Howard, 1989; Secada, Fennema, & Adajian, 1995). No theoretical framework is necessary to see that school mathematics plays a gate-keeping role in the movement of children from middle school to high school and beyond.

There are also those who question directly the "construction" of mathematics content and performance in terms most closely allied with the critical variety of social constructivism$_1$. For example, Marilyn Frankenstein (1987, 1995) systematically and prospectively uses Marxist and Freirian conceptualizations to try to change students' consciousness about mathematics practice and their own social positioning. Michael Apple, whose critical theory of curriculum presupposes many of the ideas of social constructivism$_1$, takes on the mathematics reform movement itself, pushing us to analyze how the collective construction of "effective mathematics education" serves interests of which we remain blissfully unaware.

There seems to be a strong assumption that by coupling better mathematics with new psychological theories, most of the issues of educational achievement and equity will be solved.... The psychologization of educational theory and practice—though it has brought gains with it as some of the new mathematics programs...demonstrate—unfortunately has also had a number of crucial limiting effects. It has, profoundly, evacuated critical social, political and economic considerations from the purview of curriculum deliberations. In the process of individualizing its view of students, it has lost any serious sense of the social structures and the race, gender and class relations that form these individuals. Furthermore, it is then unable to situate areas such as mathematics education in a wider social context that includes larger programs for democratic education and a more democratic society.... Without a recognition of the socially situated character of all educational policy and practice, without a recognition of the winners and losers in this sociey, without a more structural understanding of how and why schools participate in creating these winners and losers...I believe we are doomed to reproduce an endless cycle of high hopes, rhetorical reforms, and broken promises. (Apple, 1995, pp. 331–332)

## Summary

Research in mathematics education, like that in process writing, currently foregrounds numerous social aspects of teaching, learning, and disciplinary practice itself. Attention to these social aspects of learning by and large does not rely on any social constructivist theory. Rather, it originates in the experiences and insights of mathematics educators and has been reified and amplified by the concerns of the mathematics community. However, as in writing process research, one of the factors that works to amplify these social concerns is a growing awareness of theoretical work such as that described in the three clusters. Of those who carry out research on K–12 mathematics education, a number do make contact with the work of social constructivism: The second cluster, in which Piagetian constructivism expands its purview into the realm of the social, is well represented. However, even a brief overview reveals a number of researchers taking work in the other two clusters as well.

## CONCLUSIONS

The board's questions as posed cannot be answered, at least not within the space of a chapter, or perhaps even a book. Beyond the issue of the multiplex nature of "social constructivism," there are other reasons that tracing the "efficacy" of social constructivism is problematic. First, there is the fact, obvious perhaps, but not insignificant, that researchers have turned to study the social contexts of learning for a wide variety of reasons, only some of which are related to social constructivist theories. A sizable number of education researchers have looked back at the heart of collective human activity within their disciplines, seeking to identify the activities in which novices must come to participate if they are ever to hope to have mastery in the subject. Others come to education research bringing with them a vivid awareness of collective life generally, with all of its inequity and struggle. Finally, those with a commitment to teaching in classrooms bring to research a deep knowledge of the social contexts of learning, a reality more unruly and multifaceted than any theoretical framework can yet encompass. These sources of interest in social aspects of learning precede theory in most cases; yet, we can see that, in many cases, these nontheoretical sources of interest drive the search for illuminating and compatible theories. Thus, since advances in understanding of social aspects of learning and teaching arise from many quarters, it is difficult to sort out the contributions of social constructivist theories to those advances.

Second, the questions presume a "canonical" relation between theory and research (the production line metaphor) in which theory drives the planning and conduct of research, and expansion and refinement of theory is the goal. This linear relation is not common in this literature. Some researchers, notably Cole, Wertsch, and their colleagues, have used the concepts of social constructivism$_3$ in a formative and even programmatic fashion, setting out from the beginning to test and push the limits of these ideas, to explore the theory itself while studying teaching and learning. In the small sample of content-area-based research described here, however, this formative use of theory is not widely apparent. Instead, what is striking about this small sample of papers is the extent to which some researchers seem committed to adapting the tools of theory. They explore existing social constructivist theories in search of helpful distinctions, categorizations, and explanatory concepts, yet at the same time they are unwilling to subordinate their account of the complexity of their research sites to those theories. Their gaze is held by the multidimensional, intractably complex scene of the learner and teacher in the classroom. Social constructivist theories offer "tools to think with," in the famous phrase, but the thinking remains to be done by the researcher acting in concert with those tools in the midst of learning environments.

Could there be one social constructivism? Even if one accepts that research on teaching and learning has a tremendously complicated focus, still the theories presented here seem to offer potentially powerful tools for analysis. Couldn't a more coherent and unified approach be constructed, one social constructivist theory adapted to the needs of education? Students often ask why different theoretical approaches cannot simply be combined. Couldn't we graft together Vygotskian and constructivist approaches and set them within a critical social constructivism?

In setting out the earlier informal typology of social constructivisms, I did not go into detail about fundamental incompatibilities between the clusters, beyond showing their different emphases. However, this should not be read as implying that there are no fundamental incompatibilities. Three thoughtful discussions of this issue can be found in Cobb (1994a), Confrey (1995), and Hatano (1993). Each points out potential incompatibilities between Vygotskian and constructivist theoretical perspectives, although Confrey is the least sanguine about the combinatory potential. Yet, each offers something crucial for our understanding of learning. Confrey argues persuasively that a Vygotskian approach by itself cannot give an account of the heart of mathematics learning. An "exclusive reliance on 'mathematizing' as 'the interactive constitution of a social practice' could lead social constructivist researchers to overlook much of what Piaget demonstrated and to underestimate or underinvestigate the strength and diversity of individual students' constructive processes" (Confrey, 1995, p. 219).

Within the third cluster alone, sociocultural-historical theory, there are incompatibilities and conflicts. The deep differences between Leont'ev and Vygotsky discussed by Cole (1995) are only one example of cluster-internal incompatibilities. Cole states that approaches to psychology that "take the social and cultural foundations of human nature as the starting point for their analyses" are receiving more attention than they have in the last 70 years or so. However, "nowhere are these ideas so highly developed that it is possible to refer to them as a mature scientific paradigm with generally well-accepted theoretical foundations, a methodology, and a well-delineated set of prescriptions for relating theory to practice" (Cole, 1995, p. 187).

On a more global scale, Apple's concerns (1995) point to another kind of incompatibility. On one hand, the cognitive demands of "content-heavy" subject areas such as mathematics and science require that attention be allocated to individually centered, "internalist" accounts of learning, as constructivists and traditional content area specialists have done. On the other hand, such approaches lead, as Apple points out, to conceptualizations of mathematics learning and performance that ignore our obligations to the collective. It is naive to think that it will be easy to graft together a truly critical theory that will simultaneously illuminate the global and collective concerns of society, the social nature of knowledge construction in every content area, the nature of individual learning within a local collective, and the complex relation between an individual and the content itself (Gee, 1996, makes a similar point).

Furthermore, there are incompatibilities between any of these theories and the "folk theories" of teaching and learning held by the public. These incompatibilities are likely to cause problems with the "mainstreaming" of any social constructivist theory. Even if theorists forged a common view of, for example, the collective nature of higher cognitive functions, any vision that is true to the real intentions of social constructivist[3] theories would be very hard indeed for nontheoreticians to accept. The idea that knowledge and learning are situated in the individual is so firmly embedded in Western educational traditions that even if theoreticians could forge a common understanding, its use in public settings outside the academy would no doubt be subject to withering response from the beginning. The current struggles over state assessments, particularly in California, remind us of how deeply political ideas about learning and knowledge can become.

When we move from the consideration of learning to the consideration of knowledge, further chasms appear, differentially distributed across the subject matter areas. Consider the subfield of history education in relation to the ideas in the first cluster. Many practitioners and researchers might be prepared to agree on the "socially constructed" nature of historical "fact." Far fewer mathematics practitioners and researchers will agree that progress has been made in sociologists' attempts to render the content of mathematics as socially constructed (even Bloor, 1987, doubts that progress). Moreover, in neither case is it clear what is implied for practice.

So should these incompatibilities be taken to mean that there cannot be a coherent social constructivist theory that will inform and even shape research on teaching and learning? On the contrary, in the studies reviewed here, I see evidence of a slow evolution toward such a state of affairs. A partially parallel example from another field might illustrate this view. Within linguistics, there is a division of sorts between two communities.[19] On one hand, there are those who might be called "field linguists," researchers who spend their time investigating and describing in detail the grammars and lexicons of individual, often unwritten, languages. On the other hand, there are those who might be called "theoretical linguists," who spend their time constructing and supporting theories about the universal characteristics of language. Of course, the theoreticians must be accountable to data, and the field workers must eschew analytic idiosyncrasy in order to contribute new knowledge to the field. However, different outlooks divide the two communities. The field worker tends to believe that no theory yet constructed is equal to the task of providing an account of any one language, so complex is the organismic reality of any language. The theoretician tends to see descriptive work as uninterestingly loaded with particularistic details. Yet, over time, each community has come to accept parts of the other: A theoretical construct turns out to have great utility for field linguists; a phenomenon discovered in the field changes the focus of a theoretical enterprise. Each community remains largely separate from the other: The field linguists will resist any theory that does not provide a powerful new understanding of the complex reality they are immersed in; the theoretical linguists will ignore the mass of detail that remains outside the scope of their lens. Yet, as each community adheres to its own goals over time, it is nevertheless changed and enriched by an ongoing mutuality of interest and exchange of ideas.

Research on teaching and learning suffers the same burden as linguistic field research: It aims to understand something that cannot yet be encompassed. But, in addition to its surpassingly complex focus, education research carries an additional burden: Those who carry out such research have an obligation to a world of practice. The goal of their understanding is the betterment of human lives, with all of the difficult analysis and decision making that entails. The inherent complexity of teaching and learning— and the moral imperative they carry—defines the context of education research and renders it an order of magnitude more challenging than research in purely academic human sciences. In this context, we can see why the production line metaphor implied in the editors' questions fails. But perhaps something better than the production line can be envisioned: communities of education researchers, theorists, and practitioners, among which a variety of mutual and reciprocal relationships exist, driven both by the desire to understand teaching and learning and by the desire to fulfill our responsibilities toward all members of our collective.

## NOTES

[1]The board and editors of *RRE* obviously intended these questions as an impetus for exploration, not as a set of exam questions to be strictly adhered to. I employ here, however, a rhetorical strategy of using the literal questions as a foil for organizing my discussion. The reader might infer a criticism of the editors on my part; this is not my intention. The editors graciously agreed from the beginning to my taking this apparently uncooperative stance.

[2]This selection criterion thus reduces the sample from which important works might be drawn. There are other selection criteria as well (some mentioned later) that further reduce the generality of any conclusions that might be drawn from this chapter.

[3]Berger and Luckmann define *reality* as "a quality appertaining to phenomena that we recognize as having a being independent of our own volition...we cannot 'wish them away'"; *knowledge* is the certainty that phenomena are real (p. 1).

[4]Collins (1996) is an updated and considerably reconceptualized analysis of the same data. It is an excellent example of how microanalysis of discourse may provide insights into the maintainance of the social order through classroom practices.

[5]Sacks and Schegloff were not interested in conversational structure for itself, as discourse analysts are interested in the structure of discourse. Rather, they saw ordinary conversations as a form of social bedrock and as providing complex and easily available material upon which to hone their analytical tools as well. Everyday conversation thus provides a great deal of evidence for the taken-for-granted and yet continually maintained nature of social reality.

[6]In proposing this "subcluster," I am not implying that these writers were influenced by those discussed earlier. For example, Freire (1970) proposes the "banking concept" versus the "problem-posing concept" of education. His own experience as a teacher and his reading of Marx and other philosophers are the source of this "social constructivist" analysis. Other members of this cluster have equally unique and influential intellectual histories.

[7]"Constructivism" (unmodified) is presented here primarily in Piagetian terms. There are certainly other parsings of work in the field that may be of greater utility. For example, Phillips (1995) presents a discussion of constructivism that slices through some of the same works mentioned here at a different angle, revealing certain philosophical and ideological elements that are obscured in this chapter. On another note, in the journalistic world, the unmodified term *constructivism* has its own set of misreadings, as the following phrase from a recent newspaper article about a charter school indicates: "the school uses a curriculum that is constructivist, or project-based." These misreadings, which are not reviewed here, add a further layer of obfuscation to the compound "social constructivism."

[8]This implies that "discovery learning" is not by any means a synonym for constructivist learning, as Thompson (1995) points out, among others. In fact, the assumptions of that pedagogy are quite different from those of most radical constructivists.

[9]For a useful note on the naming conventions of Vygotskian and Soviet work, see Cole (1995, Footnote 1, pp. 212–213).

[10]There are several Vygotskian ideas that have played a role in education research but are not dealt with here as a result of length limitations. Among the most important of these are the importance of play in learning and development (Vygotsky, 1978) and the contrast between everyday concepts and scientific concepts (Vygotsky, 1986).

[11]Greeno (1997) addresses some of these dichotomies from a somewhat different angle, contrasting situative and cognitive perspectives on learning, their presuppositions and analytic

advantages. His article goes a long way toward spelling out implications of the differences that are either ignored or merely touched on in this chapter.

[12]Emig makes clear that, at that time, one of her major influences was Priscilla Tyler, an essentially unpublished professor of English education who nevertheless had a great impact on a number of figures who did publish (Emig, 1983, p. 61).

[13]Of course, Graves's collaborators and colleagues, including Lucy Calkins, Jane Hansen, Don Murray, Nancie Atwell, and other writers and teachers in the writing process tradition, must be mentioned, although space precludes any further analysis of their work.

[14]After this chapter was essentially completed, I encountered a chapter by Courtney Cazden on different "readings" of Vygotsky found in published works on writing pedagogy (Cazden, 1996). Space limitations prevent my going into any detail, but readers should consult Cazden's work for an insightful discussion that fills in many areas I have missed.

[15]Recall that I limited my inquiry in this section to K–12 process writing. Fortunately for me, this puts the extensive body of research on college composition off limits. Yet, it is worth pointing out that unsurprisingly, in the college composition literature, the tension between individual and social abides as well. Brandt (1992) provides a fascinating ethnomethodological analysis of a protocol recording a graduate student's attempts to write a Modern Language Association (MLA) abstract. Her larger point is to seek a way through the impasse between hermeneutic approaches to composition and cognitivist approaches (best exemplified by Flower & Hayes, 1981; but see Flower et al., 1990, for a cognitivist attempt to integrate the individual and the social).

In the college composition literature, one finds a greater attention to the work in the first cluster, with its critical and sociological aspects. An interesting illustration of the disjunction can be found in Pat Bizzell's review of Rafoth and Rubin's *The Social Construction of Written Communication* (1989). Bizzell, a scholar of composition in college and beyond, takes the editors to task for neglecting the critical and sociological meanings of social constructivism. Their chapters, many of which concern K–12, lack a unified theoretical perspective but display frequent references to the third cluster in relation to the face-to-face interaction that is at the heart of classroom teaching and learning.

[16]In some cases (although not included in this writing process research review), researchers actually revisit finished research, using categories of a different framework to reinvestigate their original findings. For example, Clay and Cazden (1990) reinterpret Reading Recovery from a Vygotskian perspective. Clay did not create Reading Recovery with Vygotskian theory in mind; it was based on her own theory of reading and on her experiences with teachers and children (Clay & Cazden, 1990, p. 206). Clay and Cazden seek to understand Reading Recovery more deeply by applying Vygotskian concepts such as forms of mediation and scaffolding interaction within the ZPD to the interaction that forms the heart of Reading Recovery sessions between teacher and child. Another example is Moll et al.'s analysis of *The Social Construction of Lessons in Two Languages* (Moll, Diaz, Estrada, & Lopes, 1992). Here Moll et al. present a microanalysis of two reading lessons in a bilingual program, one advanced and one beginning, in Vygotskian terms. The structures and processes are very familiar, but the systematic application of sociocultural-historical constructs provides a new parsing of the internal structures underlying what might look like the same old lessons. A third example is Gavelek and Raphael (1996), who provide a Vygotskian analysis of classroom discussion about texts and their meanings. The analysis is intended as more than an account of their own research on book clubs and talk about text; it attempts to offer a retroactive, theorized perspective on "how and why different ways of talking about text can be so important for learning to read literature" applicable to far more than their own work (p. 182).

[17]Some would argue that an emphasis on the social contexts of learning can be found in Piaget's work. Von Glasersfeld (1995, p. 11) addresses those who have criticized Piaget for being unconcerned with the social: Although Piaget did not spend much time on how social interaction supported accommodation, he nevertheless asserted its importance time and

again. Von Glasersfeld himself, building on Kant's work, speaks to the most elemental aspect of social interaction, the construction of the "other." This construction is prior (by quite a ways) to any development of intersubjectivity, prior to later learning about convention, and he argues that it is entailed by any form of "social constructivism" that might be proposed by mathematics educators.

[18]See also Jere Confrey's work along with colleagues at Cornell, where this same practice is explicitly motivated by radical constructivism.

[19]Of course, the usual disclaimers apply about the caricatured nature of the following description. The social history of any discipline can be represented in a number of ways, all versions supported and rejected by central members of that discipline. This is a personal version rendered for the purposes of this chapter.

## REFERENCES

Apple, M. W. (1982). *Education and power.* Boston: Routledge & Kegan Paul.

Apple, M. W. (1995). Taking power seriously: New directions in equity in mathematics education and beyond. In W. G. Secada, E. Fennema, & L. B. Adajian (Eds.), *New directions for equity in mathematics education* (pp. 329–348). Cambridge, England: Cambridge University Press.

Bakhtin, M. M. (1986). *Selections: Speech genres and other late essays* (C. Emerson & M. Holquist, Eds., and V. W. McGee, Trans.). Austin: University of Texas Press.

Ball, D. (1993). With an eye on the mathematical horizon: Dilemmas of teaching elementary school mathematics. *Elementary School Journal, 93,* 373–397.

Bauersfeld, H. (1995). The structuring of the structures: Development and function of mathematizing as a social practice. In L. P. Steffe & J. Gale (Eds.), *Constructivism in education* (pp. 137–158). Hillsdale, NJ: Erlbaum.

Berger, P. L., & Luckmann, T. (1967). *The social construction of reality: A treatise in the sociology of knowledge.* New York: Anchor.

Bizzell, P. (1989). [Review of *The social construction of written communication*]. *College Composition and Communication, 40,* 483–486.

Bloor, D. (1987). The living foundations of mathematics [Review of *The ethnomethodological foundations of mathematics*]. *Social Studies of Science, 17,* 337–358.

Bloor, D. (1991). *Knowledge and social imagery* (2nd ed.). Chicago: University of Chicago Press.

Bourdieu, P., & Passeron, J. C. (1977). *Reproduction in education, society and culture.* Beverly Hills, CA: Sage.

Brandt, D. (1992). The cognitive as the social: An ethnomethodological approach to writing process research. *Written Communication, 9,* 315–355.

Britton, B., Burgess, T., Martin, N., McLeod, A., & Rosen, H. (1975). The development of writing abilities (11–18): A report from the Schools Council Project on written language of 11–18 year olds, based at the University of London Institute of Education, 1966–71. Urbana, IL: National Council of Teachers of English.

Brown, A., Ash, D., Rutherford, M., Nakagawa, K., Gordon, A., & Campione, J. C. (1993). Distributed expertise in the classroom. In G. Salomon (Ed.), *Distributed cognitions: Psychological and educational considerations* (pp. 188–228). New York: Cambridge University Press.

Brown, A., Campione, J. C., Webber, L. S., & McGilly, K. (1992). Interactive learning environments: A new look at assessment and instruction. In B. Gifford & M. C. O'Connor (Eds.), *Changing assessments: Alternative views of aptitude, achievement and instruction* (pp. 121–211). Boston: Kluwer.

Bruner, J. (1960). *The process of education.* Cambridge, MA: Harvard University Press.

Cazden, C. B. (1996). Selective traditions: Readings of Vygotsky in writing pedagogy. In D. Hicks (Ed.), *Discourse, learning and schooling* (pp. 165–185). Cambridge, England: Cambridge University Press.

Clay, M. M., & Cazden, C. B. (1990). A Vygotskian interpretation of Reading Recovery. In L. Moll (Ed.), *Vygotsky and education: Instructional implications and applications of sociohistorical psychology* (pp. 206-222). Cambridge, England: Cambridge University Press.

Cobb, P. (1994a). Where is the mind? Constructivist and sociocultural perspectives on mathematical development. *Educational Researcher, 23*(7), 13–20.

Cobb, P. (1994b). Constructivism in mathematics and science education. *Educational Researcher, 23*(7), 4.

Cobb, P. (in press). Cultural tools and mathematical learning: A case study. *Journal for Research in Mathematics Education.*

Cobb, P., Wood, T., & Yackel, E. (1993). Discourse, mathematical thinking, and classroom practice. In E. A. Forman, N. Minick, & C. A. Stone (Eds.), *Contexts for learning: Sociocultural dynamics in children's development* (pp. 91–119). New York: Oxford University Press.

Cohen, D. K. (1990). The revolution in one classroom: The case of Mrs. Oublier. *Educational Evaluation and Policy Analysis, 12,* 311–329.

Cole, M. (1995). Socio-cultural-historical psychology: Some general remarks and a proposal for a new kind of cultural-genetic methodology. In J. V. Wertsch, P. del Rio, & A. Alvarez (Eds.), *Sociocultural studies of mind* (pp. 187–214). Cambridge, England: Cambridge University Press.

Cole, M. (1996). *Cultural psychology: A once and future discipline.* Cambridge, MA: Belknap Press.

Collins, J. (1986). Differential treatment and reading instruction. In J. Cook-Gumperz (Ed.), *The social construction of literacy* (pp. 117–137). New York: Cambridge University Press.

Collins, J. (1996). Socialization to text: Structure and contradiction in schooled literacy. In M. Silverstein & G. Urban (Eds.), *Natural histories of discourse* (pp. 203-228). Chicago: University of Chicago Press.

Confrey, J. (1995). How compatible are radical constructivism, sociocultural approaches, and social constructivism? In L. P. Steffe & J. Gale (Eds.), *Constructivism in education* (pp. 185–225). Hillsdale, NJ: Erlbaum.

Cook-Gumperz, J. (Ed.). (1986). *The social construction of literacy.* New York: Cambridge University Press.

Cuoco, A., Goldenberg, E. P., & Mark, J. (1996). Habits of mind: An organizing principle for mathematics curricula. *Journal of Mathematical Behavior, 15,* 375–402.

Davis, P. J., & Hersh, R. (1981). *The mathematical experience.* Boston: Houghton Mifflin.

Delpit, L. (1986). Skills and other dilemmas of a progressive Black educator. *Harvard Educational Review, 56,* 379–385.

Delpit, L. (1988). The silenced dialogue: Power and pedagogy in educating other people's children. *Harvard Educational Review, 58,* 280–298.

Dewey, J. (1916). *Democracy and education.* New York: Free Press.

Diaz, R., Neal, C. J., & Amaya-Williams, M. (1990). The social origins of self-regulation. In L. Moll (Ed.), *Vygotsky and education: Instructional implications and applications of sociohistorical psychology* (pp. 127-154). Cambridge, England: Cambridge University Press.

Dyson, A. H. (1993). *Social worlds of children learning to write in an urban primary school.* New York: Teachers College Press.

Dyson, A. H. (1997). *Writing superheroes: Contemporary childhood, popular culture, and classroom literacy.* New York: Teachers College Press.

Edelsky, C. (1991). *With literacy and justice for all: Rethinking the social in language and education.* London: Falmer.

Eder, D. (1986). Organizational constraints on reading group mobility. In J. Cook-Gumperz (Ed.), *The social construction of literacy* (pp. 138–155). Cambridge, England: Cambridge University Press

Ellsworth, E. (1989). Why doesn't this feel empowering? Working through the repressive myths of critical pedagogy. *Harvard Educational Review, 59,* 297–324.

Emig, J. (1983). *The web of meaning: Essays on writing, teaching, learning and thinking* (D. Goswami & M. Butler, Eds.). Portsmouth, NH: Heinemann.

Flower, L., & Hayes, J. R. (1981). A cognitive process theory of writing. *College Composition and Communication, 32,* 365–387.

Flower, L., Stein, V., Ackerman, J., Kantz, M., McCormick, K., & Peck, W. (1990). *Reading to write: Exploring a cognitive and social process.* New York: Oxford University Press.

Forman, E. A., Minick, N., & Stone, C. A. (Eds.). (1993). *Contexts for learning: Sociocultural dynamics in children's development.* New York: Oxford University Press.

Frankenstein, M. (1987). Critical mathematics education: An application of Paolo Freire's epistemology. In I. Shor (Ed.), *Freire for the classroom: A sourcebook for liberatory teaching* (pp. 180–210). Portsmouth, NH: Heinemann.

Frankenstein, M. (1995). Equity in mathematics education: Class in the world outside the class. In W. Secada, E. Fennema, & L. B. Adajian (Eds.), *New directions for equity in mathematics education* (pp. 165–190). Cambridge, England: Cambridge University Press.

Freedman, S. W. (1987). *Response to student writing* (NCTE Research Report No. 23). Urbana, IL: National Council of Teachers of English.

Freedman, S. W. (1994). *Exchanging writing, exchanging cultures: Lessons in school reform from the United States and Great Britain.* Cambridge, MA: Harvard University Press.

Freire, P. (1970). *Pedagogy of the oppressed.* New York: Continuum.

Gavelek, J. R., & Raphael, T. E. (1996). Changing talk about text: New roles for teachers and students. *Language Arts, 73,* 182–192.

Gee, J. P. (1990). *Social linguistics and literacies.* Basingstoke, England: Falmer.

Gee, J. P. (1996). Vygotsky and current debates in education: Some dilemmas as afterthoughts to *Discourse, learning and schooling.* In D. Hicks (Ed.), *Discourse, learning and schooling* (pp. 269–282). Cambridge, England: Cambridge University Press.

Gilyard, K. (1996a). African American in process. In K. Gilyard, *Let's flip the script: An African American discourse on language, literature and learning* (pp. 87–96). Detroit, MI: Wayne State University Press.

Gilyard, K. (1996b). The social responsibility that writing is—and writing instruction too. In K. Gilyard, *Let's flip the script: An African American discourse on language, literature and learning* (pp. 21–27). Detroit, MI: Wayne State University Press.

Giroux, H. A. (1983). *Theory and resistance in education.* South Hadley, MA: Bergin & Garvey.

Graff, H. J. (1979). *The literacy myth.* New York: Academic Press.

Graves, D. H. (1983). *Writing: Teachers and children at work.* Portsmouth, NH: Heinemann.

Greeno, J. (1997). On claims that answer the wrong questions. *Educational Researcher, 26*(1), 5–17.

Hatano, G. (1993). Time to merge Vygotskian and constructivist conceptions of knowledge acquisition. In E. A. Forman, N. Minick, & C. A. Stone (Eds.), *Contexts for learning: Sociocultural dynamics in children's development* (pp. 153–166). New York: Oxford University Press.

John-Steiner, V., & Souberman, E. (1978). Afterword. In L. S. Vygotsky, *Mind in society: The development of higher psychological processes* (M. Cole, V. John-Steiner, S. Scribner, & E. Souberman, Eds., pp. 121–133). Cambridge, MA: Harvard University Press.

Lampert, M. (1990). Connecting inventions with conventions. In L. P. Steffe & T. Wood (Eds.), *Transforming children's mathematics education: International perspectives* (pp. 253–264). Hillsdale, NJ: Erlbaum.

Lampert, M. (1991). Connecting mathematical teaching and learning. In E. Fennema, T. P. Carpenter, & S. J. Lamon (Eds.), *Integrating research on teaching and learning mathematics* (pp. 121–152). Albany, NY: State University of New York Press.

Lampert, M., Rittenhouse, P., & Crumbaugh, C. (1996). Agreeing to disagree: Developing sociable mathematical discourse in school. In D. R. Olson & N. Torrance (Eds.), *Handbook of psychology and education: New models of learning, teaching and school* (pp. 731–764). Oxford, England: Basil Blackwell.

Langer, J., & Applebee, A. N. (1987). *How writing shapes thinking: A study of teaching and learning* (NCTE Research Report No. 22). Urbana, IL: National Council of Teachers of English.

Lave, J. (1988). *Cognition in practice*. Cambridge, England: Cambridge University Press.

Lave, J., & Wenger, E. (1991). *Situated learning: Legitimate peripheral participation*. New York: Cambridge University Press.

Lensmire, T. J. (1994). Writing workshop as carnival: Reflections on an alternative learning environment. *Harvard Educational Review, 64,* 371–391.

Lynch, M. (1985). Discipline and the material form of images: An analysis of scientific visibility. *Social Studies of Science, 15,* 37–66.

Mehan, H. (1979). *Learning lessons*. Cambridge, MA: Harvard University Press.

Mehan, H. (1996). The construction of an LD student: A case study in the politics of representation. In M. Silverstein & G. Urban (Eds.), *Natural histories of discourse* (pp. 253–276). Chicago: University of Chicago Press.

Mehan, H., & Wood, H. (1975). *The reality of ethnomethodology*. New York: Wiley.

Minick, N. (1987). The development of Vygotsky's thought: An introduction. In L. S. Vygotsky, *Collected works* (R. Rieber & A. Carton, Eds., and N. Minick, Trans., Vol. 1, pp. 17–36). New York: Plenum.

Moll, L. (Ed.). (1990). *Vygotsky and education: Instructional implications and applications of sociohistorical psychology*. Cambridge, England: Cambridge University Press.

Moll, L., Diaz, S., Estrada, E., & Lopes, L. M. (1992). Making contexts: The social construction of lessons in two languages. In M. Saravia-Shore & S. F. Arvizu (Eds.), *Cross-cultural literacy: Ethnographies of communication in multiethnic classrooms* (pp. 339–366). New York: Garland.

Moses, R. P. (1994). Remarks on the struggle for citizenship and math/science literacy. *Journal of Mathematical Behavior, 13,* 107–111.

Moses, R. P., Kamii, M., Swap, S., & Howard, J. (1989). The Algebra Project: Organizing in the spirit of Ella. *Harvard Educational Review, 59,* 423–443.

National Council of Teachers of Mathematics. (1988). *Number concepts and operations in the middle grades*. Reston, VA: Author.

National Council of Teachers of Mathematics. (1989). *Curriculum and evaluation standards for school mathematics*. Reston, VA: Author.

National Research Council. (1989). *Everybody counts: A report to the nation on the future of mathematics education*. Washington, DC: National Academy Press.

Nemirovsky, R. (1994). On ways of symbolizing: The case of Laura and the velocity sign. *Journal of Mathematical Behavior, 13,* 389–422.

Phillips, D. C. (1995). The good, the bad, and the ugly: The many faces of constructivism. *Educational Researcher, 24*(7), 5–12.

Polya, G. (1957). *How to solve it: A new aspect of mathematical method* (2nd ed.). Garden City, NY: Doubleday.

Prawat, R. S. (1995). Misreading Dewey: Reform, projects, and the language game. *Educational Researcher, 24*(7), 13–22.

Rogoff, B. (1995). Observing sociocultural activity on three planes: Participatory appropriation, guided participation, and apprenticeship. In J. V. Wertsch, P. del Rio, & A. Alvarez (Eds.), *Sociocultural studies of mind* (pp. 139–164). New York: Cambridge University Press.

Rogoff, B., Mosier, C., Mistry, J., & Goncu, A. (1993). Toddlers' guided participation with their caregivers in cultural activity. In E. A. Forman, N. Minick, & C. A. Stone (Eds.), *Contexts for learning: Sociocultural dynamics in children's development* (pp. 230–253). New York: Oxford University Press.

Schegloff, E., & Sacks, H. (1973). Opening up closings. *Semiotica, 8,* 289–327.

Schoenfeld, A. H. (1985). *Mathematical problem solving.* New York: Academic Press.

Schoenfeld, A. H. (1987). *Cognitive science and mathematics education.* Hillsdale, NJ: Erlbaum.

Scribner, S., & Cole, M. (1981). *The psychology of literacy.* Cambridge, MA: Harvard University Press.

Secada, W., Fennema, E., & Adajian, L. B. (Eds.). (1995). *New directions for equity in mathematics education.* Cambridge, England: Cambridge University Press.

Simon, M. A., & Blume, G. W. (1996). Justification in the mathematics classroom: A study of prospective elementary teachers. *Journal of Mathematical Behavior, 15,* 3–31.

Star, L. (1983). Simplification in scientific work: An example from neuroscience research. *Social Studies of Science, 13,* 206–228.

Steffe, L. P. (1988). Children's construction of number sequences and multiplying schemes. In *Number concepts and operations in the middle grades* (pp. 119–140). Reston, VA: National Council of Teachers of Mathematics.

Steffe, L. P., & Gale, J. (Eds.). (1995). *Constructivism in education.* Hillsdale, NJ: Erlbaum.

Sudnow, D. (1978). *Ways of the hand: The organization of improvised conduct.* Cambridge, MA: Harvard University Press.

Thompson, P. (1995). Constructivism, cybernetics, and information processing: Implications for technologies of research on learning. In L. P. Steffe & J. Gale (Eds.), *Constructivism in education* (pp. 123-133). Hillsdale, NJ: Erlbaum.

Volosinov, V. N. (1971). Reported speech. In L. Metejka & K. Pomorska (Eds.), *Readings in Russian poetics: Formalist and structuralist views* (pp. 149–175). Cambridge, MA: MIT Press.

von Glasersfeld, E. (1995). A constructivist approach to teaching. In L. P. Steffe & J. Gale (Eds.), *Constructivism in education* (pp. 3–15). Hillsdale, NJ: Erlbaum.

Vygotsky, L. S. (1978). *Mind in society: The development of higher psychological processes* (M. Cole, V. John-Steiner, S. Scribner, & E. Souberman, Eds.). Cambridge, MA: Harvard University Press.

Vygotsky, L. S. (1981). The genesis of higher mental functions. In J. V. Wertsch (Ed.), *The concept of activity in Soviet psychology.* Armonk, NY: Sharpe.

Vygotsky, L. S. (1986). *Thought and language* (A. Kozulin, Ed. and Trans.). Cambridge, MA: MIT Press. (Original work published 1934)

Wertsch, J. V. (Ed.). (1985a). *Vygotsky and the social formation of mind.* Cambridge, MA: Harvard University Press.

Wertsch, J. V. (Ed.). (1985b). *Culture, communication and cognition: Vygotskian perspectives.* Cambridge, England: Cambridge University Press.

Wertsch, J. V. (1990). The voice of rationality in a sociocultural approach to mind. In L. Moll (Ed.), *Vygotsky and education: Instructional implications and applications of sociohistorical psychology* (pp. 111–126). Cambridge, England: Cambridge University Press.

Wertsch, J. V. (1991). *Voices of the mind: A sociocultural approach to mediated action.* Cambridge, MA: Harvard University Press.

Wertsch, J. V. (1995). The need for action in sociocultural research. In J. V. Wertsch, P. del Rio, & A. Alvarez (Eds.), *Sociocultural studies of mind* (pp. 56–74). Cambridge, England: Cambridge University Press.

Wertsch, J. V., del Rio, P, & Alvarez, A. (Eds.). (1995). *Sociocultural studies of mind.* Cambridge, England: Cambridge University Press.

Wertsch, J. V., & Stone, C. A. (1985). The concept of internalization in Vygotsky's account of the genesis of higher mental functions. In J. V. Wertsch (Ed.), *Culture, communication and cognition: Vygotskian perspectives* (pp. 162–179). Cambridge, England: Cambridge University Press.

Willis, P. (1977). *Learning to labor.* Lexington, MA: Heath.

Manuscript received October 1, 1997
Accepted December 15, 1997

# Chapter 3

# The Development of Children's Motivation in School Contexts

ALLAN WIGFIELD
University of Maryland

JACQUELYNNE S. ECCLES
University of Michigan

DANIEL RODRIGUEZ
University of Maryland

## OVERVIEW

Research on student motivation has burgeoned in the last 20 years. We have learned much about the nature of students' motivation, how it develops, how it relates to students' school performance, and how it is influenced by different teacher practices, classroom environments, and school environments (for reviews of the research on motivation, see Eccles, Wigfield, & Schiefele, 1998; Pintrich & Schunk, 1996). Very broadly, motivation theorists are interested in the "whys" of human behavior: what moves people to act (see Weiner, 1992). In terms of school performance, researchers studying school motivation look at factors such as the choices students make about which academic activities to do, their persistence in continuing the activities, and the degree of effort they expend.

But what determines individuals' choices, effort, and persistence at different academic activities? Over the last 25 years, many motivation researchers have focused on students' self-perceptions and interests and on how their self-perceptions and interests regulate their achievement behaviors, such as choice, persistence, and performance (Eccles et al., 1998; Pintrich & Schunk, 1996; Renninger, Hidi, & Krapp, 1992; Schunk & Meece, 1992; Schunk & Zimmerman, 1994). Because of this emphasis on *self* variables, much of the research on motivation has focused on motivation as a characteristic of the individual. However, there has been increasing recognition of the importance of social influences on learning and motivation (Eccles et al., 1998; Marshall, 1992; McCaslin & Good, 1996).

Indeed, many researchers and theorists now posit that learning is an inherently social activity (Marshall, 1992; McCaslin & Good, 1996; Shuell, 1996; Vygotsky,

The writing of this chapter was supported in part by a grant from the Spencer Foundation to Allan Wigfield and by Grant HD17553 from the National Institute for Child Health and Human Development to Jacquelynne S. Eccles, Allan Wigfield, Phyllis Blumenfeld, and Rena Harold. The views expressed are solely the responsibility of the authors.

1978). Learning in classrooms is not done in isolation; instead, it occurs in the context of relationships with teachers and peers (Webb & Palincsar, 1996). These relationships, along with the different roles that emerge for students and teachers in various classrooms, strongly influence how students learn. Furthermore, opportunities for social interactions around learning have been shown to improve children's achievement in reading and other areas (e.g., Guthrie et al., 1996; Slavin, 1996). This more social conceptualization of learning has important implications for conceptualizations of motivation (see Hickey, 1997) and how children's motivation develops. It is increasingly clear that the social organization of classrooms and schools, and children's interactions with peers and teachers, have major influences on students' motivation (Eccles et al., 1998; Juvonen & Wentzel, 1996; Maehr & Midgley, 1996; Ryan & Stiller, 1991).

In this chapter, we discuss how the social organization of classrooms and group processes in classrooms influence student motivation. We begin the chapter with a review of some of the crucial constructs prevalent in current motivation theory and discuss how children's motivation develops during the school years. Because of space limitations, our review of these topics is relatively brief. More detailed reviews of this work can be found in Eccles et al. (1998), Pintrich and Schunk (1996), and Weiner (1992). We then discuss the influence of different social organizations of classrooms on students' motivation, focusing especially on teacher practices and classroom structure and how they influence motivation. To complement the section on the development of motivation, we next discuss how school structures change as children move from elementary into secondary school and how such changes affect students' motivation. Finally, we consider the peer group and motivation. It is important to note at the outset that, in this chapter, we consider motivation in two fundamental ways. In the first section, we focus on how motivation influences students' behaviors; thus, motivation is the causal variable. In the sections on socialization, we focus on factors that influence motivation; thus, motivation as an outcome is considered.

## THE NATURE OF STUDENT MOTIVATION

Researchers now have assessed many different constructs that are crucial aspects of students' motivation. To organize our discussion of these constructs, we separate them into two broad groups (see also Eccles et al., 1998). One set involves self-perception constructs that include individuals' sense of their competence and agency to achieve different outcomes. Another set concerns the purposes individuals have for engaging in different activities and their interest in and valuing of the activities. We begin with the first set of constructs.

### Individuals' Sense of Competence and Control

#### Ability and Efficacy Beliefs

Many researchers interested in motivation (e.g., Bandura, 1977, 1986, 1997; Eccles et al., 1983; Nicholls, 1984, 1990; Wigfield, 1994) focus on students' beliefs about their ability and efficacy to perform achievement tasks as crucial motivational mediators of achievement behavior. Ability beliefs are children's evaluations of their competence in different areas. Researchers have documented that children's and adolescents' ability beliefs relate to and predict their performance in different achievement domains such as math and reading, even when previous performance is controlled (e.g., Eccles et al., 1983; Meece, Wigfield, & Eccles, 1990; Nicholls, 1979a). A construct related to individuals' ability beliefs is their expectancies for success. Expectancies refer to children's sense of how well they will do on an upcoming task, instead of their general belief of how good they are at the task (see Stipek, 1984). These beliefs also predict children's performance on different tasks; when children think they can accomplish a task, they are more likely to do so.

Bandura's (1977, 1997) construct of self-efficacy also deals with individuals' expectancies about being able to do tasks; however, Bandura defined self-efficacy as a generative capacity in which different subskills are organized into courses of action (see also Schunk, 1991). Bandura (1977) proposed that individuals' efficacy expectations for different achievement tasks are a major determinant of activity choice, willingness to expend effort, and persistence (see also Bandura, 1997). In work with school-aged children, Schunk and his colleagues (see Schunk, 1991, for a review) have clearly demonstrated that students' sense of efficacy relates to their academic performance (see also Zimmerman, Bandura, & Martinez-Pons, 1992). They also have shown that training students both to be more efficacious and to believe they are more efficacious improves their achievement in different subject areas such as math and reading.

Researchers interested in competence and efficacy beliefs currently are debating the similarities and differences between these belief constructs (see Pajares, 1996). This debate will provide important definitional clarity to these constructs. However, for our purposes, the general conclusion from this work is that when individuals have a positive sense of their ability and efficacy to do a task, they are more likely to choose to do the task, persist at it, and maintain their effort. Efficacy and competence beliefs predict future performance and engagement even when previous performance is taken into account.

## Control and Autonomy Beliefs

Researchers interested in individuals' control beliefs initially made a major distinction between internal and external locus of control (e.g., Crandall, Katkovsky, & Crandall, 1965; Rotter, 1954). Internal control means the individual believes that he or she controls the outcome; external control means the outcome is determined by other things. Researchers have confirmed the positive association between internal locus of control and academic achievement (see Findley & Cooper, 1983) and elaborated broader conceptual models of control (e.g., Connell, 1985; Weiner, 1979, 1985). Connell (1985), for example, added unknown control as a third control belief category and argued that younger children are particularly likely to use this category. Weiner included locus of control as one of the crucial dimensions in his attribution theory. Skinner (1995) defined several kinds of perceived control beliefs and emphasized the importance of perceived contingency between individuals' actions and their success for developing positive motivation.

Connell and Wellborn (1991) integrated control beliefs into a broader theoretical framework based on the psychological needs for competence, autonomy, and relatedness (see also Deci & Ryan, 1985; Ryan, 1992; Ryan & Stiller, 1991). They linked control beliefs to competence needs: Children who believe they control their achievement outcomes should feel more competent. They hypothesized that the extent to which these needs are fulfilled is influenced by the following contextual characteristics: amount of structure, degree of autonomy provided, and level of involvement in the children's activities. When the family, peer, and school contexts support children's autonomy, develop their competence, and provide positive relations with others, children's motivation (which Connell and Wellborn conceptualized as *engagement*) will be positive, and they will become fully engaged in different activities such as schoolwork. When one or more of the needs are not fulfilled, children will become disaffected (see Connell, Spencer, & Aber, 1994; Skinner & Belmont, 1993). This theory is especially relevant to this chapter because of the focus on relatedness as something that influences engagement in achievement activities. We return to it in the sections on how relations with teachers and peers influence motivation.

## Individuals' Intrinsic Motivation, Interests, Values, and Goals

Although theories dealing with competence, expectancy, and control beliefs provide powerful explanations of individuals' performance on different kinds of achievement activities, these theories do not systematically address another important motivational question: Does the individual want to do the task? Even if people are certain they can do a task and think they can control the outcome, they may not want to engage in it. Once the decision is made to engage in a task or activity, there are different reasons for doing so. The constructs discussed next focus on these aspects of motivation.

### Intrinsic and Extrinsic Motivation

A basic distinction in the motivation literature is between intrinsic motivation and extrinsic motivation (see Deci & Ryan, 1985; Harter, 1981). When individuals are intrinsically motivated, they engage in activities for their own sake and out of interest in the activity. Csikszentmihalyi's (1988) notion of "flow" may represent the ultimate form of intrinsic motivation. He described flow as feelings of being immersed and carried by an activity, as well as feeling in control of one's actions and the surrounding environment. Flow is possible only when people feel that the opportunities for action in a given situation match their ability to master the challenges. By contrast, when extrinsically motivated, individuals engage in activities for instrumental or other reasons, such as receiving a reward.

Deci, Ryan, and their colleagues (e.g., Deci, Vallerand, Pelletier, & Ryan, 1991) went beyond the extrinsic-intrinsic motivation dichotomy in their discussion of *internalization*, the process of transferring the regulation of behavior from outside to inside the individual. They defined several levels in the process of moving from external to more internalized regulation: *external* (regulation coming from outside the individual), *introjected* (internal regulation based on the individual's feelings that he or she should or has to engage in the behavior), *identified* (internal regulation of behavior that is based on the utility of that behavior, such as studying hard to get into college), and, finally, *integrated* (regulation based on what the individual thinks is valuable and important). Even though the integrated level is self-determined, it does not reflect intrinsically motivated behavior (Deci, 1992). Intrinsic motivation occurs only when the individual is interested in the behavior, which may not be the case even at the integrated level of regulation.

Ryan and Stiller (1991) also argued against the simple intrinsic-extrinsic dichotomy. Like Connell and Wellborn (1991), they focused on the importance of engagement in learning as a crucial motivational construct. They also argued that students are more likely to be engaged when they have internalized a value for learning. When students have internalized values for learning, they will engage themselves in learning tasks and activities, even if the activities are not of particular interest to them. Thus, these internalized values are crucial to student engagement. We return later to aspects of classroom social structures that promote or inhibit student engagement.

## Interest

A construct closely related to the notion of intrinsic motivation is interest (see Alexander, Kulikowich, & Jetton, 1994; Hidi, 1990; Krapp, Hidi, & Renninger, 1992; Renninger & Wozniak, 1985; Schiefele, 1991, 1996a, 1996b; Tobias, 1994). Researchers studying interest differentiate between individual and situational interest. As the label implies, individual or personal interest is a characteristic of the individual, and it is conceptualized as either a relatively stable disposition or an active state. In discussing what individual interest consists of, Renninger (1990) suggested that it includes both knowledge and value about a topic or object. By contrast, situational interest stems from conditions in the environment (see Krapp et al., 1992). Krapp et al. argued that situational interest generates curiosity, leading individuals to explore the topic further.

Individuals' personal interests have important implications for their subsequent activity (see Renninger, 1990). Much of the research on individual interest has focused on its relation to quality of learning (see Alexander et al., 1994; Renninger, Hidi, & Krapp, 1992; Schiefele, 1996a). In general, there are significant but moderate relations between interest and text learning. More important, interest is more strongly related to indicators of deep-level learning, such as recall of main ideas, coherence of recall, responding to deeper comprehension questions, and representation of meaning, than it is to surface-level learning, such as responding to simple questions or verbatim representation of text (Schiefele, 1996a; Schiefele & Krapp, in press).

Researchers studying situational interest have focused on the characteristics of academic tasks that create interest (e.g., Anderson, Shirey, Wilson, & Fielding, 1987; Hidi & Baird, 1986, 1988; Teigen, 1987). Among others, several text features have been found to arouse situational interest: personal relevance, novelty, activity level, and comprehensibility (Hidi & Baird, 1986). Empirical evidence has provided strong support for the relation between situational interest and text comprehension and recall (see reviews by Schiefele, 1996b; Wade, 1992). Furthermore, Hidi and Berndorff (1996) have argued that situational interest can lead to individual interest and intrinsic motivation. This point is a crucial one for this chapter; features of activities that individuals do in school can increase their personal interest in the activities.

Although interest is a powerful motivator, Deci (1992) noted that not all motivated behavior reflects interest. Individuals often do things that are not necessarily of interest to them but have other purposes. This brings us to the notions of (a) subjective valuing of activities and (b) achievement goals.

### Individuals' Subjective Task Values

Eccles and her colleagues have defined different ways in which individuals can value activities such as schoolwork (see Eccles et al., 1983; Wigfield & Eccles, 1992). Eccles et al. (1983) outlined four motivational components of task value: attainment value, intrinsic value, utility value, and cost. They defined attainment value as the personal importance of doing well on the task. Drawing on self-schema and identity theories (e.g., Markus & Wurf, 1987), they also linked attainment value to the relevance of engaging in a task for confirming or disconfirming salient aspects of one's self-schema. That is, because tasks provide the opportunity to demonstrate aspects of one's actual or ideal self-schema, such as masculinity, femininity, and/or competence in various domains, tasks will have higher attainment value to the extent that they allow the individual to confirm salient aspects of these self-schemata (see Eccles, 1984, 1987).

Intrinsic value is the enjoyment the individual gets from performing the activity. This component of value is similar to the construct of intrinsic motivation, as defined by Harter (1981) and by Deci and his colleagues (e.g., Deci & Ryan, 1985; Ryan, Connell, & Deci, 1985), and to the constructs of interest and flow, as defined by Csikszentmihalyi (1988), Renninger (1990), and Schiefele (1991).

Utility value is determined by how well a task relates to current and future goals, such as career goals. A task can have positive value to a person because it facilitates important future goals, even if he or she is not interested in the task for its own sake. For instance, students often take classes that they do not particularly enjoy but that they need in order to pursue other interests, to please their parents, or to be with their friends. In one sense, then, this component captures the more "extrinsic" reasons for engaging in a task. But it also relates directly to individuals' internalized short- and long-term goals.

Finally, Eccles and her colleagues identified "cost" as a critical component of value (Eccles, 1987; Eccles et al., 1983). Cost is conceptualized in terms of the negative aspects of engaging in the task, such as performance anxiety and fear of both failure and success, as well as the amount of effort that is needed to succeed and the lost opportunities that result from making one choice rather than another.

Eccles and her colleagues have found that individuals' task values predict course plans and enrollment decisions in mathematics, physics, and English and involvement in sport activities, even after prior performance levels have been controlled

(Eccles et al., 1983, 1995; Eccles, Adler, & Meece, 1984; Eccles & Harold, 1991; Meece et al., 1990). They have also shown that both expectancies and values predict career choices (see Eccles, 1994).

## Achievement Goal Orientations

Recently, researchers have become interested in children's achievement goals and their relation to achievement behavior (see Ames & Ames, 1989; Meece, 1991, 1994). Several different approaches have emerged. Bandura (1986) and Schunk (1990, 1991) focus on goals' proximity, specificity, and level of challenge and have shown that specific, proximal, and somewhat challenging goals promote both self-efficacy and improved performance. Other researchers have defined and investigated broader goal orientations (e.g., Ames, 1992a, 1992b; Blumenfeld, 1992; Butler, 1993; Dweck & Leggett, 1988; Nicholls, 1984). For example, Nicholls and his colleagues (e.g., Nicholls, 1979b; Nicholls, Cobb, Yackel, Wood, & Wheatley, 1990) defined two major kinds of motivationally relevant goal patterns or orientations: ego-involved goals and task-involved goals. Individuals with ego-involved goals seek to maximize favorable evaluations of their competence and minimize negative evaluations of competence. Questions such as "Will I look smart?" and "Can I outperform others?" reflect ego-involved goals. In contrast, with task-involved goals, individuals focus on mastering tasks and increasing their competence. Questions such as "How can I do this task?" and "What will I learn?" reflect task-involved goals. Nicholls also discussed a third type of goal orientation: work avoidance. As its label suggests, work avoidance refers to attempting to do as little academic work as possible in school.

Dweck and her colleagues provided a complementary analysis (e.g., Dweck & Elliott, 1983; Dweck & Leggett, 1988) distinguishing between performance goals (like ego-involved goals) and learning goals (like task-involved goals). Similarly, Ames (1992b) distinguished between the association of performance goals (like ego-involved goals) and mastery goals (like task-focused goals) with both performance and task choice. With ego-involved (or performance) goals, children try to outperform others, and they are more likely to engage in tasks they know they can do. Task-involved (or mastery-oriented) children choose challenging tasks and are more concerned with their own progress than with outperforming others.

Goal theories are currently very popular among researchers interested in both the determinants of performance and task choice (e.g., Butler, 1989a, 1989b) and the restructuring of schools to enhance motivation (e.g., Ames, 1992a; Maehr & Midgley, 1996). By and large, consistent support for the benefits of task-involved or learning goals is emerging. However, the categorization of children's goals as ego or task involved oversimplifies the complexity of motivation. Researchers are broadening notions of achievement goal orientations in important ways. As mentioned earlier, Nicholls, Cheung, Lauer, and Patashnick (1989) defined another important goal orientation, work avoidance, which unfortunately may characterize many students' motivation. In a somewhat similar vein, Elliott and Harackiewicz (1996) discussed how students' performance goals can lead them to either approach achievement situations or avoid such situations. This focus on avoidance motivation is an important new direction in the work on achievement goals.

Another important issue regarding goals concerns their domain specificity versus generality. Some researchers study students' goal orientations for specific domains; for instance, Meece (1991, 1994) studied students' goals for science. Other researchers have argued that students' goal orientations are more general. Duda and Nicholls (1992) found that students' goal orientations toward sport and academics formed factors that bridged the two domains. That is, the mastery goal orientation factor emerging in their analyses included items from both sport and academic domains. By contrast, students' perceived competence was more domain specific. Duda and Nicholls concluded that students' goal orientations appear to be quite general, at least across the domains they studied. Stipek and Gralinski (1996) provided further evidence that students' goal orientations generalize across different academic subject areas. More research is needed on the domain specificity or generality of students' goal orientations.

There is a growing body of research on how different classroom organizational characteristics influence children's goal orientations; we discuss that work later.

## Multiple Goal Perspectives

Researchers including Ford (1992) and Wentzel (1991b) have adopted a more complex perspective on goals and motivation, arguing that there are many different kinds of goals individuals can have in school settings. For example, Wentzel (e.g., Wentzel, 1991a, 1993, 1996) has examined the multiple goals of adolescents in school settings. Wentzel's view on goals differs from the views of theorists such as Dweck and Nicholls in that she focuses on the content of children's goals to guide and direct behavior rather than the criteria a person uses to define success or failure (i.e., mastery vs. performance). In this sense, Wentzel's goals are like the goals and self-schemas that relate to attainment value hierarchies in the Eccles et al. expectancy value model.

Wentzel has focused on both academic and social goals as being important predictors of children's achievement (see Wentzel, 1996). She makes the important point that children's academic motivation is not the only motivational predictor of school performance; children's social motivation must be considered as well (see also Goodenow, 1993; Urdan & Maehr, 1995; Wentzel & Wigfield, in press). Wentzel (1989) found that the goals related to school achievement include seeing oneself as successful, dependable, wanting to learn new things, and wanting to get things done. Higher achieving students have higher levels of social responsibility and higher achievement goals than lower achieving students (for a review, see Wentzel, 1991a, 1991b). Similarly, Wentzel (1994) documented the association among middle school children's prosocial goals of helping others, academic prosocial goals such as sharing learning with classmates, peer social responsibility goals such as following through on promises made to peers, and academic social responsibility goals such as doing what the teacher says to do. Prosocial goals (particularly academic prosocial goals) related positively to peer acceptance. Interestingly, academic responsibility goals related negatively to peer acceptance but positively to acceptance by teachers. Furthermore, positive prosocial and academic goals related positively to prosocial behaviors (as rated by teachers) and negatively to irresponsible behaviors. And, finally, the pursuit of positive social goals was facilitated by perceived support from teachers and peers. Like Connell and Wellborn's (1991) discussion of relatedness, this work is central to this chapter because of its focus on links between social and academic aspects of motivation.

In further work on this topic, Patrick, Hicks, and Ryan (1997) assessed relations of middle-school students' academic self-efficacy, social self-efficacy, and social goals. They found that students' academic and social self-efficacy with peers and teachers were related. Children's endorsement of responsibility goals was related to their sense of efficacy in relating to their teacher. Furthermore, children's social self-efficacy and social goals predicted their academic self-efficacy. These results provide further support for the notion that social aspects of motivation are important not only in terms of children's relations with teachers and peers but also for their academic motivation and achievement.

To conclude this section, researchers have identified a number of important constructs that are part of students' motivation. We have discussed these constructs separately, and, indeed, much of the research on these motivational constructs has focused on just one (or at most two) of the constructs. Yet the constructs are related, and increasingly researchers are examining links among them. For instance, we now know that competence beliefs, achievement values, and intrinsic motivation relate positively to one another (Eccles & Wigfield, 1995; Harter & Connell, 1984; Ryan & Stiller, 1991). Thus, when children think they are competent, they are more likely to be motivated for intrinsic reasons. Furthermore, positive competence beliefs, more intrinsic motivations, and learning goals lead to greater persistence, choices of more challenging activities, and higher levels of engagement in different activities (Ames, 1992b; Dweck & Leggett, 1988; Pintrich & De Groot, 1990). Similarly, having positive efficacy beliefs fosters setting more challenging goals (Schunk, 1991). These links need to be studied further in future research.

### Regulating Achievement Outcomes: Self-Regulation and Co-Regulation

Motivation theorists also study the specific ways children regulate their behavior to meet their goals (e.g., see Schunk & Zimmerman, 1994). Some have suggested links between motivational beliefs and the use of particular cognitive strategies (e.g., Alexander et al., 1994; Pintrich, Marx, & Boyle, 1993). Kuhl (1987) and Corno and Kanfer (1993) argued for the distinction between motivation and volition, with motivation guiding decisions about engaging in particular activities and volition guiding the behaviors used to attain the goal. Broadly, these theorists focus on two issues: how motivation is translated into regulated behavior and how motivation and cognition are linked.

Reviewing the extensive literature on the self-regulation of behavior is beyond the scope of this chapter (see Borkowski, Carr, Rellinger, & Pressley, 1990; Schunk & Zimmerman, 1994). We briefly focus on the work of Zimmerman, Schunk, and their colleagues, because they directly link motivation to self-regulation. Zimmerman

(1989) described self-regulated students as being metacognitively, motivationally, and behaviorally active in their own learning processes and in achieving their own goals. Following Bandura (1986), Zimmerman posited reciprocally related personal, environmental, and behavioral determinants of self-regulated learning that allow individuals to control the extent to which they are self-regulated through personal and behavioral actions and choices. However, he also acknowledged that context is important in that some environments vary in how much latitude for choice of activities or approaches is afforded.

According to Zimmerman (1989), self-regulated learners have three important characteristics. First, they use a variety of self-regulated strategies (active learning processes that involve agency and purpose). Second, self-regulated students believe they can perform efficaciously. Third, self-regulated students set numerous and varied goals for themselves. Furthermore, self-regulated learners engage in three important processes: self-observation (monitoring of one's activities), self-judgment (evaluation of how well one's performance compares with a standard or with the performance of others), and self-reactions (reactions to performance outcomes). When these reactions are favorable, particularly in response to failure, students are more likely to persist. As proposed by attribution theorists, the favorableness of people's reaction to failure is determined by how they interpret their difficulties and failures. Zimmerman and Bonner (in press) discuss the advantages of attributing difficulties to ineffective strategy use rather than to a more general attribution of not trying.

In discussing self-efficacy and self-regulation, Schunk (1994) emphasized the interactive and synergistic relations among goal setting, self-evaluation, and self-efficacy. He has discussed goals in two ways. Initially, he argued and demonstrated that when goals are proximal, specific, and challenging, they are most effective in motivating children's behavior and increasing their sense of self-efficacy (Schunk, 1990, 1991). Schunk (1994) also discussed how self-efficacy might be influenced by the learning and performance goal types discussed earlier, suggesting that self-efficacy should be higher under learning than under performance goals; some research supports this claim (e.g., Elliott & Dweck, 1988; Meece, Blumenfeld, & Hoyle, 1988).

In contrast to the focus on self-regulation, McCaslin and Good (1996) recently proposed the term *co-regulation* as a way to socially situate the learner. They described co-regulation as "the process by which the social/instructional environment supports or scaffolds the individual via her relationships within the classroom, relationships with teachers and peers, objects and setting, and ultimately, the self. Internalization of these supportive relationships empowers the individual to seek new challenges within co-regulated support" (p. 660). McCaslin and Good stated that although self-regulation may be the ultimate goal for learning, co-regulation is necessary to reach that goal. Teachers and other students must provide support and motivation in order for any given student to learn (see also Goodenow, 1993). McCaslin and Good described the following as being crucial in co-regulation: opportunities made available in different classrooms, the kinds of tasks presented to students and the amount of choice allowed in them, the kinds of goals students have, and students' own self-evaluations. The crucial point for our purposes is again the recognition of the social nature of learning and how interactions with others are critical to students' motivation and achievement.

## THE DEVELOPMENT OF MOTIVATION

The motivation constructs discussed in the previous sections undergo important changes during childhood and adolescence; these changes are the focus of this section. A major reason for discussing the research on these changes is that this information is crucial for understanding how group processes and the social organizations of classrooms influence students' motivation. For instance, classroom practices such as ability grouping probably affect younger and older students' self-evaluations differently, in part because younger and older children have differing conceptions of their ability.

### The Development of Competence-Related Beliefs

Developmental theorists such as Harter (1983) proposed that children begin with broad understandings of whether they are "smart" or "dumb" that later develop into a more fine-grained and differentiated understanding of their competencies across different activities. Researchers examining this hypothesis with factor-analytic approaches have found that even very young elementary school children distinguish among their self-perceptions of competence in different domains (e.g., Eccles, Wigfield, Harold, & Blumenfeld, 1993; Harter, 1982; Marsh & Hocevar, 1985). For example, Eccles et al. (1993) and Marsh and his colleagues (Marsh, Barnes, Cairns, & Tidman, 1984; Marsh, Craven, & Debus, 1991) demonstrated that even kindergarten and first-grade children's beliefs about their competencies are clearly differentiated across many different domains, including math, reading, music, sports, general school ability, physical appearance, and both peer and parent relations.

Another kind of change in children's competence-related beliefs is that their levels on different tasks decline across the elementary school years and into the middle school years (see Dweck & Elliott, 1983; Eccles & Midgley, 1989; Stipek & Mac Iver, 1989; Wigfield, Eccles, Mac Iver, Reuman, & Midgley, 1991). To illustrate, Nicholls (1979a) found that most first graders ranked themselves near the top of the class in reading ability, and there was no correlation between their ability ratings and their performance level. In contrast, 12-year-olds' ratings were more dispersed and correlated highly with school grades (.70 or higher). Similar results have emerged in cross-sectional and longitudinal studies of children's competence beliefs in a variety of academic and nonacademic domains (e.g., Eccles et al. 1993; Marsh, 1989; Wigfield et al., 1997). These declines, particularly for math, often continue into and through secondary school (Eccles et al., 1983, 1989; Wigfield et al., 1991).

Expectancies for success also decrease during the elementary school years. In most laboratory-type studies, 4- and 5-year-old children expect to do quite well on specific tasks, even after repeated failure (e.g., Parsons & Ruble, 1977; Stipek, 1984). Stipek (1984) argued that young children's optimistic expectancies may reflect hoped-for outcomes rather than real expectations; in addition, Parsons and

Ruble (1977) suggested that, since young children's skills do improve rapidly, high expectancies for future success may be based on experience (see also Dweck & Elliott, 1983). Across the elementary school years, however, children's expectancies for success become more sensitive to both success and failure experiences and more accurate or realistic in terms of their relation to actual performance history (see Eccles, Midgley, & Adler, 1984; Parsons & Ruble, 1977; Stipek, 1984).[1]

The declines in children's competence-related beliefs have been explained in two main ways. First, children become much better at understanding, interpreting, and integrating the evaluative feedback they receive, and they engage in more social comparison with their peers; this leads them to become more accurate or realistic in their self-assessments, which means that some children will see themselves as being less competent (see Dweck & Elliott, 1983; Nicholls, 1984; Ruble, 1983; Stipek & Mac Iver, 1989). Indeed, researchers have found that children's competence beliefs relate more closely to their performance as they get older (e.g., Nicholls, 1979a; Wigfield et al., 1997).

Second, because school environments change in ways that make evaluation more salient and competition between students more likely, some children's self-assessments will decline as they get older (e.g., see Blumenfeld, Pintrich, Meece, & Wessels, 1982; Eccles & Midgley, 1989; Eccles, Midgley, & Adler, 1984; Stipek & Daniels, 1988). We return to these points later, especially the point about changes in school environments, because it deals directly with how the social organization of schools influences motivation.

Interestingly, children's self-efficacy beliefs appear to increase rather than decrease. Shell, Colvin, and Bruning (1995) found that 4th graders had lower self-efficacy beliefs for reading and writing than did 7th and 10th graders, and the 7th graders' efficacy beliefs were lower than 10th graders' beliefs (see Zimmerman & Martinez-Pons, 1990, for similar findings). The inconsistency in the findings regarding self-efficacy and competence beliefs probably reflects measurement differences. Shell et al. measured children's estimates of their efficacy on specific reading and writing skills, which should be higher among older children. Measures of competence beliefs tend to be more general (see Pajares, 1996).

## Development of Control and Agency Beliefs

During middle childhood and beyond, there appears to be an increase in perceptions of internal control as children get older (see Skinner & Connell, 1986). However, based on a series of studies of children's understanding of skill versus chance events, Weisz (1984) concluded that the developmental sequence is more complex. The kindergarten children in these studies believed that outcomes of chance tasks were due to effort, whereas the oldest groups (eighth graders and college students) believed that such outcomes were due to chance; fourth graders were confused about the distinction. Thus, in this work, the youngest children had strong internal control beliefs, so strong, in fact, that they believed in internal control over outcomes even when none was possible, suggesting that with age children came to understand better which kinds of events they can and cannot control. Similarly,

Connell (1985) found a decrease in the endorsement of all three of his locus of control constructs (internal control, control by powerful others, and unknown control) from Grades 3 through 9. The findings regarding unknown control beliefs suggest that older children have a clearer understanding of what controls their achievement outcomes than do younger children. However, the older children rated the other two sources of control as less important as well.

Skinner (1990, 1995) emphasized the importance of success itself for developing positive control beliefs and discussed how children's understanding of causality and explanations for outcomes change over age. She found that the structure of children's control beliefs became more complex as children got older. Like Connell (1985), she also found that beliefs about unknown control and powerful others decreased across age levels.

## Development of Interest and Intrinsic Motivation

Travers (1978) suggested that only "universal" interests would be evident in very young children (e.g., the search for structure). Later, children's interests should become more differentiated and individualized. Roe and Siegelman (1964) proposed that the earliest differentiation occurs between interest in the world of physical objects and interest in the world of people. Todt (1990) argued that this early differentiation eventually leads to individual differences in interests in the social versus the natural sciences.

A second major change in children's interests, occurring between 3 and 8 years of age, regards the formation of gender-specific interests. According to Kohlberg (1966), the acquisition of gender identity leads to gender-specific behaviors, attitudes, and interests. Children strive to behave consistently with their gender identity and, thus, evaluate activities or objects consistent with their gender identity more positively than other activities or objects. As a consequence, boys and girls develop gender-role-stereotyped interests (see Eccles, 1987; Renninger & Wozniak, 1985; Ruble & Martin, 1998). For instance, Wigfield et al. (1997) found that elementary-school-aged girls were more interested in instrumental music and reading than were boys, whereas boys were more interested in sports than were girls.

As is the case with children's competence beliefs, children's academic intrinsic motivation and interest have been found to decline across the school years; these results have occurred in studies of European and American children, and such decreases are especially true for the natural sciences and mathematics (e.g., Eccles et al., 1993; Harter, 1981; Hedelin & Sjoberg, 1989; Helmke, 1993; Lehrke, Hoffmann, & Gardner, 1985; Wigfield et al., 1997) and during the early adolescent years. Pekrun (1993) found that intrinsic motivation stabilized after eighth grade.

Baumert (1995) argued that the decline in school-related interests during adolescence reflects a more general developmental process in which adolescents discover new fields of experience that lead to new interests and reduce the dominant influence of school. In contrast, other researchers have suggested that changes in a number of instructional variables, such as clarity of presentation, monitoring of what happens in the classroom, supportive behavior, cognitively stimulating experiences, self-concept of the teacher (e.g., educator vs. scientist), and achievement pressure, may contribute to declining interest in school mathematics and science (e.g., Eccles & Midgley, 1989).

## Development of Subjective Task Values

Eccles, Wigfield, and their colleagues examined age-related changes in both the structure and mean levels of children's valuing of different activities. In Eccles et al. (1993), Eccles and Wigfield (1995), and Wigfield et al. (1997), children's competence-expectancy beliefs and subjective values within the domains of math, reading, and sports formed distinct factors at all grade levels. Thus, even during the very early elementary grades, children appear to have distinct beliefs about what they are good at and what they value. The distinctions among the importance, utility, and interest components of subjective task value appear to differentiate more gradually (Eccles et al., 1993; Eccles & Wigfield, 1995). Children in the early elementary grades differentiate task value into two components: interest and utility/importance. In contrast, children in Grades 5 through 12 differentiate task value into the three major subcomponents (attainment value/personal importance, interest, and utility value) outlined by Eccles et al. (1983). These results suggest that the interest component differentiates out first, followed later by the distinction between utility and attainment value.

As with competence-related beliefs, researchers generally find age-related declines in children's valuing of certain academic tasks (e.g., Eccles et al., 1983, 1993; see Eccles & Midgley, 1989; Wigfield & Eccles, 1992). For instance, Wigfield et al. (1997) found that children's beliefs about the usefulness and importance of math, reading, instrumental music, and sports activities decreased over time. In contrast, the children's interest decreased only for reading and instrumental music (not for either math or sports). The decline in valuing of math continues through high school (Eccles et al., 1983). Eccles et al. (1989) and Wigfield et al. (1991) also found that children's ratings of both the importance of math and English and their liking of these school subjects decreased across the transition to junior high school. In math, students' importance ratings continued to decline in seventh grade, whereas their importance ratings of English increased somewhat during seventh grade.

## Development of Children's Goals

There has been little work on how children's goals develop. Although Nicholls documented that both task goals and ego goals are evident by second grade (Nicholls et al., 1989, 1990), he also suggested that an ego goal orientation becomes more prominent for many children as they get older as a result of both developmental changes in their conceptions of ability and systematic changes in school context. Dweck and her colleagues (e.g., Dweck & Leggett, 1988) also predicted that, as they get older, children are more likely to adopt performance goals as they come to view intelligence as stable (entity view), because an entity view of intelligence is linked to performance goals. Recently, Meece and Miller (1996) found that, in the third and fourth grades, children's learning and performance goals decreased, and their work avoidance goals increased. More work charting the development of children's goal orientations is needed.

The relations of goals to performance should also change with age as the meaning of ability and effort change and as the social conditions under which tasks are performed change. In a series of studies examining how competitive and noncompetitive conditions, along with task and ego-focused conditions, influence preschool-aged and elementary-school-aged children's interests, motivation, and self-evaluations, Butler identified several developmental changes. First, competition decreased children's subsequent interest in a task only among those children who had also developed a social-comparative sense of ability (Butler, 1989a, 1990). Competition also increased older, but not younger, children's tendency to engage in social comparison (Butler, 1989a, 1989b). Second, although children of all ages engaged in social comparison, younger children seemed to be doing so more for task mastery reasons, whereas older children did so to assess their abilities (Butler, 1989b). Third, whereas 5-, 7-, and 10-year-old children's self-evaluations were equally accurate under mastery conditions, 5- and 7-year-olds inflated their performance self-evaluations more than 10-year-olds under competitive conditions (Butler, 1990). Apparently, the influence of situationally induced performance goals on children's self-evaluations depends on the children's age and cognitive sophistication. Finally, Butler and Ruzany (1993) found that patterns of socialization influence both ability assessments and reasons for social comparison: Kibbutz-raised Israeli children adopted a normative ability concept at a younger age than city-reared Israeli children. However, only the urban children's reasons for engaging in social comparison were influenced by their concept of ability: Once they adopted a normative view, they used social comparison to compare their abilities with those of other children. In contrast, the kibbutz children used social comparison primarily for mastery reasons, regardless of their conception of ability.

Developmental studies of multiple goals are badly needed. We know very little about how these kinds of multiple goals emerge during childhood and whether the relation of these different goals to performance varies across age and context.

In summary, researchers studying the development of children's motivation have found that motivation changes in important ways across the middle childhood and early adolescent years. Children's self-perceptions, interests, values, and goals become differentiated and established during this time. Particularly during middle childhood and early adolescence, children's beliefs and values tend to decline. Children's competence and efficacy beliefs become more closely tied to indicators of their performance. These changes are important to keep in mind as we review how social organizations of classrooms and group processes influence children's motivation; thus, we revisit some of these points in subsequent sections.

## THE SOCIAL ORGANIZATION OF CLASSROOMS
## AND STUDENTS' MOTIVATION

How do different social organizational structures in classrooms and instructional practices influence students' motivation? We focus in this section on relations between students and teachers and their impact on motivation, emphasizing the motivation constructs discussed in the earlier sections. We begin at the relatively broad level of overall classroom and school climate and their influence on motivation and then discuss more specific factors, with a special focus on classroom goal structure and ability grouping practices. We then move to more specific teaching practices and their influences on motivation. Our review does not capture all aspects of classroom organization and teacher practices; instead, we focus on the factors most often studied by motivation theorists. Interested readers also should see other reviews for further discussion of these issues, including Eccles et al. (1998), McCaslin and Good (1996), Maehr and Midgley (1996), Pintrich and Schunk (1996), and Wigfield, Eccles, and Pintrich (1996).

### Classroom- and School-Level Factors

### Classroom and School Climate and Student Motivation

Researchers studying teacher influence on motivation initially focused on the impact of teachers' personal characteristics and teaching style on children's overall achievement, motivation, satisfaction, and self-concept. Many investigators studied the association between teacher warmth/supportiveness and student motivation (particularly the value attached to working hard) and performance. However, because much of this early work was flawed methodologically, the results are difficult to interpret (see Dunkin & Biddle, 1974, for a review).

More recently, researchers studying classroom climate have separated factors such as teacher personality and warmth from teacher instruction and managerial style. They found that the effects of "climate" are dependent on other aspects of teachers' beliefs and practices. For instance, Moos and his colleagues have shown that student satisfaction, personal growth, and achievement are maximized only when teacher warmth and supportiveness are accompanied by efficient organization, stress on academics, and provision of focused, goal-oriented lessons (Fraser & Fisher, 1982; Moos, 1979; Trickett & Moos, 1974). Furthermore, these practices are more common among teachers who believe they can influence their students' performance and future achievement potential (Brookover, Beady, Flood, Schweitzer, & Wisenbaker, 1979; Rutter, Maughan, Mortimore, & Ouston, 1979).

Recently, researchers have extended this general approach to the climate of the entire school. They found that schools vary in climate, teachers' sense of efficacy, and general expectations regarding student potential. Variations in these dimensions influence the motivation of both teachers and students in very fundamental ways (e.g., Maehr & Midgley, 1996; Rutter et al., 1979). The work of Maehr, Midgley, and their colleagues is a good example of this school organizational perspective (e.g., Maehr & Anderman, 1993; Maehr & Midgley, 1996). These investigators have focused primarily on some of the important motivation constructs we have discussed in this chapter, students' goal orientations and beliefs about ability. They suggest that school-level policies and practices (such as those promoting ability tracking, comparative performance evaluations, retention, and ego instead of mastery focus) undermine the motivation of both teachers and students through their impact on the goals these individuals bring to the learning environment (cf. Mac Iver, Reuman, & Main, 1995). These researchers have conducted extensive collaborative work to restructure elementary and middle schools to emphasize mastery- rather than ability-focused goals in order to foster the motivation of students.

## Classroom Goal Structure, Cooperative Learning, and Student Motivation

Ames (1984) discussed how different goal structures used in the classroom affect students' self-evaluation and motivation. She focused on three different goal structures. *Individualized* structures occur when each student is judged on his or her own performance. In this structure, any student can succeed if he or she works hard. The performance of other students does not affect the evaluation of any given student. *Competitive* structures mean that some students are winners and others losers; that is the essence of competition. Ames noted that competition makes social comparison and judgments of ability especially salient. *Cooperative* structures mean that group members share in rewards or punishments; the overall group's performance is key (although individuals often are accountable as well).

Ames (1984) discussed some of the motivational outcomes of these different structures; the structures influence in, particular, children's ability-related beliefs and goal orientations. In general, students focus more on self-evaluations of their ability under competitive goal structures. Winners' ability beliefs are enhanced, and losers' are diminished. Overall, differences in self-perceptions of ability are heightened under competitive conditions. With individualistic structures, students' mastery goals are heightened; the main focus is on improving one's own skills. Ability perceptions probably are less salient, because the focus is on effort and improvement. There is little concern for others, however, because each individual determines his or her own achievement. Cooperative goal structures foster an emphasis on shared effort and interdependence rather than ability. The social group becomes more the focus, and the group outcome is especially salient; thus, social goals may be enhanced. Individuals' own ability perceptions become less crucial; rather, the group's performance is emphasized.

A major approach to instruction that uses cooperative goal structures is cooperative learning. Generally, cooperative learning involves students working together in groups rather than on their own or competing with others. There are a variety of types of cooperative learning; these are described by Kagan (1985), Slavin (1995), and Webb and Palincsar (1996). For instance, in "jigsaw" each student in a group is given part of the material that he or she needs to learn, and the student shares this material with the other members of the group. In "team games tournaments," students form into groups to learn material and then compete against other groups to earn points for their team.

There now is an extensive literature on cooperative learning's effects on children (for reviews, see Johnson & Johnson, 1989, 1994; Sharan & Sharan, 1992; Slavin, 1995, 1996). Researchers have found that cooperative learning has many positive effects. When teachers adopt a cooperative instructional and reward structure in their classrooms, achievement often improves, social relations are more positive, and students' motivation is enhanced (see Sharan & Shaulov, 1990). Both learning and motivation appear to be maximally facilitated in cooperative learning situations that are characterized by both group goals and individual accountability (Slavin, 1995). Such situations appear to create positive interdependence and stimulating group inquiry, which, in turn, arouse social and academic motivational goals and prevent the "free rider effect," or the problem of some children receiving good evaluations because their group does well, even if they did not contribute to the group (Stevens & Slavin, 1995).

Researchers have assessed how some of the different aspects of student motivation we have discussed are affected by cooperative learning. Students' liking of school and/or liking of different school subjects often has been assessed, and, as just mentioned, most studies of cooperative learning show that students' attitudes are more positive in classrooms in which cooperative learning is used extensively. Stevens and Slavin (1995) assessed students' beliefs about their ability in different subject areas along with their liking of the subjects. They found that students in cooperative elementary schools did have higher perceived ability in reading and math than students in "traditional" schools; however, there were no differences in students' liking of the different subjects between the two groups (Stevens and Slavin suggested that this may have been due to problems with their attitude measures). Overall, cooperative learning appears to have a positive impact on some of the motivational constructs we have been discussing.

Most of the research on cooperative learning has taken place in elementary schools. As we noted earlier, students' motivational characteristics change across the school years, and so it is important to assess how practices such as cooperative learning affect students of different ages. Recently, Nichols (1996, in press) assessed cooperative learning's effects on a number of the motivation constructs we are discussing in this chapter, including persistence, self-regulation, self-efficacy, intrinsic/extrinsic motivation, and goal orientation. Nichols has examined the effects of cooperative learning on these constructs in studies of high school students in mathematics classes. Students in the studies learned geometry either through cooperative learning techniques or through more traditional methods. Their motivation was measured via a questionnaire. Students in the cooperative learning groups (in comparison with those in more traditional instruction) showed more positive self-regulation and self-efficacy, higher intrinsic motivation, and a stronger focus on mastery goals, with the differences between groups often increasing over time. The students in cooperative learning also stated a stronger desire to please their teachers and their friends, providing further evidence for cooperative learning's positive effects on social outcomes.

Although cooperative learning appears to have many desirable outcomes, it does pose challenges for teachers. Structuring activities cooperatively requires extensive planning, and record keeping can be challenging as well. There are questions concerning the kinds of subject areas for which cooperative learning is most effective.

Another important issue in cooperative learning is group composition. Slavin (1990) and other researchers generally recommend that groups be heterogeneous in terms of children's ability level as well as other characteristics such as race and gender. There is a growing body of research on how group composition influences student interaction in the group, and a major implication of this work is that group composition indeed has important influences on how groups operate (see Webb & Palincsar, 1996, for a review). Webb and Palincsar noted that children with middle levels of ability may be ignored in heterogeneous groups; high-ability children benefit by being leaders and teachers, and low-ability children benefit from the high-ability children's teaching. Furthermore, mixed-race groups can be dominated by White children, and mixed-sex groups can be dominated by boys. Thus, care must be taken in constructing groups, and teachers are advised to change groups frequently.

The reasons for the positive effects of cooperative learning on student motivation and achievement still are not completely understood. Slavin (1996) discussed different alternative models for the effects of cooperative learning: the motivational perspective, the social cohesion perspective, the developmental perspective, and the cognitive elaborative perspective. According to the motivational perspective, students, when working in groups, know that the only way they can reach their own goals is for the group to be successful. Therefore, they are motivated to help others in the group and work hard so that the group does succeed. Thus, cooperative learning creates a "group incentive" system in which individuals work together to achieve their own goals. Of course, this contrasts dramatically with competitive reward structures, in which one person's success means another's failure.

Slavin (1996) attempted to integrate the four perspectives into one model. He proposed that group goals facilitate students' own motivation to learn, as well as their motivation to encourage and help their groupmates to learn. This motivation will lead students to tutor one another, engage in peer modeling, and provide other cognitive elaborations. It also will lead to greater social cohesiveness in the group. Thus, in Slavin's model, motivation is the key, producing social, cognitive, and academic outcomes.

Ames (1992b) discussed how classroom grouping and other practices influence students' achievement goal orientations and other aspects of motivation (see Blumenfeld, 1992, for an expansion and critique of some of Ames's ideas). Ames, following Epstein (1988), focused on several aspects of motivation—classroom tasks, authority structure, recognition, grouping, evaluation, and time—and used the acronym TARGET to describe them. Each of these aspects can influence whether students develop a more task-involved or a more ego-oriented goal orientation. In describing these influences, we focus on practices that facilitate a task-involved goal orientation (or mastery goal orientation, to use Ames's term). *Tasks* that are diverse, interesting, and challenging foster students' task-involved goals, as do tasks students think they have a reasonable chance to complete. When the *author-*

*ity* in classrooms is structured such that students have opportunities to participate in decision making and take responsibility for their own learning, students
are more task involved. *Recognition* of students' effort (instead of recognition
of only ability) and giving all students a chance to achieve recognition (rather
than only the "best" students) foster task involved-goals. As discussed earlier,
task-involved goals are fostered when cooperative *grouping* is used and students
have opportunities to work with a heterogeneous mix of classmates. When teachers *evaluate* students' progress and mastery rather than only their outcomes and
provide students opportunities to improve, task involvement is more likely. Finally, *time* refers to how instruction is paced. Crucial elements for fostering task
involvement are varying the amounts of time available for different students to
complete their work and helping students learn to plan their own work schedule
and organize how they progress through the work. Ames (1992a, 1992b) argued
cogently that such practices will allow more students to remain positively motivated in the classroom, in that they will have more positive competence beliefs
and task-involved goals (see also Stipek, 1996).

It should be clear from the work just reviewed that much progress has been made
toward understanding how these different school and classroom features influence
students' motivation. Yet, much more work is needed to understand how various
instructional strategies interact with each other in a single context (e.g., the classroom) to affect motivation and learning (Ames, 1992b; Blumenfeld, 1992). Most
teachers in American schools use a mix of mastery-oriented and
performance-oriented strategies. For example, they may use mastery-oriented tasks
and allow the students appropriate levels of autonomy but still rely primarily on
social comparative evaluation strategies, and children often engage in social comparison and competition even in mastery-oriented classrooms (Crockenberg &
Bryant, 1978). We know little about the best combination of these features to support
a mastery-oriented motivational orientation. Nor do we know when, and if, the
collection of motivational dimensions actually clusters together within the individual. More work is needed to determine how these motivational components
interrelate with each other and with other motivational constructs to influence
behavior. Of particular importance is the need to study the interaction of multiple
goals as well as the contextual characteristics influencing the relative salience of
various achievement, social, and moral goals in particular settings.

Students' own beliefs about effective instructional and motivational strategies
need to be considered as well. Results of two studies are illustrative. Nolen and
Nicholls (1993) found that students and teachers often had different views on the
effectiveness of motivational practices; for instance, students thought extrinsic
rewards were more effective, and praise less effective, than teachers did. Furthermore, Thorkildsen, Nolen, and Fournier (1994) found that some children believed
practices promoting meaningful learning were most fair, others favored practices
emphasizing the importance of effort, and still others focused on practices involving extrinsic reward. If students' ideas about appropriate motivational strategies do
not mesh with teachers' ideas and practices, students' motivation might not be
enhanced.

## Ability Grouping Practices

Students are grouped by ability in two main ways. In elementary schools, children are often grouped by ability within classrooms for instruction in subjects such as reading and math. In middle schools and high schools, between-classroom ability grouping, or tracking, is used more. These practices are controversial (e.g., Oakes, 1985) and have attracted much attention. Despite an extensive amount of research, however, few strong and definitive answers have emerged regarding their impact on motivation (see Fuligni, Eccles, & Barber, 1995; Gamoran & Mare, 1989; Kulik & Kulik, 1987; Slavin, 1990). The situation is complicated by the fact that there are conflicting hypotheses about the likely direction and the magnitude of the effects of ability grouping on motivation. The best justification for these practices derives from a person-environment fit perspective: People will be more motivated to learn if the material can be adapted to their current competence level. There is some evidence consistent with this perspective for students placed in high-ability classrooms, high within-class ability groups, and college tracks (Dreeben & Barr, 1988; Fuligni et al., 1995; Gamoran & Mare, 1989; Kulik & Kulik, 1987; Pallas, Entwisle, Alexander, & Stulka, 1994). The results for students placed in low-ability and noncollege tracks do not confirm this hypothesis. By and large, when long-term effects are found for this group of students, they are negative, primarily because these students are often provided with inferior educational experience and support (Dreeben & Barr, 1988; Pallas et al., 1994). Such results are consistent with a social stratification theoretical perspective. But it is important to note that these negative effects appear to result from the stereotypically biased implementation of ability grouping programs. A different result might emerge for the low-competence students if the teachers implemented the program more in keeping with the goals inherent in the person-environment fit perspective, that is, by providing high-quality instruction and motivational practices tailored to the current competence level of the students.

One important concern about ability grouping is determining the relevant social comparison group for particular students. Ability grouping should narrow the range of possible social comparisons and thus lead to declines in the ability self-perceptions of higher ability individuals and increases in the ability self-perceptions of lower ability individuals. The few existing studies support this position. For example, Reuman, Mac Iver, Eccles, and Wigfield (1987) found that being placed in a low-ability math class in the seventh grade led to an increase in self-concept of math ability and a decrease in test anxiety; conversely, being placed in a high-ability math class led to a decrease in self-concept of math ability (see also Reuman, 1989). Similarly, Marsh, Chessor, Craven, and Roche (1995) found that being placed in a gifted and talented program led to a decline over time in students' academic self-concepts. It should be noted, however, that Pallas et al. (1994) found no evidence of within-class ability grouping in reading effects on ability self-concepts and performance expectations during the early elementary school years once the effect of ability group placement on actual achievement level was controlled. However, if children compare *across* ability groups, then students in lower tracks should end up with less positive ability beliefs, and those in the higher tracks more positive ability beliefs.

## Teacher Beliefs, Practices, and Support of Students

### Teaching Practices Linked to Self-Evaluation and Motivation

Rosenholtz and Simpson (1984) discussed a set of teaching practices that affect motivation because they make ability differences in classroom especially salient to the students. These practices include whole group (vs. more individualized) instruction, ability grouping (vs. heterogeneous grouping), and public (vs. private) feedback. Rosenholtz et al. assumed that the first practice listed in each pair increases the salience of students' ability as crucial to success in the classroom and focuses students more on social comparisons with others. The practices also promote extrinsic motivators and ego-focused learning goals. All of these factors probably reduce children's motivation for learning, especially their beliefs about their competence. Such effects are particularly likely for low-performing children because, as these children become more aware of their relative low standing, they are likely to adopt a variety of ego-protective strategies that undermine learning and mastery (Covington, 1992). The little available research provides preliminary support for these hypotheses (e.g., Mac Iver, 1987; Rosenholtz & Rosenholtz, 1981). However, Stipek (1996) noted that these practices interact in complex ways that still are not fully understood.

It is obvious that grades and test scores influence students' self-evaluations by providing them with important information about their academic performance. However, it is not only the information itself but its form of presentation that is crucial. Public methods for charting progress, such as wall posters detailing amount or level of work completed, provide readily accessible information that students can use to compare themselves with one another (Rosenholtz & Rosenholtz, 1981). In addition, teachers who frequently contrast students' performances, grant privileges to "smart" children, or award prizes for "best" performance may increase the importance of ability as a factor in classroom life and heighten the negative affect associated with failure (see Ames, 1992b). When there are few clear winners and many losers, relative performance will be more salient to children, and thus social comparison will be emphasized (Nicholls, 1979b). In contrast, in mastery-oriented classrooms, everyone who performs adequately can experience success. As a result, youngsters in mastery-oriented rooms are more likely to focus on self-improvement than social comparison, to perceive themselves as able, and to have high expectations for success (Ames, 1992b). Finally, when variations in evaluations are either attributed to entity-based differences in competence or used as a controlling strategy rather than primarily for information on progress, intrinsic motivation is reduced (Kage & Namiki, 1990). Motivation researchers suggest that evaluation practices focusing on students' mastery and improvement are better at fostering and maintaining motivation than are social normative, competitive, or controlling evaluation practices (see Ames, 1992b; Maehr & Midgley, 1996).

## Teacher Control and Use of Rewards

As discussed earlier, researchers such as Deci and Ryan (1985), Ryan and Stiller (1991), and Connell and Wellborn (1991) have argued that intrinsic motivation—and, more particularly, internalization of the value of learning—leads to student engagement. Classroom contexts can greatly influence students' engagement; the degree of teacher versus student control is one crucial part of this. Deci, Ryan, Connell, and their colleagues have discussed how teachers who are overly controlling and do not provide an adequate amount of autonomy support undermine students' sense of autonomy, which can also undermine their intrinsic motivation and engagement. Support for this hypothesis has been found in both laboratory and field-based studies (e.g., Boggiano et al., 1992; Deci, Schwartz, Sheinman, & Ryan, 1981; Grolnick & Ryan, 1987; Ryan & Grolnick, 1986; see Ryan & Stiller, 1991, for a review).

Skinner and Belmont (1993) built on this work by looking at predictors of students' engagement, defined in both behavioral and emotional terms. The theoretical model for this study was Connell and Wellborn's (1991) model of engagement. As discussed earlier, Connell and Wellborn proposed that students have three fundamental needs (competence, autonomy, and relatedness) and that when context supports these needs, students will be engaged in the activities that they do. Skinner and Belmont measured teachers' and students' perceptions of teachers' provision of clear structure in the classroom, their support of autonomy, and their emotional involvement with students. They also measured teachers' and students' perceptions of students' behavioral and emotional engagement in the classroom. They found that students' behavioral engagement was predicted most strongly by teachers' ability to structure the classroom clearly. Student emotional engagement was predicted most by teachers' positive involvement with students. Furthermore, students' behavior influenced teachers' treatment of students across the school year; therefore, the effects must be thought of as reciprocal. The most crucial finding of the study for this chapter, however, concerns the impact of teachers' positive involvement with students on students' emotional engagement; the implication of this finding is that positive relations with teachers are crucial to motivation.

Other researchers also have looked at the impact of control and autonomy on student motivation and achievement. Turner (1995, 1997) studied how classroom contexts influence different aspects of young students' motivation for literacy activities. She distinguished between open and closed literacy activities. Open activities are ones that allow students choice, require strategy use, and facilitate student involvement and persistence. Because students choose the activities, they often are more interested in them. In contrast, closed activities are more constrained, both in terms of students' choices about whether and how to engage in them and in terms of the cognitive demands of the activity. Turner (1995) found that in classrooms where tasks are more open, students were more engaged in literacy activities, used more elaborate strategies, and were much more interested in literacy activities.

Au and her colleagues (Au, 1997; Au, Scheu, Kawakami, & Herman, 1990) discussed the importance of students' ownership of their activities as a crucial contributor to the development of literacy skills. Arguing that ownership is especially important for many minority students, they developed reading curricula in Hawaii to help foster the development of literacy skills, including ownership, in native Hawaiians, a group that traditionally has done poorly in school. The reading and writing activities in the Kamehameha Elementary Education Program (KEEP) curricula promote ownership by making the materials culturally relevant to the children. Evaluations of the program have shown that students are strongly engaged in the literacy activities and have a strong sense of ownership over the activities. Initially, improvement in the children's reading performance was not dramatic; in more recent evaluations, however, 80% of the students in the KEEP program were at or above grade level in reading.

One crucial point of debate relevant to the topic of control and autonomy is whether extrinsic rewards should be used by teachers to motivate students and, if they are used, how they should be administered. The use of rewards by teachers is a common practice in many schools; the rewards can be tangible (e.g., extra privileges) or verbal (e.g., praise). Yet, many motivation theorists, particularly theorists who believe intrinsic motivation has many positive effects on students' learning, have argued that, under certain conditions, the use of such rewards can undermine students' sense of control and autonomy over their achievement outcomes and reduce their intrinsic motivation (e.g., Deci & Ryan, 1985; Lepper, 1988; Ryan & Stiller, 1991). This is particularly true when students already possess intrinsic motivation for the activity in question; Lepper, Greene, and Nisbett (1973) used the compelling phrase "turning play into work" to describe such effects. In addition to the "turning play into work" issue, Ryan and Stiller discussed how extrinsic rewards can change students' perception of control from the sense that they control their own achievement outcomes to the sense that the teacher is controlling them. In Ryan and Stiller's view, this change undermines students' motivation to engage in the activity. These researchers thus have advocated careful and judicious use of extrinsic rewards in classroom settings.

Cameron and Pierce (1994) performed a meta-analysis of the research on the effects of rewards on intrinsic motivation and concluded that, in general, rewards do not undermine intrinsic motivation. They stated that the only time rewards appear to undermine intrinsic motivation is when expected tangible rewards are given to students. Ryan and Deci (1996), Kohn (1996), and Lepper, Keavney, and Drake (1996) all provided vigorous critiques of Cameron and Pierce's work, focusing on the way in which the meta-analysis was conducted (in particular, their focus on overall effects rather than on more particular conditions under which rewards affect intrinsic motivation) and the ways in which effects were included in the analysis. They further argued that Cameron and Pierce knew the answer they wanted to obtain from the meta-analysis before they began, which biased their approach to the analysis. In a response to their critics, Cameron and Pierce (1996) defended their meta-analytic practices and did not change their conclusion that, overall, rewards do not undermine intrinsic motivation.

We cannot resolve this debate here, although we do believe that Cameron and Pierce's critics raised a number of important issues that the authors did not completely rebut in their reply. Most important is Cameron and Pierce's focus on the overall effects of reward rather than a more fine-grained consideration of the various conditions under which rewards may or may not undermine intrinsic motivation. As Lepper et al. (1996) and Ryan and Deci (1996) emphasized, focusing on overall effects is both simplistic and misleading. In this regard, it is important to note that Lepper et al. (1996) and Ryan and Deci (1996) stated that they are not completely opposed to the use of extrinsic rewards; there are conditions under which such rewards can foster student motivation. This debate has served the important function of moving away from the "overall effects" question to a closer consideration of when extrinsic rewards should and should not be used.

## Social Support From Teachers

Birch and Ladd (1996) discuss how teachers and peers can facilitate (or sometimes debilitate) children's early adjustment to school and school motivation. There appear to be several aspects of students' relations with teachers that are key: closeness, dependency, and conflict. Close relations with teachers provide support to students and facilitate their school involvement. In contrast, dependency and conflict relate negatively to children's school motivation. When children are too dependent on teachers, they are less likely to adjust well to the classroom and, thus, are less positively motivated. Conflict with teachers is negatively related to both students' involvement in school and their regard for school (how much they like it).

Birch and Ladd (1996) focused on children's early adjustment to school, particularly relations with teachers during the primary grades. Other researchers have found that relations with teachers during middle school influence students' motivation. Goodenow (1993) found that students' perceptions of support from teachers and their sense of belongingness in their classrooms related strongly to their perceived valuing of the schoolwork they were doing. Similarly, Wentzel (in press) found that students' academic goals and performance were strongly related to their sense that their middle school teachers were "caring." This work provides further evidence of the important influence of positive teacher-student relations on student motivation.

## SCHOOL TRANSITIONS AND CHANGES IN STUDENT MOTIVATION

In the previous sections, we discussed some classroom practices that can facilitate or debilitate aspects of students' motivation. Anderman and Maehr (1994), Eccles and Midgley (1989), Eccles et al. (1998), Harter (1996), and Wigfield et al. (1996) discussed how many classroom and school environments move from practices that foster mastery goals and intrinsic motivation to practices that promote an ego goal orientation in students. Such practices also can contribute to the declines in students' academic competence beliefs, interest, and intrinsic motivation discussed earlier (see also Eccles, Wigfield, Midgley, et al., 1993). Many of these changes occur as children move from elementary to middle school and may be at least partially attributable to the larger size and structure of the middle school. We focus here on the particular changes in teacher-student relations and social organizations of classrooms and schools. Those most relevant to our discussion include changes in authority differential, the "personal" character of student-teacher relations, the organization of instruction, and the stability of peer networks.

First, as students move into middle school, they experience major changes in authority relationships. Middle school classrooms, as compared with elementary school classrooms, are characterized by a greater emphasis on teacher control and discipline and fewer opportunities for student decision making, choice, and self-management (e.g., Brophy & Evertson, 1976; Midgley & Feldlaufer, 1987; Moos, 1979).

Second, middle school classrooms, as compared with elementary school classrooms, often are characterized by less personal and positive teacher-student relationships (see Eccles & Midgley, 1989). For example, Trebilco, Atkinson, and Atkinson (1977) found that students reported less favorable interpersonal relations with their teachers after the transition to secondary school than before. Similarly, Feldlaufer, Midgley, and Eccles (1988) found that both students and observers rated junior high school math teachers as less friendly, less supportive, and less caring than the teachers the same students had 1 year earlier in the last year of elementary school. As discussed earlier, positive and emotionally warm relations with teachers relate to students' motivation and adjustment in the classroom.

Third, the shift to middle school is associated with systematic changes in the organization of instruction. In particular, students experience increases in practices such as whole-class task organization and between-classroom ability grouping (see Eccles & Midgley, 1989). As mentioned earlier, such changes are likely to increase social comparison, concerns about evaluation, and competitiveness, all of which could foster an ego goal orientation and a stronger focus on perceived competence (see Rosenholtz & Simpson, 1984). For children doing less well in school, such changes should lead to a decrease in their competence beliefs.

Finally, peer networks are disrupted when children change schools. Many times friends are separated from one another, and it takes some time for children to reestablish social networks. Wigfield et al. (1991) found that children's sense of social competence was lowest immediately after the transition to junior high school, in comparison with before the transition or later in junior high school. Such disruptions could influence children's academic motivation as well. Peers and motivation are considered in more detail in the next section.

In summary, after the transition to middle school, many aspects of the classroom and school organization seem to have negative effects, particularly on students' competence beliefs, achievement goals, and intrinsic motivation for learning. As mentioned earlier, Maehr and Midgley (1996) present a detailed account of an attempt to change the organization of a middle school using principles from achievement goal theory, the TARGET approach discussed by Ames (1992a, 1992b). Through collaborations with teachers and school administrators, many practices in the school were changed in order to facilitate mastery rather than ability-focused goal orientations. Maehr and Midgley's account of the process of reorganizing the school is fascinating, and many positive results did occur as a consequence of the change. However, the researchers encountered many difficult issues throughout the process, including resistance to change, difficulties in adjusting the rigid middle school bell schedule, and parents' objections that their high-achieving students did not receive enough recognition. These difficulties illustrate the continuing challenges inherent in school reform efforts.

## THE PEER GROUP AND STUDENTS' MOTIVATION

In this discussion of social influences on motivation, we have focused primarily on teacher-student relations and on characteristics of classroom organizations that influence students' motivation. Peers are another important social influence on motivation (see Webb & Palincsar, 1996, for a review of the research on group processes in the classroom). In this section, we focus on several crucial ways peers influence each other's learning and motivation.

### Friendship and Motivation

In Connell and Wellborn's (1991) model of motivation, relatedness is considered a major need. Relations with peers are an important way children can fulfill their need for relatedness. There has been much research focused on the relations among social competence, academic success, and motivation. Children are able to focus more of their attention on learning if they feel socially supported and well liked by both their peers and the adults in their learning context and if they feel that they belong (Goodenow, 1993; Ladd, 1990; Wentz-Gross, Siperstein, Untch, & Widaman, 1997). Researchers have found that children who are accepted by their peers and who have good social skills do better in school and have more positive motivation. Furthermore, social competence and social support can help ease school transitions, including the transition from home to school (Ladd, 1990). In contrast, socially rejected and highly aggressive children are at risk for poorer achievement and motivation (e.g., Asher & Coie, 1990; Ladd & Price, 1987; Parker & Asher, 1987; Wentzel, 1991b, 1993; for further discussion and review, see Berndt & Keefe, 1996; Birch & Ladd, 1996). Moreover, it appears that both the quantity of children's friendships with peers and the quality of the friendships are important; in fact, the quality of children's friendships may be especially key, particularly as children move into adolescence (see Berndt & Keefe, 1996). We should note that the major motivational constructs studied in this work are children's liking/disliking of school and school involvement/avoidance; thus, in certain respects, only limited aspects of motivation have been assessed by these researchers.

We discussed earlier research on teachers' relations with students and students' motivation. Birch and Ladd (1996) have encouraged researchers to examine the effects on motivation of different kinds of support teachers and peers provide children. They raised questions about the potential compensatory roles teachers and peers might provide. Perhaps students with poor peer relations compensate by relating well with teachers; the converse also could be the case. Or perhaps each type of relationship is tied to a particular aspect of children's school adjustment and motivation. These interesting questions await future research.

## Communities of Learners

Another important aspect of the work on cooperative learning discussed earlier is the role of peers as colearners. Doing learning activities in a social context is usually considered more "fun," and that perception alone may enhance students' motivation (Slavin, 1990; Stevens & Slavin, 1995). Peers can also help each other understand and learn the material through group discussion, sharing of resources, modeling academic skills, and interpreting and clarifying the tasks for each other (Schunk, 1987; Schunk & Zimmerman, 1997; Sieber, 1979). Each of these characteristics should influence achievement through its impact on children's expectations for success, their valuing of the activity, and their focus on learning rather than performance goals.

Other researchers also have noted the benefits of social interaction and collaboration for children's motivation and achievement. We focus on some illustrative work in the literacy field; other examples can be found in Oldfather and Dahl (1994) and Santa Barbara Discourse Group (1992). Turner (1995, 1997) noted that another benefit of open literacy tasks is that they allow opportunities for social collaboration. The social activities children engaged in took many forms, including modeling, peer tutoring, and discussion of the materials being read. The importance of these activities resided not just in the results students produced but in the processes of learning. Turner discussed the importance of the class working together to create a community of literacy learners rather than being either unconnected or competing individuals.

Guthrie and his colleagues (e.g., Guthrie et al., 1996; Guthrie & McCann, 1997) developed a reading instructional program, Concept Oriented Reading Instruction, designed to facilitate students' engagement in literacy and literacy skills. A crucial aspect of the program is collaboration with peers to facilitate students' skills and thematic understandings, along with their motivation. Thus, researchers increasingly are realizing how social collaboration can enhance students' motivation and performance.

## Help Seeking From Peers

One important focus of work on motivation that relates to the notion of communities of learners is students' help seeking. Nelson Le Gall and her colleagues (e.g., Nelson Le Gall & Glor-Sheib, 1985; Nelson Le Gall & Jones, 1990) and Newman and his colleagues (e.g., Newman, 1990, 1994; Newman & Goldin, 1990; Newman & Schwager, 1995) have developed models of children's help seeking; both groups stress the difference between appropriate and inappropriate help seeking. Appropriate help seeking (labeled *instrumental* help seeking by Nelson Le Gall and *adaptive* help seeking by Newman) involves (a) deciding that one does not understand how to complete a problem after having tried to solve it on one's own, (b) figuring out what and whom to ask, (c) developing a good question to obtain the needed help, and (d) processing the information received appropriately in order to complete the problem-solving task. Instrumental help seeking can foster motivation by keeping children engaged in an activity when they experience difficulties. Indeed, Newman has found that children are most likely to seek adaptive help when they are self-regulated, possess strong competence beliefs, and have mastery-oriented learning goals (see Newman, 1994).

It is important to note that, in general, children in elementary and secondary school do not frequently engage in help seeking either in classroom settings (Nelson Le Gall & Glor-Scheib, 1985) or when they are strongly encouraged to do so in a laboratory study (e.g., Newman & Schwager, 1995). This finding suggests that many children view help seeking as an admission that they cannot complete a problem on their own, an admission that is hard for them to make.

A number of factors influence children's willingness to seek help. These include both personal factors, such as children's motivation (e.g., competence beliefs, values, and goals) and affective reactions (e.g., Does help seeking cause embarrassment?), and contextual factors, such as classroom environment. Furthermore, there are some interesting individual and developmental differences in children's help seeking. For instance, Nelson Le Gall and DeCooke (1987) found that, among elementary-school-aged children, boys are more likely than girls to be asked for help (even though girls often perform better than boys in elementary school). Despite this overall difference, each sex prefers asking for help from same-sex peers. In a study of third-, fifth-, and seventh-grade children, Newman and Goldin (1990) found two interesting developmental differences in children's help seeking. At all ages, children who enjoyed challenge were more likely to seek help. In the two younger age groups, greater dependency related to help seeking; however, among the seventh graders, a greater focus on independent mastery related to help seeking. Furthermore, the seventh graders were more sensitive to both the costs (looking stupid, being embarrassed) and the benefits of help seeking than were the younger children.

Equally important, if not more important, are the environmental factors. Children are more likely to seek help when teachers are warm and supportive and organize the instruction around learning or task goals rather than performance or ego goals, when they work in small groups rather than in whole-class situations, and when they work on certain kinds of tasks or activities (e.g., math) rather than other kinds of achievement tasks (see Newman, 1994, for a full review).

The studies of classroom goal structure and help seeking are particularly relevant to this chapter. Newman and Schwager (1995) gave third- and sixth-grade children math reasoning problems under either learning or performance goal conditions and examined the ways in which children asked for help. Children in the learning goal condition were more likely to ask if their answers were correct; Newman and Schwager interpreted this as a desire to receive corrective feedback about their performance. Sixth graders were less likely to seek help in the performance goals condition than in the learning goals condition, and they attempted to complete as many problems as possible as quickly as possible. In a somewhat similar study, Butler and Neuman (1995) assessed help seeking under learning (task focus, in their terminology) and performance (ego focus) conditions. They also assessed children's explanations for why they and other children do not seek help when it is needed. They found that second- and sixth-grade children were more likely to ask for help in the task condition than in the ego goal condition. The sixth graders in the ego goals condition were more likely than children in the other groups to say that another child would not ask for help to avoid looking stupid.

Ryan and Pintrich (1997) assessed early adolescents' perceptions of the benefits and threats of seeking help. They hypothesized that students with a positive sense of competence (both cognitive and social) and with task-focused achievement goals should be more likely to seek help, whereas those with a low sense of competence and performance goals should avoid help seeking. Moreover, they proposed that students' attitudes toward help seeking (seeing it as a threat or benefit) would mediate the relations just discussed. Using regression analyses, they found that perceived cognitive and social competence predicted negatively students' attitude that help seeking was threatening. Children with task-focused goals were more likely to see help seeking as beneficial, whereas those with relatively stronger performance goals saw it as a threat. Cognitive and social competence negatively predicted avoidance of help seeking, whereas children's task-focused goals directly and positively predicted adaptive help seeking. Furthermore, the attitudinal variables mediated some of the links among perceived competence, achievement goals, and help seeking. These results provide further evidence that students who perhaps need the most help (those with a lower sense of competence) are the ones least likely to engage in help seeking (see Ryan, Hicks, & Midgley, 1997, for further evidence regarding this point).

## Peer Group Influences on Student Motivation

Much of the early work on peer influences on school achievement focused on the negative effects of peer groups on adolescents' commitment to doing well in school (e.g., Coleman, 1961). Investigators now have examined the specific mechanisms by which peer groups can have either a positive or negative effect on motivation across various activity settings. These researchers document that children join together in peer groups sharing similar motivational orientations and activity preferences and that such groupings reinforce and strengthen their existing motivational orientation and activity preferences over time (e.g., Berndt & Keefe, 1996; Berndt, Laychak, & Park, 1990; Kindermann, McCollam, & Gibson, 1996). Whether such effects are positive or negative depends on the nature of the peer groups' motivational orientation. High-achieving children who seek out other high achievers as friends develop even more positive academic motivation over time. By contrast, low achievers who join a low-achieving peer group should become even less motivated to do school work and more motivated to engage in other activities more consistent with their peer group's values (see Brown, 1990; Kindermann, 1993; Kindermann et al., 1996). Furthermore, the ways in which groups operate can either facilitate or debilitate motivation and achievement. Webb and Palincsar

(1996) discussed some of the difficulties that can occur in group learning (including the free rider effect discussed earlier) and the problem of certain children dominating the group. Thus, the effects of groups on children's motivation are complex and depend greatly on how the group is structured and the kinds of interactions that occur within the group.

Why are children influenced by their peers? Berndt and Keefe (1996) suggested several mechanisms to explain these influences. First, children want and need social approval, particularly from others whom they like. To gain social approval, they will do things their friends like. Whether this has positive or negative effects on motivation and achievement depends on who children's friends are. If they are high achievers, then the effects should be positive; if they are low achievers, problems could arise. Second, children often identify closely with their friends and, thus, act similarly to them; this is particularly likely during the early adolescent years. Third, children's friends provide important information about their own competence, and Berndt and Keefe made the intriguing suggestion that children often compete with their friends to enhance their own sense of self. For instance, high achievers may compete with one another for good grades. This competition may interfere with friendships if pushed too far, but it probably is a motivator for children.

The role of peer group influences is likely to vary across age. Peers may play an especially important role vis-à-vis motivation and achievement during adolescence for two reasons: Adolescents are more aware of, and concerned about, peer group acceptance and spend much more unsupervised time with peer groups than younger children. Consequently, adolescents should be especially vulnerable to peer group influences on their goals, interests, and values. In addition, however, the potential negative impact of peers may be especially problematic for some adolescents' academic achievement motivation. For example, early adolescents rate social activities as very important and as more enjoyable than most other activities, particularly academic activities (Eccles et al., 1989; Wigfield et al., 1991). Furthermore, early adolescents' physical appearance and social acceptance are more important predictors of their general self-esteem than their perceptions of their cognitive competence (Harter, 1990). Consequently, to the extent that one's peer group devalues academic achievement relative to other goals and activities, adolescents should shift their focus away from academic pursuits in order to maintain peer acceptance.

The work on the institutional consequences of ability grouping provides an example of these processes. Several researchers (e.g., Dreeben & Barr, 1988; Eder & Felmlee, 1984) have suggested that ability grouping influences motivation and achievement, in part, by its influence on one's peer group. The evidence of this effect is mixed for the elementary school years. But it is more likely to be true in the adolescent years, when between-class ability grouping and curricular tracking become more common. These institutional practices result in much greater segregation of peer groups based the courses they are taking (Fuligni et al., 1995; Rosenbaum, 1980; Vanfossen, Jones, & Spade, 1987). Consequently, we should expect greater evidence of social stratification effects of ability grouping on students' motivation during the high school years.

# CONCLUSION

In this chapter, we have discussed the nature of students' academic motivation and its relation to important behavioral outcomes such as performance in different academic subjects, choices of which activities to pursue, effort exerted, and persistence. We noted that much of the work on students' motivation over the last 25 years has focused on a variety of student self-perceptions, along with students' interests, values, and goals, as crucial components of motivation. These constructs mediate students' performance, choices, and efforts. We also discussed the development of these different aspects of motivation, describing how students' motivation often declines during the school years and relates more closely to their actual performance.

We reviewed the large and growing body of research on how different school and classroom environmental factors influence students' motivation, and we discussed peer groups and motivation. Unfortunately, findings from many different studies suggest that the declines in motivation we discussed often can be traced to changes in the classroom environment and teaching practices; this seems to be particularly true as students move from elementary to middle school. On a more positive note, we also discussed a number of teaching practices and environmental conditions that can facilitate students' self-perceptions, values, interests, and goals. We also noted that peers often can have a positive influence on each other's motivation. We close this chapter with a discussion of some important issues remaining to be addressed in these different areas.

One issue concerns how the many different motivation constructs we discussed are influenced together by different social features of classrooms (see Stipek, 1996). We defined numerous aspects of students' motivation in the first section of the chapter. Yet, researchers assessing the ways in which different social factors in the school environment influence motivation often assess only certain of these aspects. For instance, researchers focus on students' goal orientations perhaps, or competence beliefs, but not a number of motivation constructs. Or they define and assess motivation in more general terms than those used in the literature on motivation; the research on cooperative learning's effects on motivation is one example of this. To obtain a more complete understanding of the influences of different social and environmental factors on motivation, one must assess motivation more fully.

We also must consider more closely how multiple aspects of motivation influence students' choices of different activities and their performance. This often has been done in studies within the academic domain (e.g., Meece et al., 1990; Pintrich & De Groot, 1990; Wigfield & Guthrie, 1997). Also, there is growing interest in how different kinds of motivation, particularly social and academic motivation, influence students' performance (e.g., Juvonen & Wentzel, 1996; Wentzel & Wigfield, in press). Wentzel and Wigfield (in press) discuss how social and academic goals may interact to influence students' performance and how different classroom factors influence both social and academic goals. But the study of the joint influence of social and academic motivation on students' outcomes is just beginning, and much more work remains to be done in this important new research area. Crucial issues that researchers need to consider carefully are the degree to which the constructs of social and academic motivation are similar or different and the interplay of these constructs in influencing students' outcomes (see Wentzel & Wigfield, in press, for further discussion).

Another crucial issue is how motivation should be conceptualized as theorists move to the view that learning is an inherently social activity. If learning truly is a social phenomenon and individuals cannot be separated from their social context, what is the role of self-perceptions in motivating students' behavior? Some might argue that they are irrelevant. Others believe that self-perceptions still are important, but perhaps in modified form (for further discussion, see Hickey, 1997; Marshall, 1992). Our point is that a truly social approach to learning may be incompatible with the things that many motivation researchers study. This incompatibility encompasses different levels, from relevant constructs to ways of studying motivation.

We of course believe strongly that the motivation constructs we discussed, including those conceived of primarily as self-perceptions, have strong relevance to students' educational outcomes and so deserve continued conceptual and research attention. Yet, as social constructivist models become more prevalent, it is increasingly important to consider the influence of these models on ways of conceptualizing motivation. One issue is which constructs prevalent in social cognitive approaches to motivation are compatible with social constructivist approaches. Theorists have begun to discuss this issue. For instance, both Marshall (1992) and Blumenfeld (1992) focused on students' goal orientations as at least partly compatible with social constructivist views. But they also noted some limitations in prevalent views of goal orientations. Oldfather and Dahl (1994) discussed intrinsic motivation from a social constructivist perspective, conceptualizing it as the continuing impulse to learn. They defined this impulse as ongoing engagement in learning that comes from the learner's social construction of meaning and stated that it is characterized by learners' involvement, curiosity, and search for understanding. Their construct thus is similar to intrinsic motivation but clearly takes on a more social constructivist flavor.

Theorists are incorporating these constructs into models of motivation. For instance, Hickey (1997) presented what he called a principled, pragmatic model of motivation compatible with social constructivist views of learning. His model includes the beliefs and goals of individuals, socially defined constructs, and their interactions. McCaslin and Good (1996) developed a model of co-regulated learning that includes individuals' self-perceptions (such as self-efficacy and attributions for success and failure) and goals and the social/environmental characteristics of classrooms. They also noted that the reciprocal relations of learners' individual motives and characteristics of their social environments are crucial to co-regulated learning. While important steps, these models have not yet received much research attention.

Adopting the view that students' motivation is influenced strongly by their learning environment implies that motivation is situation specific (see Paris & Turner, 1994; Wigfield, 1997). Yet, there is interesting discussion in the field about this issue; in particular, there is discussion of how constructs may differ in their generality or specificity. In his review of research on self-efficacy and competence beliefs, Pajares (1996) noted that self-efficacy usually is defined in very task-specific terms, whereas competence beliefs often are defined more generally. Wigfield and Guthrie (1997) present evidence for domain-specific reading motivation constructs. Students' interests probably are relatively specific. As we discussed earlier, however, students' goal orientations actually may generalize across different domains, such as academics and sports (Duda & Nicholls, 1992).

What now is needed is a clearer categorization of motivation constructs in terms of their generality and specificity. Such a categorization would lead to a better understanding of which constructs are more likely to be influenced by different environmental factors and social influences and which may be more stable across different environments. One example of this approach is Boekaerts's (1996) categorization system of different levels of situations, along with different levels of individuals' personality characteristics, and their relations to learning. The levels range from broad, general characteristics of both situations and individuals to very specific, unique aspects of both situations and people. This conceptualization allows for a clearer understanding of how characteristics of the person interact with characteristics of the situation to influence learning outcomes.

The methods used in research on motivation are another important concern. Hickey (1997) noted that self-report measures, a hallmark of social cognitive motivation research, may miss important contextual influences on motivation. Such measures also do not capture students' experiences as they are in the midst of an activity. There are other methodologies that can capture more fully these subjective experiences. Boekaerts and her colleagues (e.g., Boekaerts, 1997; Seegers & Boekaerts, 1993) developed an "on-line motivation" questionnaire that assesses students' motivation as they are doing different tasks. Seegers and Boekaerts found that "on-line" assessments were the strongest direct predictors of outcomes such as task performance and emotions. Csikszentmihalyi's experience sampling methodology is another good example of a method for measuring individuals' experiences as they are taking place (see Csikszentmihalyi & Nakamura, 1989).

The study of the reciprocal relations of school and classroom environmental factors and student motivation also poses important methodological challenges. As Stipek (1996) pointed out, the interactive influence of different school and classroom factors on students' motivation has not been studied fully. Detailed ethnographic studies are one way to look at the complex interplay of classroom environmental factors and students' motivation (e.g., Oldfather & McLaughlin, 1993). Quantitative approaches can be used as well, and one particularly promising approach is hierarchical linear modeling (HLM) (Bryk & Raudenbush, 1992). With HLM, researchers can examine both individual differences in motivation and classroom effects on it. Anderman and Young (1994) used HLM to study students' goal orientations in science classrooms. They found individual differences in students' goal orientations but also effects of particular classroom practices on students' goal orientations. Uncovering these different influences on students' goal orientations, along with other aspects of motivation, is an important task for future research.

As we hope is clear from the research reviewed in this chapter, much has been learned about the nature of students' motivation and how it is influenced by the social learning environments students experience. The complexity of these relations, as well as their situation specificity, means that much work remains to be done in this area.

## NOTE

[1]In contrast to these early studies using self-report measures, researchers using different methodologies (either asking different kinds of questions or observing young children's reactions to their performance on different tasks) have recently shown that not all young children are optimistic about their abilities. In Heyman, Dweck, and Cain's (1993) study, some preschool children already reacted negatively to failure, reporting that their failures mean that they are not good people. Similarly, in Stipek, Recchia, and McClintic (1992), preschool children as young as 2 years of age reacted both behaviorally and emotionally to failure experiences.

## REFERENCES

Alexander, P. A., Kulikowich, J. M., & Jetton, T. L. (1994). The role of subject-matter knowledge and interest in the processing of linear and nonlinear texts. *Review of Educational Research, 64,* 201–252.

Ames, C. (1984). Competitive, cooperative, and individualistic goal structures: A cognitive-motivational analysis. In R. E. Ames & C. Ames (Eds.), *Research on motivation in education* (Vol. 1). San Diego: Academic Press.

Ames, C. (1992a). Achievement goals and the classroom motivational climate. In D. H. Schunk & J. L. Meece (Eds.), *Student perception in the classroom* (pp. 327–348). Hillsdale, NJ: Erlbaum.

Ames, C. (1992b). Classrooms: Goals, structures, and student motivation. *Journal of Educational Psychology, 84,* 261–271.

Ames, C., & Ames, R. (Eds.). (1989). *Research on motivation in education: Vol. 3. Goals and cognitions.* San Diego, CA: Academic Press.

Anderman, E. M., & Maehr, M. L. (1994). Motivation and schooling in the middle grades. *Review of Educational Research, 64,* 287–309.

Anderman, E. M., & Young, A. J. (1994). Motivation and strategy use in science: Individual differences and classroom effects. *Journal of Research in Science Teaching, 31,* 811–831.

Anderson, R. C., Shirey, L. L., Wilson, P. T., & Fielding, L. G. (1987). Interestingness of children's reading material. In R. E. Snow & M. J. Farr (Eds.), *Aptitude, learning, and instruction: Vol. 3. Conative and affective process analyses* (pp. 287-299). Hillsdale, NJ: Erlbaum.

Asher, S. R., & Coie, J. D. (Eds.). (1990). *Peer rejection in childhood.* New York: Cambridge University Press.

Au, K. H. (1997). Ownership, literacy achievement, and students of diverse cultural backgrounds. In J. T. Guthrie & A. Wigfield (Eds.), *Reading engagement: Motivating readers through integrated instruction* (pp. 168–182). Newark, DE: International Reading Association.

Au, K. H., Scheu, J. A., Kawakami, A. J., & Herman, P. A. (1990). Assessment and accountability in a whole literacy curriculum. *The Reading Teacher, 43,* 574–578.

Bandura, A. (1977). Self-efficacy: Toward a unifying theory of behavioral change. *Psychological Review, 84,* 191–215.

Bandura, A. (1986). *Social foundations of thought and action: A social cognitive theory.* Englewood Cliffs, NJ: Prentice Hall.

Bandura, A. (1997). *Self-efficacy: The exercise of control.* New York: W. H. Freeman.

Baumert, J. (1995, April). *Gender, science interest, teaching strategies and socially shared beliefs about gender roles in 7th graders—A multi-level analysis.* Paper presented at the annual meeting of the American Educational Research Association, San Francisco.

Berndt, T. J., & Keefe, K. (1996). Friends' influence on school adjustment: A motivational analysis. In J. Juvonen & K. Wentzel (Eds.), *Social motivation: Understanding school adjustment.* New York: Cambridge University Press.

Berndt, T. J., Laychak, A. E., & Park, K. (1990). Friends' influence on adolescents' academic achievement motivation: An experimental study. *Journal of Educational Psychology, 82,* 664–670.

Birch, S. H., & Ladd, G. W. (1996). Interpersonal relationships in the school environment and children's school adjustment: The role of teachers and peers. In J. Juvonen & K. Wentzel (Eds.), *Social motivation: Understanding school adjustment.* New York: Cambridge University Press.

Blumenfeld, P. C. (1992). Classroom learning and motivation: Clarifying and expanding goal theory. *Journal of Educational Psychology, 84,* 272–281.

Blumenfeld, P., Pintrich, P. R., Meece, J., & Wessels, K. (1982). The formation and role of self-perceptions of ability in elementary school classrooms. *Elementary School Journal, 82,* 401–420.

Boekaerts, M. (1996). Personality and the psychology of learning. *European Journal of Personality, 10,* 377–404.

Boekaerts, M. (1997). *Motivated learning: The study of student\*situation transactional units.* Manuscipt submitted for publication.

Boggiano, A. K., Shields, A., Barrett, M., Kellam, T., Thompson, E., Simons, J., & Katz, P. (1992). Helplessness deficits in students: The role of motivational orientation. *Motivation and Emotion, 16,* 271–296.

Borkowski, J. G., Carr, M., Rellinger, E., & Pressley, M. (1990). Self-regulated cognition: Interdependence of metacognition, attributions, and self-esteem. In B. Jones & L. Idol (Eds.), *Dimensions of thinking and cognitive instruction* (Vol. 1). Hillsdale, NJ: Erlbaum.

Brookover, W., Beady, C., Flood, P., Schweitzer, J., & Wisenbaker, J. (1979). *School social systems and student achievement: Schools can make a difference.* New York: Praeger.

Brophy, J. E., & Evertson, C. M. (1976). *Learning from teaching: A developmental perspective.* Boston: Allyn & Bacon.

Brown, B. B. (1990). Peer groups and peer culture. In S. S. Feldman & G. R. Elliott (Eds.), *At the threshold: The developing adolescent* (pp. 171–196). Cambridge, MA: Harvard University Press.

Bryk, A. S., & Raudenbush, S. W. (1992). *Hierarchical linear models: Applications and data analysis methods.* Newbury Park, CA: Sage.

Butler, R. (1989a). Interest in the task and interest in peers' work: A developmental study. *Child Development, 60,* 562–570.

Butler, R. (1989b). Mastery versus ability appraisal: A developmental study of children's observations of peers' work. *Child Development, 60,* 1350–1361.

Butler, R. (1990). The effects of mastery and competitive conditions on self-assessment at different ages. *Child Development, 61,* 201–210.

Butler, R. (1993). Effects of task- and ego-achievement goals on information seeking during task engagement. *Journal of Personality and Social Psychology, 65,* 18–31.

Butler, R., & Neuman, O. (1995). Effects of task and ego achievement goals on help-seeking behaviors and attitudes. *Journal of Educational Psychology, 87,* 261–271.

Butler, R., & Ruzany, N. (1993). Age and socialization effects on the development of social comparison motives and normative ability assessments in kibbutz and urban children. *Child Development, 64,* 532–543.

Cameron, J., & Pierce, W. D. (1994). Reinforcement, reward, and intrinsic motivation: A meta-analysis. *Review of Educational Research, 64,* 363–423.

Cameron, J., & Pierce, W. D. (1996). The debate about rewards and intrinsic motivation: Protests and accusations do not alter the results. *Review of Educational Research, 66,* 39–51.

Coleman, J. S. (1961). *The adolescent society.* New York: Free Press.

Connell, J. P. (1985). A new multidimensional measure of children's perception of control. *Child Development, 56,* 1018–1041.

Connell, J. P., Spencer, M. B., & Aber, J. L. (1994). Educational risk and resilience in African American youth: Context, self, and action outcomes in school. *Child Development, 65,* 493–506.

Connell, J. P., & Wellborn, J. G. (1991). Competence, autonomy, and relatedness: A motivational analysis of self-system processes. In R. Gunnar & L. A. Sroufe (Eds.), *Minnesota symposia on child psychology* (Vol. 23, pp. 43–77). Hillsdale, NJ: Erlbaum.

Corno, L., & Kanfer, R. (1993). The role of volition in learning and performance. In L. Darling-Hammond (Ed.), *Review of research in education* (Vol. 29). Washington, DC: American Educational Research Association.

Covington, M. V. (1992). *Making the grade: A self-worth perspective on motivation and school reform.* New York: Cambridge University Press.

Crandall, V. C., Katkovsky, W., & Crandall, V. J. (1965). Children's beliefs in their own control of reinforcements in intellectual-academic achievement situations. *Child Development, 36,* 91–109.

Crockenberg, S., & Bryant, B. (1978). Socialization: The "implicit curriculum" of learning environments. *Journal of Research Development in Education, 12,* 69–78.

Csikszentmihalyi, M. (1988). The flow experience and its significance for human psychology. In M. Csikszentmihalyi & I. S. Csikszentmihalyi (Eds.), *Optimal experience* (pp. 15-35). Cambridge, England: Cambridge University Press.

Csikszentmihalyi, M., & Nakamura, J. (1989). The dynamics of intrinsic motivation: A study of adolescents. In C. Ames & R. Ames (Eds.), *Research on motivation in education.* San Diego, CA: Academic Press.

Deci, E. L. (1992). The relation of interest to the motivation of behavior: A self-determination theory perspective. In K. A. Renninger, S. Hidi, & A. Krapp (Eds.), *The role of interest in learning and development* (pp. 43–71). Hillsdale, NJ: Erlbaum.

Deci, E. L., & Ryan, R. M. (1985). *Intrinsic motivation and self-determination in human behavior.* New York: Plenum.

Deci, E. L., Schwartz, A. J., Sheinman, L., & Ryan, R. M. (1981). An instrument to assess adults' orientations toward control versus autonomy with children: Reflections on intrinsic motivation and perceived competence. *Journal of Educational Psychology, 73,* 645–650.

Deci, E., L., Vallerand, R. J., Pelletier, L. C., & Ryan, R. M. (1991). Motivation and education: The self-determination perspective. *Educational Psychologist, 26,* 325–346.

Dreeben, R., & Barr, R. (1988). Classroom composition and the design of instruction. *Sociology of Education, 61,* 129–142.

Duda, J. L., & Nicholls, J. G. (1992). Dimensions of achievement motivation in schoolwork and sport. *Journal of Educational Psychology, 84,* 290–299.

Dunkin, M., & Biddle, B. (1974). *The study of teaching.* New York: Holt, Rinehart & Winston.

Dweck, C. S., & Elliott, E. S. (1983). Achievement motivation. In P. H. Mussen (Ed.), *Handbook of child psychology* (Vol. 4, 3rd ed., pp. 643–691). New York: Wiley.

Dweck, C. S., & Leggett, E. (1988). A social-cognitive approach to motivation and personality. *Psychological Review, 95,* 256–273.

Eccles, J. S. (1984). Sex differences in achievement patterns. In T. Sonderegger (Ed.), *Nebraska Symposium on Motivation* (Vol. 32, pp. 97–132). Lincoln: University of Nebraska Press.

Eccles, J. S. (1987). Gender roles and women's achievement-related decisions. *Psychology of Women Quarterly, 11,* 135–172.

Eccles, J. S. (1994). Understanding women's educational and occupational choice: Applying the Eccles et al. model of achievement-related choices. *Psychology of Women Quarterly, 18,* 585–609.

Eccles, J. S., Adler, T. F., Futterman, R., Goff, S. B., Kaczala, C. M., Meece, J. L., & Midgley, C. (1983). Expectancies, values, and academic behaviors. In J. T. Spence (Ed.), *Achievement and achievement motivation* (pp. 75–146). San Francisco: W. H. Freeman.

Eccles, J. S., Adler, T. F., & Meece, J. L. (1984). Sex differences in achievement: A test of alternate theories. *Journal of Personality and Social Psychology, 46,* 26–43.

Eccles, J. S., & Harold, R. D. (1991). Gender differences in sport involvement: Applying the Eccles' expectancy-value model. *Journal of Applied Sport Psychology, 3,* 7–35.

Eccles, J. S., & Midgley, C. (1989). Stage/environment fit: Developmentally appropriate classrooms for early adolescents. In R. Ames & C. Ames (Eds.), *Research on motivation in education* (Vol. 3, pp. 139–181). New York: Academic Press.

Eccles, J., Midgley, C., & Adler, T. (1984). Grade-related changes in the school environment: Effects on achievement motivation. In J. G. Nicholls (Ed.), *The development of achievement motivation* (pp. 283–331). Greenwich, CT: JAI Press.

Eccles, J. S., & Wigfield, A. (1995). In the mind of the achiever: The structure of adolescents' academic achievement related-beliefs and self-perceptions. *Personality and Social Psychology Bulletin, 21,* 215–225.

Eccles, J. S., Wigfield, A., Flanagan, C., Miller, C., Reuman, D., & Yee, D. (1989). Self-concepts, domain values, and self-esteem: Relations and changes at early adolescence. *Journal of Personality, 57,* 283–310.

Eccles, J. S., Wigfield, A., Harold, R., & Blumenfeld, P. B. (1993). Age and gender differences in children's self- and task perceptions during elementary school. *Child Development, 64,* 830–847.

Eccles, J. S., Wigfield, A., Midgley, C., Reuman, D., Mac Iver, D., & Feldlaufer, H. (1993). Negative effects of traditional middle-schools on students' motivation. *Elementary School Journal, 93,* 553–574.

Eccles, J. S., Wigfield, A., & Schiefele, U. (1998). Motivation to succeed. In W. Damon (Series Ed.) & N. Eisenberg (Vol. Ed.), *Handbook of child psychology* (5th ed., Vol. 3). New York: Wiley.

Eder, D., & Felmlee, D. (1984). The development of attention norms in ability groups. In P. L. Peterson, L. C. Wilkinson, & M. Hallinan (Eds.), *The social context of instruction: Group organization and group processes* (pp. 189–208). Orlando, FL: Academic Press.

Elliott, A. J., & Harackiewicz, J. M. (1996). Approach and avoidance achievement goals and intrinsic motivation: A mediational analysis. *Journal of Personality and Social Psychology, 70,* 968–980.

Elliott, E. S., & Dweck, C. S. (1988). Goals: An approach to motivation and achievement. *Journal of Personality and Social Psychology, 54,* 5–12.

Epstein, J. L. (1988). Effective schools or effective students: Dealing with diversity. In R. Haskins & B. MacRae (Eds.), *Policies for America's public schools: Teacher equity indicators.* Norwood, NJ: Ablex.

Feldlaufer, H., Midgley, C., & Eccles, J. S. (1988). Student, teacher, and observer perceptions of the classroom environment before and after the transition to junior high school. *Journal of Early Adolescence, 8,* 133–156.

Findley, M. J., & Cooper, H. M. (1983). Locus of control and academic achievement: A literature review. *Journal of Personality and Social Psychology, 44,* 419–427.

Ford, M. E. (1992). *Human motivation: Goals, emotions, and personal agency beliefs.* Newbury Park, CA: Sage.

Fraser, B. J., & Fisher, D. L. (1982). Predicting students' outcomes from their perceptions of classroom psychosocial environment. *American Educational Research Journal, 19,* 498–518.

Fuligni, A. J., Eccles, J. S., & Barber, B. L. (1995). The long-term effects of seventh-grade ability grouping in mathematics. *Journal of Early Adolescence, 15,* 58–89.

Gamoran, A., & Mare, R. D. (1989). Secondary school tracking and educational inequality: Compensation, reinforcement, or neutrality? *American Journal of Sociology, 94,* 1146–1183.

Goodenow, C. (1993). Classroom belonging among early adolescent students: Relationships to motivation and achievement. *Journal of Early Adolescence, 13,* 21–43.

Grolnick, W. S., & Ryan, R. M. (1987). Autonomy in children's learning: An experimental and individual difference investigation. *Journal of Personality and Social Psychology, 52,* 890–898.

Guthrie, J. T., & McCann, A. D. (1997). Characteristics of classrooms that promote motivations and strategies for learning. In J. T. Guthrie & A. Wigfield (Eds.), *Reading engagement: Motivating readers through integrated instruction* (pp. 128–148). Newark, DE: International Reading Association.

Guthrie, J. T., Van Meter, P., McCann, A., Wigfield, A., Bennett, L., Poundstone, C., Rice, M. E., Faibisch, F., Hunt, B., & Mitchell, A. (1996). Growth in literacy engagement: Changes in motivations and strategies during Concept-Oriented Reading Instruction. *Reading Research Quarterly, 31,* 306–325.

Harter, S. (1981). A new self-report scale of intrinsic versus extrinsic orientation in the classroom: Motivational and informational components. *Developmental Psychology, 17,* 300–312.

Harter, S. (1982). The Perceived Competence Scale for Children. *Child Development, 53,* 87–97.

Harter, S. (1983). Developmental perspectives on the self-system. In P. H. Mussen (Ed.), *Handbook of child psychology* (Vol. 4, pp. 275–385). New York: Wiley.

Harter, S. (1990). Causes, correlates and the functional role of global self-worth: A life-span perspective. In J. Kolligian & R. Sternberg (Eds.), *Perceptions of competence and incompetence across the life-span* (pp. 67–98). New Haven, CT: Yale University Press.

Harter, S. (1996). Teacher and classmate influences on scholastic motivation, self-esteem, and the level of voice in adolescents. In J. Juvonen & K. Wentzel (Eds.), *Social motivation: Understanding school adjustment.* New York: Cambridge University Press.

Harter, S., & Connell, J. P. (1984). A model of children's achievement and related self-perceptors of competence, control, and motivational orientation. In J. G. Nicholls (Ed.), *Advances in motivation and achievement* (Vol. 23, pp. 219–250). Greenwich, CT: JAI Press.

Helmke, A. (1993). The development of learning from kindergarten to fifth grade. *Journal of Educational Psychology, 7,* 77–86.

Hedelin, L., & Sjoberg, L. (1989). The development of interests in the Swedish comprehensive school. *European Journal of Psychology of Education, 4,* 17–35.

Heyman, G. D., Dweck, C. S., & Cain, K. M. (1993). Young children's vulnerability to self-blame and helplessness: Relationships to beliefs about goodness. *Child Development, 63,* 401–415.

Hickey, D. T. (1997). Motivation and contemporary socio-constructivist instructional perspectives. *Educational Psychologist, 32,* 175–193.

Hidi, S. (1990). Interest and its contribution as a mental resource for learning. *Review of Educational Research, 60,* 549–571.

Hidi, S., & Baird, W. (1986). Interestingness—A neglected variable in discourse processing. *Cognitive Science, 10,* 179–194.

Hidi, S., & Baird, W. (1988). Strategies for increasing text-based interest and students' recall of expository texts. *Reading Research Quarterly, 23,* 465–483.

Hidi, S., & Berndorff, D. (1996, June). Situational interest and learning. Paper presented at the Seeon Conference on Gender and Interest, Kloster, Seeon, Germany.

Johnson, D. W., & Johnson, R. T. (1989). *Cooperation and competition: Theory and research.* Edina, MN: Interaction.

Johnson, D. W., & Johnson, R. T. (1994). *Learning together and alone: Cooperative, competitive, and individualistic learning* (4th ed.). Boston: Allyn & Bacon.

Juvonen, J., & Wentzel, K. R. (Eds.) (1996). *Social motivation: Understanding school adjustment.* New York: Cambridge University Press.

Kagan, S. (1985). Dimensions of cooperative classroom structures. In R. Slavin, S. Sharan, S. Kagan, R. Hertz-Lazarowitz, C. Webb, & R. Schmuck (Eds.), *Learning to cooperate, cooperating to learn* (pp. 67–96). New York: Plenum.

Kage, M., & Namiki, H. (1990). The effects of evaluation structure on children's intrinsic motivation and learning. *Japanese Journal of Educational Psychology, 38*, 36–45.

Kindermann, T. A. (1993). Natural peer groups as contexts for individual development: The case of children's motivation in school. *Developmental Psychology, 29*, 970–977.

Kindermannn, T. A., McCollam, T. L., & Gibbson, E., Jr. (1996). Peer networks and students' classroom engagement during childhood and adolescence. In J. Juvonen & K. Wentzel (Eds.), *Social motivation: Understanding children's school adjustment.* Cambridge, England: Cambridge University Press.

Kohlberg, L. (1966). A cognitive-development analysis of children's sex-role concepts and attitudes. In E. E. Macoby (Ed.), *The development of sex differences.* (pp. 82–172). Stanford, CA: Stanford University Press.

Kohn, A. (1996). By all available means: Cameron and Pierce's defense of extrinsic motivators. *Review of Educational Research, 66*, 1–4.

Krapp, A., Hidi, S., & Renninger, K. A. (1992). Interest, learning and development. In K. A. Renninger, S. Hidi, & A. Krapp (Eds.), *The role of interest in learning and development* (pp. 3–25). Hillsdale, NJ: Erlbaum.

Kuhl, J. (1987). Action control: The maintenance of motivational states. In F. Halisch & J. Kuhl (Eds.), *Motivation, intention, and volition* (pp. 279–307). Berlin: Springer-Verlag.

Kulik, J. A., & Kulik, C. L. (1987). Effects of ability grouping on student achievement. *Equity & Excellence, 23,* 22–30.

Ladd, G. W., & Price, J. M. (1987). Predicting children's social and school adjustment following the transition from preschool to kindergarten. *Child Development, 58*, 1168–1189.

Lehrke, M., Hoffmann, L., & Gardner, P. L. (Eds.). (1985). *Interests in science and technology education.* Kiel, Germany: Institut fur die Padagogik der Naturwissenschaften.

Lepper, G., Greene, D., & Nisbett, R. E. (1973). Undermining children's intrinsic interest with extrinsic rewards: A test of the "overjustification" hypothesis. *Journal of Personality and Social Psychology, 28*, 129–137.

Lepper, M. R. (1988). Motivational considerations in the study of instruction. *Cognition and Instruction, 5*, 289–310.

Lepper, M. R., Keavney, M., & Drake, M. (1996). Intrinsic motivation and extrinsic rewards: A commentary on Cameron and Pierce's meta-analysis. *Review of Educational Research, 66*, 5–32.

Mac Iver, D. (1987). Classroom factors and student characteristics predicting students' use of achievement standards during ability self-assessment. *Child Development, 58*, 1258–1271.

Mac Iver, D. J., Reuman, D. A., & Main, S. R. (1995). Social structuring of school: Studying what is, illuminating what could be. *Annual Review of Psychology, 46*.

Maehr, M. L., & Anderman, E. M. (1993). Reinventing schools for early adolescents: Emphasizing task goals. *Elementary School Journal, 93*, 593–610.

Maehr, M. L., & Midgley, C. (1996). *Transforming school cultures.* Boulder, CO: Westview Press.

Markus, H., & Wurf, E. (1987). The dynamic self-concept: A social psychological perspective. *Annual Review of Psychology, 38*, 299–337.

Marsh, H. W. (1989). Age and sex effects in multiple dimensions of self-concept: Preadolescence to early adulthood. *Journal of Educational Psychology, 81*, 417–430.

Marsh, H. W., Barnes, J., Cairns, L., & Tidman, M. (1984). Self-Description Questionnaire: Age and sex effects in the structure and level of self-concept for preadolescent children. *Journal of Educational Psychology, 76*, 940–956.

Marsh, H. W., Chessor, D., Craven, R., & Roche, L. (1995). The effects of gifted and talented programs on academic self-concept: The big fish strikes again. *American Educational Research Journal, 32*, 285–319.

Marsh, H. W., Craven, R. G., & Debus, R. (1991). Self-concepts of young children 5 to 8 years of age: Measurement and multidimensional structure. *Journal of Educational Psychology, 83,* 377–392.

Marsh, H. W., & Hocevar, D. (1985). The application of confirmatory factor analyses to the study of self-concept: First and higher-order factor structures and their invariance across age groups. *Psychological Bulletin, 97,* 562–582.

Marshall, H. H. (1992). Seeing, redefining, and supporting student learning. In H. H. Marshall (Ed.), *Redefining student learning: Roots of educational change* (pp. 1-32). Norwood, NJ: Ablex.

McCaslin, M., & Good, T. L. (1996). The informal curriculum. In D. C. Berliner & R. C. Calfee (Eds.), *Handbook of educational psychology* (pp. 622–670). New York: Macmillan.

Meece, J. L. (1991). The classroom context and students' motivational goals. In M. Maehr & P. Pintrich (Eds.), *Advances in motivation and achievement* (Vol. 7, pp. 261–286). Greenwich, CT: JAI Press.

Meece, J. L. (1994). The role of motivation in self-regulated learning. In D. H. Schunk & B. J. Zimmerman (Eds.), *Self-regulation of learning and performance* (pp. 25–44). Hillsdale, NJ: Erlbaum.

Meece, J. L., Blumenfeld, P. B., & Hoyle, R. H. (1988). Students' goal orientations and cognitive engagement in classroom activities. *Journal of Educational Psychology, 80,* 514–523.

Meece, J. L., & Miller, S. D. (1996, April). *Developmental changes in children's self-reports of achievement goals, competence, and strategy use during the late elementary years.* Paper presented at the annual meeting of the American Educational Research Association, New York City.

Meece, J. L., Wigfield, A., & Eccles, J. S. (1990). Predictors of math anxiety and its consequences for young adolescents' course enrollment intentions and performances in mathematics. *Journal of Educational Psychology, 82,* 60–70.

Midgley, C., & Feldlaufer, H. (1987). Students' and teachers' decision-making fit before and after the transition to junior high school. *Journal of Early Adolescence, 7,* 225–241.

Moos, R. H. (1979). *Evaluating educational environments.* San Francisco: Jossey-Bass.

Nelson Le Gall, S., & DeCooke, P. A. (1987). Same sex and cross-sex help exchanges in the classroom. *Journal of Educational Psychology, 79,* 67–71.

Nelson Le Gall, S., & Glor-Sheib, S. (1985). Help seeking in elementary classrooms: An observational study. *Contemporary Educational Psychology, 10,* 58–71.

Nelson Le Gall, S., & Jones, E. (1990). Cognitive-motivational influences on task-related help-seeking behavior of Black children. *Child Development, 61,* 581–589.

Newman, R. S. (1990). Children's help-seeking in the classroom: The role of motivational factors and attitudes. *Journal of Educational Psychology, 82,* 71–80.

Newman, R. S. (1994). Adaptive help-seeking: A strategy of self-regulated learning. In D. H. Schunk & B. J. Zimmerman (Eds.), *Self-regulation of learning and performance: Issues and educational applications* (pp. 283–301). Hillsdale, NJ: Erlbaum.

Newman, R. S., & Goldin, L. (1990). Children's reluctance to seek help with schoolwork. *Journal of Educational Psychology, 82,* 92–100.

Newman, R. S., & Schwager, M. T. (1995). Students' help-seeking during problem solving: Effects of grade, goal, and prior achievement. *American Educational Research Journal, 32,* 352–376.

Nicholls, J. G. (1979a). Development of perception of own attainment and causal attributions for success and failure in reading. *Journal of Educational Psychology, 71,* 94–99.

Nicholls, J. G. (1979b). Quality and equality in intellectual development: The role of motivation in education. *American Psychologist, 34,* 1071–1084.

Nicholls, J. G. (1984). Achievement motivation: Conceptions of ability, subjective experience, task choice, and performance. *Psychological Review, 91,* 328–346.

Nicholls, J. G. (1990). What is ability and why are we mindful of it? A developmental perspective. In R. J. Sternberg & J. Kolligian (Eds.), *Competence considered* (pp. 11–40). New Haven, CT: Yale University Press.

Nicholls, J. G., Cheung, P., Lauer, J., & Patashnick, M. (1989). Individual differences in academic motivation: Perceived ability, goals, beliefs, and values. *Learning and Individual Differences, 1,* 63–84.

Nicholls, J. G., Cobb, P., Yackel, E., Wood, T., & Wheatley, G. (1990). Students' theories of mathematics and their mathematical knowledge: Multiple dimensions of assessment. In G. Kulm (Ed.), *Assessing higher order thinking in mathematics* (pp. 137–154). Washington, DC: American Association for the Advancement of Science.

Nichols, J. D. (1996). Cooperative learning: A motivational tool to enhance student persistence, self-regulation, and efforts to please teachers and parents. *Educational Research and Evaluation, 2,* 246–260.

Nichols, J. D. (in press). The effects of cooperative learning on student achievement and motivation in a high school geometry class. *Contemporary Educational Psychology.*

Nolen, S. B., & Nicholls, J. G. (1993). Elementary school pupils' beliefs about practices for motivating pupils in mathematics. *British Journal of Educational Psychology, 63,* 414–430.

Oakes, J. (1985). *Keeping track: How schools structure inequality.* New Haven, CT: Yale University Press.

Oldfather, P., & Dahl, K. (1994). Toward a social constructivist reconceptualization of intrinsic motivation for literacy learning. *Journal of Reading Behavior, 26,* 139–158.

Oldfather, P., & McLaughlin, J. (1993). Gaining and losing voice: A longitudinal study of students' continuing impulse to learn across elementary and middle school contexts. *Research in Middle Level Education, 17,* 1–25.

Pajares, F. (1996). Self-efficacy beliefs in academic settings. *Review of Educational Research, 66,* 543–578.

Pallas, A. M., Entwisle, D. R., Alexander, K. L., & Stulka, M. F. (1994). Ability-group effects: Instructional, social, or institutional? *Sociology of Education, 67,* 27–46.

Paris, S. G., & Turner, J. C. (1994). Situated motivation. In P. Pintrich, D. Brown, & C. E. Weinstein (Eds.), *Student motivation, cognition, and learning: Essays in honor of Wilbert J. McKeachie* (pp. 213–237). Hillsdale, NJ: Erlbaum.

Parker, J. G., & Asher, S. R. (1987). Peer relations and later personal adjustment: Are low-accepted children at risk? *Psychological Bulletin, 102,* 357–389.

Parsons, J. E., & Ruble, D. N. (1977). The development of achievement-related expectancies. *Child Development, 48,* 1075–1079.

Patrick, H., Hicks, L., & Ryan, A. M. (1997). Relations of perceived social efficacy and social goal pursuit to self-efficacy for academic work. *Journal of Early Adolescence, 17,* 109–128.

Pekrun, R. (1993). Facets of adolescents' academic motivation: A longitudinal expectancy-value approach. In M. Maehr & P. Pintrich (Eds.), *Advances in motivation and achievement* (pp. 139–189). Greenwich, CT: JAI Press.

Pintrich, P., & De Groot, E. V. (1990). Motivational and self-regulated learning components of classroom academic performance. *Journal of Educational Psychology, 82,* 33–40.

Pintrich, P. R., Marx, R. W., & Boyle, R. A. (1993). Beyond cold conceptual change: The role of motivational beliefs and classroom contextual factors in the process of conceptual change. *Review of Educational Research, 63,* 167–199.

Pintrich, P. R., & Schunk, D. H. (1996). *Motivation in education: Theory, research, and applications.* Englewood Cliffs, NJ: Merrill-Prentice Hall.

Renninger, K. A. (1990). Children's play interests, representation, and activity. In R. Fivush & J. Hudson (Eds.), *Knowing and remembering in young children* (pp. 127–165). Cambridge, England: Cambridge University Press.

Renninger, K. A., Hidi, S., & Krapp, A. (Eds.). (1992). *The role of interest in learning and development.* Hillsdale, NJ: Erlbaum.

Renninger, K. A., & Wozniak, R. H. (1985). Effect of interest on attentional shift, recognition, and recall in young children. *Developmental Psychology, 21,* 624–632.

Reuman, D. A. (1989). How social comparison mediates the relation between ability-grouping practices and students' achievement expectancies in mathematics. *Journal of Educational Psychology, 81,* 178–189.

Reuman, D. A., Mac Iver, D., Eccles, J., & Wigfield, A. (1987, April). *Changes in students' mathematics motivation and behavior at the transition to junior high school.* Paper presented at the annual meeting of the American Educational Research Association, Washington, DC.

Roe, A., & Siegelman, M. (1964). *The origin of interests.* Washington, DC: American Personnel and Guidance Association.

Rosenbaum, J. E. (1980). Social implications of educational grouping. In *Review of research in education* (Vol. 7, pp. 361–401). Washington, DC: American Educational Research Association.

Rosenholtz, S. J., & Simpson, C. (1984). The formation of ability conceptions: Developmental trend or social construction? *Review of Educational Research, 54,* 31–63.

Rosenholtz, S. R., & Rosenholtz, S. J. (1981). Classroom organization and the perception of ability. *Sociology of Education, 54,* 132–140.

Rotter, J. B. (1954). *Social learning and clinical psychology.* Englewood Cliffs, NJ: Prentice Hall.

Ruble, D. (1983). The development of social comparison processes and their role in achievement-related self-socialization. In E. T. Higgins, D. N. Ruble, & W. W. Hartup (Eds.), *Social cognition and social development: A sociocultural perspective* (pp. 134–157). New York: Cambridge University Press.

Ruble, D. N., & Martin, N. (1998). Gender. In W. Damon (Series Ed.) & N. Eisenberg (Vol. Ed.), *Handbook of child psychology* (Vol. 3, 5th ed.). New York: Wiley.

Rutter, M., Maughan, B., Mortimore, P., & Ouston, J. (1979). *Fifteen thousand hours: Secondary schools and their effects on children.* Cambridge, MA: Harvard University Press.

Ryan, A. M., Hicks, L., & Midgley, C. (1997). Social goals, academic goals, and avoiding help seeking in the classroom. *Journal of Early Adolescence, 17,* 152–171.

Ryan, A. M., & Pintrich, P. R. (1997). "Should I ask for help?" The role of motivation and attitudes in adolescents' help seeking in math class. *Journal of Educational Psychology, 89,* 329–341.

Ryan, R. M. (1992). Agency and organization: Intrinsic motivation, autonomy, and the self in psychological development. In J. Jacobs (Ed.), *Nebraska Symposium on Motivation* (Vol. 40, pp. 1–56). Lincoln: University of Nebraska Press.

Ryan, R. M., Connell, J. P., & Deci, E. L. (1985). A motivational analysis of self-determination and self-regulation in education. In C. Ames & R. Ames (Eds.), *Research on motivation in education: Vol. 2. The classroom milieu* (pp. 13–51). London: Academic Press.

Ryan, R. M., & Deci, E. L. (1996). When paradigms clash: Comments on Cameron and Pierce's claim that rewards do not undermine intrinsic motivation. *Review of Educational Research, 66,* 33–38.

Ryan, R. M., & Grolnick, W. S. (1986). Origins and pawns in the classroom: Self-report and projective assessments of individual differences in children's perceptions. *Journal of Personality and Social Psychology, 50,* 550–558.

Ryan, R. M., & Stiller, J. (1991). The social contexts of internalization: Parent and teacher influences on autonomy, motivation, and learning. In M. L. Maehr & P. R. Pintrich (Eds.), *Advances in motivation and achievement* (Vol. 7). Greenwich, CT: JAI Press.

Santa Barbara Classroom Discourse Group. (1992). Constructing literacy in classrooms: Literate action as social accomplishment. In H. H. Marshall (Ed.), *Redefining student learning: Roots of educational change* (pp. 119–150). Norwood, NJ: Ablex.

Schiefele, U. (1991). Interest, learning, and motivation. *Educational Psychologist, 26,* 299–323.

Schiefele, U. (1996a). *Motivation and learning with text.* Gottingen, Germany: Hogrefe.

Schiefele, U. (1996b). Topic interest, text representation, and quality of experience. *Contemporary Educational Psychology, 21,* 3–18.

Schiefele, U., & Krapp, A. (in press). Topic interest and free recall of expository text. *Learning and Individual Differences.*

Schunk, D. H. (1987). Peer models and children's behavioral change. *Review of Educational Research, 57,* 149–174.

Schunk, D. H. (1990). Goal setting and self-efficacy during self-regulated learning. *Educational Psychologist, 25,* 71–86.

Schunk, D. H. (1991). Self-efficacy and academic motivation. *Educational Psychologist, 26,* 207–231.

Schunk, D. H. (1994). Self-regulation of self-efficacy and attributions in academic settings. In D. H. Schunk & B. J. Zimmerman (Eds.), *Self-regulation of learning and performance.* Hillsdale, NJ: Erlbaum.

Schunk, D. H., & Meece, J. L. (Eds.). (1992). *Student perceptions in the classroom.* Hillsdale, NJ: Erlbaum.

Schunk, D. H., & Zimmerman, B. J. (Eds.). (1994). *Self-regulation of learning and performance.* Hillsdale, NJ: Erlbaum.

Schunk, D. H., & Zimmerman, B. J. (1997). Developing self-efficacious readers and writers: The role of social and self-regulatory processes. In J. T. Guthrie & A. Wigfield (Eds.), *Reading engagement: Motivating readers through integrated instruction* (pp. 34–50). Newark, DE: International Reading Association.

Seegers, G., & Boekaerts, M. (1993). Task motivation and mathematics achievement in actual task situations. *Learning and Instruction, 3,* 133–150.

Sharan, S., & Shaulov, A. (1990). Cooperative learning, motivation to learn, and academic achievement. In S. Sharan (Ed.), *Cooperative learning: Theory and research.* New York: Praeger.

Sharan, Y., & Sharan, S. (1992). *Expanding cooperative learning through group investigation.* New York: Teachers College Press.

Shell, D. F., Colvin, C., & Bruning, R. H. (1995). Self-efficacy, attribution, and outcome expectancy mechanisms in reading and writing achievement: Grade-level and achievement-level differences. *Journal of Educational Psychology, 87,* 386–398.

Shuell, T. J. (1996). Teaching and learning in a classroom context. In D. C. Berliner & R. C. Calfee (Eds.), *Handbook of educational psychology* (pp. 726–764). New York: Macmillan.

Sieber, R. T. (1979). Classmates as workmates: In formal peer activity in the elementary school. *Anthropology and Education Quarterly, 10,* 207–235.

Skinner, E. A. (1990). Age differences in the dimensions of perceived control during middle childhood: Implications for developmental conceptualizations and research. *Child Development, 61,* 1882–1890.

Skinner, E. A. (1995). *Perceived control, motivation, and coping.* Thousand Oaks, CA: Sage.

Skinner, E. A., & Belmont, M. J. (1993). Motivation in the classroom: Reciprocal effects of teacher behavior and student engagement across the school year. *Journal of Educational Psychology, 85,* 571–581.

Skinner, E. A., & Connell, J. P. (1986). Control understanding: Suggestions for a developmental framework. In M. M. Baltes & P. B. Baltes (Eds.), *The psychology of control and aging.* Hillsdale, NJ: Erlbaum.

Slavin, R. E. (1990). Achievement effects of ability grouping in secondary schools: A best-evidence synthesis. *Review of Educational Research, 60,* 471–499.

Slavin, R. E. (1995). *Cooperative learning: Theory, research, and practice* (2nd ed.). Boston: Allyn & Bacon.

Slavin, R. E. (1996). Research on cooperative learning and achievement: What we know, what we need to know. *Contemporary Educational Psychology, 21,* 43–69.

Stevens, R. J., & Slavin, R. E. (1995). The cooperative elementary school: Effects on students' achievement, attitudes, and social relations. *American Educational Research Journal, 32,* 321–351.

Stipek, D. J. (1984). The development of achievement motivation. In R. Ames & C. Ames (Eds.), *Research on motivation in education* (Vol. 1, pp. 145–174). New York: Academic Press.

Stipek, D. J. (1996). Motivation and instruction. In D. C. Berliner & R. C. Calfee (Eds.), *Handbook of educational psychology* (pp. 85–113). New York: Macmillan.

Stipek, D. J., & Daniels, D. H. (1988). Declining perceptions of competence: A consequence of changes in the child or in the educational environment? *Journal of Educational Psychology, 80,* 352–356.

Stipek, D. J., & Gralinski, J. H. (1996). Children's beliefs about intelligence and school performance. *Journal of Educational Psychology, 88,* 397–407.

Stipek, D. J., & Mac Iver, D. (1989). Developmental change in children's assessment of intellectual competence. *Child Development, 60,* 521–538.

Stipek, D. J., Recchia, S., & McClintic, S. M. (1992). *Self-evaluation in young children.* Monographs of the Society for Research in Child Development, 57(2, Serial No. 226).

Teigen, K. H. (1987). Intrinsic interest and the novelty-familiarity interaction. *Scandinavian Journal of Psychology, 28,* 199–210.

Thorkildsen, T. A., Nolen, S. B., & Fournier, J. (1994). What is fair? Children's critiques of practices that influence motivation. *Journal of Educational Psychology, 86,* 475–486.

Tobias, S. (1994). Interest, prior knowledge, and learning. *Review of Educational Research, 64,* 37–54.

Todt, E. (1990). Development of interest. In H. Hetzer (Ed.), *Applied developmental psychology of children and youth.* Wiesbaden, Germany: Quelle & Meyer.

Travers, R. M. W. (1978). *Children's interests.* Unpublished manuscript.

Trebilco, G. R., Atkinson, E. P., & Atkinson, J. M. (1977, November). *The transition of students from primary to secondary school.* Paper presented at the annual conference of the Australian Association for Research in Education, Canberra.

Trickett, E. J., & Moos, R. H. (1974). Personal correlates of contrasting environments: Student satisfaction in high school classrooms. *American Journal of Community Psychology, 2,* 1–12.

Turner, J. C. (1995). The influence of classroom contexts on young children's motivation for literacy. *Reading Research Quarterly, 30,* 410–441.

Turner, J. C. (1997). Starting right: Strategies for engaging young literacy learners. In J. T. Guthrie & A. Wigfield (Eds.), *Reading engagement: Motivating readers through integrated instruction* (pp. 183–204). Newark, DE: International Reading Association.

Urdan, T. C., & Maehr, M. L. (1995). Beyond a two-goal theory of motivation and achievment: A case for social goals. *Review of Educational Research, 65,* 213–244.

Vanfossen, B. E., Jones, J. D., & Spade, J. Z. (1987). Curriculum tracking and status maintenance. *Sociology of Education, 60,* 104–122.

Vygotsky, L. S. (1978). *Mind in society: The development of higher psychological processes.* Cambridge, MA: Harvard University Press.

Wade, S. E. (1992). How interest affects learning from text. In K. A. Renninger, S. Hidi, & A. Krapp (Eds.), *The role of interest in learning and development* (pp. 255–277). Hillsdale, NJ: Erlbaum.

Webb, N. M., & Palincsar, A. S. (1996). Group processes in the classroom. In D. C. Berliner & R. C. Calfee (Eds.), *Handbook of educational psychology* (pp. 841–873). New York: Macmillan.

Weiner, B. (1979). A theory of motivation for some classroom experiences. *Journal of Educational Psychology, 71,* 3–25.

Weiner, B. (1985). An attributional theory of achievement motivation and emotion. *Psychological Review, 92,* 548–573.

Weiner, B. (1992). *Human motivation: Metaphors, theories, and research.* Newbury Park, CA: Sage.

Weisz, J. P. (1984). Contingency judgments and achievement behavior: Deciding what is controllable and when to try. In J. G. Nicholls (Ed.), *The development of achievement motivation* (pp. 107–136). Greenwich, CT: JAI Press.

Wentz-Gross, M., Siperstein, G. N., Untch, A. S., & Widaman, K. F. (1997). Stress, social support, and adjustment of adolescents in middle school. *Journal of Early Adolescence, 17,* 129–151.

Wentzel, K. R. (1989). Adolescent classroom grades, standards for performance, and academic achievement: An interactionist perspective. *Journal of Educational Psychology, 81*, 131–142.

Wentzel, K. R. (1991a). Relations between social competence and academic achievement in early adolescence. *Child Development, 62,* 1066–1078.

Wentzel, K. R. (1991b). Social competence at school: Relation between social responsibility and academic achievement. *Review of Educational Research, 61,* 1–24.

Wentzel, K. R. (1993). Does being good make the grade? Social behavior and academic competence in middle school. *Journal of Educational Psychology, 85,* 357–364.

Wentzel, K. R. (1994). Relations of social goal pursuit to social acceptance, and perceived social support. *Journal of Educational Psychology, 86,* 173–182.

Wentzel, K. R. (1996). Social goals and social relationships as motivators of school adjustment. In J. Juvonen & K. R. Wentzel (Eds.), *Social motivation: Understanding school adjustment.* New York: Cambridge University Press.

Wentzel, K. R. (in press). Student motivation in middle school: The role of perceived pedagogical caring. *Journal of Educational Psychology.*

Wentzel, K. R., & Wigfield, A. (in press). Academic and social motivational influences on students' academic performance. *Educational Psychology Review.*

Wigfield, A. (1994). Expectancy-value theory of achievement motivation: A developmental perspective. *Educational Psychology Review, 6,* 49–78.

Wigfield, A. (1997). Reading motives: A domain-specific approach to motivation. *Educational Psychologist, 32,* 59–68.

Wigfield, A., & Eccles, J. (1992). The development of achievement task values: A theoretical analysis. *Developmental Review, 12,* 265–310.

Wigfield, A., Eccles, J., Mac Iver, D., Reuman, D., & Midgley, C. (1991). Transitions at early adolescence: Changes in children's domain-specific self-perceptions and general self-esteem across the transition to junior high school. *Developmental Psychology, 27,* 552–565.

Wigfield, A., Eccles, J. S., & Pintrich, P. R. (1996). Development between the ages of eleven and twenty-five. In D. C. Berliner & R. C. Calfee (Eds.), *The handbook of educational psychology.* New York: Macmillan.

Wigfield, A., Eccles, J. S., Yoon, K. S., Harold, R. D., Arbreton, A., Freedman-Doan, K., & Blumenfeld, P. C. (1997). Changes in children's competence beliefs and subjective task values across the elementary school years: A three-year study. *Journal of Educational Psychology, 89,* 451–469.

Wigfield, A., & Guthrie, J. T. (1997). Relations of children's motivation for reading to the amount and breadth of their reading. *Journal of Educational Psychology, 89,* 420–432.

Zimmerman, B. J. (1989). A social cognitive view of self-regulated learning. *Journal of Educational Psychology, 81,* 329–339.

Zimmerman, B. J., Bandura, A., & Martinez-Pons, M. (1992). Self-motivation for academic attainment: The role of self-efficacy beliefs and personal goal setting. *American Educational Research Journal, 29,* 663–676.

Zimmerman, B. J., & Bonner, S. (in press). A social cognitive view of strategic learning. In C. E. Weinstein & B. L. McCombs (Eds.), *Strategic learning: Skill, will, and self-regulation.* Mahwah, NJ: Erlbaum.

Zimmerman, B. J., & Martinez-Pons, M. (1990). Student differences in self-regulated learning: Relating grade, sex, and giftedness to self-efficacy and strategy use. *Journal of Educational Psychology, 82,* 51–59.

Manuscript received August 15, 1997
Accepted December 24, 1997

# Chapter 4

# Discourse Analysis, Learning, and Social Practice: A Methodological Study

JAMES PAUL GEE
Department of Curriculum and Instruction, University of Wisconsin-Madison

JUDITH L. GREEN
University of California, Santa Barbara[1]

In the past two decades, the study of discourse has become an important theoretical perspective for those concerned with the study of learning in social settings. Discourse analysis approaches have been developed to examine ways in which knowledge is socially constructed in classrooms and other educational settings. By studying discursive activity within classrooms and other social settings, researchers have provided new insights into the complex and dynamic relationships among discourse, social practices, and learning. Specifically, this body of work has provided understandings of the ways in which opportunities for learning are constructed across time, groups, and events; how knowledge constructed in classrooms (and other educational settings) shapes, and is shaped by, the discursive activity and social practices of members; patterns of practice simultaneosuly support and constrain access to the academic content of the "official" curriculum; and how opportunities for learning are influenced by the actions of actors beyond classroom settings (e.g., school districts, book publishers, curriculum developers, legislators, and community members) (for recent syntheses and conceptual analyses, see Hicks, 1995; Luke, 1995).

Discourse analysis approaches used to examine such educational issues draw on discourse theories and methods developed in other disciplines (e.g., applied linguistics, law, literary studies, psychology, sociolinguistics, and sociology, among others) (see van Dijk, 1985, for a comprehensive look at the issue of discourse theory and method across disciplines, including education). However, educational researchers have not merely taken up and applied existing approaches. They have also contributed to the development of discourse theories and methods as they have adopted and adapted existing approaches and constructed new approaches to address questions of importance to education as a discipline.[2]

Given the complex and continuing nature of life in classrooms and other educational settings, educational researchers often combine discourse analysis with ethnographic approaches to examine questions of what counts as learning in a local setting, how and when learning occurs, and how what is learned at one point in time becomes a sociocultural resource for future learning for both the group and the individual. Through this combined approach, educational researchers are able to examine how educational processes and practices are constructed across time by members of the classroom; how students take up, resist, or fail to learn academic content through these processes and practices; and how discourse processes and practices shape what counts as knowing, doing, and being within and across events in classrooms and other educational settings (e.g., staff rooms, psychoeducational diagnostic team meetings, parent-teacher conferences, and testing situations).[3]

One way to understand the value of the approaches that combine discourse analysis with ethnography is that each represents a *logic-of-inquiry*, or what Birdwhistell (1977) calls a *logic-in-use*. This logic-of-inquiry influences the ways in which learning can be studied in social settings, the questions that can be asked, the research decisions and procedures used, and the ways of reporting and representing findings. Our goal in this chapter is to propose a conceptual framework for constructing a logic-of-inquiry for studying learning in social settings that uses different forms of discourse analyses guided by an ethnographic perspective in theoretically coherent ways.[4] The discussion of the framework and its application is presented in three parts. In the first part, we describe the theoretical perspective on discourse and language underlying the proposed framework. In the second part, we illustrate how this framework can be used to study learning as a sociocultural activity in communities of practice. In the third part, we discuss issues of vality and implications for theory, research, and practice.

## CONSTRUCTING A LOGIC-OF-INQUIRY: THEORY-METHOD RELATIONSHIPS

Concern for understanding why a theoretically grounded logic-of-inquiry is needed was articulated by Birdwhistell (1977) two decades ago: "The interdependence of theory and methodology can be hidden by exclusive focus upon either philosophy or technique. Once separated, only the most sophisticated can reconstitute them into investigatory practice" (p. 104). He was led to this conclusion by a review of the literature he undertook when his students asked whether Margaret Mead and Gregory Bateson had a methodology. Their question surprised, amazed, and challenged him, since he thought that he had made visible the importance of considering theory-method relationships guiding his and others' research.

This literature review also led him to conclude that, while this was a general trend across research perspectives, it was particularly true of a number of researchers from disciplines concerned with "what is termed 'direct observation'" (p. 104). He found that these researchers had a tendency to "reject the use of theory except as a device for the interpretation of data" (p. 104). In addition, his analysis led him to conclude that this was not a new tendency; rather, it was one that was ongoing:

I have come to the conclusion that the past twenty-five years have seen a separation of theory from methods of research procedure. This tendency becomes manifest in the choice and analysis of import of problem, in the location of observational site, in the preliminary isolation of data, in the development of relevant, consistent and explicit techniques of observation, in the recording and storage of data, in the orientation of rules of evidence, and, finally, in the methods of data and evidence assessment and presentation that permit and assist in ordering reexamination, and research. (pp. 104–105)

An analysis of the literature on observational research in education shows a parallel condition for those engaged in many forms of direct observational research in education (Evertson & Green, 1986). Extending Birdwhistell's (1977) observations to this chapter, we argue that to create a coherent logic-of-inquiry, an understanding of the sociocultural nature of discourse, social practice, and learning is necessary. Without such understanding, researchers will not be able to engage with and use ethnographically grounded methods of discourse analysis in theoretically appropriate ways.

Our purpose in making visible the theory-method relationships grounding the proposed framework is twofold. First, we view this knowledge as critical, since each decision about method implicates the use of particular theories and the exclusion of others, and each decision about theory entails related decisions about method. Second, such knowledge is needed to understand what philosopher Kenneth Strike (1974) calls the expressive potential of a theoretical language. Strike argues that each research program has an expressive potential that places limits on what can be discussed and what phenomena can be described in and through that language. He also argues that the choice of language (theoretical orientation), with all of its related conventions for use, inscribes a particular view and set of understandings about the phenomena under study. From this perspective, then, there is the relationship of the language to the actions, problems, and processes of a researcher. Viewed in this way, a logic-of-inquiry is a way of working as a researcher, a theoretically coherent research approach, and a language of the research that has a particular expressive potential.

## A THEORETICAL PERSPECTIVE
## ON DISCOURSE AND LANGUAGE

In this section, we present a theoretical orientation to language as a sociocultural practice and social resource of a group, and, in so doing, we demonstrate that discourse analysis entails more than writing talk down and reading the transcript. Specifically, we show that an ethnographically grounded approach to discourse analysis involves a particular perspective on discourse and social action through language that forms an orienting framework for research design and implementation (e.g., data collection cycles or processes) as well for data analysis, interpretation, and explanation.

The discussion is presented in four parts. In the first part, we present four key dimensions of language as social action and cultural resource that provide a foundation for our ethnographically grounded approach to discourse analysis: situated meanings, cultural models, reflexivity, and an ethnographic perspective. In the second part, we describe key elements for constructing a logic-of-inquiry. In the third part, we present an argument about how, through language, members engage in a range of construction processes within and across time and events: world building, activity building, identity building, and connection building. Finally, in the fourth section, we examine the concept of social languages and show how members of a social group, through oral and written texts, construct local or situated meanings, identities, and worlds that vary across situations or events.

## Situated Meanings, Cultural Models, and Reflexivity

We begin the discussion of discourse and language by introducing two types of meaning that attach to words and phrases in actual use: situated meanings and cultural models. After a brief discussion of these two notions, we turn to a discussion of an important and related property of language-in-use, a property ethnomethodologists call *reflexivity*. Through these constructs, we examine language as social action with a focus on what members of a social group are accomplishing through their discourse, rather than focusing solely on language form or function.

### Situated Meanings and Cultural Models

A situated meaning is an image or pattern that we (participants in an interaction) assemble "on the spot" as we communicate in a given context, based on our construal of that context and on our past experiences (Agar, 1994; Barsalou, 1991, 1992; A. Clark, 1993; H. H. Clark, 1996; Gee, 1996; Gumperz, 1982a; Hofstadter, 1997; Kress, 1985; Levinson, 1983; Wittgenstein, 1953). For example, consider the following two utterances: "The coffee spilled, get a mop" and "The coffee spilled, get a broom." In the first case, triggered by the word *mop* (a lexical cue), a hearer (or reader) may assemble the situated meaning as something like "dark liquid we drink" for "coffee," by using his or her experience in similar situations. In the second case, triggered by the word *broom* and personal experience in such matters, a hearer (or reader) may assemble a situated meaning as something like "grains that we make our coffee from" or "beans from which we grind coffee."

These contrasting cases provide a point of departure for the discussion of situated meaning. However, in a real context, there are many more signals as to how to go about assembling situated meanings for words and phrases. Gumperz (1982a) called such cues (or clues) *contextualization cues*. They include prosodic and nonverbal cues such as pitch, stress, intonation, pause, juncture, proxemics (distance between speakers, spatial organization of speakers), eye gaze, and kinesics (gesture, body movement, and physical activity), in addition to lexical items, grammatical structures, and visual dimensions of context. Such cues provide information to participants about the meaning of words and grammar and how to move back and forth between language and context (situations). For example, it is not possible to determine the meaning of the word *okay* without considering the way it was said and its context of use. Consider each of the following questions about the delivery of this lexical item: Was it said with a rising intonation after a person offered a suggestion (a way of asking for confirmation)? Was it said with great excitement (a way of given praise)? Was it said at the beginning of a message (a request for attention)? Or was it said slowly in between messages by a speaker (as a placeholder to the hearer that one is thinking and wants to maintain one's turn at talk) (Green & Harker, 1982)? These are not signals of fixed and decontextualized meanings; rather, they are clues that people draw on to construct and negotiate situated meanings within and across particular events (see Duranti & Goodwin, 1992, for a cross-disciplinary discussion of context and meaning construction).

From this perspective, situated meanings do not simply reside in individual minds;

very often, they are negotiated between people in and through social interaction (Billig, 1987; Edwards & Potter, 1992; Goffman, 1981; M. H. Goodwin, 1990; Gumperz, 1992). For example, if a partner in a relationship says something like "I think good relationships shouldn't take work," a good part of the ensuing conversation might involve mutually negotiating (directly, or indirectly through inferencing) what "work" is going to mean for the people concerned in this specific context as well as in the larger context of their ongoing relationship. Furthermore, as conversations—and, indeed, relationships—develop, participants often continually revise their situated meanings.

Words such as *work* and *coffee* seem, at a folk or commonsense level, to have more general meanings than are apparent in the sorts of situated meanings we have discussed so far. This is because words are also associated with "cultural models." Cultural models are "story lines," families of connected images (like a mental movie), or (informal) "theories" shared by people belonging to specific social or cultural groups (Cole, 1996; D'Andrade & Strauss, 1992; Geertz, 1983; Holland & Quinn, 1987; Spradley, 1980). Cultural models "explain," relative to the standards (norms) of a particular social group, why words have the range of situated meanings they do for members and shape members' ability to construct new ones. They also serve as resources that members of a group can use to guide their actions and interpretations in new situations.

Cultural models are usually not stored in any one person's head but are distributed across the different sorts of "expertise" and viewpoints found in a group (Hutchins, 1995; Shore, 1996), much like a plot of a group-constructed (oral or written) story in which different people have different bits of information, expertise, and interpretations that they use to contribute to the plot being negotiated. Through this process of joint construction of text, then, members construct local meanings that they draw on to mutually develop a "big picture." This process can be illustrated if we consider further the example of coffee. The cultural model connected to "coffee" is, for some of us (depending on our local opportunities), something like the following: Berries are picked (Somewhere? From some sort of plant?) and then prepared (How?) as beans or grain to be made later into a drink, as well as into flavorings (How?) for other foods. In addition, some of us may have experiences with drinking coffee in coffee bars or coffeehouses, experiences that extend the general model in particular ways: Different types of coffee, drunk in different ways, have different social and cultural implications (e.g., marking particular types of status). Furthermore, members who work in a coffee bar, or the processing plant, will have still other dimensions to add to the cultural model. In this way, members, through their experiences, expand their personal cultural repertoires for meaning construction related to "coffee" while simultaneously expanding the cultural model of the group (see Kantor, Green, Bradley, & Lin, 1992, and Fernie, Davies, Kantor, & McMurray, 1993, for a discussion of this process in relation to developing cultural repertoires for being a student in a classroom).

Viewed in this way, a cultural model is a group's construction that becomes a resource that an individual may call on to guide his or her actions. Furthermore, such models, constructed within a particular context, may link with others in complex ways to create more complex models. These models become framing models that particular members or groups within a society draw on to guide their actions in particular domains of life (for a discussion of how this applies to research on classrooms as cultures, see Gee, 1992; Lin, 1993; and Santa Barbara Classroom Discourse Group, 1992).

To clarify this process further, we draw on a conceptualization of culture framed by cognitive anthropologists James Spradley and Charles Frake.[5] We find that this definition of culture can be applied to—and is consonant with—our notion of cultural models. Spradley (1980) proposed viewing culture as a cognitive map that is constantly being redrawn to serve as a guide for acting and interpreting our experience. Drawing on Frake (1977), he argued that

culture is not simply a cognitive map that people acquire in whole or in part, more or less accurately, and then learn to read. People are not just map-readers; they are map-makers. People are cast out into imperfectly charted, continually revised sketch maps. Culture does not provide a cognitive map, but a set of principles for map making and navigation. Different cultures are like different schools of navigation designed to cope with different terrains and seas. (Frake, cited in Spradley, 1980, p. 9)

This perspective on culture, along with work in symbolic anthropology on local knowledge (Geertz, 1983), suggests that what we have called cultural models are not fixed but are open to modification, expansion, and revision by members as they interact across time and events. This perspective also suggests that cultural models (whether local or broader framing models) constitute a set of principles for actions in particular cultural domains and for particular cultural processes (e.g., coffee making and drinking, child rearing, being a student in a classroom).

The dynamic process involved in constructing a cultural model can be seen if we consider how notions of coffee have changed in the last decade. The coffee bar (e.g., Starbucks) is a recent cultural space and phenomenon within the U.S. context. Ten or more years ago, such coffee bars were exotic or did not exist in many regions of the United States (and other countries), even though coffeehouses were part of the 1960s culture for particular groups. As coffee bars have become more and more common, they have become taken-for-granted dimensions of life for increasing numbers of people within and across social groups. In addition, the language and action[6] associated with such coffee establishments have become shared by larger segments of U.S. society, thus expanding the cultural model associated with "coffee." This model can be understood as a linked network of local or situated cultural models consisting of principles of practice that help to guide the thinking, social practices, and communicative resources of particular sociocultural groups or subgroups within a society, as well as individuals within these groups (for a discussion of cultural models at a national level, see Del Rio & Alvarez, 1995; for a discussion of how opportunities are shaped and local models are negotiated, see Tuyay, Jennings, & Dixon, 1995).

To further illustrate the notion of a framing model and principles of practice, we consider a second, more socially complex and consequential example: the cultural model that some members of particular groups in the United States use in raising young children. This model, drawing on work by Harkness, Super, and Keefer

(1992), can be summarized as follows: Children are born dependent on their parents and later go through various stages during which they often engage in disruptive behaviors in pursuit of their growing desire for independence. This cultural model integrates sets of principles of practice for defining and shaping what counts as child, child rearing, stages, development, and independence, as well as other dimensions of this complex cultural process. These principles of practice also help parents take action with their children and explain their children's actions and development in terms of values that their group (or subgroup) holds (e.g., independence, in this case in contrast to collective accountability in other groups). As in the case of "coffee," these models are not fixed but are continually revised and developed (consciously and unconsciously) in interaction with others in the group, as well as through exposure to various books and other media (cultural artifacts) (for a discussion of how particular social groups view children differently, see Strauss, 1992, and Whiting & Whiting, 1959; for related discussion of differences in cultural perspectives of children's socialization and language acquisition, see Corsaro & Miller, 1992, and Ochs, 1983, respectively).

From this theoretical position, not all of the bits and pieces of cultural models or principles of practice are consciously in people's heads, and different bits and pieces are shared across different people and groups. Through interactions, members appropriate the bits and pieces available to them within a social group, and these bits and pieces often become part of people's taken-for-granted social practices. In this way, members construct—and, at times, reconstruct—cultural models socially significant to appropriate participation within their social group (for a discussion of communicative competence in relationship to appropriate participation, see Gumperz, 1986; Hymes, 1974). In addition, cultural models, and combinations of such models in framing models, need not be completely consistent or complete for an individual or for the social group. Rather, they are always subject to revision, modification, and reconstruction as needed by members of the group. Furthermore, depending on the opportunities of particular groups, individual members may have more or less access to and, therefore, knowledge of such models.[7]

This view of the situated nature of meaning and the constructed nature of cultural knowledge places particular demands on discourse analysts. The task of the discourse analyst is to construct representations of cultural models by studying people's actions across time and events. In closely observing the concerted actions among members, examining how and what members communicate, and interviewing members (see Briggs, 1986, and Mishler, 1986, for discussions of the constructed nature of interviews), the analyst asks questions about the patterns of practice that make visible what members need to know, produce, and interpret to participate in socially appropriate ways (Heath, 1982). By means of such questions, the analyst can examine, for example, what members construct together, what they hold each other accountable to, and how they view the actions of others. In this way, the analyst identifies the principles guiding members' practices within and across contexts as well as the types of worlds, identities, and actions they construct and display in and through their talk and actions.

## What Is Meant by an Ethnographic Perspective

One way to approach the study of cultural models is through the use of an ethnographic perspective to guide a discourse analysis. While this approach is not the same as doing ethnography, Green and Bloome (1983, 1997) argue that the cultural perspective guiding ethnography can be productively used in discourse studies (hence the term *ethnogaphic perspective*). One way to assess how discourse and ethnographic perspectives are conceptually related is through the definition of the phenomenon of study in ethnography by Spindler and Spindler (1987):

> Within any social setting, and any social scene within a setting, whether great or small, social actors are carrying on a culturally constructed dialogue. This dialogue is expressed in behavior, words, symbols, and in the application of cultural knowledge to make instrumental activities and social situations *work* for one. We learn the dialogue as children, and continue learning it all of our lives, as our circumstances change. This is the phenomenon we study as ethnographers—the dialogue of action and interaction. (p. 2)

In summarizing the goals and purpose of ethnography in this way, they place the study of "dialogue" in the center of the work, whether that dialogue be through discourse or through action. Discourse analysis, then, when guided by an ethnographic perspective, forms a basis for identifying what members of a social group (e.g., a classroom or other educational setting) need to know, produce, predict, interpret, and evaluate in a given setting or social group to participate appropriately (Heath, 1982) and, through that participation, learn (i.e., acquire and construct the cultural knowledge of the group). Thus, an ethnographic perspective provides a conceptual approach for analyzing discourse data (oral or written) from an emic (insider's) perspective and for examining how discourse shapes both what is available to be learned and what is, in fact, learned.[8]

Two key tasks facing ethnographers are central to understanding an ethnographic perspective on discourse analysis: exploration of part-whole, whole-part relationships and the use of contrastive relevance. According to Erickson (1979), "One goal...of the ethnographer is to arrive at a holistic understanding of the overall historical, cultural, or social context, whether that whole be an entire society or the beginning of a single lesson" (p. 1). Thus, he argues that the size of the "bit of life" being examined does not matter. What matters is how one approaches the analysis. Hymes (1977) described the second task as one of contrastive relevance. By using a contrastive analysis approach, the ethnographer is able to demonstrate the functional relevance of the "bit of life, or language and actions within that bit" (p. 92). This approach provides a way of demonstrating

> that a particular choice counts as a difference within the frame of reference...to discover what meaning and choices of meaning lead to changes in form. One works back and forth between form and meaning in practice to discover the individual devices and codes of which they are a part. (p. 92)

Contrast can occur at any level of analysis; the size of the unit does not matter. The key is to show the relevance of this contrast in understanding what members are doing together. An ethnographic perspective, then, involves analyzing the choices of words and actions that members of a group use to engage with each other within and across time, actions, and activity. Having described briefly what we mean by an ethnographic perspective, we now turn to a discussion of the framework we have developed for constructing an ethnographically grounded discourse analysis, or a logic-of-inquiry.

## Reflexivity: Perspectives on the Joint Construction of Social Action

In this section, we examine an important property of language, reflexivity, and its implication for studying learning as social activity. By "reflexivity" we mean the way in which language always takes on a specific meaning from the actual context in which it is used, while, simultaneously, helping to construct what we take that context to mean and be in the first place. We will discuss several different perspectives on reflexivity below to create a broader perspective on how language gives meaning to and gets meaning from social activity. The different perspectives we discuss are clearly related, though they constitute somewhat different lenses through which to investigate language and social activity. As part of our discussion, we examine the implications of these perspectives for creating a conceptually coherent logic-of-inquiry for the study of learning in social settings.

We begin with a discussion of reflexivity, as defined by Mehan (1979) from an ethnomethodological perspective, that focuses on how members structure (organize) conversational and social activity.[9] We then consider perspectives that focus on the negotiated nature of action, activity, content (text), and context. Constructs to be considered include the distinction between language and speech, speaker-hearer relationships, contexts as socially constructed, and intertextuality and intercontextuality as interactionally accomplished and socially significant. Each perspective argues for the need to consider sequences of connected talk and action, not simply individual utterances such as those provided in the coffee examples. This discussion is meant to be illustrative and not comprehensive, given the extensive body of work that exists across disciplines.

*Ethnomethodology and reflexivity.* To illustrate the ways in which ethnomethodologists view reflexivity, we consider two examples, one we describe and one from Mehan's (1979) research on social organization in the classroom. We begin by considering how this perspective on reflexivity helps to explain the following brief interaction between colleagues observed in an office corridor: Speaker 1: "How are ya?" Speaker 2: "Fine." Mehan (1979) describes how the relationship between these two utterances can be conceptualized.

In extended sequences...co-occurrence relationships bind initiation and reply acts.... The co-occurrence relationships within these interactional sequences are "reflexively" established (Garfinkel, 1967; Garfinkel & Sacks, 1970). Given the first part of a sequence (an initiation act or an initiation-reply pair), the second part of the sequence is conditionally relevant (Schegloff, 1968). That is, the appearance of the first part of a sequence makes the appearance of a second part prospectively possible. The actual appearance of the second part of the sequence gives meaning to the first part of the sequence.... Thus individual acts of speech are not autonomous. The meaning of a given speech act is not contained within its internal structure. Instead, meaning resides in the reflexive assembly of initiation, reply, and evaluation acts into interactional sequences. (p. 102)

From this perspective, the first utterance is understood to be an initiation in the form of a question that is followed by an appropriate (expected) type of response. Using the notion of co-occurrence relationship described by Mehan, we can see that the initiating act, a question, placed a social obligation on the hearer to respond; that is, it required cooperative completion of an activity by the participant to whom the question was directed to complete the conversational symmetry of this exchange sequence.

Although this discourse sequence is brief (it consists of only two utterances or two turn exchanges), it illustrates succinctly how reflexivity works as a means of structuring the activity between these speakers. If we now consider a more extended sequence from Mehan's (1979) research, we can obtain an expanded picture of how he used this approach to examine longer sequences in order to identify ways that members organize school structures through language-in-use. In his book *Learning Lessons: Social Organization in the Classroom*, Mehan presents an analysis of how

classroom turn-taking rules, like other normative rules, are tacit (Cicourel, 1973; Garfinkel, 1967). They are seldom formulated, listed, or stated in so many words. When interviewed, participants provide only idealized versions of procedures. The rules for normal operation can be made visible, however, by specifying the conditions that constitute their violation. Rule violations, in turn, can be located by looking for action that participants take in the absence of the expected forms of interaction. (p. 102)

One of the central findings of Mehan's study was the identification of the three-part initiation-response-evaluation act structure cited previously. One area of analysis using this "machinery" (Mehan's term) as an analytic tool was that of the turn-allocation apparatus of classroom lessons. Through this analysis, Mehan identified three techniques for turn allocation: individual nominations, invitations to bid, and invitations to reply. The following is an example of an individual nomination technique:

| INITIATION | RESPONSE | EVALUATION |
|---|---|---|
| 3:15<br>T: Now, what can you think, can you think of something to eat? | Many: Snakes<br><br>Many: (raise hands) Snakes. | T: Wait a minute, wait a minute<br>T: Wait a minute, raise your hand. Raise your hand. Give people a chance to think |

In this example, Mehan argues that the "evaluative activity marks the absence of the expected form of interaction" (p. 102). From an ethnomethodological perspective, the evaluative activity portion of the structure was obligatory given that the students violated the co-occurrence relationship between speaker and respondent. That is, its existence was not an arbitrary imposition by the researcher; rather, it was necessitated by the actions of members. When members failed to provide the expected response, the next act was obligated by this violation of expectations. Evaluation of such violations made visible, to participants and analysts alike, the "recovery work being done there to reestablish normal operations" (p. 102). Analysis of such points revealed the interactional activity that "supports the normative order of classroom lessons under normal circumstances" (p. 102). Through analysis of such patterns of action among participants, then, Mehan (1979) engaged in "an exhaustive analysis of behavior in the flow of events" (p. 37) that was part of a larger ongoing analysis he called constitutive ethnography:

The continuous flow of activity depicted on videotape or film is segmented into sequential phases and hierarchical components. This analysis continues until the researchers have derived a small set of recursive rules that completely describes the structure and structuring of events (McDermott, 1976). (p. 37)

This example shows how the theoretical perspective of ethnomethodology has a particular expressive potential that shapes what can be discussed, how the researcher engages in analytic work, and how questions of import shape the claims that can be made. This perspective also provides a particular way of talking about the relationship between language and activity and speaker-hearer relationships. Furthermore, the discussion shows how discourse analysis was grounded by an ethnographic perspective, one theoretically consistent with ethnomethodology.

*A dialogic perspective and speaker-hearer relationships.* Bakhtin (1986) provides another perspective on reflexivity in his distinction between language and speech and his conceptualization of the dialogic nature of speaker-hearer relationships. Bakhtin draws a distinction between language and speech communication that frames his perspective on speaker-hearer relationships. By contrasting a speech communion (dialogic) perspective with a linguistic perspective, he defines speaker-hearer relationships as reflexive. He argues that, from a linguistic perspective,

language is regarded from the speaker's standpoint as if there were only one speaker who does not have any necessary relation to other participants in speech communication. If the role of the other is taken into account at all, it is the role of a listener, who understands the speaker only passively. The utterance is adequate to its object (i.e., the content of the uttered thought) and to the person who is pronouncing the utterance. (p. 67)

From a dialogic perspective, this relationship is complex and interconnected:

Any understanding of live speech, a live utterance, is inherently responsive, although the degree of this activity varies extremely. Any understanding is embued with response and necessarily elicits it in one form or another: the listener becomes the speaker.... An actively responsive understanding of what is heard (a command, for example) can be directly realized in action (the execution of an order or command that has been understood and accepted for execution), or it can remain for the time being, a silent responsive understanding (certain speech genres are intended for this kind of responsive understanding...), but this is, so to speak, responsive understanding with a delayed reaction. (Bakhtin, 1986, pp. 68–69)

Thus, for Bakhtin (1986), speakers and hearers are not separate entities. Rather, each is implicated in the actions (speaking and hearing) of the other. Speakers do not speak to hearers who simply receive the speech (hear). Rather, a speaker expects a response, immediate or delayed, which in turn shapes how and what the speaker says. As Bakhtin (1986) noted:

> Sooner or later what is heard and actively understood will find its response in the subsequent speech or behavior of the listener. In most cases, genres of complex cultural communication are intended precisely for this kind of actively responsive understanding with delayed action. Everything we have said here also pertains to written and read speech, with the appropriate adjustments and additions. (pp. 69)

Building on this, he argues that, in a dialogue, a response is not automatic; rather, "each rejoinder...has the specific quality of completion that expresses a particular position of the speaker, to which one may respond or may assume, with respect to it, a responsive position" (p. 72). Bakhtin, then, sees the speaker-hearer relationship as placing an obligation on the listener that serves as completion.

While this perspective appears to overlap with the ethnomethodological one, the assumptions and theoretical basis guiding this work differ from those of the ethnomethodologists. For Bakhtin, reflexivity of language is part of the very nature of the speaker-hearer relationships, but that moment of dialogue or communion may not lead to an explicit structuring of the next move by participants or even to an expected response. The focus for Bakhtin, then, is on interpretation and meaning construction, not on structuring social order. Bakhtin (1986) argues that "in reality any communication...addressed to someone or evoking something, has a particular purpose, that is, it is a real link in the chain of speech communion in a particular sphere of human activity or everyday life" (p. 83).

This brief discussion is not meant to be a definition of Bakhtin's theory; rather, it is meant to show how different ways of conceptualizing common constructs (e.g., speech in contrast to language, and speaker-hearer relationships) affect how reflexivity in social activity can be understood. From this perspective:

> Language is realized in the form of individual concrete utterances (oral and written) by participants in the various areas of human activity. These utterances reflect the specific conditions and goals of each such area not only through their content (thematic) and linguistic style, that is, the selection of lexical, phraseological, and grammatical resources of the language, but above all through their compositional structure. All three of these aspects—thematic content, style, and compositional structure—are inseparably linked to the *whole* of the utterance and are equally determined by the specific nature of the particular sphere of communication. Each separate utterance is individual, of course, but each sphere in which language is used develops its own *relatively stable* types of these utterances. These we may call *speech genres.*

> The wealth and diversity of speech genres are boundless because the various possibilities of human activity are inexhaustible, and because each sphere of activity contains an entire repertoire of speech genres that differentiate and grow as the particular sphere develops and becomes more complex. (Bakhtin, 1986, p. 60)

By relating this definition to the previous ones, we can see further the social and contextual nature of speech and the difference between a unit of "speech communion" (p. 67) and units of language (i.e., words and sentences). Central to this difference is that units of speech communion reflect the active understanding that members of a speech community signal to each other.

The dialogic or speech communion perspective of Bakhtin (1986), like the ethnomethodological perspective, can be viewed as a language of a research program that has a particular expressive potential (Strike, 1974). However, this language differs from ethnomethodology in particular ways that implicate different sets of phenomena of interest, questions to be examined, units to analyze, ways of conceptualizing and conducting that analysis, and the types of claims and explanations constructed. While both focus on the social construction of social activity, they frame that focus differently. Those seeking to use these perspectives need to understand the effect of this difference on their research and need to assess which perspective best fits their purpose.

*Microethnography and the social construction of context.* To further expand the view of reflexivity, we examine a third perspective, one that provides information about the ways in which contexts (situations) are socially constructed. Erickson and Shultz (1981), drawing on work on face-to-face interactions across a number of disciplines (i.e., anthropology, psycholinguistics, sociolinguistics, sociology), argue that contexts are not given:

Rather, contexts are constituted by what people are doing and where and when [and with whom] they are doing it. As McDermott...puts it succinctly, people in interaction become environments for each other. Ultimately, social contexts consist of mutually shared and ratified definitions of situation and in the social actions persons take on the basis of these definitions (Mehan et al.). [Furthermore]...interactionally constituted environments are embedded in time and can change from moment to moment. With each context change, the roles and relationships among participants are redistributed to produce different configurations of concerted actions...(Blom & Gumperz, 1972). Mutual rights and obligations of interactants are continually amenable to subtle readjustment (Cicourel, 1972) into different configurations of concerted actions that can be called participant structures (cf. Philips, 1972, 1974), or coherently co-occurring sets (cf. Ervin-Tripp, 1972). These structures include ways of speaking, listening, getting the floor and holding it, and leading and following. (p. 148)

Erickson and Shultz's perspective shows the dynamic, interpretive, and reflexive nature of members' actions and how, through these actions, members shape— and, in turn, are shaped by— the context being constructed. Furthermore, these authors argue that, along with shaping context, members are also constructing situated definitions of roles and relationships, rights and obligations, and cultural models (participant structures). Like cultural models, then, contexts are not given or static; they are also subject to negotiation, modification, and change, and these changes are interactionally accomplished by participants.

For these researchers, reflexivity is seen in what members orient to, how they coordinate (or fail to coordinate) interactions, what positions (roles and relationships) they take, and what rights and obligations they hold each other accountable for. Viewed in this way, content and context are reflexively related, shaping the meanings, activity, and positions that members construct. By using a microethnographic approach, they are able to examine the moment-by-moment interactions that lead to the construction of social participation structures (Erickson & Shultz, 1981) and to academic task structures (Erickson, 1982). These two types of structures are dynamically and interactively accomplished in and through the same moments in time, place, and actors.

In this brief discussion, we again see a research language that describes the ways in which members of a social group construct the structures of everyday life. Again, the units and processes of analysis differ from those previously discussed. This difference influences what can be studied, how, in what ways, under what conditions, and with what outcomes. Furthermore, a comparative analysis across perspectives shows that Erickson and Shultz and Mehan (1979) drew on each other's perspectives in mutually informing ways.

*Sociolinguistics, ethnography, intertextuality, and intercontextuality.* The final perspective that we examine is work by Bloome and his colleagues (Bloome & Bailey, 1991; Bloome & Egan-Robertson, 1993) on intertextuality. As part of this discussion, we also include the work of Floriani (1993) on intercontextuality, since this work builds on that of Bloome and his colleagues. Collectively, these two bodies of work provide a view of reflexivity that ties different moments in time together, providing a way of understanding how members draw on past texts (oral or written) and practices (ways of being with and constructing text) to construct present texts and/or to implicate future ones. In addition, they describe and illustrate the value of a set of criteria for identifying intertextuality as socially constructed. These criteria can be used to apply a range of phenomena, including reflexivity, if we take an emic perspective as the goal (e.g., Floriani, 1993).

Bloome and Bailey (1992) propose the following conceptualization of and criteria for intertextuality, arguing that

> whenever people engage in a language event, whether it is a conversation, a reading of a book, diary writing, etc., they are engaging in intertextuality. Various conversational and written texts are being juxtaposed. Intertextuality can occur at many levels and in many ways.... Juxtaposing texts, at whatever level, is not in itself sufficient for intertextuality. Intertextuality is a social construction. The juxtaposition must be interactionally recognized, acknowledged and have social significance.... In classrooms, teachers and students are continuously constructing intertextual relationships. The set of intertextual relationships they construct can be viewed as constructing a cultural ideology, a system for assigning meaning and significance to what is said and done and socially defining participants. (p. 49)

This dynamic and constructed view of intertextuality suggests that members and analysts alike must consider how members, through their interactions, propose, acknowledge, recognize, and interactionally construct as socially significant past, current, and future texts and related actions. For both members and researchers, then, these actions constitute a set of criteria for examining intertextuality as a cultural resource.

This perspective on intertextuality builds on Bakhtin's view of language as social activity to argue that

> language is...social because any language act is a response to other acts, both those that preceded it and those that will follow (Bakhtin, 1935/1981). The meaning of an utterance or other language act derives not from the content of its words, but rather from its interplay with what went before and what will come later....

When language is viewed as part of an ongoing dialogue, as part of how people act and react to each other, then language is seen not as meaning per se but as meaningful, strategic action that is materially realized. That is, in order to engage in a dialogue, regardless of whether that dialogue is a face-to-face conversation or something else (e.g., an exchange of letters), people must do so in ways such that their actions and intentions can be understood by others in the event. (Bloome & Egan-Robertson, 1993, p. 309)

From this perspective, intertextuality is a form of reflexivity that can be identified in and across the actions of members as they construct the events of daily life. Like Mehan and Erickson, such analyses are grounded by an ethnographic approach to the study of language as social action. The particular theoretical orientation guiding this work draws on sociolinguistics and cultural anthropology (Green & Bloome, 1997).

Floriani (1993) expands the notion of intertextuality by proposing a related concept, what she calls *intercontextuality*. In an ethnographic study of discourse among members of a sixth-grade classroom, she observed students signaling actions and practices used in previous events (e.g., "like in the Island Project"). For members of this class, this phrase carried with it historical importance as well as social relevance of previously constructed cultural models that they now drew on to guide their participation in the current activity. She also found that members signaled future use of current texts and practices (e.g., "Tomorrow, we will use these data to construct estimated graphs in each group"). Thus, her work demonstrates how reflexivity crosses time and events within this classroom.

Floriani (1993), in building on the work of Bloome (as well as Erickson & Shultz, 1981, among others), who in turn builds on the work of Bakhtin (1986), demonstrates further the potential of bringing conceptually coherent constructs together to frame an enhanced logic-of-inquiry. These examples, then, show the intertextual nature of a logic-of-inquiry, as well as the complex web of theoretical perspectives needed to frame analysis of life in classrooms and other educational settings.[10]

*Reconsidering reflexivity.* Through our brief discussion of these four perspectives on reflexivity, we have attempted to make visible the theoretical language used by each group of researchers and how each provides a particular choice of phenomena, the way in which phenomena are conceptualized, the set of analysis procedures, and the type of explanations that can be constructed. In this way, we sought to make visible factors that researchers need to consider to construct a theoretically coherent logic-of-inquiry. While we have highlighted similarities and differences among perspectives through this discussion of reflexivity, we have also shown that, across these different perspectives, there is a common understanding that language simultaneously reflects reality ("the way things are") and constructs (construes) it in a certain way.

Furthermore, regardless of which perspective a researcher selects, if she or he accepts reflexivity as an important property of language or speech communion (in Bakhtin's, 1986, terms; i.e., of social activity), then the implications for the construction of a logic-of-inquiry are clear. The choice of reflexivity means that to examine how people learn in and through interactions with others, analysts will use an ethnographically grounded discourse analysis approach to analyze and represent sequences of talk within particular events and will examine ties among such sequences across time and events in classrooms and other social settings. Furthermore, they will construct theoretically appropriate transcriptions (Ochs, 1983) that show concern for the reflexive, socially constructed, and interactive nature of the social situation (Green, Franquiz, & Dixon, 1997).[11]

## CONSTRUCTING A LOGIC-OF-INQUIRY: TOWARD A CONCEPTUALLY COHERENT APPROACH TO LINKING DISCOURSE ANALYSES

In the preceding discussion of language and discourse, we described ways of understanding how language simultaneously reflects and constructs the situation in which it is used. In this section, we describe two sets of elements that are central to an understanding of the relationships among discourse, social practices, and learning and illustrate how they can be used to analyze written artifacts from a classroom. The first set of elements we call *the MASS system* (*m*aterial, *a*ctivity, *s*emiotic, and *s*ociocultural aspects of discourse), and the second we call building tasks (i.e., what is accomplished through discourse that simultaneously shapes the discourse and social practices).

### The MASS System

To identify key aspects of an ethnographically grounded approach to discourse analysis, we focus on "situation," because it is a key unit of analysis (segment of social life) for which discourse analysis is used across a number of current theoretical perspectives, including applied linguistics, conversational analysis, education, ethnomethodology, linguistic anthropology, linguistics, sociocultural psychology, social semiotics, and sociology.[12] The dimensions of situation that are presented in this section are those that a broad range of researchers across disciplines view as central to understanding the socially constructed nature of knowledge.

Four inextricably connected components or aspects of a situation are identified: a material aspect, an activity aspect, a semiotic aspect, and a sociocultural aspect (see Hymes, 1974, and Ochs, 1996, for conceptual discussions of the interconnections). The *material aspect* consists of actors, place (space), time, and objects present (or referred to) during interaction (e.g., Bloome & Bailey, 1992; A. Clark, 1997; Fairclough, 1992; Hanks, 1990; Latour, 1991; Levinson, 1996). The *activity aspect* refers to the specific social activity or interconnected chains of activity (events) in which the participants are engaging; activities (events) are, in turn, made up of a sequence of actions (e.g., Erickson & Shultz, 1981; Green & Wallat, 1981; Leont'ev, 1978, 1981; Mehan, 1979; Rogoff, 1990; Searle, 1969; Spradley, 1980; Wertsch, 1981, 1991).

The *semiotic aspect* refers to situated meanings and cultural models connected to various "sign systems" such as language, gestures, images, or other symbolic systems (e.g., Golden, 1990; C. Goodwin, 1981; Gumperz, 1992; Kress, 1996; Kress & van Leeuwen, 1996). The *sociocultural aspect* refers to the personal, social, and cultural knowledge, feelings, and identities (cognition, affect, and identity are all equally important here) relevant in the interaction, including sociocultural knowledge about sign systems, activities, and the material world (i.e., all of the other aspects just described) (e.g., Gee, 1992, 1996; Gumperz, 1982a, 1982b; Hanks, 1995; John-Steiner, Panofsky, & Smith, 1994; Palmer, 1996; Scollon & Scollon, 1981; Sperber & Wilson, 1986; Spradley, 1980; Toolan, 1996; Ungerer & Schmid, 1996; Volosinov, 1973). These four aspects constitute the MASS system.

We present these aspects as separate categories for hueristic purposes. In actuality, they cannot be separated. However, since it is not possible during analysis to consider all of these aspects simultaneously, it is necessary for an analyst to foreground particular aspects while backgrounding others. The key to the analysis, then, is a form of part-whole relationship for the units being analyzed. Across different analyses, a broader, more holistic picture can be developed. Thus, these four aspects constitute a system (an interconnected network) within which each of the components or aspects simultaneously gives meaning to all of the others and obtains meaning from them. By using the MASS system, the researcher can move back and forth among meaning, activity, sociocultural practices, and form. This contrastive exploration can occur within a social situation and across time, place, and events.

To illustrate the relationship between everyday activity and this analytic perspective, we draw on an excerpt from a community essay (a cultural artifact) written by Arturo, a fifth-grade student in a bilingual classroom. This essay was taken from a discourse analysis of the community essays written by Arturo and his classmates in the 1994–1995 school year that was part of a larger ethnographic study of the social construction of knowledge in his bilingual classroom; this investigation, in turn, was part of a larger ongoing ethnography conducted in the participating teacher's classrooms.[13] The excerpt is as follows:

> In our Tower community, we have our own language as well as the languages we bring from outside (like Spanish and English) which helped us make our own language. So, for example, someone that is not from our classroom community would not understand what insider, outsider, think twice, notetaking/notemaking, literature log, and learning log mean... These words are all part of the common Tower community language and if someone new were to come in, we would have to explain how we got them and what they mean. We also would tell them that we got this language by reports, information, investigations, and what we do and learn in our Tower community. (Green & Yeager, 1995, p. 26)

In this excerpt, Arturo uses particular words (the material and sociocultural aspect) to describe (the semiotic aspect) a range of social and academic tasks facing him and his colleagues (activity aspect). Through these choices, he demonstrates knowledge about how members are constructing life within this community of practice. He contrasts the insider position with the outsider position to illustrate his claim that, for all, the community (material and sociocultural aspects) was evolving rather than fixed (material aspect). Specifically, he claims that, together, they constructed a language of the classroom (a material and sociocultural resource) through the languages that they brought: Spanish and English (material, activity, semiotic, and sociocultural aspects). In making this claim, Arturo demonstrated his awareness of the discourse (way of talking [sociocultural aspect]) used in this classroom (Gee, 1996; Ivanic, 1994), his knowledge that life in the classroom is both predictable and variable over time (Santa Barbara Classroom Discourse Group, 1992; Tuyay,

Floriania, Yeager, Dixon, & Green, 1995), and his understanding that activity and classroom events and actors' actions and meanings (texts) have material substance. Furthermore, in explaining that such sociocultural knowledge entails more than the names of "objects" or "activities," he makes explicit what members—as well as outsiders—needed to know, understand, and produce in order to participate in socially appropriate ways in this ongoing group and how such knowledge is gained through activity (life as text). In this way, he makes visible what is entailed in what a student entering in the middle of a previous year called "becoming just one of everyone else" (Green & Dixon, 1993). In other words, he identified the particular terms and their meanings (semiotic aspect) that guided his activity in the classroom and that marked him as an "insider."

Moreover, through his use of contrastive relevance, he demonstrated understanding of the ways in which his identity within this class was socially constructed and tied to particular positions that were available to him as a bilingual speaker (e.g., insiders, outsiders, English and Spanish speakers, Tower language speaker, we, our Tower community). His final statement shows that "group" (community) existed for him (material and sociocultural aspects) and that it was constituted by common understandings of collective activity and sociocultural knowledge of objects, actors, processes, and practices (Edwards & Mercer, 1987): "We also would tell them that we got this language by reports, information, investigations, and what we do and learn in our Tower community." In electing to write about these aspects of community construction, he demonstrated understanding that membership in a community is more than just being in the same physical space with a group of people. Furthermore, through the use of this particular type of writing convention (contrast, a sociocultural resource), Arturo described what was entailed in being an insider and in moving from outsider to insider (an activity aspect and a sociocultural aspect).

The MASS system provided a set of aspects that we drew on to examine the life world that Arturo inscribed. This example illustrated ways in which the MASS system can be used to inform analysis of texts written (artifacts) in and about particular communities of practice to obtain an emic perspective on what is learned and accomplished in educational settings. It also showed the value of this approach in developing a grounded perspective on student knowledge of social practices and the social construction of everyday life. Furthermore, the analysis revealed the interconnected nature of the different aspects of the MASS system in actual situations.

## On What Members Build in and Through Discourse: Illustrative Examples

As we have argued in the previous sections, people do not talk for talk's sake or write for writing's sake. Rather, they talk (and write) for a purpose (i.e., to communicate with others in order to accomplish "things" with them or to show what they have learned). In this section and the next, we describe briefly several interconnected social building tasks that members construct in and through their oral or written texts. By using an ethnographic perspective, we provide a way to view what speakers and writers are doing socially through these tasks: world building, activity building, identity building, and connection building. These building tasks are illustrative of a larger group of tasks that can be identified (e.g., gender building, building power relationships). They are ones that we see as relevant to studying learning as a sociocultural process (see Hicks, 1995, for a comprehensive review of what is learned and constructed through discourse).

As the discussion of the discourse of Arturo's essay showed, his text contained "cues" or "clues" (Gumperz, 1982a) that we used to construct a re-presentation (an analysis) of the world inscribed, to examine the positions (roles and relationships) inscribed for the actors in that world, and to analyze the activities inscribed as possible for these actors and the identities Arturo saw for himself in relation to membership in this classroom. In the example that follows, we illustrate how this process of construction or building is accomplished in the moment-by-moment interactions among members and how, through these moments, particular opportunities for learning, connection building, activity, and world building are constructed. Specifically, through this example, we show the ways in which the intertextual and intercontextual connections that are built support student learning.

To illustrate how a discourse analysis can make visible the intertextual and intercontextual by examining connection building, we present an analysis of a brief interaction between Arturo's teacher and another class member. This interaction occurred midway through a 2.5-month cycle of activity (Tuyay, Floriani, Yeager, Dixon, & Green, 1995) that served to introduce the processes and practices of social science to help students understand point of view.

As indicated in Table 1, this interaction was initiated by Jared with the claim "I don't understand. Can you explain what you mean about looking at things from a different angle." The teacher took up (Collins, 1987) Jared's problem and engaged in a dialogue with him that drew on a range of intertextual and intercontextual ties to previous activities, texts, and events. The column labeled textual references identifies those that we were able to locate in the ethnographic data set. In this brief example, we see how the participants used these references to past texts and contexts, across the months preceding this particular interaction, as a heuristic for helping Jared understand what he was to do in the current task (activity aspect) and to clarify the meaning of point of view (semiotic aspect). Thus, through an examination of what the teacher and Jared signaled as intertextually and intercontextually important and socially (and academically) significant, we are able to see how the teacher supported Jared in clarifying his understanding of both the task at hand and the concept of point of view.

This brief analysis highlights the potential relationship between in-the-moment analyses and ethnographic analyses of sociocultural aspects of life within a particular community of practice. Once the references are identified, it is possible to reenter the data and examine each of these moments in time to identify the social processes and practices that were constructed, the meanings that were developed, and what counted as appropriate actions and knowledge within each event or point in time reference. This example also illustrates how, within an activity as well as over time, worlds, identities, activity, and connections are built.

**TABLE 1**
**Jared and the Teacher Talk About the 3 Pigs Project**

**POINT OF VIEW:** *(Social Science Activity—3 Pigs project—conversation reconstructed by the teacher. This occurred prior to Jared revising his drawing of the three pigs' events from the point of view of an ethnographer or detective)*

| Actor | Dialogue | Textual Reference |
|-------|----------|-------------------|
| J: | I don't understand. Can you explain what you mean about looking at things from a different angle? | • teacher's talk "looking at things from a different angle" as text |
| T: | Well, remember the video of our first day that we observed? We were the ethnographers then. | • past actions from first day<br>• video as text<br>• actions of ethnographers |
| J: | OK. | |
| T: | What were you able to see? | • memory of events as text |
| J: | S & V & N moving around, changing tables . . . | • actions of everyday actors<br>• class discussion as text |
| T: | Now, if someone watching that video who wasn't here the first day wanted to know if you were in the class, would they be able to tell? | • point of view of outsider<br>• needing to use insider knowledge<br>• teacher leading inquiry |
| J: | Not really. | • memory as insider |
| T: | Why? | • leading inquiry |
| J: text | Because of where the camera was<br><br>pointed. | • seeing through camera angle as text |
| T: | Exactly. From the angle of the camera, there were things you could observe and see and things you could not see and what you couldn't see was maybe as important as what you could see. | • point of view as the relationship between the camera angle, what can be seen or not seen<br>• actions of observer<br>• strategy that text does not represent the whole |
| J: | OK. I get it. | • further internalizing |
| T: | So, you know, you have to position our scientist or ethnographer . . . | • further referent of positioning to illustrate point of view |
| J: | So he's looking at it from a certain angle, probably. | • current dialogue using text |
| T: | You've got it. | • confirming Jared's understanding the social and academic practices as well as the concept |

To highlight these dimensions of social activity more clearly, we offer the following definitions:

1. *World building:* assembling situated meanings about "reality," present and absent, concrete and abstract (Gee, 1996; Gee, Hull, and Lankshear, 1996).

2. *Activity building:* assembling situated meanings about what activity or activities are going on, composed of what specific actions.

3. *Identity building (socially situated):* assembling situated meanings about what identities are relevant to the interaction (written text), with their concomitant attitudes and ways of feeling, ways of knowing and believing, as well as ways of acting and interacting (Carbaugh, 1996; Gee, 1992, 1996; Gumperz, 1982b; Fernie, Davies, Kantor, & McMurray, 1993; Wieder & Pratt, 1990).

4. *Connection building:* making assumptions about how the past and future of an interaction, verbally and nonverbally, are connected to the present moment and to each other (after all, interactions always have some degree of continuous coherence; e.g., Bloome & Egan-Robertson, 1993; Floriani, 1993; Halliday & Hasan, 1976).

As suggested previously, these dimensions are common to each social situation. However, they do not exhaust all of the dimensions of social life that are built in and through the day-to-day interactions among members of a group. Others have shown how power, gender, access, literacy, and views of science, among other dimensions of human activity, are socially constructed. We invite readers to add to these dimensions and expand this framework. To support this effort, we present a way of intersecting the social building tasks with the language (discourse) aspects in the MASS system to form a frame that can be used to more systematically guide the construction of a logic-of-inquiry and the selection and use of relevant forms of discourse analysis. Table 2 provides a summary of the intersecting dimensions and representative questions.

As indicated in Table 2, it is possible to select more than one aspect to use in examining the oral and written discourse constructed by members of a social group or used by an individual member to complete a personal or group-defined task. Each building task, language aspect, and question provides particular information and requires particular analytic processes and procedures. No single study or analysis will use all of these elements or questions. Rather, in each analysis, the researcher will select those that are relevant to the questions being examined and the data being analyzed. Taken together, they form a more comprehensive picture of the social world, the actors and their actions, and what the actors are accomplishing socially.

## Redefining Language: Social Languages
## As a Basis for Discourse Analysis

In presenting two examples from the work of Gee, we show how this framework can be used across types of data and discursive situations as well as across groups that differ in terms of age (elementary students, college students, and working scientists), mode (oral and written), and context (classrooms, science articles, conversations in social spaces). The discussion of these two examples serves an

**TABLE 2**
**An Example of the MASS Framework and Related Questions**

| Building Task | MASS Aspect | Representative Questions |
|---|---|---|
| World Building | Semiotic Aspect | What are the sign systems being used in the situation (e.g., speech, writing, images, and gestures)? |
| | | What situated meanings of the words and phrases (and gestures and images) do members construct and/or signal to each other in the situation? |
| | | What cultural models do members signal are being used to connect and integrate these situated meanings to each other? |
| | | When a frame clash occurs between different interpretations of situation or use of cultural models, what do members do and what consequences does it have for each, as well as the group? |
| | | What institutions, communities of practice, and/or discourses are being (re-)produced in this situation and how are they being transformed in the act? |
| | Material Aspect | When, where, with whom, and under what conditions are members interacting? |
| | | What meanings and values seem to be attached to places, times, bodies, objects, artifacts, and institutions relevant in this situation? |
| | | What name is given to this event/ situation, and to activity (if provided)? |
| | | What situated modes and forms of language practices and processes are used as resources by members in this event? |
| Activity Building | Activity Aspect | On what is time being spent in this situation/event (i.e., what is the larger activity to which members are orienting in this situation)? |
| | | What subactivities and sequences of these compose this activity? |
| | | What actions (down to the level of things like "requests for reasons") compose these subactivities and activities? |
| Identity Building | Sociocultural Aspect | What norms and expectations, roles and relationships, and rights and obligations are constructed by, and/or signalled by, relevant members (the group) to guide participation and activity among participants in the event? |
| | | What personal, social, and cultural knowledge and beliefs (cognition), feelings (affect), and identities (roles and relationships, positions) seem to be relevant to the situation? |

TABLE 2 (continued)

| Building Task | MASS Aspect | Representative Questions |
|---|---|---|
| Identity Building | Sociocultural Aspect | How are these identities signalled by members and/or constructed in the interactions among members?<br>How are they transformed in and through the actions, responses, and collective activity in the situation (questions about situated meanings and cultural models will already bear on this)? |
| Connection Building | Semiotic Aspect | What sorts of connections (intertextual ties)—looking backward and/or forward—are made within utterances?<br>What sorts of connections (intertextual ties)—looking backward and/or forward—are made across utterances and large stretches of the interaction?<br>What sorts of connections (intertextual ties) are proposed, recognized, acknowledged, and interactionally made to previous or future interactions (activity) and texts, to other people, ideas, things, institutions, and discourses outside the current interaction?<br>In what ways are the intertextual ties constructed within and across events (at each level of analysis) socially significant? |
| | Sociocultural Aspect | What sorts of connections (intercontextual ties) are made to previous or future interactions, to other people, ideas, things, institutions, and discourses outside the current interaction?<br>What sorts of connections (intercontextual ties) are made to previous processes and practices (cultural patterns) and proposed, recognized, and acknowledged as socially significant outside the currentinteraction?<br>Which processes, practices, and discourses do members draw on from previous events/situations to guide the actions in the current situation (e.g., text construction)? |

additional purpose, that of revisiting the issue of what we mean by language. If we are to examine the relationships among discourse, learning, and social practice, we must understand this concept we call "language." Therefore, before presenting these examples and the contrastive analyses, we discuss what counts as language within our discourse analysis perspective.

What is important to discourse analysis is that all languages are composed of many different social languages (Bakhtin, 1981, 1986). Each social language uses somewhat different and characteristic grammatical resources to carry out the four building tasks described earlier. All of us control many different social languages and switch among them in different contexts. In that sense, no one is monolingual.

It is important, as well, to note that often social languages are not "pure"; rather, people mix ("hybridize") them in complex ways for specific purposes. It is sometimes quite difficult to know whether it is best to say that someone is switching from one social language to another ("code switching") or that they are mixing two languages to assemble, for a given context, a transformed (even novel) social language (which may historically come to be seen as a "pure" and different social language in its own right). Of course, it is more important, in a discourse analysis, to recognize this matter than to settle it. People can even mix or switch between different social languages that are drawn from different languages.

In these two examples of social languages at work, keep in mind that discourse analysis is an analysis of social languages, not an analysis of language (like "English") per se. The first example is the case of Jane, an upper-middle-class, Anglo-American young woman in her 20s who was attending one of Gee's courses on language and communication. As part of the class, Jane recorded herself talking to her parents and to her boyfriend in different locations. In both cases, she decided to discuss a story the class had discussed earlier so as to be sure that, in both contexts, she was talking about the same thing.

In the story she chose, a character named Abigail wants to get across a river to see her true love, Gregory. A river boat captain (Roger) says he will take her only if she consents to sleep with him. Desperate to see Gregory, Abigail agrees to do so. But when she arrives and tells Gregory what she has done, he disowns her and sends her away.

Students in class had been asked to rank order the characters in the story from the most offensive morally to the least. Jane had selected Gregory as the least moral character as a result of this activity. This, then, is the historical context of the situation that she brought to the retelling of the story she selected.

In explaining to her parents why she thought Gregory was the worst (least moral) character in the story, the young woman said the following:

Well, when I thought about it, I don't know, it seemed to me that Gregory should be the most offensive. He showed no understanding for Abigail, when she told him what she was forced to do. He was callous. He was hypocritical, in the sense that he professed to love her, then acted like that.

Earlier, in a discussion with her boyfriend in an informal setting, she had also explained why she thought Gregory was the worst character. In this context, she said:

What an ass that guy was, you know, her boyfriend. I should hope, if I ever did that to see you, you would shoot the guy. He uses her and he says he loves her. Roger never lies, you know what I mean?

When we approach the analysis of this discourse using a contrastive approach to examining its semiotic aspects, it is clear that Jane has used two different forms of language. The differences (different "cues" to how the situation is to be construed) between Jane's two social languages are apparent in her two texts. To her parents, she carefully hedges her claims ("I don't know..."; "It seemed to me..."); to her boyfriend, she makes her claims straight out. To her boyfriend, she uses terms such as *ass* and *guy*, while to her parents she uses more formal terms such as *offensive, understanding, callous, hypocritical,* and *professed.* She also uses a more formal sentence structure with her parents ("It seemed to me that..."; "He showed no understanding for Abigail, when..."; "He was hypocritical in the sense that...") than she does with her boyfriend ("...that guy, you know, her boyfriend"; "Roger never lies, you know what I mean?"). Jane repeatedly addresses her boyfriend as "you," thereby noting his social involvement as a listener, but she does not directly address her parents in this way. In talking to her boyfriend, she leaves several points to be inferred, points that she spells out more explicitly to her parents (e.g., her boyfriend must infer that Gregory is being accused of being a hypocrite from the information that, although Roger is bad, "at least he does not lie, which Gregory did in claiming to love Abigail").

Through her choices of words, syntax, and content, Jane makes visible and recognizable two different versions of who she is and who her parents and boyfriend are (identity building), as well as what she and they are doing together (activity building). In one case, her language choices indicate that she is taking up the position of "a dutiful and intelligent daughter." This can be seen in the fact that, although she is a college student, she is having dinner with her parents. Furthermore, the language register she chose to use with her parents supports a more formal situation. In contrast, her language choices with her boyfriend indicate that she has positioned herself as "a girlfriend being intimate with her boyfriend."

By contrasting Jane's talk on the same topic across two settings with different types of actors, we show how a discourse analysis can be used to make visible the repertoires members have for interacting and communicating with different audiences. It demonstrates the situated nature of language choice. If all languages are social languages, and all instances of language use situated uses, then the implications for the study of learning in social context become clear. Rather than assuming that a single example provides an accurate picture of what students know, contrastive situations may be more productive. In contrasting what members display as learning, knowing, and understanding across different interactants with different situational contexts, a fuller picture may be obtained. Without the contrastive case (at whatever level, and using whatever types of resources, e.g., phonemic, intonational, lexical, different cultural expectations, texts, events, periods of time, people), we question the level of certainty in assessments of learning (Heap, 1980) that can exist when only one instance or context of use is considered. This leaves unexamined what the student can do or display as learning under other conditions (Giddens, 1990) and, thus, limits the degree of certainty about the claims that can be made. For example, we raise the question of how Jane would be assessed as a storyteller had the informal interaction with her boyfriend been the only example used. Certainly, her ability to use more formal registers would not have been understood (for a historical discussion of this issue related to African-American speakers of English, see Labov, 1969).

The second example of social languages at work comes from the "professional" domains. Biologists and other scientists often write for a range of journals, each with a particular type of audience. Thus, they write one way in professional journals aimed at other members of their particular intellectual community of science (e.g., biology), with all of its conventions and expectations for appropriate form and substance (content) (Bazerman, 1989; Toulmin, 1970, 1972), and they write another way in popular science magazines. These two ways of writing involve different activities and display different identities. From this perspective, a popular science article is not merely a "translation" or "simplification" of the professional article.

To illustrate these differences in language, purpose, and outcome, we present a contrastive analysis of two extracts. The first comes from a professional journal, and the second comes from a popular science magazine; both are written by the same biologist on the same topic (the example is from Myers, 1992, p. 150).

> 1. Experiments show that *Heliconius* butterflies are less likely to oviposit on host plants that possess eggs or egg-like structures. These egg mimics are an unambiguous example of a plant trait evolved in response to a host-restricted group of insect herbivores. (professional journal)

> 2. *Heliconius* butterflies lay their eggs on *Passiflora* vines. In defense the vines seem to have evolved fake eggs that make it look to the butterflies as if eggs have already been laid on them. (popular science)

By examining the cues in the two texts, we again see a difference in the language used. However, as our analysis will show, while the topic appears to be the same, the content differs, and this difference provides the grounds for examining the issue of identity building (among other social dimensions of interest, including issues of power and gender). The first extract, from a professional scientific journal, refers to the conceptual structure of a specific theory within the scientific discipline of biology.

Let us consider, then, how these two different social languages build different worlds, identities, activities, and connections. The first extract, from a professional scientific journal, is about the conceptual structure of a specific theory within the scientific discipline of biology. The subject of the initial sentence is "experiments," a methodological tool in natural science. The subject of the next sentence is "these egg mimics": Note how plant parts are named, not in terms of the plant itself, but in terms of the role they play in a particular theory of natural selection and evolution, namely "coevolution" of predator and prey (that is, the theory that predator and prey evolve together by shaping each other). Note also, in this regard, the earlier "host plants" in the preceding sentence, rather than the "vines" of the popular passage.

In the second sentence, the butterflies are referred to as "a host-restricted group of insect herbivores," which points simultaneously to an aspect of scientific methodology (like "experiments" did) and to the logic of a theory (like "egg mimics" did). Any scientist arguing for the theory of coevolution faces the difficulty of demonstrating a causal connection between a particular plant characteristic and a particular predator when most plants have many different sorts of animals attacking them. A central methodological technique to overcome this problem is to study plant groups (like Passiflora vines) that are preyed on by only one or a few predators (in this case, Heliconius butterflies). "Host restricted group of insect herbivores," then, refers to both the relationship between plant and insect that is at the heart of the theory of coevolution and to the methodological technique of picking plants and insects that are restricted to each other so as to "control" for other sorts of interactions.

The first passage, then, is concerned with scientific methodology and a particular theoretical perspective on evolution. On the other hand, the second extract, from a popular science magazine, is not about methodology and theory, but about animals in nature. The butterflies are the subject of the first sentence and the vine is the subject of the second. Further, the butterflies and the vine are labeled as such, not in terms of their role in a particular theory. The second passage is a story about the struggles of insects and plants that are transparently open to the trained gaze of the scientist. Further, the plant and insect become "intentional" actors in the drama: The plants act in their own "defense" and things "look" a certain way to the insects, there are "deceived" by appearances as humans sometimes are.

These two examples replicate in the present what, in fact, is a historical difference. In the history of biology, the scientist's relationship with nature gradually changed from telling stories about direct observations of nature (seeing) to carrying out complex experiments to test complex theories (Bazerman, 1989) and manage uncertainty (Myers, 1990). This change was caused, in part, by the fact that mounting "observations" of nature led scientists, not to consensus, but to growing disagreement as to how to describe and explain such observations (Shapin & Schaffer, 1985). "Seeing" became more and more mediated by theory and technology. This problem led, in turn, to the need to convince the public that such uncertainty did not damage the scientist's claim to be able to "see" and know the world in some relatively direct way, a job now carried out by much "popular science" writing. Note, here, then, too, how changing institutions play into the analysis of our texts, and how our analysis of these texts, in turn, helps illuminate the current and past workings of these institutions.

These two texts build different worlds (here the "nature-as-lab" versus "nature as open to the gaze"), different identities (here the experimenter/theoretician versus the careful observer of nature) and different activities (the professional contribution to science and the popularization of it). Further, they create very different sorts of connections: one creates, inside and outside the text, a chain of links in a theory; the other creates, inside and outside the text, a chain of links in seeing and in nature.

The worlds, identities, activities, and connections these texts, like all texts, build are licensed by specific socially and historically shaped practices and institutions representing the values and interests of distinctive groups of people. If we can use the term "politics" to mean any place where social interests and "social goods" are at stake, then all language-in-use is political in a quite straightforward sense (Fairclough, 1989, 1995; Lee, 1992; van Dijk, 1993). Since this is true, politics is an integral part of any discourse analysis; it is part of any full description of a social language and of the four building tasks that social languages allow us to carry out.

## An Interactive Approach to the Study of Learning in Communities of Practice

The discussion to this point has focused on establishing the conceptual and theoretical basis of the MASS system and framework for the study of learning in social settings and on illustrating particular elements and uses of the system. In the previous section, we showed how this system can be applied to different types of texts, groups, and social situations, with only a brief discussion of how this relates to the study of learning as a sociocultural process. In this section, we examine the relationships among discourse analysis, learning, and social practice in classrooms more explicitly. To do this, we need to add to our framework a sociocultural perspective on learning. This perspective, in different forms, guides our individual perspectives on learning. Here we present a mutually constructed view that examines learning within communities of practice. As argued here, this view of learning adds an explanatory aspect to the MASS framework, one that is needed for the current argument but not one that is central to all instances of use of the system. Viewed in this way, theories of learning are part of a broader framework that enhances the expressive potential of our research language when we focus on the study of learning in social settings.

One way to see the difference between these perspectives on theory is to revisit the distinction that Birdwhistell (1977) drew about the relationship of theory to method. The MASS system is a theoretically driven approach to discourse analysis that we use to analyze particular types of learning situations. Sociocultural theory is a theoretically framed approach to the study of learning and development as social constructions (e.g., John-Steiner, Panofsky & Smith, 1994; Lave, 1996; Rieber & Carton, 1987; Rogoff, 1990; Souza Lima, 1995; Wertsch, 1991). Given the common view of the social construction of knowledge and the focus on material, activity, semiotic, and sociocultural aspects of this process, we view these theories as mutually informing. From this perspective, we see a view of learning that focuses only on changing representations in people's heads as one that fails to engage the full range of semiotic, material, activity, and sociocultural aspects of situations that we have stressed previously. In bringing these perspectives together, we construct a logic-of-inquiry that provides resources for the study of the relationships among discourse, learning, and social practices that neither perspective can provide alone. In the next section, we show how these perspectives can be used to create a discourse-oriented analysis of learning in social settings. We then illustrate how this enhanced perspective can be used in the study of learning in a social situation.

### Learning in Classrooms: A Sociocultural Perspective

The perspective on discourse analysis that we have developed so far encourages us to take a particular perspective on learning. As we illustrated previously, discourse analysis is as much (or more) about what is happening among people out in the world (anthropology and sociology) as it is about what is happening in their minds (psychology). The approach to learning that is most compatible with an ethnographically grounded perspective on discourse analysis is one that defines learning as changing patterns of participation in specific social practices within communities of practice (Lave, 1988, 1996; Lave & Wenger, 1991; Rogoff, 1990; Rogoff & Lave, 1984; Souza Lima, 1995; Wertsch, 1981, 1991).

This view of learning requires us to see that people's activities are part of larger "communities of practice"; that is, groups of people who affiliate over time and events engage in tasks or work of a certain sort. This is the case whether they are students in an elementary school classroom, members of a street gang, members of an academic discipline, affiliates of a "cause," or participants in a specific business organization. Such communities of practice produce and reproduce themselves through the creation of a variety of social processes and practices. Within social processes, and through interactions constituting and constituted by social practices, they "apprentice" new members.

Many perspectives focus on production and reproduction (e.g., critical theory, sociology); each brings with it a particular view of this process, from a factory model to a human reproduction model. To frame the way in which we view this process, we draw on work on childhood socialization as framed by Corsaro, text construction through discourse as framed by Fairclough (1992), and work from a sociohistorical perspective as framed by Souza Lima (1995). Gaskin, Miller, and Corsaro (1993) argue that the relationship is interactive, dynamic, and recursive (a form of reflexivity), one in which the child is socialized to a culture and transforms that culture. Gaskin et al. argue for a dynamic view of

*productive-reproductive* to emphasize the creative nature of this process and to convey, in line with Giddens (1984), the duality of social structure. Giddens (1984, p. 25) argues that "the social structural properties of social systems are both medium and outcome of the practices they recursively organize" (see also Ochs and Schieffelin, 1984). This view of social structure provides the basis for the claim that the cultural-developmental process is not linear but reproductive. It is reproductive in that what children do with adults and other children involves the creative use, refinement, and transformation of available cultural resources.... In this view, socialization is not merely a matter of acquiring or appropriating culture at the level of the individual child but also a collective process of innovative or interpretive reproduction. (1993, p. 7)

From this perspective, as members interact with children and with others in their environments within particular institutional or social settings, they are simultaneously structuring and being structured by the actions between and among others. Viewed in this way, structures are not "out there" but are constructed as members interact with each other; a community of practice is constituted out of actions and situations (across time and space).

Fairclough (1993) captures this dynamic at the level of discourse. He proposed a three-dimensional framework that views

each discursive event [as having] three dimensions or facets: it is a spoken or written language text, it is an instance of discourse practice involving the production and interpretation of text, and it is a piece of social practice.... The connection between text and social practice is seen as being mediated by discourse practice: on the one hand, processes of text production and interpretation are shaped by (and help shape) the nature of the social practice, and on the other hand the production shapes (and leaves "traces" in) the text, and the interpretive process operates upon "cues" in the text. (p. 136)

Viewed in this way, we can examine a text or interaction in terms of the social practices and discourse practices used. Furthermore, we can examine the text for traces of previous (and future/implicated) practices (e.g., for intertextual and intercontextual ties). The commonality of this perspective with the more macrosocial perspective of Corsaro and Giddens supports a dynamic and constructed view of learning. From these perspectives, learning, like text and social structure, is an outcome of the moment-by-moment and over-time actions of members of a social group. Moreover, if we use Bloome and Egan-Robertson's (1993) criteria for intertextuality, we can see members proposing, recognizing, acknowledging, and interactionally accomplishing situated definitions of what counts as learning that they view as socially significant to the group. This view of learning is a dynamic one. It is situated in particular contexts of practice, and it is, to a large extent, discursive in nature.

One way to view this perspective on learning has been framed succinctly by Souza Lima (1995). Building on sociohistorical theory, she argues that

we have two dimensions of development [and, by implication, learning]: one that resides in the individual and the other in the collectivity. Both are interdependent and create each other. Historically created possibilities of cultural development are themselves transformed by the processes through which individuals acquire the cultural tools that are or become available in their context. (Souza Lima, 1995, pp. 447–448)

From this perspective, then, learning and development are in a reflexive relationship, as are the individual and collective.

These three perspectives provide different, yet intersecting, perspectives on collective-individual relationships. A logic-of-inquiry that draws on them will view each local group as a type of community of practice in which members, through their face-to-face interactions (discourse as activity, as well as other forms of activity), construct the very patterns of practice that define the community. Thus, as members interact across time and events, they are continually defining and redefining what counts as community through the norms and expectations, roles and relationships, and rights and obligations constructed. Within such communities of practice, individual members are afforded access to particular events and spaces; thus, they have particular opportunities for learning and for acquiring the social and cultural processes and practices of group membership. However, if we take Corsaro's perspective, this process is not a "bring them into the culture view." Rather, members have agency and thus take up, resist, transform, and reconstruct the social and cultural practices afforded them in and through the events of everyday life.

This view of learning, then, suggests that an analyst must examine the collective as an entity that has a "material reality" and consider individuals and their actions in relationship to the opportunities for learning they are afforded while simultaneously examining how members, through their interactions, are shaping and being shaped by the texts they are jointly constructing. Thus, the analysis must include the moment-by-moment, bit-by-bit construction of texts (oral and written), the chains of concerted actions among members, the role of prior and future texts in connecting these "bits of life," and what members take from one context to use in another. In this way, the analyst can build a grounded view of the cultural models, social practices, and discourse practices that members draw on "to learn."

While this is the ideal case, as we have argued, it is possible to examine a "slice of life" from this perspective to obtain an emic perspective on social participation and, through that, both opportunities for learning and situated views of what counts as learning. Given space limits, we illustrate what a "slice of life" analysis that focuses on examining opportunities for learning (Tuyay, Jennings, & Dixon, 1995) can show when viewed through the MASS system proposed in this chapter.

By conceptualizing learning through the notion of opportunities for learning (collective constructions) and opportunities to learn (individual opportunities), we establish a means of examining collective-individual development, learning as individual and collective activity, and discourse practices as socially constituted by and constitutive of learning opportunities. In this way, we can begin to examine the complex and dynamic relationships among discourse, learning, and social practice. Furthermore, as shown subsequently, we are able to identify the cultural ideologies and models that members bring to, inscribe in, and construct through the texts of classroom life by examining the processes and practices in which these members engage.

## An Example of the Discursive Construction of Opportunities for Learning

The "slice of life" we examine comes from data on science reform being analyzed by Gee. The data that we consider are derived from a videotape of a classroom lesson and an accompanying booklet produced as a resource for teacher professional development in science education (Rosebery, Puttick, & Bodwell, 1996; all subsequent page and transcript references refer to this booklet). These cultural artifacts (i.e., teacher materials) present science in action in a second-grade classroom in Concord, Massachusetts (the town's real name is used in the materials), an affluent town west of Boston. We selected these materials not to critique them but to show the complexity involved in understanding what counts as an opportunity for learning and how such opportunities are not mere activities but are constructed through activity among members on a moment-by-moment (or line-by-line) basis as they construct a common text.

The analysis of Gee's (and Green's previous) example, in this chapter, is a slightly modified version that resulted from dialogue among our perspectives. Our joint question that arose from the dialogue with these data became "What counts as learning, and how is this shaped in and through the actions of actors?"

This question was analyzed in two parts. In the first part, we examined the written materials provided. Just as we examined Arturo's text and the scientist's texts for cues to meanings, activity, sociocultural models, identity, and other aspects of building tasks, we approached this text in the same manner. After completing that analysis, we examined the videotape data to explore what counts as learning science as represented by the actions and interactions of members of the second-grade class. At each point in our analysis, we tried to maintain an emic perspective; consider a part-whole, whole-part relationship; and use contrastive relevance as a guiding principle.

Building on the MASS system, we saw the authors of the booklet and the videotape as building a particular world, along with identities, activities, and connections, through their language and discourse choices as well as their choices of semiotic systems (e.g., written language, oral language, graphic materials, videotaped records of science lessons). The following excerpt from the booklet provides both an introduction to their perspective on science and an introduction to the videotape. In the booklet, they state that the videotape represents

the story of a class of second graders who designed experiments to investigate their questions about plant growth, focusing on the work of one group [of three girls] that wanted to study the effects of light. In small groups, the students planned, designed, and conducted experiments over a period of four weeks. At the end, each group presented their observations to the rest of their classmates and invited them to help interpret their data. In this way their teacher...introduced them to scientific ways of thinking and talking, which was the goal for this unit. (p. 4)

By examining the situated meanings of the words in this text (i.e., the cues to who the actors are and what they were doing together), we were able to examine what constitutes scientific ways of thinking and talking. The authors initiate this segment of text by calling it "a story." They continue by describing who the actors are, what they are doing together over time and events, what the sequence of activity entailed, what roles and relationships and patterns of organization occurred, and what types of interaction requirements were framed. They end this segment of text by stating that, through these patterns of actions and practices, the teacher "introduced [the students] to scientific ways of thinking and talking, which was the goal for this unit" (p. 4).

In this way, the authors construct a "telling case" (Mitchell, 1984), a case that makes visible theoretically what had not necessarily been visible before. We call it a telling case for two reasons: It was constructed as an instructional tool to use with teachers to help them acquire new knowledge of science pedagogy and it makes visible to us, as analysts, a particular understanding (not the only understanding) of what counts as doing and teaching science to the actors involved in the processes represented in the text.

The actors identified are second graders who were working in small groups over a 4-week period. The actors on whom the videotape focused were three girls who worked together over the period to study the effects of light. These girls (as was the case for members of each of the groups) were expected to interact with rest of their classmates and their teacher in particular groupings (whole-class, small-group, and small-group–whole-class interactions) at particular points in time for particular purposes (at one point to design the experiment, at a second point to conduct the experiment, and at a third point to invite help in interpreting their data from other class members). By analyzing the chains of activity and by examining who the actors were in each of these chains (Spradley, 1980, calls this process a domain analysis), we were able to identify a range of configurations, all of which were collective, including the teacher, who was framed in relationship to the students and different types of groups. Furthermore, by examining the actions that these actors took among themselves and with others, we were able to identify a shift in the frame for the activity and, through this, a shift in the model of science being constructed.

We began the analysis by examining, through consideration of the words used by the authors, the language of the booklet for the sorts of situated meanings given to words such as *experiment, data, observation, interpret,* and *science* (and related terms) and the cultural models seemingly attached to them. The analysis showed that the passage involved many words for "scientific work" but that that work did not accumulate in terms of results in any strong manner. For Example, consider how in the passage from the booklet quoted above the students conduct "experiments over a period of four weeks." While these students, it turns out, discover, however tentatively, that "more light makes plants grow better," they are not asked, in the last part of the quoted passage, to share their "results" or "findings" with the wole class. Rather, they are asked to present their "observations" and "invite" the whole group to help them "interpret" their "data."

This initial examination of the booklet gave us our own tentative hypothesis, one that we could test further by an examination of the actual classroom interaction. It looks as if the booklet shifts from one model of science to another. In the first case, it treats science as a form of work in stages that is meant to issue in a result (the classical experimental model of science). In the second case, it treats science as a form of looking or witnessing through which one gains "observations" (data) that need interpretation much like literary texts do. The booklet, in a sense, seems to add the second model onto the first one as its final stage. Rather than attempting to contest or support the results of the girls' experiment, the whole group is asked to discuss different ways of interpreting the observaitons the gils have made on the way to gaining their results.

We then turned to the actual classroom interaction to which the booklet was but an introduction. Our analysis, of the booklet and the interaction, is grounded both in an emic perspective on what members appeared to need to know and do to accomplish their tasks in socially appropriate ways within their emerging community of practice and in a more etic perspective based on our own coultural expectations and knowledge of research directions in science education. We try to keep these perspectives separate. However, given the interactive and responsive nature of this work, this is not always possible.

Let us turn now to that classroom interaction. The teacher starts his instructional sequence by encouraging the children, in small group discussions, to come up with predictions.

Transcript Segment 1

*Krysta:* I thought maybe it was going to grow best um over by the window and at the grow plant table.

*Lia:* Yeah.

*Teacher:* Do you think it will grow like—really good in the grow table and the window and not at all in the other places?

*Krysta:* Maybe not at all in the closet.

*Teacher:* Okay.

*Ceysa:* Because that would be pretty dark.

In this discussion with their teacher (Transcript 1, booklet pp. 17–18), the three girls on whom the booklet and video materials focus construct a group-accomplished prediction something like the following: "Light causes plants to grow better (or be healthier)." We call this a group prediction, since each member of the group contributed a "piece" to the prediction. In the way in which they add to the interaction, the three girls signal their involvement with the task and their expected interpretations and understandings of the contrast.

One way to view the teacher's choice of actions (i.e., his response to the students' initial thoughts) is to see him as positioning the students to respond in particular ways: to think about other places where the plant might not grow well. The students' actions show that they take up this position and respond appropriately. They take up his strategy of comparing places.

In the following transcript segment (Transcript 2, pp. 18–19), the teacher engaged in actions we have labeled guidance (scaffolding).

Transcript Segment 2

*Lia:* Maybe they're a little bit more green if they're healthier....

*Teacher:* Okay, so maybe it's not— maybe it's greenness too.

*Lia:* Yeah.

*Teacher:* All right.

*Lia:* Or whatever color it is....

*Ceysa:* And like they're standing up straighter and dead ones sort of hang down.

*Teacher:* Okay, so like if they're limping over....

*Ceysa:* A lot....

In this sequence, we see the teacher eliciting from the girls a decision that "green-ness" and "straightness," and not "height" alone, are criterial attributes of having "grown better" or of "health." In this way, he jointly constructs an answer with the students.

After such small-group discussion work, the girls actually run their experiment, placing plants in various light conditions, ranging from plants grown 24 hours a day under a grow light to plants grown 24 hours a day in a dark closet and in various other conditions (e.g., in a window that is light in the day and dark at night).

The experiment was successful, by and large confirming predictions. Some of the plants grown in the closet (a low light condition) had, however, grown tall, although they were pale yellow (not green) and droopy (not straight). Thus, however anomalous their height, the plants were not healthy by the criteria the girls had decided upon, and so their prediction was supported nonetheless.

Across these segments, then, we were able to see the types of opportunities for learning afforded these girls. As indicated in the activity aspects of these situations, the girls were given a range of opportunities: They were able to jointly construct a prediction and to learn from the teacher appropriate types of actions to take to test the prediction (to place the plants in different places, each with different conditions). They were also afforded the opportunity to compare and contrast plant growth under the varying conditions. Through these opportunities, they were afforded the further opportunity to explore and take up a particular language of science.

After the girls had finished their experimental work, there was a full class discussion in which the girls first gave a brief presentation on their experiment, displaying their plants. Then, as the booklet states, the other children were "invited" to help the girls "make sense of their data." This part of the curriculum involves an entire class in "sense-making discussion." This description, obtained by observing the actual actions and activity among members, provides insights into the questions that we had after analyzing the author's description in the "booklet." The girls were able to present the visual as well as oral evidence to the group. In this way, they were given an opportunity to discuss and describe their experiment.

However, this activity was not the final activity; rather, a period of sense making occurred.

Transcript 3 provides us with a base for examining what counted as "inviting interpretation." Analysis of this transcript showed that the activity has changed in an important way, from small-group discussions devoted to planning and carrying out "hands on" science activities to large-group discussions devoted to "making sense" (a "minds on," not "hands on," activity).[14] As the segment that follows will show, concomitant with this change in activity, the sorts of identities and related talk the teacher and children adopt (or are expected to adopt) change as well. This change in identity is reflected in who can speak, who is recognized as knowing, and whose knowledge and/or comments are accepted. While a full discourse analysis would be needed to trace these changes and to assess what students in different organizational contexts (the group, individuals within the group, and the small-group members) learned, the following segment illustrates what can be identified through this type of contrastive analysis.

The following is an extended example from the whole-class discussion that shows some of the diversity of talk generated in and supported by this situation (pp. 32–37):

*Teacher:* Does anybody have any idea about why those [pale plants grown in the closet] might be that color [i.e., not green]?

*Lia:* Karen?

*Karen:* Because, um, that's in the dark and it doesn't get any light maybe.

*Girl:* It does get a little light.

*Girl:* It gets the teeniest bit.

*Girl:* Aleisha?

*Aleisha:* I think it's that color because it doesn't get that much light, and, it—it has—and plants grow with light, so.

*Krysta:* Michael?

*Michael:* Well, I think these are—there are these special rays in light that make it turn green and it's not getting those rays, so it won't turn green.

*Michael:* Like a laser and a light beam are almost the sa- are almost different- I mean they are different kinds of light. So, maybe there's this kind of light in the air that maybe we can't see, but maybe the plants need it maybe to turn green.

*Anna:* I think, um, the rays, um, gives the plant food, and um, they like store the food in the leaves and cotyledon, and the food like makes it turn green? And stuff.

*Michael:* Yeah, that sounds like an idea behind my idea.

*Will:* Um, maybe it's not the light. Maybe it's heat....

[discussion about heat and air and other things]

*Teacher:* This never turned green. These became green for some reason, and that never became green.

The teacher poses the opening question and asks whether anybody has any idea about why the less green plants (grown in the closet) might be less green (we consider the actual form of this utterance in the next section). Lia then takes up the role of calling on people who are raising their hands (note that the three experimenters get to call on classmates) and calls on Karen to respond to the teacher's question. She says: "Because, um, that's in the dark and it doesn't get any light maybe." Her "um," her "maybe," and the form of this utterance (with a raising pitch at the end) indicate that she is treating the answer to this question as "news." Her response is contradicted by another girl, whose own response is also qualified by a third girl.

Aleisha is then called on to respond. She states that she too "thinks" that the answer has to do with light. Her response, however, is a slightly expanded restatement of information already on the floor. By not adding new information, she shows that she also believes this is "news" and open to "speculation." No one responds to her statement. Neither student's responses indicate they are aware of the epistemological status of the claim they are making about light, namely that it follows from the logic of the experiment the girls have carried out and presented to the group. Furthermore, Aleisha uses the generalization "and plants grow with light, so" as a piece of general knowledge unconnected to the experiment the girls have carried out.

Following Aleisha's turn, Michael and Anna engage in talk that more genuinely takes off from where the girls' experiment has ended, and they attempt to help the girls explain (not just "interpret") their "results." Explanation requires going beyond the mere causal claim, which the girls' work has established, that "light causes plants to grow better (healthier)" by discussing things that might mediate between light and health. Michael introduces "different kinds of light" and things "plants need." Anna goes yet further and introduces a true mediating variable (between "light" and "health"), namely "food," which the plants which "store in the leaves and cotyledon" and which "[make them] turn green."

This explanatory talk is, however, not followed up on, and Will returns the group to another type of talk that our analysis showed was pervasive in the whole discussion, namely talk about what variables were and were not controlled in the experiment (part of the earlier activity of experimental design). Will suggests that heat, and not light, might be the important causal variable.

After the talk about heat to which Will's contribution gives rise, the teacher says, "These [the plants that had been given ample light] became green for some reason." The teacher's "for some reason" implies that this reason is waiting to be discovered as "news" through the process of discussion (much as Karen and Aleshia had assumed). But that is exactly what the girls' experiment was designed to discover.

Our analysis shows that the pattern of talk shaped particular opportunities and, at the same time, precluded others. Through analysis of the chains of action supported by the teacher, we found that the children had entered a different activity, one in which the causal claim "Light makes plants grow better (healthier)" is again "up for grabs." In the prior activity sequence (experimentation), it was, however, the end product, the achievement. This contrast of outcomes pointed us to the need to think about the relationships between the different activities in this overall instructional sequence and to ask questions about the purpose of each type of activity: What were the students expected to know as a result of each phase of activity? What views of science were visible in each phase? Who had access to these views? Whose views counted in each?

To examine these questions, we focused our analysis not on the general sequence of activity but the specific types of actions that the students were able to perform in the group phase in contrast to the small-group phase. Building on the theoretical view that all activities are composed of subactivities and that subactivities are composed of smaller actions, each of which recruits different forms of language, we identified a range of actions that the children could take in the large-group discussion activity: "explaining," "guessing," "hypothesizing," "critiquing," "questioning," "suggesting," and others. We also identified a general characteristic of such an activity in this discussion. These actions occurred and interrupted each other in a fairly flexible way, depending, in part, on how different children interpreted the teacher's questions, other students' contributions, and the activity they took themselves to be in.

Such "hybridity" raised interesting questions about how different children in the discussion assemble situated meanings and begin to form cultural models; how they begin (or fail) to learn and use different social languages; what identities they do or do not take on; and how these relate to the identities they have taken on in other activities in this classroom and elsewhere.

We can see that, in this discussion, Michael and Anna function quite differently from many of the other speakers in regard to their language and what they take the activity to be. Our analysis showed that Michael and Anna consistently, here and elsewhere in the discussion, treated the task as adding an explanation to the girls' achievement of the causal claim that light makes plants grow better and healthier. Thus, by contrasting a pattern observed at one point in the discussion, we were able to obtain a picture of a more general case for Michael and Anna and then contrast this with other students. In this way, we constructed an argument that they took up different identities, through the types of actions they took with each other and in relationship to the content and activity of others.

The actions taken by the actors and the activity jointly constructed across phases of this event confirmed our initial hypothesis that two different views of science were being constructed at different points in this instructional unit. In one phase, students had an opportunity to engage in "an experimental model of science," one centered around a sequence of logically related activities: making a prediction, designing an experiment (e.g., controlling variables), gathering data, interpreting data and looking for anomalies, confirming or disconfirming (aspects of) the initial prediction, and then seeking to find a deeper explanation (in this case, for why light makes plants grow better and healthier).

Students also had an opportunity to participate in and to construct a second model (what we might call the "sense-making model") that was centered around the idea that people make sense through open-ended (i.e., less sequenced and constrained) collaborative talk with each other, pooling their knowledge and building upon each other's contributions in a quite egalitarian way. Work on the sociology of science suggests that both of these cultural models are used by laboratory scientists (e.g., Knorr-Cetina, 1983, 1995; Latour & Woolgar, 1986). However, in the astrophysics lab that they studied, Garfinkel, Lynch, and Livingston (1981) found that the astronomers, through their negotiations, transformed an observed phenomenon in their data from an "evidently-vague IT which was an object-of-sorts with neither demonstrable sense nor reference, to a 'relatively finished object'" (p. 135), an independent Gallilean pulsar.

The observed activity in the classroom, however, did not lead to this type of conclusion. What seemed to happen, in this case, is that some children treated the discussion as just such an explanatory endeavor, while others (with the implied permission of the teacher, as indicated in his actions) treated it as a more autonomous activity in which the experimental work already done could be revisited in ways that sometimes ignored what had already been accomplished. This appeared to return the girls, who were at the end of a set of tasks, back to where they began. While we cannot determine from these data whether knowledge did not "accumulate," for the girls or the group, what we can see is that there was a lack of resolution or a shared consensus, elements that Toulmin (1970) and others who have studied the history of science suggest characterize science communities.

Such a lack of resolution led us to wonder why this "sense-making" activity (with its great hybridity and open-endedness) was positioned as the last step of an activity sequence based on the experimental model. It also raised further questions about where an activity might be placed that would support the construction of "deeper explanations of one's successful prediction." We wondered how the developers saw the action of the students and how they would actually use this videotape segment with teachers. This issue led us to ask further questions: What model of science did the developers seek to support? Did they see a conflict between the two models here? Finally, was this example selected to raise questions such as these so that the group of teachers might challenge their views and discuss the implications of each model?

While these questions cannot be answered at this time through the present discourse analysis, the questions we raise are ones that can be examined further in future studies. Some might respond that the simple answer to this analysis would be to move to a more direct instruction model. However, past research has not shown that this simple answer will promote the type of learning and learners that reform efforts, regardless of perspective, desire.

What logic-of-inquiry demonstrated was that a range of different approaches to discourse analysis were needed to examine the complex patterns constructed in these written and oral texts. It also illustrated the interactive-responsive nature of this type of discourse analysis, in which one analysis provides a basis for comparison with others or in which an analysis of one type of data generates hypotheses that can be examined further through analysis of a second type of data. By examining the over-time construction of activity and examining cues to shifts in activity, we were able to present evidence of a tension between two models of doing science in this classroom. The data selected, therefore, formed a telling case that raised issues not visible at the outset.

What the analysis did not do was equally telling. From these data, we could not generalize to all classrooms. Nor can we determine how these materials are used. While we identified questions about the materials, these questions are not a critique of this professional development effort. Rather, they are questions that can shape new discussions around these materials, ones that will examine issues about the models of science and science pedagogy that teachers and others (reform agents) seek to promote and use.

## A CLOSING AND AN OPENING: ON IMPLICATIONS FOR RESEARCH, THEORY, POLICY, AND PRACTICE

This chapter has focused on what is involved in constructing a logic-of-inquiry that is theoretically driven and conceptually coherent. The analysis of the science data from Gee's study of science reform showed that an ethnographically grounded logic-of-inquiry can be used to make visible the ways in which models of science are constructed in and through the moment-by-moment and over-time actions of members. This work combines with a growing body of work using discourse analysis and ethnographic perspectives to examine what counts as science, how science is learned in different types of classrooms, and how opportunities arise for learning science content and science practices (e.g., Bleicher, 1994; Carlsen, 1992; Crawford, Chen, & Kelly, 1997; Kelly & Crawford, 1997; Moje, 1997). These studies provide insights into the ways in which differential opportunities for learning are afforded students in classrooms and how everyday life is consequential in different ways for different students. Furthermore, they contribute new understandings of the students' agency in this process.

What our analyses in this chapter illustrate is that, by using a logic-of-inquiry in which we moved back and forth between segments of activity (and across time and events) and by contrasting the patterns identified, we were able to make visible (a) differences in models of pedagogy constructed at different times by the same group of actors, (b) differences in models of science used by a scientist in writing about his research for different audiences, and (c) differences in registers used by an individual with different types of partners and similarities in claims about life in the classroom with the same teacher in different years. In each of these analyses, we needed to move between meaning aspects (semiotic), material aspects, activity aspects, and sociocultural aspects to identify ties among patterns across time, sources of influence on observed actions, and the ways in which collective and individual actions, identities, and patterns of interaction were constructed and socially significant. No single point in the analysis would have been sufficient, and no single approach would have provided the information obtained through the logic-of-inquiry we constructed across levels and types of discourse analysis. Only through the use of multiple data sources, multiple approaches to discourse analysis, and a contrastive analysis were we able to identify these similarities and differences and to understand the conditions that gave rise to them.

Given this view of research as social action, we have to consider how analyses such as the ones presented here might be used to inform educational stakeholders, including researchers, educators, and policymakers, interested in ways of supporting equity of access to educational processes and practices. Rather than pose recommendations for change, we have elected to present a discussion of what constitutes validity as a closing to this chapter.

What constitutes validity for a discourse analysis? Validity is not constituted by arguing that the analysis "reflects reality" in any simple way (Carspecken, 1996; Mishler, 1990) for two reasons. First, humans construct their realities, although what is "out there," beyond human control, places serious constraints on this construction (thus, "reality" is not "only" constructed). Second, just as language is always reflexively related to situations so that both make each other meaningful, so too is discourse analysis. The analysis interprets its data in a certain way, and those data, so interpreted, render the analysis meaningful in certain ways and not others.

These two considerations do not mean that discourse analyzes are "subjective," that they are just the analyst's "opinion." Validity for discourse analysis is based on the following three elements; (a) *Convergence*: A discourse analysis is more, rather than less, valid (validity is not once and for all; all interpretations are open to ongoing discussion and dispute), the more different analyzes of the same data or related data, or different analytic tools applied to the same data yield similar results; (b) *Agreement*: Answers to our questions are more convincing the more both "native speakers" of the social languages in the data and other discourse analysts (who accept our basic theoretical assumptions and tools) agree that the analysis reflects how such social languages actually can function in such settings. The native speakers do not need to know why or how their social languages so function, just that they can. (c) *Coverage*: the analysis is more valid the more it can be applied to related sorts of data. This includes being able to make sense of what has come before and after the situation being analyzed and being able to predict the sorts of things that might happen in related sorts of situations.

Why does this constitute validity? Because it is highly improbable that a good many answers to different questions (i.e., data from different sources), the perspectives of different "inside" and "outside" observers, and additional data sets, will converge unless there is good reason to trust the analysis. This, of course, does not mean the analysis is true or correct in every respect. Empirical science is social and accumulative in that investigators build on each other's work in ways that, in the long run, we hope, improves it. It does mean, however, that a "valid" analysis explains things that any future investigation of the same data, or related data, will have to take seriously into account.

We can also point out that it is highly improbable that answers to many of the questions facing those concerned about learning in social contexts require generalizable strategies or recommendations. It is much more probable that they require local, situated answers. Indeed, when a teacher is faced with a decision about what to do for "Sue" and what to do for "Sonia," the answers needed may be quite different. From this perspective, then, equal treatment, if it means the "one-size-fits-all" model, may not be equitable. Therefore, what is needed is not a single recommendation or definition of learning but, rather, a way of examining the individual-collective relationships that constitute the "local" opportunities for learning that students and others experience in educational settings and examining how and what students gain from such opportunities. As this chapter has shown, such an approach must be able to answer different questions, provide a means of analyzing data from different sources, and be able to account for differences in the perspectives of different "inside" and "outside" observers. In addition, it must be provide a basis for the analyst to move across types of data in theoretically coherent ways. Finally, it needs to provide evidence of the logic-of-inquiry that supported the multiple analyses.

If these conditions can be met, then it will be possible for investigators to build on each other's work in ways that in the long run, we hope, expand and enhance this work, individually and collectively. Such building tasks, however, will need to be based on a firm foundation of coherence of theoretical perspectives, not consistency alone. In that way, we can expand the expressive potential of our individual languages and perspectives and construct a more general perspective, one with greater expressive potential. We believe that Kenneth Strike's (1974) view of expressive potential will be one of the key tests of the validity of this new language. The questions that must be asked, then, are the following: What is the expressive potential of this perspective for the phenomena of importance to a certain individual? What types of questions does it allow the individual to answer? and Which questions cannot be answered using this approach?

## NOTES

[1]As a member of the Santa Barbara Classroom Discourse Group, my contributions are both individual and collective. My contribution was shaped by members of this group and related colleagues, both historically and in the moments of writing. Therefore, in addition to the contributions of Hugh Mehan to the direction and production of this chapter, I would like to acknowledge contributions by particular members of the group and colleagues who interacted with me and provided data for this chapter: Carol Dixon and Greg Kelly, University of California, Santa Barbara; LeAnn Putney, University of Nevada, Las Vegas; Ana Floriani, Illinois Wesleyan University; Elaine Vine, University of Canterbury, New Zealand; David Bloome, Vanderbilt University; and Beth Yeager, McKinley Elementary School.

[2]Studies of learning in social settings combining ethnography and discourse analysis have been undertaken from a number of theoretical perspectives: anthropological (e.g., Gilmore & Glatthorn, 1982; Cook-Gumperz, 1986; Bloome, 1987; Green & Bloome, 1997; Green & Dixon, 1993; Green & Wallat, 1981), social semiotic (Christie, 1995; Lemke, 1990), social psychological (Edwards & Mercer, 1987), and sociological (e.g., Bernstein, 1996; Mehan, 1979; Heap, 1991).

[3]Examples of these combined approaches can be found in educational research handbooks across disciplines (e.g., literacy education, science education and teaching), in research monographs, and in edited volumes, as well as previous volumes of *RRE*. Furthermore, in the last decade, major research journals across educational research disciplines have become more receptive to studies that use discourse-analytic perspectives and methodologies. Discourse-analytic approaches have been developed to study the relationship between discourse and schooling practices (e.g., Cazden, 1986; Cazden, John, & Hymes, 1972; Green, 1983; Green & Wallat, 1981; Mehan, 1979, 1985; Sinclair & Coulthard, 1975; Stubbs, 1983; Wilkinson, 1982), discourse and learning in classrooms (e.g., Duran, 1995; Edwards & Furlong, 1978; Edwards & Mercer, 1987; Gee, Michaels, & O'Connor, 1992; Green & Harker, 1988; Gumperz, 1986; Mehan, 1979), discourse and other forms of observational (Evertson & Green, 1986) and qualitative research (Erickson, 1986), discourse and science (Kelly & Green, 1997; Lemke, 1997), and discourse and literacy research (Baker & Luke, 1991; Bloome, 1987; Bloome & Green, 1984; Cook-Gumperz, 1986; Gee, 1996; Green & Dixon, 1993). The preceding articles, monographs, and collections are illustrative and not all inclusive. They were selected to provide information about and access to a broad range of approaches.

Work by individual authors and groups of authors can be found in major educational research journals. Discourse-analytic studies can now be found in the *American Educational Research Journal, Anthropology and Education Quarterly, Cognition and Instruction, Elementary School Journal, Harvard Education Review, Journal of Classroom Interaction, Journal of Literacy Research, Journal of Research in Science Teaching, Linguistics and Education, Reading Research Quarterly, Research in the Teaching of English,* and the *TESOL Quarterly,* among others, attesting to the growing interest in the insights afforded by this research perspective.

[4]We argue that what is needed is a set of approaches that cohere in theoretically oriented ways, and not a consistent set of methods, given the range and type of data collected within an ethnographic study or studies guided by ethnographic perspectives. What remains constant in this approach is the theoretical perspective and approach that guides selection and analysis of particular methods of analysis. This approch allows us to be responsive to the type of data being analyzed and the questions being examined. To use a consistent set, selected on an a priori basis, would require that we impose a logic on the data rather than constructing one in response to the type of data under examination.

[5]We recognize that there are a number of different perspectives on culture in anthropology. However, we have elected to use the cognitive anthropology perspective articulated by Frake (1977) and Spradley (1980) for heuristic purposes. We recognize the limitations of this work but find it productive in the current context. Given that Spradley died in 1980, we do not know whether, or how, he would have modified his work in the face of the criticism of cognitive anthropology by Geertz (1983) or in the face of the criticisms by others. Thus, we view this theory as a material resource and not as a fixed statement of reality.

[6]Drawing on Spradley (1980), we use the term *action* rather than *behavior*, since in communicative situations, participants act purposefully. As we have argued, through their use of contextualization cues, they signal to others their meanings and intentions.

[7]For a seminal collection of discourse and ethnographic studies that examine this issue in the area of language and schooling, see Cazden, John, and Hymes (1972); in the area of literacy and schooling, see Bloome (1987; Cook-Gumperz, 1986); for a seminal article on how, through language, members of the schooling culture structure school structures and thus access to learning, see Mehan (1979).

[8]We distinguish here between members' perspectives and members' perceptions. The first is a point of view (angle of vision) from which to view the event, situation, and analysis. The latter requires interviewing participants in a local situation about what they perceived.

[9]For a discussion of related constructs and approaches, see Bauman (1986), Duranti and Goodwin (1992), Gumperz and Levinson (1996), Harre and Gillett (1994), Hymes (1996), Lynch (1993), and Pickering (1995). For overviews of an important and quite specialized approach to discourse analysis, "conversation analysis," that studies the ways in which language in social interaction produces and reproduces "order" in society, see Goodwin and Heritage (1990), Heritage (1984), Psathas (1995), and Wootton (1989).

[10]For examples of other linked programs of research using discourse analysis in education, see Cook-Gumperz (1986); Fernie, Davies, Kantor, and McMurray (1993); Gee, Michaels, and O'Connor (1992); Gilmore and Glatthorn (1982); Green and Dixon (1993); Kantor, Miller, and Fernie (1992). Also, see reviews by Cazden (1988) and Hicks (1995). For examples of how researchers have brought conceptually different perspectives into deliberate juxtaposition, see and Green and Harker (1988).

[11]Any speech data can be transcribed in more or less detailed ways such that we get a continuum of possible transcripts ranging from very detailed (what linguists call "narrow") to much less detailed (what linguists call "broad"). The purposes of the analysis are to determine how narrow or broad the transcript must be, what is represented, and how the transcript itself is formatted. For theoretical discussions related to transcribing, see Baker (1997); Green, Franquiz, and Dixon (1997); and Ochs (1979).

[12]Given the scope of work in this area, the citations were selected to show a range of perspectives that are currently being used to construct understandings of teaching-learning processes within educational settings. Some of these studies were conducted within education, while others were used as part of the theoretical basis of studies within education.

[13]This ethnographic research was conducted from 1991–1997. Five dissertations have been completed on data across years in this classroom, each providing an analysis of particular class essays or a whole-class analysis of essays. In addition, a number of articles have been written about life in this classroom by varying groups of authors. For a complete list of publications, please contact Judith Green (e-mail: green@education.ucsb.edu) or Carol Dixon (e-mail: dixon@education.ucsb.edu).

[14]We use these two terms, *hands on* and *minds on*, to represent a way of viewing such activities that is often discussed in science education literature.

## REFERENCES

Baker, C. (1997). Transcription and representation in literacy research. In J. Flood, S. B. Heath, & D. Lapp (Eds.), *Research on teaching literacy through the communicative and visual arts*. New York: Macmillan.

Baker, C., & Luke, A. (Eds.). (1991). *Toward a critical sociology of reading pedagogy.* Amsterdam: John Benjamins.

Bakhtin, M. (1981). *The dialogic imagination.* Austin: University of Texas Press. (Original work published 1935)

Bakhtin, M. (1986). *Speech genres and other late essays.* Austin: University of Texas Press.

Barsalou, L. W. (1991). Deriving categories to achieve goals. In G. H. Bower (Ed.), *The psychology of learning and motivation: Advances in research and theory* (Vol. 27, pp. 1–64). New York: Academic Press.

Barsalou, L. W. (1992). *Cognitive psychology: An overview for cognitive scientists.* Hillsdale, NJ: Erlbaum.

Bauman, R. (1986). *Story, performance, and event: Contextual studies of oral narrative.* Cambridge, England: Cambridge University Press.

Bazerman, C. (1989). *Shaping written knowledge.* Madison: University of Wisconsin Press.

Billig, M. (1987). *Arguing and thinking: A rhetorical approach to social psychology.* Cambridge, England: Cambridge University Press.

Birdwhistell, R. (1977). Some discussion of ethnography, theory, and method. In J. Brockman (Ed.), *About Bateson: Essays on Gregory Bateson* (pp. 103–144). New York: Dutton.

Bleicher, R. (1994). High school students presenting science: An interactional sociolinguistic analysis. *Journal of Research in Science Teaching, 31,* 697–719.

Blom, J. P., & Gumperz, J. J. (1972). Social meaning in linguistic structures: Code switching in Norway. In J. Gumperz & D. Hymes (Eds.), *Directions in sociolinguistics.* New York: Holt, Rinehart & Winston.

Bloome, D. (Ed.). (1987). *Literacy and schooling.* Norwood, NJ: Ablex.

Bloome, D., & Bailey, F. (1991). Educational contexts of literacy. *Annual Review of Applied Linguistics, 12,* 49–70.

Bloome, D., & Egan-Robertson, A. (1993). The social construction of intertextuality in classroom reading and writing lessons. *Reading Research Quarterly, 28,* 304–333.

Bloome, D., & Green, J. L. (1984). Directions in sociolinguistic study of reading. In P. D. Pearson, M. Kamil, R. Barr, & P. Mosenthal (Eds.), *Handbook on research on reading.* New York: Longman.

Briggs, C. (1986). *Learning how to ask: A sociolinguistic appraisal of the role of the interview in social science research.* Cambridge, England: Cambridge University Press.

Carbaugh, D. (1996). *Situating selves: The communication of social identities in American scenes.* Albany: State University of New York Press.

Carlsen, W. S. (1992). Closing down the conversation: Discouraging student talk on unfamiliar science content. *Journal of Classroom Interaction, 27*(2), 15–21.

Carspecken, P. F. (1996). *Critical ethnography in educational research: A theoretical and practical guide.* New York: Routledge.

Cazden, C. (1986). Classroom discourse. In M. Wittrock (Ed.), *The handbook for research on teaching* (pp. 432–463). New York: Macmillan.

Cazden, C. (1988). *Classroom discourse: The language of teaching and learning.* Portsmouth, NH: Heinemann.

Christie, F. (1995). Pedagogic discourse in the primary school. *Linguistics and Education, 7,* 221–242.

Clark, A. (1993). *Associative engines: Connectionism, concepts, and representational change.* Cambridge, England: Cambridge University Press.

Clark, A. (1997). *Being there: Putting brain, body, and world together again.* Cambridge, MA: MIT Press.

Clark, H. H. (1996). *Using language.* Cambridge, England: Cambridge University Press.

Cochran, J. (1997). What's "common" in a common curriculum: How course structure shapes disciplinary knowledge. *Journal of Classroom Interaction, 32*(2).

Cole, M. (1996). *Culture in mind.* Cambridge, MA: Harvard University Press.

Collins, J. (1987). Using cohesion analysis to understand access to knowledge. In D. Bloome (Ed.), *Literacy and schooling* (pp. 70–98). Norwood, NJ: Ablex.

Cook-Gumperz, J. (Ed.). (1986). *The social construction of literacy.* New York: Cambridge University Press.

Crawford, T., Chen, C., & Kelly, G. J. (1997). Creating authentic opportunities for presenting science: The influence of audience on student talk. *Journal of Classroom Interaction, 32*(2), 1–13.

D'Andrade, R., & Strauss, C. (Eds.). (1992). *Human motives and cultural models.* Cambridge, England: Cambridge University Press.

Del Rio, P., & Alvarez, A. (1995). Directivity: The cultural and educational construction of morality and agency. Some questions arising from the legacy of Vygotsky. *Anthropology and Education Quarterly, 26,* 384–409.

Duran, R. (Ed.). (1995). Literacy among Latinos: Focus on school contexts [Special issue]. *Discourse Processes, 19*(1).

Duranti, A., & Goodwin, C. (Eds.). (1992). *Rethinking context: Language as an interactive phenomenon.* Cambridge, England: Cambridge University Press.

Edwards, D., & Potter, J. (1992). *Discursive psychology.* London: Sage.

Edwards, V., & Furlong, A. (1978). *The language of the classroom: Meaning in classroom interaction.* London: Heinemann.

Edwards, D., & Mercer, N. (1987). *Common knowledge: The development of understanding in the classroom.* New York: Falmer.

Erickson, F. (1979). On standards of descriptive validity in studies of classroom activity (Occasional Paper #16). East Lansing, MI: Institute for Research on Teaching.

Erickson, F. (1982). Taught cognitive learning in its immediate environment: A neglected topic in the anthropology of education. *Anthropology and Education Quarterly, 13*(2), 149–179.

Erickson, F. (1986). Qualitative research. In M. Wittrock (Ed.), *The handbook for research on teaching* (pp. 119–161). New York: Macmillan.

Erickson, F., & Shultz, J. (1981). When is a context? Some issues and methods in the analysis of social competence. In J. Green & C. Wallat (Ed.), *Ethnography and language in educational settings* (pp. 147–160). Norwood, NJ: Ablex.

Ervin-Tripp, S. (1972). On sociolinguistic rules: Alternation and co-occurrence. In J. Gumperz & D. Hymes (Eds.), *Directions in sociolinguistics: The ethnography of communication.* New York: Holt, Rinehart & Winston.

Evertson, C., & Green, J. L. (1986). Observation as inquiry and method. In M. Wittrock (Ed.), *The third handbook for research on teaching* (pp. 162–213). New York: Macmillan.

Fairclough, N. (1989). *Language and power.* London: Longman.

Fairclough, N. (1992). *Discourse and social change.* Cambridge, England: Polity Press.

Fairclough, N. (1993). Critical discourse analysis and the marketization of public discourse: The universities. *Discourse and Society, 4,* 122–169.

Fairclough, N. (1995). *Critical discourse analysis.* London: Longman.

Fernie, D., Davies, B., Kantor, R., & McMurray, P. (1993). Becoming a person in the preschool: Creating integrated gender, school culture, and peer culture positionings. *Qualitative Studies in Education, 6,* 95–110.

Floriani, A. (1993). Negotiating what counts: Roles and relationships, texts and contexts, content and meaning. *Linguistics and Education, 5,* 241–274.

Frake, C. O. (1977). Plying frames can be dangerous: Some reflections on methodology in cognitive anthropology. *Quarterly Newsletter of the Institute for Comparative Human Development, 3,* 1–7.

Garfinkel, H., Lynch, M., & Livingston, E. (1981). The work of discovering science construed with materials from the optically discovered pulsar. *Philosophy of the Social Sciences, 11,* 131–158.

Gaskin, S., Miller, P. J., & Corsaro, W. A. (1993). Theoretical and methodological perspectives in the interpretive study of children. In W. A. Corsaro & P. J. Miller (Eds.), *Interpretive approaches to children's socialization.* San Francisco: Jossey-Bass.

Gee, J. P. (1992). *The social mind: Language, ideology, and social practice.* New York: Bergin & Garvey.

Gee, J. P. (1996). *Social linguistics and literacies: Ideology in discourses* (2nd ed.). London: Taylor & Francis.

Gee, J. P., Hull, G., & Lankshear, C. (1996). *The new work order: Behind the language of the new capitalism.* Boulder, CO: Westview.

Gee, J. P., Michaels, S., O'Connor, C. (1992). Discourse analysis. In M. D. LeCompte, W. Millroy, & J. Preissle (Eds.), *Handbook of qualitative research in education* (pp. 227–291). New York: Academic Press.

Geertz, C. (1983). *Local knowledge.* New York: Basic Books.

Giddens, A. (1990). *Central problems in social theory: Action, structure and contradiction in social analysis.* Los Angeles: University of California Press.

Gilmore, P., & Glatthorn, A. (1982). *Children in and out of school.* Washington, DC: Center for Applied Linguistics/Ablex.

Goffman, I. (1981). *Forms of talk.* Philadelphia: University of Pennsylvania Press.

Golden, J. (1990). *Constructing a text: Narrative symbol in childhood literature.* Berlin: Aldine de Gruyter.

Goodwin, C. (1981). *Conversational organization: Interaction between speakers and hearers.* New York: Academic Press.

Goodwin, C., & Heritage, J. (1990). Conversation analysis. *Annual Review of Anthropology, 19,* 283–307.

Goodwin, M. H. (1990). *He-said-she-said: Talk as social organization among Black children.* Bloomington: Indiana University Press.

Green, J. (1983). Teaching as a linguistic process: A state of the art. In E. Gordon (Ed.), *Review of research in education* (Vol. 10, pp. 151–252). Washington, DC: American Educational Research Association.

Green, J., & Bloome, D. (1997). Ethnography and ethnographers of and in education: A situated perspective. In J. Flood, S. Brice Heath, & D. Lapp (Eds.), *Research on teaching literacy through the communicative and visual arts* (pp. 181–202). New York: Macmillan.

Green, J., & Bloome, D. (1983). Ethnography and reading: Issues, approaches, criteria and findings. In *Thirty-second yearbook of the National Reading Conference* (pp. 6–30). Rochester, NY: National Reading Conference.

Green, J., & Dixon, C. (1993). Talking knowledge into being: Discursive practices in classrooms. *Linguistics and Education, 5,* 231–239.

Green, J., Franquiz, M., & Dixon, C. (1997). The myth of the objective transcript. *TESOL Quarterly, 31,* 172–176.

Green, J., & Harker, C. (Eds.). (1988). *Multiple perspective analyses of classroom discourse.* Norwood, NJ: Ablex.

Green, J. L., & Harker, J. O. (1992). Gaining access to learning: Controversial, social, and cognitive demands of instructional conversation. In L. C. Wilkinson (Ed.), *Communicating in the classroom* (pp. 183–222). New York: Academic Press.

Green, J., & Wallat, C. (1981). Mapping instructional conversations: A sociolinguistic ethnography. In J. Green & C. Wallat (Eds.), *Ethnography and language in educational settings* (pp. 161–205). Norwood, NJ: Ablex.

Gumperz, J. J. (1982a). *Discourse strategies.* Cambridge, England: Cambridge University Press.

Gumperz, J. J. (Ed.). (1982b). *Language and social identity.* Cambridge, England: Cambridge University Press.

Gumperz, J. (1986). Interactional sociolinguistics. In J. Cook-Gumperz (Ed.), *The social construction of literacy* (pp. 45–68). New York: Cambridge University Press.

Gumperz, J. J. (1992). Contextualization and understanding. In A. Duranti & C. Goodwin (Eds.), *Rethinking context: Language as an interactive phenomenon* (pp. 229–252). Cambridge, England: Cambridge University Press.

Gumperz, J. J., & Levinson, S. C. (Eds.). (1996). *Rethinking linguistic relativity.* Cambridge, England: Cambridge University Press.

Halliday, M. A. K., & Hasan, R. (1976). *Cohesion in English.* London: Longman.

Hanks, W. F. (1990). *Referential practice: Language and lived space among the Maya.* Chicago: University of Chicago Press.

Hanks, W. F. (1995). *Language and communicative practices.* Bolder, CO: Westview Press.

Harkness, S., Super, C. M., & Keefer, C. H. (1992). Learning how to be an American parent: How cultural models gain directive force. In R. D'Andrade & C. Strauss (Eds.), *Human motives and cultural models* (pp. 163-178). Cambridge, England: Cambridge University Press,

Harre, R., & Gillett, G. (1994). *The discursive mind.* Thousand Oaks, CA: Sage.

Heap, J. (1980). What counts as reading. Limits to certainty in assessment. *Curriculum Inquiry, 10,* 265–292.

Heap, J. (1991). A situated perspective on what counts as reading. In C. Baker & A. Luke (Eds.), *Toward a critical sociology of reading pedagogy.* Philadelphia: John Benjamins.

Heath, S. (1982). Ethnography in education: Defining the essential. In P. Gilmore & A. Glatthorn (Eds.), *Children in and out of school* (pp. 33–58). Washington, DC: Center for Applied Linguistics.

Heritage, J. (1984). *Garfinkel and ethnomethodology.* Oxford, England: Basil Blackwell.

Hicks, D. (1995). Discourse, learning, and teaching. In M. W. Apple (Ed.), *Review of research in education* (Vol. 21, pp. 49–95). Washington, DC: American Educational Research Association.

Hofstadter, D. R. (1997). *Le ton beau de Marot: In praise of the music of language.* New York: Basic Books.

Holland, D., & Quinn, N. (Eds.). (1987). *Cultural models in language and thought.* Cambridge, England: Cambridge University Press.

Hutchins, E. (1995). *Cognition in the wild.* Cambridge, MA: MIT Press.

Hymes, D. (1974). *Foundations of sociolinguistics.* Philadelphia: University of Pennsylvania Press.

Hymes, D. (1996). *Ethnography, linguistics, narrative inequality: Towards an understanding of voice.* London: Taylor & Francis.

Hymes, D. (1977). Critique. *Anthropology & Education Quarterly, 8,* 91–93.

Ivanic, R. (1994). I is for interpersonal: Discoursal construction of writer identities and the teaching of writing. *Linguistics and Education, 6*(1), 3–15.

John-Steiner, V., Panofsky, C. P., & Smith, L. W. (Eds.). (1994). *Sociocultural approaches to language and literacy: An interactionist perspective.* Cambridge, England: Cambridge University Press.

Kantor, R., Green, J., Bradley, M., & Lin, L. (1992). The construction of schooled repertoire: An interactional sociocultural perspective. *Linguistics and Education, 4,* 131–172.

Kantor, R., Miller, S., & Fernie, D. (1992). Diverse paths to literacy in a preschool classroom: A sociocultural perspective. *Reading Research Quarterly, 27,* 185–201.

Kelly, G. J., & Crawford, T. (1997). An ethnographic investigation of the discourse processes of school science. *Science Education, 81,* 533–559.

Kelly, G. J., & Green, J. (1997). What counts as science in high school and college classrooms? Examining how teachers' knowledge and classroom discourse influence opportunities for learning science. *Journal of Classroom Interaction, 32*(2), 1–3.

Knorr Cetina, K. (1992). The couch, the cathedral, and the laboratory: On the relationship between experiment and laboratory in science. In A. Pickering (Ed.), *Science as practice and culture* (pp. 113–137) Chicago: University of Chicago Press.

Kress, G. (1996). *Before writing: Rethinking paths into literacy.* London: Routledge.

Kress, G., & van Leeuwen, T. (1996). *Reading images: The grammar of visual design.* London: Routledge.

Labov, W. (1969). *The logical of non-standard English* (Georgetown Monographs on Language and Linguistics). Washington, DC: Georgetown University Press.

Latour, B. (1991). *We have never been modern.* Cambridge, MA: Harvard University Press.

Latour, B., & Woolgar, S. (1986). *Laboratory life: The construction of scientific facts.* Princeton, NJ: Princeton University Press.

Lave, J. (1988). *Cognition in practice.* Cambridge, England: Cambridge University Press.

Lave, J. (1996). Teaching, as learning, in practice. *Mind, Culture, and Activity, 3,* 149–164.

Lave, J., & Wenger, E. (1991). *Situated learning: Legitimate peripheral participation.* Cambridge, England: Cambridge University Press.

Lee, D. (1992). *Competing discourses: Perspective and ideology in language.* London: Longman.

Lemke, J. L. (1990). *Talking science.* Norwood, NJ: Ablex.

Leont'ev, A. N. (1978). *Activity, consciousness, and personality.* Englewood Cliffs, NJ: Prentice Hall.

Leont'ev, A. N. (1981). The problem of activity in psychology. In J. V. Wertsch (Ed.), *The concept of activity in Soviet psychology* (pp. 37–71). Armonk, NY: M. E. Sharpe.

Levinson, S. (1983). *Pragmatics.* Cambridge, England: Cambridge University Press.

Levinson, S. (1996). Relativity in spatial conception and description. In J. J. Gumperz & S. C. Levinson (Eds.), *Rethinking linguistic relativity* (pp. 177–202). Cambridge, England: Cambridge University Press.

Lin, L. (1993). Language of and in the classroom: Constructing the patterns of social life. *Linguistics and Education, 5,* 2367–2410.

Luke, A. (1995). Text and discourse in education: An introduction to critical discourse analysis. In M. W. Apple (Ed.), *Review of research in education* (Vol. 21, pp. 3–48). Washington, DC: American Educational Research Association.

Lynch, M. (1993). *Scientific practice and ordinary action: Ethnomethodology and social studies of science.* Cambridge, England: Cambridge University Press.

McDermott, R. P. (1976). *Kids made sense: An ethnographic account of the interactional management of success and failure in one first-grade classroom.* Unpublished doctoral dissertation, Stanford University.

Mehan, H. (1978). Structuring school structure. *Harvard Educational Review, 1,* 32–64.

Mehan, H. (1979). *Learning lessons: Social organization in the classroom.* Cambridge, MA: Harvard University Press.

Mishler, E. G. (1986). *Research interviewing: Context and narrative.* Cambridge, MA: Harvard University Press.

Mishler, E. G. (1990). Validation in inquiry-guided research: The role of exemplars in narrative studies. *Harvard Educational Review, 60,* 415–442.

Mitchell, C. J. (1984). Typicality and the case study. In R. F. Ellens (Ed.), *Ethnographic research: A guide to general conduct* (pp. 238–241). New York: Academic Press.

Moje, E. (1997). Exploring discourse, subjectivity, and knowledge in chemistry class. *Journal of Classroom Interaction, 1,* 35–44.

Myers, G. (1992). *Writing biology: Texts in the social construction of scientific knowledge.* Madison: University of Wisconsin Press.

Ochs, E. (1979). Transcription as theory. In E. Ochs & B. Schieffelin (Eds.), *Developmental pragmatics.* New York: Academic Press.

Ochs, E. (1983). From feelings to grammar: A Samoa case study. In B. Schieffelin & E. Ochs (Eds.), *Language socialization across cultures.* Cambridge, England: Cambridge University Press.

Ochs, E. (1996). Linguistic resources for socializing humanity. In J. J. Gumperz & S. C. Levinson (Eds.), *Rethinking linguistic relativity* (pp. 407-437). Cambridge, England: Cambridge University Press.

Palmer, G. B. (1996). *Toward a theory of cultural linguistics.* Austin: University of Texas Press.

Philips, S. U. (1972). Participant structures and communicative competence: Warm Springs children in community and classroom. In C. Cazden, V. John, & D. Hymes (Eds.), *Functions of language in the classroom.* New York: Teachers College Press.

Philips, S. U. (1974). *The invisible culture.* New York: Teachers College Press.

Pickering, A. (1995). *The mangle of practice: Time, agency, and science.* Chicago: University of Chicago Press.

Psathas, G. (1995). *Conversation analysis.* Thousand Oaks, CA: Sage.

Rieber, R. W., & Carton, A. S. (1987). *The collected works of L. S. Vygotsky: Vol. 1. Problems of general psychology.* New York: Plenum.

Rogoff, B. (1990). *Apprenticeship in thinking: Cognitive development in social context.* New York: Oxford University Press.

Rogoff, B., & Lave, J. (Eds.). (1984). *Everyday cognition: Its development in social context.* Cambridge, MA: Harvard University Press.

Rosebery, A. S., Puttick, G. M., & Bodwell, M. B. (1996). *"How much light does a plant need?": Questions, data, and theories in a second grade classroom.* Portsmouth, NH: Heinemann.

Santa Barbara Classroom Discourse Group. (1992). Constructing literacy in classrooms: Literate action as social accomplishment. In H. Marshall (Ed.), *Redefining student learning: Roots of educational change* (pp. 119–150). Norwood, NJ: Ablex.

Scollon, R., & Scollon, S. B. K. (1981). *Narrative, literacy, and face in interethnic communication.* Norwood, NJ: Ablex.

Searle, J. (1969). *Speech acts: An essay in the philosophy of language.* Cambridge, England: Cambridge University Press.

Shapin, S., & Schaffer, S. (1985). *Leviathan and the air-pump: Hobbes, Boyle and the experimental life.* Princeton, NJ: Princeton University Press.

Shore, B. (1996). *Culture in mind: Cognition, culture, and the problem of meaning.* New York: Oxford University Press.

Sinclair, J. M., & Coulthard, M. (1975). *Towards an analysis of discourse: The English used by teachers and pupils.* Oxford, England: Oxford University Press.

Souza Lima, E. (1995). Culture revisited: Vygotsky's ideas in Brazil. *Anthropology and Education Quarterly, 26,* 443–457.

Sperber, D., & Wilson, D. (1986). *Relevance: Communication and cognition.* Oxford, England: Blackwell.

Spindler, G., & Spindler, L. (Eds.). (1987). *Interpretive ethnography of education: At home and abroad.* Hillsdale, NJ: Erlbaum.

Spradley, J. (1980). *Participant observation.* New York: Holt, Rinehart & Winston.

Strauss, C. (1992). What makes Tony run? Schemas as motives reconsidered. In R. D'Andrade & C. Strauss (Eds.), *Human motives and cultural models* (pp. 197–224). Cambridge, England: Cambridge University Press.

Strike, K. (1974). On the expressive potential of behaviorist language. *American Educational Research Journal, 11,* 103–120.

Stubbs, M. (1983). *Discourse analysis: The sociolinguistic analysis of natural language.* Chicago: University of Chicago Press.

Toolan, M. (1996). *Total speech: An integrational linguistic approach to language.* Durham, NC: Duke University Press.

Toulmin, S. (1970). Does the distinction between normal and revolutionary science hold water? In I. Lakatos & A. Musgrave (Eds.), *Criticism and the growth of knowledge* (pp. 39–47). Cambridge, England: Cambridge University Press.

Toulmin, S. (1972). *Human understanding: Vol. 1. The collective use and evolution of concepts.* Princeton, NJ: Princeton University Press.

Tuyay, S., Floriani, A., Yeager, B., Dixon, C., & Green, J. (1995). Constructing an integrated, inquiry-oriented approach in classrooms: A cross case analysis of social, literate and academic practices. *Journal of Classroom Interactions, 30*(4), 1–15.

Tuyay, S., Jennings, L., & Dixon, C. (1995). Classroom discourse and opportunities to learn: An ethnographic study of knowledge construction in a bilingual third-grade classroom. *Discourse Processes, 10,* 75–100.

Ungerer, F., & Schmid, H. J. (1996). *An introduction to cognitive linguistics.* London: Longman.

van Dijk, T. (1972). *Some aspects of text grammars.* The Hague: Mouton.

van Dijk, T. (1977). *Text and context.* London: Longman.

van Dijk, T. (Ed.). (1985). *Handbook of discourse analysis: Vol. 1. Disciplines of discourse.* New York: Academic Press.

van Dijk, T. (1993). Principles of critical discourse analysis. *Discourse and Society, 4,* 249–283.

Volosinov, V. (1973). *Marxism and the philosophy of language.* New York: Seminar.

Vygotsky, L. S. (1978). *Mind in society: The development of higher psychological processes.* Cambridge, MA: Harvard University Press.

Wertsch, J. V. (Ed.). (1981). *The concept of activity in Soviet psychology.* Armonk, NY: M. E. Sharpe.

Wertsch, J. V. (1991). *Voices of the mind: A sociocultural approach to mediated action.* Cambridge, MA: Harvard University Press.

Whiting, J., & Whiting, B. (1959). Contributions of anthropology to methods of studying child rearing. In P. Mussen (Ed.), *Handbook of research methods in child development.* New York: Wiley.

Wieder, D. L., & Pratt, S. (1990). On being a recognizable Indian among Indians. In D. Carbaugh (Ed.), *Cultural communication and intercultural contact* (pp. 45–64). Hillsdale, NJ: Erlbaum.

Wilkinson, L. C. (Ed.). (1992). *Communicating in the classroom.* New York: Academic Press.

Wittgenstein, K. (1953). *Philosophical investigations.* New York: Macmillan.

Wootton, A. (1989). Remarks on the methodology of conversation analysis. In D. Roger & P. Bull (Eds.), *Conversation: An interdisciplinary perspective* (pp. 238–258). Clevedon, England: Multilingual Matters.

Manuscript received June 1, 1997
Accepted December 31, 1997

# Chapter 5

# Quantitative Methods for Studying Social Context in Multilevels and Through Interpersonal Relations

KENNETH A. FRANK

Michigan State University

The connection between a volume on the social organization of learning and a chapter with a title that begins with the words "Quantitative methods . . ." may not seem obvious, especially in view of the fact that so much of our recent socially grounded educational inquiry has been conducted within a qualitative or interpretive paradigm. In this chapter, I attempt to make as strong a case as possible for the importance of quantitative methods in understanding the social organization of learning. I want to argue that both at the level of macroanalysis (considering the effects of different levels of social organization, such as the district, school, and classroom) and at the level of microanalysis (examining relations among individuals in their primary social settings), quantitative methods can help us achieve important insights and understanding about the nature, causes, and consequences of social relations.

Schooling is a complex process because teachers, students, and administrators operate in a diverse set of social contexts.[1] Although they may appear to be isolated in their classroom practices (Cusick, 1983; Hargreaves, 1993; Lortie, 1977), teachers are affected by their social contexts, as they are influenced by others' orientations to teaching and classroom practices (e.g., Rowan, 1990; Trent, 1992; Wilson & Ball, 1991; Zeichner & Gore, 1989). Although principals may make many of the official decisions regarding school policies and practices (Callahan, 1962; Greenfield, 1975; Ingersoll, 1994; Levine & Lezotte, 1990; Smith, Prunty, & Dwyer, 1981), institutional contexts defined across most schools determine the parameters of decision making (Meyer & Rowan, 1977; Rowan, 1995), and relations among faculty and students help generate the organizational context in which many decisions are made (Bidwell & Quiroz, 1991; Firestone & Wilson, 1985; Fuller & Izu, 1986; Johnson, 1990; Lightfoot, 1983; Little, 1984; Rosenholtz, 1989). And though a school may have general policies or structures (Coleman et al., 1966; Peshkin, 1986; Shedd & Bacharach, 1991), the experience of each student, teacher, and administrator is unique, because each person's social context is uniquely defined within and outside the school's walls (Bidwell & Kasarda, 1980; Dreeben & Gamoran, 1986; Pallas, 1988; Sorensen & Hallinan, 1976).

The social contexts are complex because they are defined at multiple levels (Barr & Dreeben, 1977, 1983; Bidwell & Kasarda, 1980; Bray & Thomas, 1995; Keeves & Sellin, 1988; Oosthoeck & van den Eeden, 1984) and through relations among a variety of people in a common setting (Barr & Dreeben, 1983; Bidwell

In addition to thanking my reviewers, I would like to thank Charles Bidwell for his thoughtful comments on an earlier draft of this work.

& Kasarda, 1980; Dreeben & Barr, 1988; Epstein & Karweit, 1983; Gamoran, 1987; Lazersfeld & Menzel, 1961; Miskel & Ogawa, 1988; Staessens, 1993; Schein, 1985). Each individual—whether student, teacher, or administrator—experiences "multilevels" of the school as an institution, a unique organization, and a unique set of individual experiences. Institutionalized aspects of schooling include the authority of teachers, systems for grouping by ability, courses offered within departments, definitions of special education, and evaluation according to external criteria (e.g., standardized multiple-choice tests, portfolio assessment). These institutions are established outside of the school walls and, therefore, can be defined in terms of relations and processes of widely shared societal understandings of schooling (DiMaggio & Powell, 1991; Mehan, Hertweck, & Meihls, 1986; Meyer & Rowan, 1991; Waller, 1932). For example, Pallas, Entwisle, Alexander, and Stluka (1994) argue that "ability grouping is pervasive because it is taken for granted as a rational way to organize instruction to improve students' achievement" (p. 29), even though students may be matched to groups through a nonrational process (DeLany, 1991; Riehl & Pallas, 1992). As teachers develop understandings of subject matter and expectations for learning, they too encounter institutionalized aspects of schooling that are defined beyond the walls of the school. For example, teachers' approaches to teaching are affected by the subject they teach (Bidwell, Frank, & Quiroz, 1997; Grossman & Stodolsky, 1995), the sector in which they teach (Bryk, Lee, & Holland, 1993), and the values and norms associated with the socioeconomic status of the students they teach (Metz, 1990).

The school as an organization also affects the schooling experience. As members of a school interact and influence one another, they develop shared understandings, educational practices, and mechanisms for decision making (Bidwell et al., 1997; Bird & Little, 1986; Johnson, 1990; Lightfoot, 1983; Little, 1984; Rosenholtz, 1989; Rowan, 1990). For example, faculty, administrators, and students construct shared meanings of gender (Canada & Pringle, 1995; Hall & Sandler, 1982; Nias, 1989; see Brophy, 1985, for a review), with important effects on students' achievement and attitudes (Lee, Marks, & Byrd, 1994). In the aggregate, these relations partly define the school as a unique organization that affects each person in the school (Alexander & Pallas, 1985; Barker & Gump, 1964; Barr & Dreeben, 1983; Bryk & Driscoll, 1988; Gamoran, 1987; Lazersfeld & Menzel, 1961; McDermott & Aron, 1978; Mehan et al., 1986; Miskel & Ogawa, 1988; Ogbu, 1978; Sarason, 1971; Schein, 1985; Spradley & McCurdy, 1972; Staessens, 1993). Gamoran (1991) refers to this as the additive model, in which schooling experiences equally affect each student.

But schooling experiences are unique for each individual, partly through the unique actions of other people to which each person is exposed and partly through the unique background experiences that each person brings to the school that frames the school experience (Bidwell & Kasarda, 1980; Murnane, 1975; Pallas, 1988; Sorensen & Hallinan, 1976; Summers & Wolfe, 1977). For example, students will encounter markedly different schooling experiences depending on the track to which they are assigned (Alexander, Cook, & McDill, 1978; Eder, 1981; Hansell & Karweit, 1983; Heyns, 1974; Oakes, 1985; Sorensen, 1984). Moreover, the institution of tracking tends to reproduce existing differences in students' prior experiences, which vary according to socioeconomic background or race (Bowles & Gintis, 1976; Hollingshead, 1949; Lee & Bryk, 1989; Oakes, 1985; Rosenbaum, 1976). Gamoran (1991) refers to this as the interactive model, in which the effects of schooling characteristics interact with student characteristics to shape schooling experiences.

Much of our understanding of the complexity of the organization of schooling comes from analyses of qualitative data. In particular, research has recently focused on the institutions of schooling as well as elements unique to teachers and classrooms within a school, thus differentiating the multilevels at which schooling occurs (e.g., Anstead & Goodson, 1993; Mehan, 1992; Riehl & Pallas, 1992). For example, micro-ethnographic analyses have characterized laws and cultural institutions that define the contexts for decisions regarding students' needs for special education (e.g., Erickson & Shultz, 1982; Mehan, 1992; Mehan et al., 1986).

Traditional methods for quantitative analyses have a moderate capacity to address the complex process of schooling. Using the general linear model (i.e., regression and analysis of variance), one can estimate the effects of attributes of people on their schooling experiences, and, through multiple regression, one can control for important covariates. Furthermore, using terms representing the interaction of two attributes, one can model how effects of attributes vary across contexts (e.g., Hannaway & Talbert, 1993). But the interpretation of significance values based on distributional assumptions (i.e, parametric analyses) typically requires that error terms—the part of an outcome that cannot be explained by observed factors—be *independent* and identically distributed. This assumption is in direct contrast to the characterization of schools as complex organizations partially defined by *relations among people* affiliated with the school.

Until recently, most quantitative analyses including more than one person affiliated with a given school simply did not account for dependencies among the observations (e.g., Bowles & Gintis, 1976; Coleman et al., 1966; Dreeben & Gamoran, 1986; Epstein & Karwait, 1983; Kilgore & Pendleton, 1993). These analyses used models that did not represent the nested nature of the phenomena, with negative consequences for statistical inference (Bryk & Raudenbush, 1992). Others have met the statistical assumption of independent error terms by analyzing data aggregated to the school level; thus, they have eliminated the difficulty introduced by dependencies among observations within a single school (e.g., Hannaway & Talbert, 1993), by analyzing data from a few schools and accounting for school effects through fixed effects estimation (e.g., Hallinan, 1992), or by analyzing observations from different schools (e.g., Chew, 1992). Although we can learn of commonalities across schools from such data, theoretical and mathematical models built from these data necessarily ignore the complex processes within schools as organizations. In these cases, the statistical tail is doing the wagging.

In this chapter, I consider two recent advances in quantitative methods that can help us to understand schooling as a complex process. First, *multilevel models* help account for one source of dependency among teachers and students, the common schools with which they are affiliated. Multilevel models also can be used to represent and estimate how characteristics of individuals covary according to school context. Second, quantitative analyses of *social network* data (e.g., who talks to whom or who influences whom) can help characterize and model the effects of *inter*dependencies among the people in a school. In the next section, I illustrate the importance of multilevel models by reviewing work by Lee and Smith (1995) representing some of the effects of social contexts, such as student socioeconomic status and school engagement in restructuring, as well as the interaction of these two effects. I then discuss social network analysis as a way of identifying the intraschool processes that generate differences in social contexts of schooling. I conclude by calling for extensions of social network analysis to a multilevel framework so as to more adequately capture the social processes of schooling.

## MULTILEVEL MODELS: EFFECTS OF SOCIAL CONTEXTS AT THE INDIVIDUAL AND SCHOOL LEVELS

In the preceding section, I distinguished between social context defined at the level of the school (in terms of shared understandings, school culture, decision making, etc.) and social context defined at the level of individuals (e.g., in terms of students' socioeconomic background or the subject taught by a teacher). Effects at multiple levels can be addressed with multilevel models, and in this section I familiarize the reader with multilevel models through a discussion and graphical representation of Lee and Smith's (1995) application estimating school and student effects on student achievement (for a full introduction to multilevel models, see Bryk & Raudenbush, 1992; Goldstein, 1995; Longford, 1993; Raudenbush & Bryk, 1988). I then discuss recent developments in multilevel models that have particular applications to the study of social contexts in schools.

Multilevel models, introduced in education in the 1980s, are ideally suited to incorporating features of social contexts defined at the level of the individual and school (Burstein, 1980; Goldstein, 1987; Raudenbush & Bryk, 1986, 1988). Indeed, many of the initial applications incorporated elements of both student context (e.g., socioeconomic status, curricular track placement) and school context (e.g., sense of community, size) (Bryk & Raudenbush, 1988; Lee & Bryk, 1989; Raudenbush & Bryk, 1986, 1988). Multilevel models expand the types of questions that can be asked by incorporating terms typically not specified in single-level models and provide more powerful tests and accurate estimates of effects at each level.

The relatively recent example in Lee and Smith (1995) represents the power of these analyses when combined with nationally representative data such as that from the National Educational Longitudinal Study (NELS).[2] The following multilevel model represents a simplified version of one of the analyses conducted by Lee and Smith:

*At the student level (level* 1):
*gain in achievement*$_{ij}$ = $\beta_{0j}$ + $\beta_{1j}$ *socioeconomic status*$_{ij}$ + $r_{ij}$.  (1)

*At the school level (level* 2):
$\beta_{0j} = \gamma_{00} + \gamma_{01} PCR_j + u_{0j}$, *and*
$\beta_{1j} = \gamma_{10} + \gamma_{11} PCR_j + u_{1j}$.

Several features of the model are worthy of comment. First, unlike earlier models estimated on data from the High School and Beyond study, Lee and Smith were able to incorporate measures from NELS regarding prior achievement. Lee and Smith chose to incorporate two measures of achievement (measured in 8th and 10th grades) by defining their outcome as the gain in achievement over the 2-year period (the primary alternative would have been to use 8th-grade achievement as a covariate in a model of 10th-grade achievement).

Gain scores, or difference scores, have been much criticized as "unreliable" (e.g., Bereiter, 1963; Linn & Slinde, 1977; see Willett, 1988, for a review); more recently, however, the deficiencies of difference scores have been described as "*perceived* rather than *actual, imaginary* rather than *real*" (Willett, 1988, p. 367; see also Rogosa, Brandt, & Zimowski, 1982; Rogosa & Willett, 1983; Zimmerman, Brotohusodo, & Williams, 1981). The difference score is an unbiased measure of the true change in an outcome, a reasonable measure of growth when one has data from only two time points (Willett, 1988). Moreover Allison (1990, pp. 107–109) recommends the use of the difference score partially based on whether the pretest is unrelated to the "treatment." In this case, the type of high school that a student experiences (the "treatment") is more likely to depend on geography than on the student's eighth-grade math achievement. (See also Willett, 1988, pp. 366–380, for a discussion of difference scores. See Plewis, 1991, or Friedkin & Thomas, 1997, for alternatives using pretest as a covariate. See Willms & Raudenbush, 1989, or Patterson, 1991, for alternatives using repeated cross-sectional designs.)

Next, note that the double subscript in the student-level model references observations for each student $i$ in school $j$. The second subscript, $j$, effectively allows one to conceptualize a regression in each school $j$. Thus, on the right-hand side of the student-level model, we define $\beta_0$ and $\beta_1$ uniquely for each school $j$, and we write $\beta_{0j}$ and $\beta_{1j}$. $\beta_{0j}$ represents the intercept in school $j$, thus capturing the unique average gain in achievement for students in school $j$ (assuming that the predictor, socioeconomic status, is centered around the school mean socioeconomic status; see Bryk & Raudenbush, 1992, pp. 25–31, for a discussion of centering). Similarly, $\beta_{1j}$ captures the unique relationship between socioeconomic status and gain in achievement in school $j$. Socioeconomic status, affecting the child's context in the home, has consistently been shown to affect outcomes associated with schooling such as students' aspirations, interest in school, and achievement (Apple, 1979; Bowles & Gintis, 1976; Eder, 1981; Gamoran, 1996; Hollingshead, 1949; Lee & Bryk, 1989; Lee & Smith, 1993).

Finally, the student-level model includes a unique error term for student $i$ in school $j$, $r_{ij}$, indicating that each student's gain in achievement will not be perfectly predicted by the regression equation in his or her school. In most applications of multilevel models, the errors are assumed to be normally distributed and have constant variance, $\sigma^2$, across schools. This assumption is comparable to the assumption in the general linear model in that residual variation is assumed to be constant across units.

Moving to the school-level model, the intercept and regression slopes (in this case, $\beta_{0j}$ and $\beta_{1j}$) are modeled as functions of school-level predictors (Burstein, 1980). Here Lee and Smith model school mean gains in achievement, represented by $\beta_{0j}$, as a function of whether or not the school engages in practices consistent with restructuring (PCR). PCR is a recent reform in schools challenging many of the prevailing institutions of schooling that segregate faculty and students (Carnegie Council on Adolescent Development, 1989; Carnegie Task Force on Teaching as a Profession, 1986; Lee & Smith, 1993; National Commission on Excellence in Education, 1983; Weiss, 1995). In particular, Lee and Smith defined schools as engaging in PCR, practices consistent with traditional reform (PCT), or no reform practices on the basis of items indicating the extent to which the school challenged traditional organizational structure by encouraging interdisciplinary teaching, mixed-ability classes, staff problem solving, parent volunteers, flexible class times, cooperative learning, and so forth. Note that these distinctions are defined at the level of the school and, thus, are modeled on the average gain in achievement in the school.

The $u_{0j}$ term in the model for $\beta_{0j}$ represents the unique effect of school $j$ on student gains in achievement after the effect of PCR has been controlled. That is, it can be considered the error in the model for $\beta_{0j}$. One of the basic analyses involved in multilevel modeling is a comparison of the variation (referred to as $\tau_0$) of errors at the school level and the variation ($\sigma^2$) of errors at the student level.

A key aspect of the multilevel framework is that it facilitates the specification of interaction effects crossing school-level and individual-level factors. In this case, the relationship between socioeconomic status and gain in achievement in school $j$, represented by $\beta_{1j}$, is modeled as a function of whether or not the school engages in PCR. The research question here might be as follows: Does the effect of socioeconomic status on gain in achievement depend on whether or not a school engages in PCR? The $u_{1j}$ then represent the unique component of the $\beta_{1j}$ that cannot be attributed to whether or not the school engages in PCR.

Lee and Smith estimated models similar to those in Equation 1 for gains in mathematics achievement. In an initial model, Lee and Smith differentiated between variation at the student level and variation at the school level. They found that approximately 15% of the variation in gains in mathematics achievement was between schools. While modest, this amount is not inconsequential from a policy-making standpoint. First, schools may represent the most important institutional effect on achievement, with effects of other institutions more difficult to specify. Second, we can identify and therefore potentially change those aspects of schools that are linked to achievement. Still, as I turn to an interpretation of the effects of school organization, it is helpful to keep in mind that the school-level factors used by Lee and Smith can explain at most only 15% of the variation in student achievement.

Next, Lee and Smith found that, on average, students in PCR schools gained .86 more in standardized mathematics scores than students in schools that engaged in

PCT ($\hat{\gamma}_{01} = .86, p \le .001$).[3] This is consistent with the argument that a school-level policy of restructuring can affect achievement, and the evidence is more powerful when one considers that the reported effect of PCR is net of controls for a host of other characteristics of schools (e.g., academic emphasis, course-taking patterns, and sector), as well as student composition (e.g., mean prior ability in other content areas, minority concentration, and average socioeconomic status).

Lee and Smith also found that the relationship between socioeconomic status and achievement was not as strong in schools engaged in PCR as those engaged in PCT. In schools that engaged in PCR, a one-unit increase in socioeconomic status was estimated to be associated with an increase of .16 ($\hat{\gamma}_{10} + \hat{\gamma}_{11} = .38 - .22 = .16$) in mathematics achievement, while the effect was estimated at .38 ($\hat{\gamma}_{10} = .38$) in PCT schools (the difference in the two effects was established by testing the significance of $\hat{\gamma}_{11}$, which, in this case, indicated $p \leq .01$). Thus, the advantages of high socioeconomic status are greater in schools that have not actively broken down many of the barriers that segment students and teachers.

The regression lines representing the relationship between socioeconomic status and gain in mathematics achievement in 20 hypothetical schools (10 PCT and 10 PCR) shown in Figure 1 are based on the findings of Lee and Smith. For example, the regression line for School 1 is determined by the intercept ($\beta_{01} = 1.85$) and slope ($\beta_{11} = 1.4$, indicating that the expected gain in mathematics achievement increases 1.4 units for a 1-unit increase in socioeconomic status). In Figure 1, one can roughly observe that the average intercept and slope are different between the two types of schools. The intercepts, the predicted gains in mathematics achievement for an average student, are slightly higher in PCR schools than in schools engaging in PCT (note that three of the four highest intercepts are for PCR schools, while three of the four lowest intercepts are for schools engaging in PCT). Differences among the sets of slopes are more difficult to discern, although there are several PCT schools with relatively steep slopes.

Figure 1 also helps to differentiate the two sets of error terms. Clearly, students' gains in achievement are not completely determined by any single aspect of their social contexts, in this case their socioeconomic status and the type of school they attend. Thus, the error term for Student 1 in School 1, $r_{11}$, is indicated as the deviance of the observation from the regression line, where the regression line in School 1 is given by $\beta_{01}$ and $\beta_{11}$ (to accurately represent the findings in Lee and Smith, the variance of the residuals in School 1 would have to be four times greater than the variance of the intercepts; the variance of the residuals is reduced in the figure for visual clarity). Equally as clear, the average level of gain in mathematics achievement and the relationship between gain in mathematics achievement and socioeconomic status are not completely determined by whether the school engages in PCR or PCT. Thus, the school-level errors are captured in the deviation of a given intercept, $u_{0j}$, from the overall average for that type of school, and errors in the school-level slopes are captured in the deviation of a given slope, $u_{1j}$, from the average slope for that type of school.[4] Thus, we again observe two fundamental sources of variation in schooling effects: Those associated with students and those associated with schools.

Consideration of the differences in the regression lines between the two groups relative to the variation should serve as a caution against overinterpreting effects

**FIGURE 1**

**Mathematics Gains by Socioeconomic Status Unique for Each School**

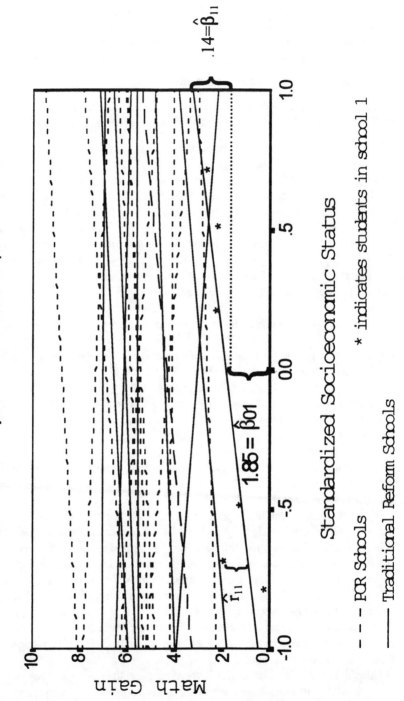

found to be significant in large samples (there were 820 schools in the sample). Nonetheless, the differences in regression lines found by Lee and Smith have important implications for school policy. Although the effect of PCR on the relationship between socioeconomic status and gain in mathematics achievement does not appear large in Figure 2 (defined for the same dimensions as the variable slopes in Figure 1), note that the predicted difference in gain in mathematics achievement between a student of moderately low socioeconomic status and a student of moderately high socioeconomic status in schools engaged in PCT would be .76, nearly three fourths of a standard deviation, while it would be only .32, about a third of a standard deviation, in PCR schools (these effects were again estimated while controlling for many of the most important alternative explanations for achievement gains). In a school engaged in *PCT* we expect a student of moderately high socioeconomic status to gain about three fourths more of a standard deviation in mathematics achievement during the first two years of high school than her schoolmate who is of moderately low socioeconomic status. In a school engaged in *PCR* we would expect this difference to be reduced by 50%, to about a third of a standard deviation. Furthermore, the effects of PCR schools just reported are in comparison with schools engaged in other, more traditional reforms. The effects of PCR on gain in mathematics achievement and on the relationship between socioeconomic status and gain in mathematics achievement would be approximately 50% stronger if comparisons were made with schools that engaged in no reform practices at all (as given in Lee & Smith, Table 6). By using multilevel models, Lee and Smith have demonstrated that the social context defined by a school's organization affects students' learning, as well as the relationship between the student's social context (in this case, measured as his or her socioeconomic status) and learning.

Multilevel models are now being broadly used to specify and estimate effects of schools on students (e.g., Gamoran, 1996; Lee & Bryk, 1989; Lee & Smith, 1993, 1996; Lee et al., 1997; Portes & MacLeod, 1996), parents (Kerbow & Bernhardt, 1993), and teachers (Bidwell et al., 1997; Lee & Smith, 1991). Many of these models become quite sophisticated at disentangling complex effects. For example, consider a two-level model of factors predicting teachers' orientations to teaching within schools (Bidwell et al., 1997). Critical among the teacher-level predictors is the teacher's subject field. As Grossman and Stodolosky (1995) demonstrated and Bidwell et al. confirmed, mathematics teachers place significantly less stress on a progressivist teaching style (e.g., engaging students in questions and answers, encouraging students to explore their own ideas) than teachers in other fields. Methodologically, the effects of subject fields were treated as fixed in Bidwell et al. by entering a series of dummy variables at the teacher level of a multilevel model. Thus, these dummy variables represent institutionalized aspects of teaching associated with teaching fields. At the second level, the model contained organizational characteristics of schools as well as random effects of schools. Multilevel models have been used to estimate effects of other institutions such as state testing practices (Schiller & Muller, 1997) and tracking (Lee & Bryk, 1989; Pallas et al., 1994). Thus, a basic two-level model can be used to explore institutional and organizational effects.

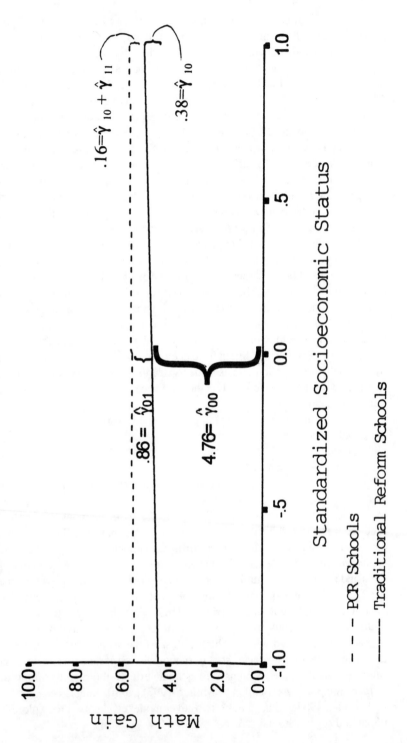

FIGURE 2
Mathematics Gains by Socioeconomic Status Averages Across Schools

- - - PCR Schools

——— Traditional Reform Schools

Because teachers teach more than one class, the preceding analysis by Bidwell et al. (1997) could be extended to three levels of classes within teachers within schools. For example, Raudenbush, Rowan, and Cheong (1993) found that as much as 64% of the variation in teaching approaches was that between classes within mathematics teachers, although the percentage of variation within teachers differed depending on subject area (science: 39%; English: 51%; social studies: 24%). In general, teachers modify their specific goals (as measured by Raudenbush et al.) from class to class more than their general orientations to teaching (as measured by Bidwell et al.), suggesting that teachers may have a general teaching style but that they adapt their approach according to the curricular track of a class, grade level, and so forth.

Three-level models also can be used to assess changes in achievement over several time periods (Level 1) as a function of student characteristics (Level 2) and school characteristics (Level 3) (see Bryk & Raudenbush, 1992, chap. 8, for a general discussion). For example, Raudenbush and Bryk (1988) extended the analysis of growth in terms of difference scores (such as in the example of Lee and Smith) to one of linear growth over several time periods. They found that about 82% of the variation in growth in mathematics achievement was between schools, as opposed to 18% within schools! This finding suggests that we need to do more to explore the causes of variation in mathematics achievement growth at the student and school levels, with potentially important policy implications.

Two-level multilevel models have also been extended to incorporate multiple sources of random effects (Rasbash & Goldstein, 1994; Raudenbush, 1993). For example, Raudenbush (1993) developed a multilevel model including random effects of the schools students attended and the neighborhoods from which they came. Thus, the models include two important cross classifications that define students' social contexts. Because neighborhoods are not nested within schools (students from the same neighborhood may attend different schools), typical two- or three-level models do not apply. The key to Raudenbush's solution is to include dummy variables representing schools in Level 1 of a multilevel model of students nested within neighborhoods. But the number of schools could potentially be large, taxing the degrees of freedom for estimating the effect associated with each dummy variable. Building on Lindley and Smith (1972), Raudenbush's approach was to consider the effects of the schools represented by the dummy variables as "exchangeable" (i.e., drawn from a common distribution). Raudenbush found that twice as much variance in student attainment could be attributed to neighborhoods as schools, thus addressing an important issue for those attempting to define the relevant social contexts for students. Raudenbush and his colleagues have followed up on this finding by exploring the effects of neighborhoods on deviant behavior (Sampson, Raudenbush & Earls, 1997).

Recent advances in the specification of the Level 1 model have allowed researchers to address how social contexts affect dichotomous outcomes such as dropout (Bryk & Thum, 1989; Rumberger, 1995) and deviant behavior (Sampson et al., 1997). These outcomes are particularly sensitive to social contexts because they represent forms of detachment from social institutions. Models with dichotomous outcomes pose special problems for maximum likelihood estimation because the likelihood based on a logit model at Level 1 cannot be directly integrated. This has been addressed either by approximating the likelihood through a second-order Taylor expansion, known as the penalized quasi-likelihood (Breslow & Clayton, 1993; Goldstein, 1991; Longford, 1993; Raudenbush, 1995), or a more extensive Laplace approximation (Yang, 1998), or by using quadrature of the Gauss-Hermite type to approximate integration over the distribution of random effects (Hedeker & Gibbons, 1996). While quadrature is theoretically appealing, it is difficult to extend to cases with multidimensional random effects (such as in considering regression coefficients as random), and it may produce less stable estimates in cases of extremely infrequent outcomes (Yosef, 1997).

Developments to incorporate multivariate outcomes in the Level 1 model also have particular application to the study of social contexts. In the illustration of his technique, Thum (1997) found that the more a school supports professional community, the more teachers spend time on the correlated behaviors of teaching activities and school governance. The multivariate approach allows one to estimate the correlation among outcomes while addressing the potential compromise of Type I error rates.

Although multilevel models have helped facilitate many important advances in our understanding of the social contexts of schools, students, and the interaction of the two levels, many of the applications of multilevel modeling have shown that the intraclass correlations (the proportion of variance between schools) are often between 10% and 33% for various measures of student achievement in various cultures (e.g., Bryk & Raudenbush, 1992; Fitz-Gibbon, 1991; Lockheed & Longford, 1991; Plewis, 1991; Raudenbush & Bryk, 1988; Zuzovsky & Aitkin, 1991). Furthermore, the intraclass correlations for measures of teachers' attitudes or orientations range as low as 10% (Bidwell et al., 1997; Lee, Dedrick, & Smith, 1991; Rowan, Raudenbush, & Kang, 1991).[5] Clearly, there is a considerable amount of variation among people within schools.

We might consider this variation to be a function of individual characteristics; if this explained most of the phenomena, however, then we would expect the proportion of variation within schools to be reduced considerably once we controlled for the likely characteristics of individuals related to the outcome. But typically only 10%–30% of the variance in achievement is explained at the student level (e.g., Bryk & Raudenbush, 1992; Fitz-Gibbon, 1991; Jacobsen, 1991; Lockheed & Longford, 1991; Pallas et al., 1994; Patterson, 1991; Raudenbush & Bryk, 1988; Zuzovsky & Aitkin, 1991). Even when controlling for a pretest (begging the question somewhat of earlier school effects), the variance explained at the student level goes up to 50%–60% (Pallas et al., 1994; Plewis, 1991). While impressive, this still leaves a considerable portion of variation unexplained even after controlling for characteristics such as race, socioeconomic status, gender, course taking, track placement, parental support, and other characteristics theoretically related to achievement. The situation for teachers in schools is no better, with only 10%–20% of the variation in teacher outcomes within schools accounted for (Bidwell et al., 1997; Lee & Smith, 1991; Rowan et al., 1991), even after control for the seniority of the teacher, the teacher's subject field, and so forth. Thus, what we know from multilevel models is that there is considerable variation among individuals within schools and much of that variation is unexplained solely in terms of the attributes of the individuals.

A place to look in accounting for further variance is in the relations among individuals within schools. Although multilevel models can incorporate characteristics ascribed to individuals or to schools as organizations, they have rarely been used to incorporate aspects of the relations among individuals that define the social contexts in which individuals work and learn. The best that multilevel models typically have done is to incorporate measures of school culture based on the aggregate perceptions of a sample of teachers that do not capture variation in individual contexts (e.g., Bryk & Driscoll, 1988) or to include measures based on individual perceptions of the global school culture that do not directly measure relations among people. Of course, the limitations just outlined would apply to any analysis of attributes of a sample of individuals that does not include relations among individuals (Coleman, 1958).

In order to move past these limitations, we must study relations among students and teachers in schools. Furthermore, if we are to refine our understandings of school processes, we cannot confine ourselves to samples of individuals in schools. We must, in at least a few schools, obtain information on all people and their relations within the school in order to capture the dynamic processes within schools. This will help us to answer questions regarding the organizational functioning of schools. For example, if a school has challenged institutionalized aspects of schooling, who generates the impetus for change, and through what channels do they persuade others to accept and adopt the change? On the student level, if a student's social context affects his or her educational aspirations, how do students determine the friendships that define social context?

While the call to study relations among people in a school may sound ambitious, it is consistent with the goal of many qualitative studies of schools. Qualitative researchers in general (Grant, 1988; Johnson, 1990; Lightfoot, 1983; Metz, 1983; Rosenholtz, 1989), and ethnographers in particular (e.g., Mehan et al., 1986; Staessens, 1993), have taken on the challenge of describing the processes through which social contexts are established and influence decisions and behaviors. For example, Mehan et al. demonstrated how a school psychologist directed the process of a committee to determine the special education placement of a student. In this case, the decision and process were quite consistent with institutionalized aspects of special education, including the tools used to assess the student, the types of educational settings considered, and the authority of the psychologist.

But typical analyses of qualitative data address only a small portion of the relations among people in a school. For example, Mehan et al. focus on relations between committee members and during committee meetings, and only small sets of relations such as those defining cliques are addressed in the work of Grant (1988), Cusick (1983), and Metz (1983). Even relations among a small set of people, however, are affected by the more general social context. In the case of decisions regarding special education described by Mehan et al. (1986), would the committee's process be the same if the entire faculty and staff were polarized with regard to how to educate students with disabilities? How does the size of the faculty affect the process of a single committee? Is there a need to coordinate practices with others in the school?

Some anthropologists and sociologists have argued that, in order to understand the context of a single relation, one must examine and characterize the entire network of interpersonal relations (Granovetter, 1973; Mitchell, 1973; Newcomb, 1950; Parsons & Shils, 1954; Simmel, 1955). Micro processes cannot be understood unless they are related to the macro structure (Collins, 1981). For example, when teachers share information or exchange opinions, are they more able to influence one another if they are members of a common professional circle than if they operate in relatively segregated regions of a school? An answer to this question would help reveal how the social context of the school affects the experiences and actions of faculty, staff, and administrators. Therefore, the contribution of ethnography can be augmented by establishing the complete context of relations, the social network, in a school. The techniques for doing so are the subject of the next section.

## EFFECTS OF SOCIAL CONTEXTS WITHIN SCHOOLS: METHODS AND MODELS IN SOCIAL NETWORK ANALYSIS

There is a deep history of analyses of the set of relations among people in schools. In fact, some of Moreno's (1934) first sociograms graphically represented the sets of relations among students in a training school. Much of the earlier work linked characteristics of students' personalities with their relative social standing (Blyth, 1958, 1960; Bonney, 1943; Boyd, 1965; Cook, 1945; Evans, 1962; French & Mensh, 1948; Gerber, 1977; Gronlund, 1950, 1959; Jennings, 1943; Northway, 1954; Olson, 1949; Powell, 1948; Zeleny, 1941), and then researchers turned to analyses of small group processes within the classroom (Flecker, 1967; King, 1960; Newcomb, 1961; Pratt, 1960; Schmuck & Schmuck, 1975). Important work in secondary schools has linked patterns of social structure to the organization of classrooms (Bossert, 1979; Epstein & Karweit, 1983; Flanders & Havumaki, 1960; Hallinan, 1976; Schmuck & Schmuck, 1975). For example, Epstein (1983, ch. 5) found when students participated in classroom decision making, distancing the classroom processes from the full guidance of the teacher, the students were more likely to develop diverse and extensive social ties. Similarly, Sheare 91978) demonstrated that modification of classroom structure can increase the low social standing experienced by students with disabilities. This low social standing may be experienced even by those who are physically mainstreamed into a regular education classroom (Bruiniks, 1978a, 1978b; Bryan, 1974; Siperstein et al., 1978), and is thus a critical issue for fully integrating students with disabilities.

Although many of these studies explored relations among students, they did not address the set of relations in a classroom as a system. Correspondingly, although their interest in social relations suggests a movement toward consideration of individuals' interdependencies, typically their *analyses* treat individuals as independent. As we move toward analyses of the entire set of relations among individuals that define the system of a classroom or school, we turn to quantitative methods used by social network analysts.

Many of the methods developed for social network analyses can be applied to analyses of the relations or interactions among the people in a school (see Scott, 1991, for an introduction to social network analysis; see Wasserman & Faust, 1994, for an encyclopedic review of social network methods; and see Wasserman & Galaskiewicz, 1994, for recent advances in social network analysis). In particular, in the following subsections, I review the techniques most relevant for the study of the social context of schooling. These techniques include graphical representation of sets of relations among people, identification of groups or subgroups of people based on the pattern of relations, modeling of attributes of people as a function of relations in the social network (influence), and modeling of the pattern of relations in a social network as a function of attributes of people (selection).

## Graphical Representations of Social Context

Coleman's (1961) *Adolescent Society* featured the construction of one of the earliest sociograms of relationships among students in a school. Through his sociograms and related analyses, Coleman demonstrated the presence of cliques of students (jocks, academic elites, etc.) that reflected emphases and actions of the faculty and of the local community, findings that were subsequently supported by Eckert (1989). The graphical representation of relationships among the students generated by Coleman (1961) and shown in Figure 3 helped to reveal how the students functioned in the social context they constructed. On one hand, the representation reveals the basic dimensions along which cliques formed. These cliques gained their salience through positive and negative sanctions of the faculty, reflecting differences in the faculty's experiences as well as values in the community. On the other hand, the graphical representation defines the context of each individual that may or may not be totally subsumed by the student's clique membership. Thus, there are some individuals who are central to a specific clique, others who span different cliques, and others who are isolated. Sociograms such as Coleman's provide an overview of social structure through which qualitative and ethnographic accounts of specific relations can be integrated.

There have been several extensions of the basic sociogram that can be applied to representing the multiple social contexts of individuals in schools. One of the fundamental problems of the original sociograms such as Coleman's was that people were located in the two dimensions arbitrarily, based on the aesthetic of the researcher (the choice to use only two dimensions is also arbitrary, although typically necessary for effective graphical representation). In an advancement, multidimensional scaling (MDS) techniques have been used to determine the location of each actor (cf. Krackhardt, Blyth, & McGrath, 1994) in a small number of dimensions.[6] Furthermore, although MDS techniques can be applied to large data sets, their application does not always result in a helpful reduction of the data. Lost is Coleman's intuitive appreciation for the importance of cliques, or subgroups, among people in a school. Inevitably, researchers who seek to interpret MDS-based sociograms draw theoretical or graphical circles around subsets of people so that they may interpret the image (e.g., Kadushin, 1995; Laumann, 1970; Nakao & Romney, 1993). But these circles are typically based on ad hoc criteria and

### FIGURE 3
### Early Sociogram of Friendships Among High School Students

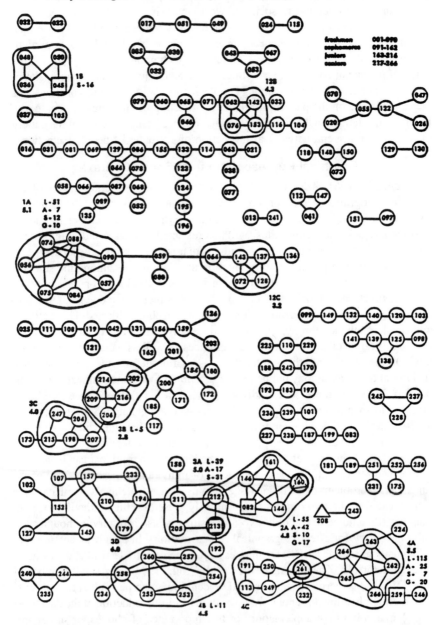

From Coleman (1961). *Adolescent Society* (p. 176). New York: The Free Press of Glencoe.

aesthetics of the researcher and cannot be defined in terms of a formal criterion for subgroup membership.

Theoretically, it is sensible to consider organizations as composed of a set of integrated cohesive subgroups. Cohesive subgroups were initially defined as those that had extensive capacity to attract and retain subgroup members (see Cartwright, 1968, and Mudrack, 1989, for reviews). From Moreno's (1934) initiation of sociometric study to Homans's (1950) and Blau's (1977) theoretical statements and Freeman's (1992) return, cohesive subgroups have been hypothesized as a crucial link between individuals and organizations. Not surprisingly, one of the strongest and most consistent theoretical images of the structure of organizations and systems is that of relations concentrated within, but not confined to, cohesive subgroups (Blau, 1977; Durkheim, 1933; Homans, 1950; Roethlisberger & Dickson, 1941; Simon, 1965). This conception is also consistent with theories defined at the level of the individual, in which people influence each other through direct relations within their subgroups and then integrate into the larger organization through relations spanning subgroup boundaries (Granovetter, 1973; Nadel, 1957).

Typically, studies of schools have relied on the formal organization in the form of departmental affiliations as a basis for defining cohesive subgroups (e.g., Johnson, 1990; Siskin, 1991). Through dense patterns of relations within departments, teachers may share a language for describing their work, orientations to teaching, mechanisms for decision making, and so forth (Johnson, 1990; Siskin, 1991). But the formal organization is not always most salient for people as the informal organization can have substantial effect on organizational processes (Burawoy, 1979; Coleman, 1958; Durkheim, 1984; Etzioni, 1961; Homans, 1950; Roethlisberger & Dickson, 1941; Selznick, 1961; Weber, 1958). In the case of schools, departments may become less salient in small schools when departments contain only a few teachers, in Catholic schools that have less of a departmental organization (partly because teachers with less training in specific subject fields are more likely to cross subject areas in their teaching) (Bryk & Frank, 1991), and even in large public schools, where there are often divisions within departments based on cohort, gender, or subfield (Metz, 1990). Indeed, part of the movement for restructuring schools calls for a reduction in departmentalization (Bryk, Lee, & Smith, 1990; Carnegie Council on Adolescent Development, 1989). Therefore, what is needed is a technique for identifying cohesive subgroups based on the pattern of relations among people instead of boundaries defined by the formal organization of the school.

In order to move beyond categories of the formal organization, methodologists have developed and used various techniques for identifying cohesive subgroups from data indicating relations among actors (e.g., Alba, 1973; Arabie & Hubert, 1990; Bock & Hussein, 1948; Borgatti, Everett, & Shirey, 1990; Cartwright & Harary, 1956; Davis, 1977; Everett, 1983; Freeman, 1992; Hubbell, 1965; Katz, 1947; Matula, 1972; Mokken, 1979; Phillips & Conviser, 1972; Reitz, 1988; Seidman & Foster, 1978). Many of the techniques involve graph-theoretic criteria (see Wasserman & Faust, 1994, for a review). First, the optimally cohesive subgroup is a clique in which all subgroup members engage in direct relations with each other. But such a definition is restrictive and "stingy" (Alba, 1973). Therefore, various efforts have been made to relax this criterion. An early approach required that each actor in a subgroup be able to reach all others in the subgroup in a minimum number of steps (Alba, 1973; Luce, 1950; Mokken, 1979). For example, the relation 1→2→3 indicates a path of two steps (or length two) connecting Actor 1 to Actor 3. A criterion could be specified such that subgroup members are all connected via paths of length one or two. This criterion can be further restricted by requiring that the connecting paths occur *within* the subgroup (Alba, 1973; Mokken, 1979). But if influence occurs through direct relations, then it may be more sensible to define cohesive subgroups in terms of direct relations rather than overall path lengths, which may be too long to transmit much influence (Burt, 1988; Hubbell, 1965). Furthermore, the definitions based on path length are restrictive in that they specify the nature of the relationship between each pair of actors within a subgroup instead of a general relationship between each actor and all others in the subgroup.

In response to the preceding concerns, Seidman and Foster (1978) and Seidman (1983) introduced definitions of subgroups based on the minimum number of relations that each actor must share with others in the subgroup or based on the maximal number of relations that can be absent between each actor and subgroup members. But the issue arises as to how to choose the minimum or maximum, and often these choices depend on post hoc interpretations of subgroup membership in terms of other characteristics of the actors. Furthermore, the application of Seidman and Foster's approach (as well as Borgatti et al.'s, 1990, extension) often results in the identification of several overlapping small clusters that are difficult to interpret (Frank, 1993; Freeman, 1992; Kadushin, 1995). Such overlapping clusters are inconsistent with many of the theoretical characterizations of systems composed of nonoverlapping subgroups. In particular, overlapping boundaries fail to establish "an inside and an outside" (Abbott, 1996, p. 872) necessary to define a sociological entity. How can we differentiate processes within subgroups from those between subgroups if two actors can simultaneously be members of the same subgroup and members of different subgroups?

Perhaps the most promising approaches for identifying nonoverlapping cohesive subgroups are those that involve goodness of fit, or statistical, criteria associated with the fitting of subgroups to social network data (e.g., Alba, 1973; Bock & Husain, 1950; Freeman, 1992; Seidman, 1983). In each case, one can conceptualize a model in which membership in the same subgroup (vs. membership in different subgroups) is used to predict whether two actors are related. The criteria measuring the fit of such models then define cohesiveness in terms of a concentration of relations within subgroups relative to the extent of relations between subgroups. These statistical measures have the advantage of allowing for relations within and across subgroup boundaries at rates that are defined relative to the data instead of absolute criteria. Thus, they accommodate variation in the data not by forcing the identification of overlapping subgroup boundaries based on fixed criteria but by allowing the identification of nonoverlapping, but permeable, subgroup boundaries.

In a recent example of the use of stochastic criteria, I defined cohesiveness in terms of the odds ratio (AD/BC) in Table 1, representing the association between membership in the same subgroup and the occurrence of relations (Frank, 1995a).

The odds ratio of Table 1 is large to the extent that actors engage in relations with members of their subgroups (Cell D) and do not engage in relations with members of other subgroups (Cell A). The odds ratio is small to the extent that actors do not engage in relations with members of their subgroups (Cell C) and actors engage in relations with others who are not in their subgroup (Cell B). Because the odds ratio is stochastic, with values on the diagonals of Table 1 essentially evaluated relative to the marginals, it accommodates variation in subgroup sizes and actors' propensities for engaging in relations (see Frank, 1995a, pp. 33–34, for a discussion).

A clustering algorithm can be used to identify nonoverlapping but permeable subgroup boundaries by assigning actors to subgroups so as to maximize the odds ratio of Table 1 (Frank, 1995a, 1996; software will be incorporated into the next release of the general social networks software package UCINET [Borgatti, Everett, & Freeman, 1992]). The representation of relations nested within cohesive subgroups then helps to establish the social contexts for individual actors, and, because the boundaries are commonly defined across all actors and do not overlap, they can also be used to characterize meaningful divisions in the pattern of relations that might affect organizational function. For example, the subgroup boundaries might reveal factions among teachers associated with differences in discipline policy, approaches to teaching, union support, and so forth.

In a recent article, I (Frank, 1996) applied my algorithm to represent the structure of professional discussions among teachers in a single school. This representation allowed me to link the pattern of professional discussions to the teachers' race and gender, as well as their orientations to teaching. I identified cohesive subgroups of teachers based on their indications of the professional discussions in which they engaged (professional discussions were measured on the basis of self-reports of teachers, who indicated the five others with whom they engaged in professional discussions most frequently and then ranked the extent of professional discussion on a scale ranging from once a month [1] to daily [4]). I then embedded the subgroup boundaries into the sociogram in Figure 4 by applying

**TABLE 1**
**Association Between Common Subgroup Membership**
**and the Realization of a Relation Between Actors**

|  |  | Relation Realized | | |
| --- | --- | --- | --- | --- |
|  |  | No | Yes |  |
| Subgroup Membership | Different | A | B | Possible relations between actors in *different* subgroups |
|  | Same | C | D | Possible relations between actors in the *same* subgroup |
|  |  | Unrealized relations | Realized relations | Total possible relations |

## FIGURE 4

### Professional Discussions Among Teachers in "Our Hamilton High"

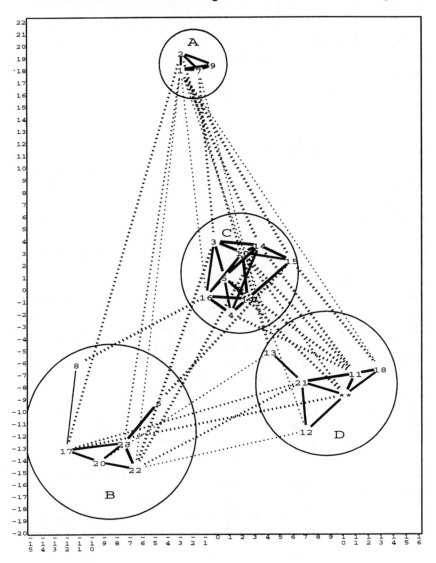

*Solid lines within subgroups, dotted lines between, thickness = frequency.*
*Scale = 4/(density of discussion*

MDS within and between subgroups (see Frank, 1996, for the technical details of this procedure). The result is a method for constructing sociograms that is consistent with Coleman's intuitive representation but applies empirically based techniques for defining subgroup membership and for representing the actors and their relations in two dimensions.[7]

Figure 4 establishes a basis for integrating qualitative data and information from survey instruments to characterize the processes through which teachers are affected by their social contexts.[8] As indicated in school documents, the student population at "Our Hamilton High" has become increasingly disadvantaged over the years as poor families have moved to the district from a nearby city and as the children of the more established wealthier families have aged. The teachers have responded in various ways to this exogenous change. Some who had difficulty adapting to the change sought early retirement. Others altered their mode of relating to the students, befriending the students whom they felt were most in need. In this sense, the school is similar to others described by Grant (1988) and Metz (1990). A core of teachers relate to the new types of students by acting as "moral agents," inculcating students into a specific set of values emphasizing citizenship and responsibility by keeping firm control of the classroom and through personal example (see Bidwell et al., 1997, for a definition and operationalization of moral agency in terms of responses to survey items [reliability = .74]).

By assigning the teachers identification numbers in the sociogram to represent their emphasis on moral agency (the lower the number, the higher the rank on moral agency), I used the image in Figure 4 as a basis for inferring processes through which teachers influenced one another (Frank, 1996). To begin, moral agency is cultivated within Subgroup A as the members of that subgroup engage in discussions with one another on a near daily basis (as indicated by the thick lines within the boundary of Subgroup A and as observed during fieldwork). Once a week or once a month, one of the teachers in Subgroup A engages in discussions with a teacher outside the subgroup (as indicated by the thinner lines between members of Subgroup A and members of other subgroups), thus possibly influencing the member of the other subgroup. The effect of these discussions is critical to integrating the subgroups into the totality of the organization, as opinions, information, and so forth that accumulate in each subgroup during daily discussions are transmitted to the other subgroup. Therefore, even teachers who do not adopt moral agency in direct response to changes in the student population may be affected, through direct and indirect discussions, by the orientations of the teachers in Subgroup A.

Although others have observed the processes through which teachers socialize one another on a dyadic level (Fuller & Izu, 1986; Grant, 1988; Hanson, 1978; Lightfoot, 1983; Metz, 1990; Rosenholtz & Simpson, 1990), Figure 4 represents the structure through which the socialization process occurs at the level of the school. Therefore, I was able to describe moral agency as being cultivated within Subgroup A and then spreading to other subgroups, where it encounters competing orientations. Of course, this process could be described with an alternative orientation being cultivated in another subgroup and then moving to the members of Subgroup A. Indeed, the image in Figure 4 suggests an equilibrium of the system, with those in Subgroup C who are mixed and moderate in their orientations mediating between the competing orientations of those at the top and bottom. Thus, the image in Figure 4 represents how processes within one subgroup may generate aspects of the organizational culture that then affect all people in the school.[9]

Images similar to Figure 4 also could be used to explore the process through which institutions penetrate the school as an organization. Who is responsible for implementing any given institution in a school, and how did they persuade others that this was a valuable practice to implement? For example, who is responsible for defining the possibilities for special education, and how did they influence others to adopt the same mind-set? One can trace such processes in images (such as in Figure 4) that combine information regarding individuals' attitudes or orientations with a helpful reduction in the representation of relations among people. Of course, images such as that in Figure 4 also have the potential to represent the relational structure through which people in schools challenge prevailing institutions, opening the possibility for studying the processes of school reform.

Graphical representations and clustering algorithms drawn from social network analysis have also been used to represent the structure of relations among students. For example, Friedkin and Thomas (1997) refined the definition of tracks and levels in high schools by analyzing the structure constructed through course-taking patterns, and Quiroz, Gonzalez, and Frank (1996) represented connections established through students' participation in extracurricular activities. Furthermore, these techniques could be used to extend earlier analyses of the friendship networks of students (Epstein, 1983; Hallinan, 1976). For example, although we may know the tendencies of students to choose others of similar gender or of higher socioeconomic status, it is helpful to know the pattern of friendship choices in classrooms that fully defines the social context in which each student learns.

Although graphical representations of the social structures within schools offer considerable potential as an aid to understanding the processes through which social contexts are defined, they do not provide a quantitative summary or formal model of the relationship between social structure and other attributes of people. To what extent do teachers influence each other's orientations? To what extent do students with similar aspirations choose to become friends? It is to these types of questions that I turn in the following subsections.

## Models of Effects Mediated by the Social Context (Influence Models)

The quantitative methods for analyzing social networks go beyond the graphical representation of the structure of a social network. In particular, models of social network processes can represent the effects of interpersonal influence that emerge out of a social context. For example, we might ask to what extent teachers' attitudes toward educating students with disabilities are influenced by the attitudes of other teachers and staff in their school. This question reflects a fundamental component of the process that ultimately affects the schooling experiences of students with disabilities (Triandis et al., 1984; Watts, 1984), which in turn is one of the most important factors in determining how teachers interact with students with disabilities (Fuchs et al., 1995; Jones & Guskin, 1984; Triadis et al., 1984).

In order to write the basic model of influence through interpersonal relations, define $w_{ii'}$ to indicate the extent or existence of a relation between individuals $i$ and $i'$, as perceived by $i$. Define $y_i$ to represent an attribute (an opinion, belief, or orientation) of person $i$ that might be influenced through relations with others. A model for $n$ people representing the influence of others on $y_i$ through interpersonal relations can be defined as

$$y_i = \rho \left[ \sum_{\substack{i'=1, \\ i' \neq i}}^{n} w_{ii'} y_{i'} \right] + e_i. \tag{2}$$

where $\rho$ represents the extent of the network effect associated with $\sum_{i'} w_{ii'} y_{i'}$, the sum of the attributes of others to whom an actor is related. As in the case of a general linear model or the Level 1 model of a multilevel mode, the errors are assumed to be independent and identically distributed and normal, with mean zero and variance $(\sigma^2)$.[10]

One possible interpretation for $\rho$ is that it indicates the effect of alters ($i'$) on ego ($i$) through the social network (Bovasso, 1996; Burt, 1987). This might occur through the process of cohesion, in which people influence one another by sharing information or persuasion (Barnes, 1972; Blau, 1977; Bott, 1971; Collins, 1981; Festinger, 1950; Homans, 1950; Mitchell, 1973), or through structural equivalence, where the $w_{ii}$ indicate the role that people occupy and the $y_i$ represent a behavior that is a function of the behaviors of others who occupy similar roles (Burt, 1987; Merton, 1957; Nadel, 1957; Radcliffe-Brown, 1940). For example, cohesion applies when students' educational decisions and aspirations are influenced through direct discussions (Davies & Kandel, 1981; Duncan, Haller, & Portes, 1968; Epstein, 1983; Hartup, 1978; Sewell, Haller, & Ohlendorf, 1970). On the other hand, students who occupy similar positions defined by curricular tracks may develop similar educational aspirations (Bowles & Gintis, 1976; Hansell & Karweit, 1983). This may be in part to achieve balance (Cartwright & Harary, 1956; Heider, 1958; Newcomb, 1961) between their aspirations and interpersonal relations.

Recently, Leenders (1995) emphasized that $\rho$ is not necessarily interpreted as the *effect* of others through interpersonal relations, because we do not know from cross-sectional data whether individuals' attributes changed as a result of the pattern of relation (influence) or whether the pattern of relation changed as a result of the attributes (selection). Similarly, Marsden and Friedkin (1994, p. 13) claim only that the direct effect of one person's response to the others through the social network is "consistent" with the presence of an influence process. Thus, Leenders describes $\rho$ as "descriptive" or as a governing factor but not necessarily as indicative of influence of actors on one another. In this sense, interpretations of analyses of cross-sectional social network data are subject to the same constraints as analyses of other cross-sectional data (Cook & Campbell, 1979). But even if $\rho$ is only "descriptive," it has the potential to represent an important characteristic of an organization: the alignment of the pattern of relations and the distribution of an attitude, behavior, or orientation (Xu, 1997).

Regardless of the interpretation of $\rho$, the unique characteristics of the dependencies in observations in social network data present challenges in the estimation of parameters such as ρ. If we define **y** as an $n \times 1$ vector of attributes, **W** as an $n \times n$ matrix representing relations, and **e** as an $n \times 1$ vector of error terms, $e_i$, we can rewrite Equation 2 in matrix form:

$$y = \rho Wy + e \tag{3}$$

For example, we might write

Attitude toward inclusion practices =
ρ (Professional discussions) × (Others' attitudes toward inclusion practices) + e, (4)

and observe the fundamental limitation in estimation of the parameter ρ: The vector **y** (attitude toward inclusion practices) appears on both sides of the equation. The result is that ordinary least squares estimates of ρ are biased (Anselin, 1988; Ord, 1975). In response, Ord described a procedure for obtaining maximum likelihood estimates of ρ that is generally available (Friedkin, 1990), although there is still work being conducted on the technical details (Dow & Leenders, 1997; Duke, 1993; Frank & Xu, 1997).

Models such as Equation 2 also can be specified and estimated for longitudinal data, estimating changes in individuals' beliefs or orientations as a function of the beliefs of the others with whom they engaged in relations in previous time periods (Friedkin & Marsden, 1994, argue that ordinary least squares estimates are unbiased for such longitudinal models). For example, Epstein (1983) found that students' self-reliance and achievement were influenced by the self-reliance and achievement of their peers at a previous time point. Friedkin (1997) and Friedkin and Johnson (1990) also developed models of the processes through which people influence one another as they move over several time points from an initial set of beliefs to a final state in which there is equilibrium between beliefs and the pattern of interaction.

Equation 2, as well as longitudinal versions of this model, can also be easily modified to incorporate other attributes of people. For example, using the data from Coleman (1961), Duke (1993) found that inclusion of peer academic performance increased the $R^2$ from .35 (for a model including gender, mental ability, and socioeconomic status) to .44 in predicting students' academic performance. Furthermore, one can include effects through multiple networks (e.g., through general discussions or lunchroom conversations) in the cross-sectional (Doreian, 1989) or longitudinal case. Therefore, models of network effects or influence can help us to identify the extent to which a set of people such as teachers or students change each other's beliefs through interaction or friendship. But the price is not cheap in terms of data collection. At a minimum, a limited version of a network effects model can be estimated by knowing the beliefs of a sample of people (egos) and the beliefs of each of the others (alters) with whom they acknowledged engaging in interactions or friendship (e.g., Epstein, 1983). Ideally, one would obtain data on all people in a given network.

## Models of the Construction of Social Context (Selection Models)

Although models such as in Equation 2 represent a largely untapped potential for representing and estimating the effects through which people in a school influence one another, the pattern of relations among the people was considered fixed over time. But the recent awareness of how teachers in a school construct their patterns of relation (Bird & Little, 1986; Darling-Hammond & McLaughlin, 1995; Little, 1993) calls for processes captured by a second set of models for analyzing social networks. For example, if we define professional discussions to either occur or not occur between individuals $i$ and $i'$ over the interval $t\text{-}h{\to}t$, as represented by $w_{ii'\ t\text{-}h{\to}t}$, we can present the following logit model for $w_{ii'\ t\text{-}h{\to}t}$:

$$\log\left(\frac{p[w_{ii'\ t\text{-}h{\to}t} = 1]}{1 - p[w_{ii'\ t\text{-}h{\to}t} = 1]}\right) = \theta_0 - \theta_1|y_{i\ t\text{-}h} - y_{i'\ t\text{-}h}|. \tag{5}$$

The left-hand side of this equation transforms, via the logit, an expression for the probability that $w_{ii'} = 1$ to the line of real numbers (Agresti, 1984). Here $\theta_0$ represents an intercept and $\theta_1$ represents the homophily effect (Blau, 1977; Feld, 1981; Festinger, Schachter, & Back, 1950; Homans, 1950), whereby people choose to engage in relations with others with similar attributes (as captured by $-|y_{i\ t\text{-}h} - y_{i'\ t\text{-}h}|$). For example, we might explore the tendency for teachers to engage in professional discussions with others of similar orientations or for students to be friendly with others of the same gender.

Again, the dependencies inherent in social network data pose interesting challenges for estimation. In obtaining estimates of the parameters in Equation 5, one's first inclination might be to use maximum likelihood techniques such as those available to estimate the parameters in logit models (e.g., Agresti, 1984). But it is difficult to define the likelihood of the parameters as a function of the data in Equation 5, because the observations are not independent. To begin, the relation between $i$ and $i'$ is not independent of the relation between $i'$ and $i$. Such dependencies are accounted for in earlier $P_1$ models of selection (Fienberg, Meyer, & Wasserman, 1985; Fienberg & Wasserman, 1981; Holland & Leinhardt, 1981; software are available in the general social networks package UCINET [Borgatti et al., 1992]) by specifying the set of relations among the dyad as the unit of analysis (including the relation from $i$ to $i'$, as well as the relation from of $i'$ to $i$). While the $p_1$ approach represents an important advancement in the estimation of parameters such as in Equation 5, the respecification of the models does not account for dependencies among pairs outside the dyad.

But a new estimation approach, developed by Frank and Strauss (1986) and Strauss and Ikeda (1990) and described by Wasserman and Pattison (1996), shows that estimates from a logit model can be used to obtain estimates while conditioning the relation between each pair of people on the relation between every other pair of people in the network. For example, we might model whether two people are friends as a function of the number of friends they have in common, the number of friends of friends they have in common, and so forth. In a key point, Strauss and Ikeda demonstrate that one need only condition on relations among sets of up to four people in order to capture all of the dependencies in a network.

The estimation of parameters in these conditioned models is based on the maximization of the pseudo-likelihood that can be obtained via standard logit estimation procedures (such as those available in SPSS and SAS), provided one controls for the full array of dependencies among the observations by incorporating sets of specifically defined independent variables in the model (the software for constructing these independent variables is available at the Web site http:// kentucky.psych.uiuc.edu/pstar/index.html). One may also use techniques based on Hubert's (1987) QAP procedure to obtain Monte Carlo–based $p$ values for outcomes measured on a continuous scale.

Models such as in Equation 5 can be used to establish whether a given factor is linked to how individuals construct their social contexts. For example, several authors have found that students prefer to establish friendships with others of the same gender, although the effect is reduced with age (e.g., Epstein, 1983; Hallinan, 1976; Leenders, 1995). Furthermore, similarity on multiple characteristics may be represented in models such as in Equation 5 in order to differentiate among factors that affect how students and teachers construct their social contexts. For teachers, we could compare the effects of a formal requirement to communicate against individual preferences for engaging in professional discussions (Darling-Hammond & McLaughlin, 1995; Selznick, 1961). For students, we could compare the effect of proximities generated by curricular tracking versus affinities based on attitudes toward education.

Although models of selection can help us understand the formation of social contexts, as was the case for models of influence, the data demands of selection models are relatively high. One can specify a limited version of a selection model by knowing the attribute of each ego and each alter with whom egos indicate a relation or engaging in communication. Ideally, one would obtain information on all of the people in a network in order to capture the complete dynamic of selection and estimate the effects of various measures of dependencies.

Combining the findings of selection models with influence models, we observe how individuals define the social contexts through which they are influenced. For example, there is some evidence that high school students are especially influenced by their closest friends (Cohen, 1971). Moreover, a recent class of models has emerged that integrates influence and selection in studies of network evolution (Carley, 1990, 1991; DeVree & Dagevos, 1994; Frank, 1995b; Frank & Fahrbach, 1997; Leenders, 1995; Stokman & Zeggelink, 1996). Although in their infancy, models of network evolution have the potential to play a critical role in the understanding of the social context of schooling. Simply by focusing on model specification, we can learn how to better represent the processes through which people construct social contexts and through which they are influenced by the social contexts they construct. These models may have important policy implications in education. For example, should a professional development program target those teachers who are already most inclined to adopt the program, at the risk of making the program an issue that factionalizes the teachers, such as is described by McLaughlin and Marsh (1979)? Consideration of such an issue points to the critical importance of teachers' social contexts in their continued learning and in the sustained function of the school (Lieberman, 1995; MacIver & Epstein, 1991; Staessens, 1993). In particular, there is increasing recognition that reforms must be holistic, addressing the processes through which teachers form relations

**FIGURE 5**
**Social Processes of Schools**

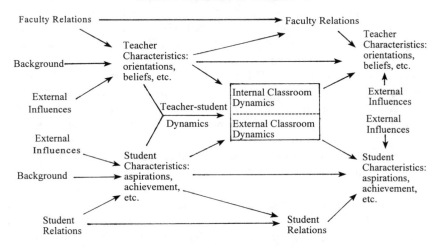

with one another and influence one another as they contribute to the construction of school culture (Darling-Hammond & McLaughlin, 1995; Goodman, 1995; Lieberman, 1995; McDonald, Smith, Turner, Finney, & Barton, 1993; Staessens, 1993; Weiss, 1995).

## A General Framework of Social Contexts in Schools

The sets of models including social network processes as predictors and outcomes represent pieces of the general framework of the social processes in schools presented in Figure 5. Building on generic models such as those included in Erbring and Young (1979) and Friedkin and Johnson (1990), the figure represents the mechanisms through which two sets of people in the school, faculty (and administrators) and students, engage in relations and influence each others' attitudes and behaviors. At the top left, faculty relations and background characteristics of teachers combine with the effects of external influences (these can include exogenous policy constraints such as legal mandates and the organization of district governance) to affect teacher characteristics such as orientation to teaching and beliefs. Relating these effects back to Equation 2, the faculty relations represent the independent variable $\Sigma_{i'}w_{ii'}y_{i'}$, and the external influences are associated with the error terms $e_i$ (note that the effect of background characteristics can also be included in the model). As we move across the top of the figure, teachers' characteristics then affect the relations in which they engage, corresponding to the processes specified in Equation 5, at which point the cycle of effects is reinitiated.

An isomorphic structure and the corresponding process are posited for students in the lower half of Figure 5. In the middle of Figure 5 is the focal point: interactions within and outside of the classroom between teachers and students. This focal point represents the processes through which two distinct sets of people, faculty (and administrators) and students, are media through which forces exogenous to the school confront one another. It is what makes schools unique (e.g.,

Ashton & Webb, 1986; Barnes, 1976; Bird & Little, 1986) and is the subject of considerable ethnographic research (e.g., Eder, 1982; Rist, 1970; Wilcox, 1982).

As an example, the exogenous effects on teachers may represent effects referred to as institutional (DiMaggio & Powell, 1991; Meyer & Rowan, 1991) or cultural (e.g., Apple, 1990; Mehan, 1992). For example, teachers may hold certain orientations toward teaching partly because of their training and exposure to the beliefs of others in their subject field outside of the school (Grossman & Stodolsky, 1995). Thus, these beliefs are partly institutionalized in the subject matter. Teachers' beliefs are then expressed in the professional discussions in which they engage, a process that is guided by aspects of the organization of the particular school. Teachers' beliefs also are expressed as classroom practices during interaction with students. The experiences of the classroom and of professional discussions with others then modify teachers' beliefs, as the cycle continues.

Coming from the student level, students' characteristics are formed on the basis of their interactions with others and their backgrounds (Apple, 1979; Bowles & Gintis, 1976; Eder, 1981; Gamoran, 1996; Hollingshead, 1949; Lee & Bryk, 1989; Lee & Smith, 1993). Much of the effect of background, such as that associated with socioeconomic status, can be considered an institutionalized aspect of the student's culture. Students' characteristics, in turn, affect the interactions with teachers within and outside of the classroom that partly define the culture of the school (e.g., Delpit, 1988; Metz, 1990). In particular, we have become increasingly aware of the challenge of classroom interaction between teachers and students who are influenced by different cultures defined within and outside of the school (e.g., Delpit, 1988). Interactions between students and teachers then affect future student relations and characteristics as the cycle is continued (e.g., Epstein, 1983). Thus, by representing social processes within schools, models of social network data capture the interplay between multiple levels of schooling (institutional, organizational, and individual) that are not completely captured by the more established multilevel models of independent individuals nested within schools.

## FUTURE RESEARCH: SOCIAL NETWORK MODELS IN MULTILEVELS

The social network models were developed in the preceding section with respect to estimating effects in a single system.[11] Thus, although the basic social network models of influence and selection can inform other research and establish a scaffold for qualitative research, they do not establish a sound basis for policy-making by comparing effects across multiple settings. It is here that multilevel models make their greatest contribution. Through the multilevel framework, the researcher can characterize the extent of variation in an outcome within and between schools and specify and estimate effects of individual- and school-level characteristics (including those effected through policies such as restructuring), as well as the interaction of individual and school characteristics.

There is also great potential to integrate multilevel models and models of social network processes. For example, a set of papers presented at the 1997 meeting of the American Sociological Association combined multilevel models with measures of social structure to assess the effects of social capital on educational outcomes (Carbonaro, 1997; Desimone, 1997; Epstein & Connors-Tadros, 1997; McNeal, 1997; Morgan & Sorensen, 1997).[12] One of the keys in this area will be to refine indices of social structure such as centralization and polarization (see Freeman, 1978, or Wasserman & Faust, 1994, for discussions of existing indices). For example, Friedkin and Thomas (1997) used social network analysis to identify course-taking positions based on the hypergraph of students' transcripts. These positions then accounted for considerable variation in student achievement, even controlling for socioeconomic status, minority status, prior achievement, and at the school level, sector. In fact, their findings indicate that once controlling for curricular positions, the effects of the covariates are dramatically reduced, indicating that the schooling experience defined by course taking patterns has a strong direct effect on achievement.

The specific models of selection and influence can also be integrated into the multilevel framework. For example, consider the following multilevel model in which the effect of teachers' influence varies randomly across schools:

At the teacher level:

$$Attitude\ toward\ inclusion_{ij} = \beta_{0j} +$$

$$\rho_j \left[ \sum_{\substack{i'=1, \\ i' \neq i}}^{n_1} professional\ discussion_{ii'j}\ Attitude\ toward\ inclusion_{i'j} \right] + e_{ij}. \quad (6)$$

*At the school level:*
$$\beta_{0j} = \gamma_{00} + u_{0j}, and$$
$$\rho_j = \gamma_0 + u_{\rho j}.$$

Here the extent of the network effect, as captured by $\rho_j$, varies randomly across schools (as captured by $u_{\rho j}$). Although some have argued that, in general, teachers have little influence over one another (Cusick, 1983; Lortie, 1977), the extent of influence may be critical to the effective implementation of professional development and innovations (Bird & Little, 1986; Darling-Hammond & McLaughlin, 1995; Little, 1984). Therefore, it is important to understand the circumstances under which the network effect is likely to be large. For example, is there a stronger network effect when a school engages in practices consistent with restructuring that are designed to facilitate relations between teachers? If there is, might that help the school to implement other reforms?

Bidwell and Bryk (1996) are already exploring models such as Equation 6 to investigate the factors that affect teachers' orientation to and engagement in teaching. They have expanded on this model by differentiating between effects within and between subgroups such as those inferred from Figure 4. On one hand, sub-group members may have more effect than others, because there is a strong ten-dency to conform to subgroup norms (e.g., Merton, 1957). On the other hand, teachers from outside a subgroup may exert greater influence as a result of the novelty of their information (this is consistent with Granovetter's, 1973, strength-of-weak-ties argument).

Specification of models such as in Equation 6 and estimation of the param-eters will require further research. As already stated, the interpretation of the typical network effect depends critically on the specification of the network relation. The interpretation of the network effect in the multilevel model will also depend on choices of centering. Furthermore, the Newton-Raphson al-gorithm for obtaining maximum likelihood estimates of the parameters in mod-els of network effects (e.g., Ord, 1975) has not been directly extended to the multilevel framework.

The selection model (Equation 5) can also be extended to multilevels. For example, Epstein (1983, chap. 5) found that friendships were more common and tended to be more integrated in schools in which the students participated in decision making. These effects would be associated with $\gamma_{01}$ and $\gamma_{11}$, re-spectively, in the following multilevel model for occurrence of friendship between students $i$ and $i'$ in school $j$ as a function of whether or not they come from the same socioeconomic status:

*At level one:*

$$\log\left(\frac{p[friendship_{ii'j}=1]}{1-p[friendship_{ii'j}=1]}\right) = \theta_{0j} + \theta_{1j} \; same \; socioeconomic \; status_{ii'j}. \quad (7)$$

*And at level two:*
$\theta_{0j} = \gamma_{00} + \gamma_{01} \; student \; participation \; in \; decision\text{-}making_j = u_{0j}$
$\theta_{1j} = \gamma_{10} + \gamma_{11} \; student \; participation \; in \; decision\text{-}making_j = u_{1j}.$

The formal model defined by Equation 7 extends Epstein's analysis by including terms representing the random variation of the slope and intercept across schools. We do not know, from Epstein's analysis, how much schools vary in the overall tendency for friendships to form, nor can we quantify how much the homophily effect associated with socioeconomic status varies across schools. Furthermore, dependencies among observations within the same school are captured in Equa-tion 7, whereas they were ignored in Epstein's analysis. Thus, models such as Equation 7 can be used to explore the extent to which relations are segregated according to ascriptive characteristics of either faculty or students. Understanding the circumstances under which segregation occurs can inform reforms attempting to reduce segregation among students or faculty.

The parameters in Equation 7 can be estimated by taking advantage of recent advancements in the estimation of selection and multilevel models. As already stated, maximum pseudo-likelihood estimates of the parameters in the model of selection can be obtained by applying ordinary logistic regression procedures while controlling for dependencies among the sets of relations. Thus, it seems sensible to extend this approach through the new procedures for maximizing the marginal likelihood (Hedeker & Gibbons, 1996) or approximations to the likelihood (Breslow & Clayton, 1993; Goldstein, 1991; Raudenbush, 1995; Yang, 1998) for multilevel models with dichotomous outcomes. As was the case with models of influence, one can even incorporate effects of subgroups by specifying a relation between a pair of people to occur either within or between subgroups (see the technical appendix in Frank & Yasumoto, 1997, for a discussion of this approach).

Because the data demands are great in order to estimate the full selection or influence model, the number of Level 2 units (e.g., schools) in the extension of these models to multilevels will be limited. It will simply be difficult to obtain observations on full populations of teachers or students in hundreds of schools. Furthermore, it is quite likely that we will rely on methods that approximate the likelihood in multilevel models including influence and selection because the techniques for obtaining maximum likelihood estimates are complex or do not yet exist in the single-level case. The combination of small numbers of Level 2 units and estimates based on approximations to the likelihood suggests that we may be turning to techniques such as Bayesian estimation via the Gibbs sampler (Seltzer, 1990), which incorporates uncertainty about estimates of the variance components to obtain standard errors of estimates.

## SUMMARY

Schooling occurs on multiple levels. Typically, the structure of multilevel models has followed the organizational structure of schools: students within classrooms within schools within districts within states within countries. Multilevel models capture effects identified with each of these levels, as well as interactions of effects across levels. Furthermore, many recent developments in estimation allow us to specify more complex multilevel models addressing a greater variety of outcomes and multiple sources of random effects.

But the social context of schooling is defined by relations among people. By studying the relations among the participants in schooling, we can begin to understand the processes through which individuals are affected by, and partially construct, schools as organizations and institutions. Institutions gain their salience as they are conducted into the school by teachers or students, and school cultures are formed through the accumulation of relations and influences among participants in schools. Our attention to these relations will require that we gather different forms of data and use quantitative methods to graphically represent relations among people as well as estimate effects on the selection of, and influence through, relations.

In the future, we may expect to see combinations of multilevel and social network models, including many we cannot now anticipate. These developments will help us understand the contexts in which students learn and teachers work. Most important, as quantitative methods become increasingly sophisticated mathematically, their application should help forge a link with others who study similar phenomena through alternate forms of inquiry.

## NOTES

[1] I define *social context* in terms of the aspects of schools as institutions and the relations among people within schools that affect the behavior of each individual affiliated with the school. In this sense, the definition is similar to other definitions put forth in this volume (see Salomon & Parkins, Chapter 1).

[2] This database is the most recent in a succession of databases collected by the federal government. Beginning with the Project Talent data collected in the 1960s, the databases were improved to include longitudinal data and information about students, teachers, and administrators (National Longitudinal Study [1972] and High School and Beyond [1980]). The NELS (1988) database included information from students in eighth grade as well as more extensive information regarding their contexts as defined by parents and teachers.

[3] Lee and Smith originally reported results in a metric allowing comparability across analyses of several outcomes and between models for intercepts and slopes in a single analysis. The results reported here have been reconverted into the original metric that represents gain in standardized achievement. Also, Lee and Smith estimated unique effects in schools that engaged in no reform practices using a separate dummy variable in Level 2 of their analyses, but these results are not reported here.

[4] Based on the results and assumptions of the model in Lee and Smith, the intercepts in Figure 1 were generated to be normally distributed with variance 3.1 (approximate normal distribution was achieved by sampling random normal deviates and then modifying on the basis of visual inspection of a normal quantile plot). The variances and shapes of the distributions were established separately among the PCT and PCR schools, thus conforming with the assumption of homogeneity of variance of Level 2 errors (see Bryk & Raudenbush, 1992, p. 200). Similarly, the slopes were generated to be normally distributed with variance .45.

[5] A notable exception is the finding in Lee and Smith (1991) that 50% of the variation in teachers' salaries was between schools, but this is somewhat expected because teachers' salaries are the result of large differences in region, urbanicity, and collective bargaining (Edwards, 1973).

[6] In reviewing methods used for social network analysis, I use the general term *actor*, which may refer to a person, organization, country, and so forth.

[7] The use of empirical criteria for defining subgroup membership also allowed me to establish procedures for determining the salience of the subgroup boundaries in terms of the pattern of relations. Specifically, because any clustering algorithm will identify some subgroups given even random data, I used Monte Carlo simulations to determine whether professional discussions were highly unlikely to be concentrated within the subgroup boundaries to the extent that they are in Figure 4 given the application of the algorithm to random data. In this case, there was less than a 1 in 100 probability of observing the concentration of discussions within the subgroup boundaries by chance alone. Furthermore, I established that the algorithm probably recovered most of the true subgroup memberships. The implication is that the subgroup boundaries were not merely imposed on a fluid pattern of relations but represented empirical tendencies in the teachers' professional discussions.

[8] I and others (Charles Bidwell and Pamela Quiroz) conducted interviews and observed teachers for several days and gathered a variety of official school documents (see Bidwell, 1998; Bidwell et al., 1997; Frank, 1993). In our interviews, our informants told us about (a) the distribution of authority and power in the school; (b) modes of decision making about curriculum, instruction, and student discipline; and (c) levels and directions of faculty involvement in these aspects of teachers' work. In addition, we shadowed our teacher-informants during entire working days (usually 2 or 3 days per teacher), taking advantage of opportunities to observe formal and informal discussions between teachers and between teachers and administrators.

[9]In Frank (1996), I noted that a comparable interpretation could not be sustained from an image constructed by embedding the boundaries of structurally similar blocks (two teachers are structurally similar to the extent that they engage in similar patterns of professional discussions) into a sociogram. While the use of structurally similar blocks has been common in other analyses, the concept and representation of cohesiveness capture the dense sets of relations that are key to characterizing the pattern of influence. In contrast, members of structurally similar blocks need not engage in relations with one another. The implication for interpretation is that there is not necessarily a concentration of influence within the block that produces commonalities in attitudes or orientations. The implication for the image is that the boundaries of the blocks overlap to the extent of being obscured. I argued that this result is consistent with longstanding theory. Although some have argued that actors who are structurally similar behave similarly (e.g., Burt, 1982; Merton, 1957; Nadel, 1957; Radcliffe-Brown, 1940; White et al., 1976), few have characterized organizations as composed of blocks of structurally similar people.

[10]Note that this model has no intercept, because Mead (1967) argues that in estimating influence one may just as well subtract out the mean value of **y** from all outcomes on the left- and right- hand sides of the equation.

The specification of $w_{ii}$ should be carefully considered so as to define a model that generates realistic values of $y$ if implemented over time. For example, the standard approach is to "row normalize" each $w_{ii}$ by specifying $w^*_{ii'} = w_{ii'}/(\Sigma_{i'} w_{ii'})$; thus, $w^*_{ii'} y_i$ represents the *relative* influence of $i'$ on $i$. Frank and Fahrbach (1997) also considered differentiating between effects of information and influence to respecify $w_{ii'}$ to produce processes typically found in complex organizations, and Friedkin and Cook (1990) considered a "polarization" parameter to govern the processes implied by Equation 2 (see Friedkin & Marsden, 1994, for other possible specifications of Equation 2).

[11]Burt (1991) and Wasserman and Faust (1994) have noted that the issue of significance testing in social network analysis requires serious consideration because one typically has data from the entire population rather than from a sample. Significance tests can be interpreted as an evaluation of phenomena sampled from a fixed time interval relative to a population of all phenomena over the duration of the system.

[12]James Coleman is once again featured prominently in this area with regard to the definition and measurement of social capital and its application to effects in schools (Coleman, 1986; Schneider & Coleman, 1993).

## APPENDIX

### Web Sites

For software availability, professional associations, publications, and web resources, etc., for multilevel models, refer to the Multilevel Models Project Web site based at the University of Montreal (comparable sites are available at the Institute of Education in London and the University of Melbourne):

http://www.medent.umontreal.ca/multilevel/

For software availability, professional associations, publications, Web resources, etc., for social network analysis, refer to the official Web site of the International Network for Social Network Analysis:

http://www.heinz.cmu.edu/project/INSNA/

## REFERENCES

Abbott, A. (1996). Things of boundaries. *Social Research, 62,* 857–882.
Agresti, A. (1984). *Analysis of categorical data.* New York: Wiley.

Alba, R. (1973). A graph-theoretic definition of a sociometric clique. *Journal of Mathematical Sociology, 3,* 113–126.

Alexander, K. L., Cook, M., & McDill, E. I. (1978). Curriculum tracking and educational stratification: Some further evidence. *American Sociological Review, 43,* 47–66.

Alexander, K. L., & Pallas, A. M. (1985). School sector and cognitive performance: When is a little a little? *Sociology of Education, 58,* 115–128.

Allison, P. D. (1990). Change scores as dependent variables in regression analysis. *Sociological Methodology, 20,* 93–114.

Anselin, L. (1988). *Spatial econometrics: Methods and models.* Amsterdam: Kluwer Academic.

Anstead, C. J., & Goodson, I. R. (1993). Structure and mediation: Glimpses of everyday life at the London Technical and Commercial High School, 1920–1940. *American Journal of Education, 102,* 55–79.

Apple, M. W. (1979). *Ideology and curriculum.* London: Routledge and Kegan Paul.

Apple, M. (1990). *Ideology and curriculum.* New York: Routledge.

Arabie, P., & Hubert, L. (1990). Block models from the bond energy approach. *Social Networks, 12,* 99-126.

Ashton, P., & Webb, R. (1986). *Making a difference: Teachers' sense of efficacy and student achievement.* New York: Longman.

Barker, R., & Gump, P. (1964). *Big school, small school: High school size and student behavior.* Stanford, CA: Stanford University Press.

Barnes, D. (1976). *From communication to curriculum.* New York: Penguin Books.

Barnes, J. (1972). Social networks. In *Anthropology Module 26* (pp. 1–29). Reading, MA: Addison-Wesley.

Barr, R., & Dreeben, R. (1977). Instruction in classrooms. In L. Shulman (Ed.), *Review of research in education* (Vol. 5). Itasca, IL: Peacock.

Barr, R., & Dreeben, R. (1983). *How schools work.* Chicago: University of Chicago Press.

Bereiter, C. (1963). Some persisting dilemmas in the measurement of change. In C. Harris (Ed.), *Problems in measuring change.* Madison: University of Wisconsin Press.

Bidwell, C., & Bryk, A. (1994, April). *How teachers' work is organized: The context and consequences of the structure of the high school workplace.* Paper presented at the annual meeting of the American Educational Research Association, New Orleans, LA.

Bidwell, C., Frank, K., & Quiroz, P. (1997). Teacher types, workplace controls, and the organization of schools. *Sociology of Education, 70*(4), pp. 285–307.

Bidwell, C., & Kasarda, J. (1980). Conceptualizing and measuring the effects of school and schooling. *American Journal of Education, 88,* 401–430.

Bidwell, C., & Quiroz, P. (1991). Organizational control in the high school workplace: A theoretical argument. *Journal of Research on Adolescence, 1,* 211–229.

Bird, T., & Little, J. (1986). How schools organize the teaching occupation. *Elementary School Journal, 86,* 493–511.

Blau, P. M. (1977). *Inequality and heterogeneity.* New York: Macmillan.

Blyth, W. (1958). Sociometry, prefects and peaceful coexistence in a junior school. *Sociology Review, 6,* 5–24.

Blyth, W. (1960). The sociometric study of children's groups in English schools. *British Journal of Educational Studies, 8,* 127–147.

Bock, R. D., & Husain, S. (1948). An adaptation of Holzinger's B-coefficients for the analysis of sociometric data. *Sociometry, 11,* 146–153.

Bonney, M. E. (1943). The relative stability of social, intellectual, and academic status in Grades 2–4 and the interrelationships between these various forms of growth. *Journal of Educational Psychology, 34,* 88–102.

Borgatti, S., Everett, M., & Freeman, L. (1992). *UCINET IV, Version 1.0 reference manual.* Natick, MA: Columbia University Press/Analytic Technologies.

Borgatti, S., Everett, M., & Shirey, P. (1990). LS sets, lambda sets, and other cohesive subsets. *Social Networks, 12,* 337–357.

Bossert, S. (1979). *Tasks and social relationships in classrooms.* New York: Cambridge University Press.

Bott, E. (1971). *Family and social network: Roles, norms and external relations.* London: Tavistock.

Bovasso, G. (1996). A network analysis of social contagion processes in an organizational intervention. *Human Relations, 49,* 1419–1435.

Bowles, S., & Gintis, H. (1976). *Schooling in capitalist America.* New York: Basic Books.

Boyd, R. D. (1965). The group as a sociopsychological setting for learning. *Review of Educational Research, 35,* 209–217.

Bray, M., & Thomas, R. M. (1995). Levels of comparison in educational studies: Different insights from different literatures and the value of multilevel analyses. *Harvard Educational Review, 65,* 472–490.

Breslow, N., & Clayton, D. (1993). Approximate inference in generalized linear mixed models. *Journal of the American Statistical Association, 88,* 9–25.

Brophy, J. (1985). Interactions of male and female students with male and female teachers. In L. Wilkinson & C. Marrett (Eds.), *Gender influence in classroom interaction* (pp. 115–142). New York: Academic Press.

Bruininks, V. L. (1978a). Actual and perceived peer status of learning disabled students in mainstream programs. *The Journal of Special Education, 12,* 51–58.

Bruininks, V. L. (1978b). Peer status and personality characteristics of learning disabled and nondisabled students. *Journal of Learning Disabilities, 11,* 29–34.

Bryan, I. (1974). Peer popularity of learning disabled children. *Journal of Learning Disabilities, 7,* 621–625.

Bryk, A., & Driscoll, M. (1988). *The school as community: Theoretical foundations, contextual influences, and consequences for students and teachers* (W. Madison, Trans.). Madison: National Center on Effective Secondary Schools, University of Wisconsin.

Bryk, A., & Frank, K. (1991). The specialization of teachers' work: An initial exploration. In S. Raudenbush & J. D. Willms (Eds.), *Schools, classrooms, and pupils* (pp. 185–202). San Diego, CA: Academic Press.

Bryk, A. S., Lee, V. E., & Holland, P. B. (1993). *Catholic schools and the common good.* Cambridge, MA: Harvard University Press.

Bryk, A., Lee, V., & Smith, J. B. (1990). High school organization and its effects on teachers and students: An interpretation summary of the research. In W. Clune & J. Witte (Eds.), *Choice and control in American education.* Newbury Park, CA: Falmer.

Bryk, A., & Raudenbush, S. W. (1988). Toward a more appropriate conceptualization of research on school effects. A three-level hierarchical linear model. *American Journal of Education, 97,* 65–108.

Bryk, A., & Raudenbush, S. W. (1992). *Hierarchical linear models.* Newbury Park, CA: Sage.

Bryk, A., Raudenbush, S. W., & Congdon, R. (1997). *Hierarchical linear models.* Chicago: Scientific Software.

Bryk, A., & Thum, Y. (1989). The effects of high school organization on dropping out: An exploratory investigation. *American Educational Research Journal, 26,* 353–383.

Burawoy, M. (1979). *Manufacturing consent: Changes in the labor process under monopoly capitalism.* Chicago: University of Chicago Press.

Burstein, L. (1980). The analysis of multilevel data in educational research and evaluation. In D. Berliner (Ed.), *Review of research in education* (Vol. 8, pp. 158–233). Washington, DC: American Educational Research Association.

Burt, R. (1982). *Toward a structural theory of action.* New York: Academic Press.

Burt, R. (1987). Social contagion and innovation: Cohesion versus structural equivalence. *American Journal of Sociology, 92,* 1287–1335.

Burt, R. S. (1988). Some properties of structural equivalence measures derived from sociometric choice data. *Social Networks, 10,* 1–28.

Burt, R. S. (1991). *STRUCTURE.* New York: Columbia University Press.

Callahan, R. (1962). *Education and the cult of efficiency.* Chicago: University of Chicago Press.

Canada, K., & Pringle, R. (1995). The role of gender in college classroom interactions: A social context approach. *Sociology of Education, 68,* 161–186.

Carbonaro, W. (1997, August). *I get by with a little help from my friends' parents: Family structure, social capital, and effects on educational outcomes.* Paper presented at the annual meeting of the American Sociological Association, Toronto, Ontario, Canada.

Carley, K. (1990). Group stability: A socio-cognitive approach. *Advances in Group Processes, 7,* 1–44.

Carley, K. (1991). A theory of group stability. *American Sociological Review, 56,* 331–354.

Carnegie Council on Adolescent Development. (1989). *Turning points: Preparing American youth for the 21st century.* Washington, DC: Author.

Carnegie Task Force on Teaching as a Profession. (1986). *A nation prepared: Teachers for the 21st century.* New York: Carnegie Forum on Education and the Economy.

Cartwright, D. (1968). The nature of group cohesiveness. In D. Cartwright & A. Zander (Eds.), *Group dynamics: Research and theory* (pp. 91-109). New York: Harper & Row.

Cartwright, D., & Harary, F. (1956). Structural balance: A generalization of Heider's theory. *Psychological Review, 63,* 277–293.

Chew, K. S. (1992). The demographic erosion of political support for public education: A suburban case study. *Sociology of Education, 65,* 280–292.

Cohen, J. (1971). *Adolescent change and peer influence.* Unpublished doctoral dissertation, University of Chicago.

Coleman, J. S. (1958). Relational analysis: The study of social organizations with survey methods. *Human Organization, 17,* 28–36.

Coleman, J. S. (1961). *Adolescent society.* New York: Free Press of Glencoe.

Coleman, J. S. (1986). Social theory, social research and theory of action. *American Journal of Sociology, 91,* 1309–1335.

Coleman, J., Campbell, E., Hobson, C., McPartland, J., Mood, A., Weinfield, J., & York, R. (1966). *Equality of educational opportunity.* Washington, DC: U.S. Government Printing Office.

Collins, R. (1981). On the microfoundations of macrosociology. *American Journal of Sociology, 86,* 984-1014.

Cook, L. (1945). An experimental sociographic study of a stratified tenth grade class. *American Sociological Review, 10,* 250–261.

Cook, T., & Campbell, D. T. (1979). *Quasi-experimentation: Design and analysis issues for field settings.* Boston: Houghton Mifflin.

Cusick, P. (1983). *The egalitarian ideal and the American high school: Studies of three schools.* New York: Longman.

Darling-Hammond, L., & McLaughlin, M. (1995). Policies that support professional development in an era of reform. *Phi Delta Kappan, 76*(8), 597-603.

Davies, M., & Kandel, D. (1981). Parental and peer influences on adolescents' educational plans: Some further evidence. *American Journal of Sociology, 87,* 363–387.

Davis, J. A. (1977). Sociometric triads as multi-variate systems. *Journal of Mathematical Sociology, 5,* 41–59.

DeLany, B. (1991). Allocation, choice, and stratification within high schools: How the sorting machine copes. *American Journal of Education, 9,* 181–207.

Delpit, L. D. (1988). The silence dialogue: Power and pedagogy in educating other people's children. *Harvard Educational Review, 58*(3), 280–298.

Desimone, L. M. (1997, August). *How does the relationship between parental involvement and eighth grade student achievement vary for children of different racial/ethnic groups?* Paper presented at the annual meeting of the American Sociological Association, Toronto, Ontario, Canada.

DeVree, J., & Dagevos, J. (1994). The structure of action and interaction: The structural similarity of systems of social science. *Journal of Mathematical Sociology, 19,* 91–127.

DiMaggio, P. J., & Powell, W. (1991). The iron cage revisited: Institutional isomorphism and collective rationality in organization fields. In W. W. Powell & P. J. DiMaggio (Eds.), *The new institutionalism in organizational analysis* (pp. 63–82). Chicago: University of Chicago Press.

Doreian, P. (1989). Two regimes of network effects autocorrelation. In M. Kochen (Ed.), *The small world* (pp. 280–295). Norwood, NJ: Ablex.

Dow, M., & Leenders, R. A. (1997, February). *The effects of measurement error on estimation procedures for network autocorrelated models.* Paper presented at the Social Network Conference, San Diego, CA.

Dreeben, R., & Barr, R. (1988). Classroom composition and the design of instruction. *Sociology of Education, 61,* 129–142.

Dreeben, R., & Gamoran, A. (1986). Race, instruction, and learning. *American Sociological Review, 51,* 660–669.

Duke, J. B. (1993). Estimation of the network effects model in a large data set. *Sociological Methods and Research, 21,* 465–481.

Duncan, O. D., Haller, A., & Portes, A. (1968). Peer influences on aspirations: A reinterpretation. *American Journal of Sociology, 74,* 119–137.

Durkheim, E. (1933). *Division of labor in society.* New York: Macmillan.

Durkheim, E. (1984). *Division of labor in society* (L. Coser, Ed., and W. Halls, Trans.). New York: Macmillan.

Eckert, P. (1989). *Jocks and burnouts: Social categories and identity in the high school.* New York: Teachers College Press.

Eder, D. (1982). Differences in communicative styles across ability groups. In L. Wilkinson (Ed.), *Communicating in the classroom.* New York: Academic Press.

Eder, D. (1981). Ability grouping as a self-fulfilling prophecy: A micro-analysis of teacher-student interaction. *Sociology of Education, 54,* 151–162.

Edwards, H. (1973). The emerging duty to bargain in the public sector. *Michigan Law Review, 71,* 885–934.

Epstein, J. L. (1983). Selection of friends in differently organized schools and classrooms. In J. L. Epstein & N. Karweit (Eds.), *Friends in school: Patterns of selection and influence in secondary schools* (pp. 73–92). New York: Academic Press.

Epstein, J. L., & Connors-Tadros, L. (1997, August). *High school teachers' reports of school-family-community partnerships.* Paper presented at the annual meeting of the American Sociological Association, Toronto, Ontario, Canada.

Epstein, J. L., & Karweit, N. (Eds.). (1983). *Friends in school: Patterns of selection and influence in secondary schools.* New York: Academic Press.

Epstein, J. L. (1983). The influence of friends on achievement and affective outcomes. In J. L. Epstein & N. Karweit (Eds.), *Friends in school: Patterns of selection and influence in secondary schools* (pp. 177–200). New York: Academic Press.

Erbring, L., & Young, A. A. (1979). Individuals and social structure: Contextual effects as endogenous feedback. *Sociological Methods and Research, 7,* 396–430.

Erickson, F., & Shultz, J. (1982). *The counselor as gatekeeper.* New York: Academic Press.

Etzioni, A. (1961). *Complex organizations: A sociological reader.* New York: Holt, Rinehart & Winston.

Evans, K. (1962). *Sociometry and education.* New York: Humanities Press.

Everett, M. (1983a). An extension of EBLOC to valued graphs. *Social Networks, 5,* 395-402.

Feld, S. L. (1981). The focused organization of social ties. *American Journal of Sociology, 86*(5), 1015–1035.

Festinger, L. (1950). Informal social communication. *Psychological Review, 57,* 271–282.

Festinger, L., Schachter, S., & Back, K. (1950). *Social pressures in informal groups.* Stanford, CA: Stanford University Press.

Fienberg, S., Meyer, M., & Wasserman, S. (1985). Statistical analysis of multiple sociometric relations. *Journal of the American Statistical Association, 80,* 51–67.

Fienberg, S., & Wasserman, S. (1981). Categorical data analysis of single sociometric relations. In S. Leinhardt (Ed.), *Analysis of single sociometric relations* (pp. 156–193). San Francisco: Jossey-Bass.

Firestone, W., & Wilson, B. (1985). Using bureaucratic and cultural linkages to improve instruction: The principal's contribution. *Educational Administration Quarterly, 21*(2), 7–30.

Fitz-Gibbon, C. T. (1991). Multilevel modelling in an indicator system. In S. Raudenbush & J. D. Willms (Eds.), *Schools, pupils, and classrooms: International studies of schooling from a multilevel perspective* (pp. 67–84). San Diego, CA: Academic Press.

Flanders, N. A., & Havumaki, S. (1960). The effect of teacher-pupil contacts involving praise on the sociometric choices of students. *Journal of Educational Psychology, 57*, 65–68.

Flecker, R. (1967). Group centered learning: A growing field and its problems. *Australian Psychologist, 2*, 31–39.

Frank, K., & Yasumoto, J. (1997, August). *Embedded in what? Variations in social structure and social capital.* Paper presented at the annual meeting of the American Sociological Association, Toronto, Ontario, Canada.

Frank, K. A. (1993). *Identifying cohesive subgroups.* Chicago: University of Chicago Press.

Frank, K. A. (1995a). Identifying cohesive subgroups. *Social Networks, 17*, 27–56.

Frank, K. A. (1995b). *Exploring interrelated structures: A system based on P1 and influence models.* Paper presented at the International Conference on Social Networks, London.

Frank, K. A. (1996). Mapping interactions within and between cohesive subgroups. *Social Networks, 18*, 93–119.

Frank, K. A., & Fahrbach, K. (1997, February). *Exploring interrelated structures: A system of longitudinal models of selection and interpersonal influence in a social network.* Paper presented at the annual meeting of the Sunbelt Social Networks Conference, San Diego, CA.

Frank, K., & Xu, J. (1997). *Maximum likelihood estimation for network effects.* Working paper, Michigan State University.

Frank, O., & Strauss, D. (1986). Markov graphs. *Journal of the American Statistical Association, 81*, 832–842.

Freeman, L. C. (1978). Segregation in social networks. *Sociological Methods and Research, 6*, 411–427.

Freeman, L. C. (1992). Filling in the blanks: A theory of cognitive categories and the structure of social affiliation. *Social Psychology Quarterly, 55*, 118–127.

French, R., & Mensh, I. (1948). Some relationships between interpersonal judgments and sociometric status in a college group. *Sociometry, 11*, 335–345.

Friedkin, N. E. (1990). SNAPS (social network analysis procedures) for Gauss. *Social Networks, 12*, 173–178.

Friedkin, N. E. (1997). *A structural theory of social influence.* Cambridge, England: Cambridge University Press.

Friedkin, N. E., & Cook, K. S. (1990). Peer group influence. *Sociological Methods and Research, 19*, 122–143.

Friedkin, N. E., & Johnson, E. C. (1990). Social influence and opinions. *Journal of Mathematical Sociology, 15*, 193–205.

Friedkin, N. E., & Marsden, P. (1994). Network studies of social influence. In S. Wasserman & J. Galaskiewicz (Eds.), *Advances in social network analysis* (pp. 1–25). Thousand Oaks, CA: Sage.

Friedkin, N. E., & Thomas, S. (1997). Social positions in schooling. *Sociology of Education, 70*(4), 239–255.

Fuchs, L., Fuchs, D., Hamlett, C., Phillips, N., & Karns, K. (1995). General educators' specialized adaptation for students with learning disabilities. *Exceptional Children, 6*(5), 440–459.

Fuller, B., & Izu, J. (1986). Explaining school cohesion: What shapes the organizational beliefs of teachers? *American Journal of Education, 94,* 501–535.

Gamoran, A. (1987). The stratification of high school learning opportunities. *Sociology of Education, 60,* 135–155.

Gamoran, A. (1991). Schooling and achievement: Additive versus interactive models. In S. W. Raudenbush & J. D. Willms (Eds.), *Schools, pupils, and classrooms: International studies of schooling from a multilevel perspective* (pp. 37–52). San Diego, CA: Academic Press.

Gamoran, A. (1996). Curriculum standardization and equality of opportunity in Scottish secondary education: 1984–90. *Sociology of Education, 69,* 1–21.

Gerber, P. (1977). Awareness of handicapping conditions and sociometric status in an integrated preschool setting. *Mental Retardation, 15*(3), 24–25.

Goldstein, H. (1987). *Multilevel models in educational and social research.* London: Oxford University Press.

Goldstein, H. (1991). Nonlinear multilevel models with an application to discrete response data. *Biometrika, 78,* 45–51.

Goldstein, H. (1995). *Multilevel statistical models* (2nd ed.). New York: Wiley.

Goodman, J. (1995). Change without difference: School restructuring in historical perspective. *Harvard Educational Review, 65,* 1–29.

Granovetter, M. (1973). The strength of weak ties: Network theory revisited. *American Journal of Sociology, 18,* 279–288.

Grant, G. (1988). *The world we created at Hamilton High.* Cambridge, MA: Harvard University Press.

Greenfield, T. (1975). Theory about organization: A new perspective and its implications for schools. In R. Campbell & R. Gregg (Eds.), *Administrative behavior in education.* London: Athlone.

Gronlund, N. E. (1950). The accuracy of teachers' judgments concerning the sociometric status of sixth-grade pupils. *Sociometry, 13,* 197–225.

Gronlund, N. E. (1959). *Sociometry in the classroom.* New York: Harper.

Grossman, P. L., & Stodolsky, S. S. (1995). Content as context: The role of school subjects in secondary school teaching. *Educational Researcher, 24*(8), 5–11.

Hall, R. M., & Sandler, B. R. (1982). *The classroom climate: A chilly one for women?* Washington, DC: Project on the Status and Education of Women, Association of American Colleges.

Hallinan, M. (1976). *Friendship formation: A continuous time Markov process* (CDE Working Paper 76–5). Madison: University of Wisconsin Center for Demography and Ecology.

Hallinan, M. T. (1992). The organization of students for instruction in the middle school. *Sociology of Education, 65,* 114–127.

Hannaway, J., & Talbert, J. E. (1993). Bringing context into effective schools research: Urban-suburban differences. *Educational Administration Quarterly, 29*(2), 164–186.

Hansell, S., & Karweit, N. (1983). Curricular placement, friendship networks, and status attainment. In J. L. Epstein & N. Karweit (Eds.), *Friends in school: Patterns of selection and influence in secondary schools* (pp. 141–162). New York: Academic Press.

Hanson, E. (1978). Organizational control in educational systems: A case study of governance in schools. In S. Bacharach (Ed.), *Organizational behavior in schools and school districts* (pp. 245–276). New York: Praeger.

Hargreaves, A. (1993). Individualism and individuality: Reinterpreting the teacher culture. In J. Little & M. McLaughlin (Eds.), *Teachers' work: Individuals, colleagues, and contexts* (pp. 51–76). New York: Teachers College Press.

Hartup, W. (1978). Children and their friends. In H. McGurk (Ed.), *Issues in childhood social development.* London: Methuen.

Hedeker, D., & Gibbons, R. (1996). MIXOR: A computer program for mixed-effects ordinal probit and logistic regression analysis. *Computer Methods and Programs in Biomedicine, 49,* 157–176.

Heider, F. (1958). *Psychology of interpersonal relations.* New York: Wiley.

Heyns, B. (1974). Social selection and stratification within schools. *American Journal of Sociology, 79,* 1434–1451.

Holland, P. W., & Leinhardt, S. (1981). An exponential family of probability distributions for directed graphs. *Journal of the American Statistical Association, 76,* 33–49.

Hollingshead, A. (1949). *Elmstown's youth.* New York: Wiley.

Homans, G. C. (1950). *The human group.* New York: Harcourt Brace.

Hubbell, C. (1965). An input output approach to clique identification. *Sociometry, 28,* 377-399.

Hubert, L. J. (1987). *Assignment methods in combinatorial data analysis.* New York: Marcel Dekker.

Ingersoll, R. M. (1994). Organizational control in secondary schools. *Harvard Educational Review, 64,* 150–172.

Jacobsen, S. (1991). The relationship between kindergarten screening measures and grade three achievement. In S. Raudenbush & J. D. Willms (Eds.), *Schools, pupils, and classrooms: International studies of schooling from a multilevel perspective* (pp. 167–184). San Diego, CA: Academic Press.

Jamieson, J. (1984). Attitudes of educators toward the handicapped. In R. Jones (Ed.), *Attitudes and attitude change in special education* (pp. 206–222). Reston, VA: The Council for Exceptional Children.

Jennings, H. H. (1943). *Leadership and isolation.* New York: Longman.

Johnson, S. (1990). *Teachers at work achieving success in our schools.* New York: Basic Books.

Jones, R., & Guskin, S. (1984). Attitudes and attitude change in special education. In R. Jones (Ed.), *Attitudes and attitude change in special education* (pp. 1–20). Reston, VA: The Council for Exceptional Children.

Kadushin, C. (1995). Friendship among the French financial elite. *American Sociological Review, 60,* 201–221.

Katz, L. (1947). On the matric analysis of sociometric data. *Sociometry, 10,* 233-241.

Kennedy, P., Northcott, W., McCauley, R., & Williams, S. (1976). Longitudinal sociometric and cross-sectional data in mainstreaming hearing impaired children in regular classrooms. *Exceptional Children, 40,* 336–342.

Keeves, J., & Sellin, N. (1988). Multilevel analysis. In J. Keeves (Ed.), *Educational research, methodology and measurement: An international handbook* (pp. 689–700). Oxford, England: Pergamon Press.

Kerbow, D., & Bernhardt, A. (1993). Parental intervention in the school: The context of minority involvement. In B. Schneider & J. S. Coleman (Eds.), *Parents, their children, and schools* (pp. 115–146). Boulder, CO: Westview Press.

Kidd, J. (1951). An analysis of social rejection in a college men's residence hall. *Sociometry, 16,* 225–334.

Kilgore, S. B., & Pendleton, W. W. (1993). The organizational context of learning: Framework for understanding the acquisition of knowledge. *Sociology of Education, 66,* 63–87.

King, C. E. (1960). The applicability of small group knowledge to the classroom situation. *Sociology and Social Research, 45,* 18–23.

Krackhardt, D., Blyth, J., & McGrath, C. (1994). Krackplot 3.0: An improved network drawing program. *Connections, 17*(2), 53–55.

Kuhlen, R., & Bretsch, H. (1947). Sociometric status and personal problems of adolescents. *Sociometry, 10,* 122–132.

Kuhlon, R. G., & Lee, B. J. (1943). Personality characteristics and social acceptability in adolescence. *Journal of Educational Psychology, 34,* 321–340.

Laumann, E. O. (1970). *The logic of social hierarchies.* Chicago: Markham.

Lazersfeld, P., & Menzel, H. (1961). On the relation between individual and collective properties. In A. Etzioni (Ed.), *Complex organizations* (pp. 422–440). New York: Holt, Rinehart & Winston.

Lee, V., & Bryk, A. (1989). A multilevel model of the social distribution of high school achievement. *Sociology of Education, 62,* 172–192.

Lee, V., Dedrick, R., & Smith, J. (1991). The effect of the social organization of schools on teacher satisfaction. *Sociology of Education, 64,* 190–208.

Lee, V. E., Marks, H. M., & Byrd, T. (1994). Sexism in single-sex and coeducational independent secondary school classrooms. *Sociology of Education, 67,* 92–120.

Lee, V. E., & Smith, J. B. (1991). Sex discrimination in teachers' salary. In S. Raudenbush & J. D. Willms (Eds.), *Schools, pupils, and classrooms: International studies of schooling from a multilevel perspective* (pp. 225–248). San Diego, CA: Academic Press.

Lee, V. E., & Smith, J. B. (1993). Effects of school restructuring on the achievement and engagement of middle-grade students. *Sociology of Education, 66,* 164–187.

Lee, V. E., & Smith, J. B. (1995). Effects of high school restructuring and size on early gains in achievement and engagement. *Sociology of Education, 68,* 241–270.

Lee, V. E., & Smith, J. B. (1996). Collective responsibility for learning and its effects on gains in achievement for early secondary school students. *American Journal of Education, 104,* 103–147.

Lee, V. E., Smith, J. B., & Croninger, R. G. (1997). How high school organization influences the equitable distribution of learning in mathematics and science. *Sociology of Education, 70,* 128–150.

Leenders, R. (1995). *Structure and influence: Statistical models for the dynamics of actor attributes, network structure and their interdependence.* Amsterdam: Thesis.

Levine, D., & Lezotte, L. (1990). *Unusually effective schools.* Madison, WI: National Center for Effective Schools Research and Development.

Lieberman, A. (1995). Practices that support teacher development. *Phi Delta Kappan, 76*(8), 591–596.

Lightfoot, S. (1983). *The good high school: Portraits of character and culture.* New York: Basic Books.

Lindley, D., & Smith, A. (1972). Bayes estimates for the linear model. *Journal of the Royal Statistical Society, Series B, 34,* 1–41.

Linn, R., & Slinde, J. (1977). The determination of the significance of change between pre- and posttesting periods. *Review of Educational Research, 47,* 121–150.

Little, J. (1984). Organizing for quality: Good teaching and good teachers. *Journal of Children and Contemporary Society, 16,* 71–84.

Little, J. (1993). Professional community in comprehensive high schools: The two worlds of academic and vocational teachers. In J. Little & M. McLaughlin (Eds.), *Teachers' work: Individuals, colleagues, and contexts* (pp. 137–163). New York: Teachers College Press.

Lockheed, M. E., & Longford, N. T. (1991). School effects on mathematics achievement gain in Thailand. In S. Raudenbush & J. D. Willms (Eds.), *Schools, pupils, and classrooms: International studies of schooling from a multilevel perspective* (pp. 131–148). San Diego, CA: Academic Press.

Longford, N. (1993). *Random coefficient models.* Oxford, England: Clarendon Press.

Lortie, D. (1977). *Schoolteacher: A sociological study.* Chicago: University of Chicago Press.

Luce, R. (1950). Connectivity and generalized cliques in sociometric groups. *Psychometrika, 15,* 169–190.

MacIver, D., & Epstein, J. (1991). Responsive practices in the middle grades: Teacher teams, advisory groups, remedial instruction, and school transition programs. *American Journal of Education, 99,* 587–622.

MacMillan, D., & Morrison, G. (1984). Sociometric research in special education. In R. Jones (Ed.), *Attitudes and attitude change in special education* (pp. 93–117). Reston, VA: The Council for Exceptional Children.

Marsden, P., & Friedkin, N. E. (1994). Network studies of social influence. *Sociological Methods and Research, 22,* 127–151.

Matula, D. (1972). K-components, clusters, and slicing in graphs. *Journal of the American Statistical Association, 22,* 459-480.

McDermott, R., & Aron, J. (1978). Pirandello in the classroom. In M. Reynolds (Ed.), *The futures of education.* Reston, VA: Council for Exceptional Children.

McDonald, J., Smith, S., Turner, D., Finney, M., & Barton, E. (1993). *Graduation by exhibition: Assessing genuine achievement.* Alexandria, VA: Association for Supervision and Curriculum Development.

McLaughlin, M., & Marsh, D. (1979). Staff development and school change. In A. Lieberman & L. Miller (Eds.), *Staff development: New demands, realities, new perspectives* (pp. 69–94). New York: Teachers College Press.

McNeal, R. B. (1997, August). *Parental involvement and dropping out of high school.* Paper presented at the annual meeting of the American Sociological Association, Toronto, Ontario, Canada.

Mead, R. (1967). A mathematical model for the estimation of interplant competition. *Biometrics, 23*(2), 189–206.

Mehan, H. (1992). Understanding inequality in schools: The contribution of interpretive studies. *Sociology of Education, 65,* 1–20.

Mehan, H., Hertweck, A., & Meihls, J. L. (1986). *Handicapping the handicapped: Decision making in students' educational careers.* Stanford, CA: Stanford University Press.

Merton, R. K. (1957). *Social theory and social structure.* Glencoe, IL: Free Press.

Metz, M. (1983). Sources of constructive social relationships in an urban magnet school. *American Journal of Education, 91,* 202–245.

Metz, M. (1990). How social class differences shape teachers' work. In M. W. McLaughlin, J. Talbert, & N. Bascia (Eds.), *The contexts of teaching in secondary schools: Teachers' realities.* New York: Teachers College Press.

Meyer, J., & Rowan, B. (1977). Institutionalized organizations: Formal structure as myth and ceremony. *American Journal of Sociology, 30,* 431–450.

Meyer, J., & Rowan, B. (1991). Institutionalized organizations: Formal structure as myth and ceremony. In W. Powell & P. J. DiMaggio (Eds.), *The new institutionalism in organizational analysis* (pp. 41–62). Chicago: University of Chicago Press.

Miskel, C., & Ogawa, R. (1988). Work motivation, job satisfaction, and climate. In N. Boyan (Ed.), *Handbook of educational administration* (pp. 279–304). New York: Longman.

Mitchell, J. (1973). Networks, norms and institutions. In J. Boissevain & J. Mitchell (Eds.), *Network analysis: Studies in human interaction* (pp. 15-36). New York: Mouton.

Mokken, R. (1979). Cliques, clubs, and clans. *Quality and Quantity, 13,* 161–173.

Moreno, J. (1934). *Who shall survive: A new approach to the problem of human interactions.* Washington, DC: Nervous and Mental Disease Publishing Co.

Morgan, S. L., & Sorensen, A. (1997, August). *Parents' friends and friends' parents: Network components of social closure and their effects on learning.* Paper presented at the annual meeting of the American Sociological Association, Toronto, Ontario, Canada.

Mudrack, P. (1989). Defining group cohesiveness: A legacy of confusion? *Small Group Behavior, 20*(1), 37–49.

Murnane, R. J. (1975). *The impact of school resources on the learning of inner city children.* Cambridge, MA: Ballinger.

Nadel, S. F. (1957). *The theory of social structure.* London: Cohen & West.

Nakao, K., & Romney, A. (1993). Longitudinal approach to subgroup formation: Re-analysis of Newcomb's fraternity data. *Social Networks, 15,* 109–131.

National Commission on Excellence in Education. (1983). *A nation at risk: The imperative for educational reform.* Washington, DC: U.S. Government Printing Office.

Newcomb, T. (1950). *Social psychology.* New York: Dryden Press.

Newcomb, T. (1961). *The acquaintance process.* New York: Holt, Rinehart & Winston.

Nias, J. (1989). *Primary teachers talking: A study of teaching as work.* New York: Routledge.

Northway, M. L. (1954). A plan for sociometric studies in a longitudinal programme of research in child development. *Sociometry, 7,* 272–281.

Oakes, J. (1985). *Keeping track: How schools structure inequality.* New Haven, CT: Yale University Press.

Ogbu, J. (1978). *Minority education and caste: The American system in cross-cultural perspective.* New York: Academic Press.

Olson, W. C. (1949). *Child development.* Boston: D. C. Heath.

Oosthoeck, H., & van den Eeden, P. (1984). *Multilevel aspects in the educational process.* London: Gordon & Breach.

Ord, K. (1975). Estimation methods for models of spatial interaction. *Journal of the American Statistical Association, 70,* 120–126.

Pallas, A. (1988). School climate in American high schools. *Teachers College Record, 89,* 541–553.

Pallas, A. M., Entwisle, D. R., Alexander, K. L., & Stluka, M. F. (1994). Ability-group effects: Instructional, social, or institutional? *Sociology of Education, 67,* 27–46.

Parsons, T., & Shils, E. (1954). *Toward a general theory of action.* Cambridge, MA: Harvard University Press.

Patterson, L. (1991). Trends in attainment in Scottish secondary schools. In S. Raudenbush & J. D. Willms (Eds.), *Schools, pupils, and classrooms: International studies of schooling from a multilevel perspective* (pp. 85–100). San Diego, CA: Academic Press.

Peshkin, A. (1986). *God's choice: The total world of a fundamentalist Christian.* Chicago: University of Chicago Press.

Phillips, D., & Conviser, R. (1972). Measuring the structure and boundary properties of groups. *Sociometry, 35,* 235-254.

Plewis, I. (1991). Using multilevel models to link educational progress with curriculum coverage. In S. Raudenbush & J. D. Willms (Eds.), *Schools, pupils, and classrooms: International studies of schooling from a multilevel perspective* (pp. 53–66). San Diego, CA: Academic Press.

Portes, A. M., & MacLeod, D. (1996). Educational progress of children of immigrants: The roles of class, ethnicity, and school context. *Sociology of Education, 69,* 255–275.

Powell, M. (1948). Comparisons of self-ratings, peer rating, and expert's rating of personality adjustment. *Educational and Psychological Measurement, 8,* 225–234.

Pratt, G. K. (1960). Group dynamics in the evaluation of classes. *Journal of Educational Sociology, 34,* 106–108.

Quiroz, P., Gonzalez, N., & Frank, K. A. (1996). Carving a niche in the high school social structure: Formal and informal constraints on participation in the extra curriculum. In A. Pallas (Ed.), *Research in sociology of education and socialization* (pp. 93–120). Greenwich, CT: JAI Press.

Radcliffe-Brown, A. (1940). On social structure. *Journal of the Royal Anthropological Society of Great Britain and Ireland, 70,* 1–12.

Rasbash, J., & Goldstein, H. (1994). Efficient analysis of mixed hierarchical and cross classified random structures using a multilevel model. *Journal of Educational and Behavioral Statistics, 19,* 337–350.

Raudenbush, S. (1993). A crossed random effects model for unbalanced data with applications in cross-sectional and longitudinal research. *Journal of Educational Statistics, 18,* 321–349.

Raudenbush, S. (1995). Hierarchical linear models to study the effects of social context on development. In J. Gottman (Ed.), *The analysis of change* (pp. 165–201). Hillsdale, NJ: Erlbaum.

Raudenbush, S., & Bryk, A. (1986). A hierarchical model for studying school effects. *Sociology of Education, 59,* 1–17.

Raudenbush, S., & Bryk, A. (1988). Methodological advances in studying effects of classrooms and schools on student learning. In *Review of research in education* (Vol. 15, pp. 423–476). Washington, DC: American Educational Research Association.

Raudenbush, S., Rowan, B., & Cheong, Y. (1993). Higher order instructional goals in secondary schools: Class, teacher, and school influences. *American Educational Research Journal, 30,* 523–553.

Reitz, K. (1988). Social groups in monastery. *Social Networks, 10,* 343-357.

Riehl, C. N., & Pallas, A. M. (1992, August). *Losing track: The dynamics of student assignment processes in high school.* Paper presented at the annual meeting of the American Sociological Association, Pittsburgh, PA.

Rist, R. (1970). Student social class and teacher expectations: The self-fulfilling prophecy in ghetto education. *Harvard Educational Review, 40,* 411–451.

Roethlisberger, F., & Dickson, W. (1941). *Management and the worker.* Cambridge, MA: Harvard University Press.

Rogosa, D., Brandt, D., & Zimowski, M. (1982). A growth curve approach to the measurement of change. *Psychological Bulletin, 90,* 726–748.

Rogosa, D., & Willett, J. (1983). Demonstrating the reliability of the difference score in the measurement of change. *Journal of Educational Measurement, 20,* 335–343.

Rosenbaum, J. (1976). *Making inequality.* New York: Wiley Interscience.

Rosenholtz, S. (1989). *Teachers' workplace: The social organization of schools.* New York: Longman.

Rosenholtz, S., & Simpson, C. (1990). Workplace conditions and the rise and fall of teachers' commitment. *Sociology of Education, 63,* 241–257.

Rowan, B. (1990). Applying conceptions of teaching to organizational reform. In R. Elmore (Ed.), *Restructuring schools: The next generation of educational reform.* San Francisco: Jossey-Bass.

Rowan, B. (1995). The organizational design of schools. In S. Bacharach & B. Mundell (Eds.), *Images of schools* (pp. 11–42). Thousand Oaks, CA: Corwin Press.

Rowan, B., Raudenbush, S. W., & Kang, S. J. (1991). School climate in secondary schools. In S. W. Raudenbush & J. D. Willms (Eds.), *Schools, pupils, and classrooms: International studies of schooling from a multilevel perspective* (pp. 203–224). San Diego, CA: Academic Press.

Rumberger, R. W. (1995). Dropping out of middle school: A multilevel analysis of students and schools. *American Educational Research Journal, 32,* 583–625.

Sampson, R., Raudenbush, S., & Earls, T. (1997). Neighborhoods and violent crime: A multilevel study of collective efficacy. *Science, 277,* 918–924.

Sarason, S. (1971). *The culture of the school and the problem of change.* Boston: Allyn & Bacon.

Schein, E. (1985). *Organizational culture and leadership: A dynamic view.* San Francisco: Jossey-Bass.

Schiller, K., & Muller, C. (1997, August). *Expectations, external examinations, and the process of educational attainment.* Paper presented at the annual meeting of the American Sociological Association, Toronto, Ontario, Canada.

Schmuck, R. A., & Schmuck, P. A. (1975). Group processes in the classroom. Dubuque, IA: Wm. C. Brown Co.

Schneider, B., & Coleman, J. S. (1993). *Parents, their children and schools.* Boulder, CO: Westview Press.

Scott, J. (1991). *Social network analysis.* New York: Sage Publications.

Seidman, S. (1983). LS sets and cohesive subsets of graphs and hypergraphs. *Social Networks, 5,* 92–96.

Seidman, S., & Foster, B. (1978). A graph-theoretic generalization of the clique concept. *Journal of Mathematical Sociology, 6,* 139–154.

Seltzer, M. (1990). *The use of data augmentation in fitting hierarchical models to educational data.* Unpublished doctoral dissertation, University of Chicago.

Selznick, P. (1961). Foundations of the theory of organization. In A. Etzioni (Ed.), *Complex organizations* (pp. 18-31). New York: Holt, Rinehart & Winston.

Sewell, W., Haller, A., & Ohlendorf, G. (1970). The educational and early occupational attainmenet process: Replication and revision. *American Sociological Review, 35,* 1014–1027.

Sheare, J. B. (1978). The impact of resource programs upon the self-concept and peer acceptance of learning disabled children. *Psychology in the Schools, 15,* 406–412.

Shedd, J. B., & Bacharach, S. B. (1991). *Tangled hierarchies: Teachers as professionals and the management of schools.* San Francisco: Jossey-Bass.

Simmel, G. (1955). *Conflict and the web of group affiliations* (K. Wolff, Trans.). Glencoe, IL: Free Press.

Simon, H. A. (1965). The architecture of complexity. In L. von Bertalanffy & A. Rapaport (Eds.), *General systems: Yearbook of the Society for General Systems* (Vol. 10, pp. 63–76). Ann Arbor, MI: Society for the Advancement of General Systems Theory.

Siskin, L. (1991). Departments as different worlds: Subject subcultures in secondary schools. *Educational Administration Quarterly, 27*(2), 134–160.

Smith, L., Prunty, J., & Dwyer, D. (1981). A longitudinal nested systems model of innovation and change in schooling. In S. Bacharach (Ed.), *Organizational behavior in schools and school districts* (pp. 127–160). New York: Praeger.

Sorensen, A. B. (1984). The organizational differentiation of students in schools. In H. Oosthoeck & P. van den Eeden (Eds.), *Multilevel aspects in the educational process* (pp. 25–43). London: Gordon & Breach.

Sorensen, A. B., & Hallinan, M. (1976). A stochastic model for change in group structure. *Social Science Research, 5,* 43–61.

Spradley, J., & McCurdy, D. (1972). *The cultural experience: Ethnography in complex society.* Chicago: SRA Associates.

Staessens, K. (1993). Identification and description of professional culture in innovating schools. *Qualitative Studies in Education, 6,* 111–128.

Stokman, F., & Zeggelink, E. (1996). Is politics power or policy oriented? A comparative analysis of dynamic access models in policy networks. *Journal of Mathematical Sociology, 21,* 77–111.

Strauss, D., & Ikeda, M. (1990). Pseudolikelihood estimation for social networks. *Journal of the American Statistical Association, 85,* 204–212.

Summers, A., & Wolfe, B. (1977). Do schools make a difference? *American Economic Review, 67,* 639–652.

Thum, Y. (1997). Hierarchical linear models for multivariate outcomes. *Journal of Educational and Behavioral Statistics, 22*(1), 77–108.

Trent, S. (1992). *Collaboration between special educators and regular educators: A cross case analysis.* Unpublished doctoral dissertation, University of Virginia, Charlottesville.

Triandis, H., Adamopoulos, J., & Brinberg, D. (1984). Perspectives and issues in the study of attitudes. In R. Jones (Ed.), *Attitudes and attitude change in special education* (pp. 21–41). Reston, VA: The Council for Exceptional Children.

Waller, W. (1932). *The sociology of teacher.* New York: Wiley.

Wasserman, S., & Faust, K. (1994). *Social networks analysis: Methods and applications.* New York: Cambridge University Press.

Wasserman, S., & Galaskiewicz, J. (1994). *Advances in social network analysis.* Twelve Oaks, CA: Sage Publications.

Wasserman, S., & Pattison, P. (1996). Logit models and logistic regressions for univariate and bivariate social networks: I. An introduction to Markov graphs. *Psychometrika, 61,* 401–426.

Watts, W. (1984). Attitude change: Theories and methods. In R. Jones (Ed.), *Attitudes and attitude change in special education* (pp. 41–69). Reston, VA: The Council for Exceptional Children.

Weber, M. (1958). *From Max Weber: Essays in sociology* (H. Gerth & C. Mills, Trans.). New York: Oxford University Press.

Weiss, C. H. (1995). The four "I's" of school reform: How interests, ideology, information, and institution affect teachers and principals. *Harvard Educational Review, 65,* 571–592.

White, H., Boorman, S., & Breiger, R. (1976). Social structure from multiple networks. *American Journal of Sociology, 81,* 730-781.

Wilcox, K. (1982). Differential socialization in the classroom: Implications for equal opportunity. In G. Spindler (Ed.), *Doing the ethnography of schooling.* New York: Harcourt Brace & World.

Willett, J. (1988). Questions and answers in the measurement of change. In *Review of research in education* (Vol. 15, pp. 224–241). Washington, DC: American Educational Research Association.

Willms, J., & Raudenbush, S. (1989). A longitudinal hierarchical linear model for estimating school effects and their stability. *Journal of Educational Measurement, 26,* 209–232.

Wilson, S., & Ball, D. (1991). *Changing visions and changing practices: Patchworks in learning to teach mathematics for understanding* (Research Report 91–2). East Lansing: National Center for Research on Teacher Learning, Michigan State University.

Xu, J. (1996). *Solution methods for spatial linear models.* Unpublished apprenticeship paper, Michigan State University.

Yang, M. (1998). *Increasing the efficiency in estimating multilevel Bernoulli models.* Unpublished doctoral dissertation, Michigan State University.

Yosef, M. (1997). *Two-level hierarchical mixed-effects logistic regression analysis: A comparison of maximum likelihood and penalized quasi-likelihood.* Unpublished manuscript, College of Education, Michigan State University.

Zeichner, K., & Gore, J. (1989). *Teacher socialization.* East Lansing: National Center for Research on Teacher Learning, Michigan State University.

Zeleny, L. D. (1941). Status: Its measurement and control in education. *Sociometry, 4,* 193–204.

Zimmerman, D., Brotohusodo, T., & Williams, R. (1981). The reliability of sums and differences of test scores: Some new results and anomalies. *Journal of Experimental Education, 49,* 177–186.

Zuzovsky, R., & Aitkin, M. (1991). Curricular change and science achievement in Israeli elementary schools. In S. Raudenbush & J. D. Willms (Eds.), *Schools, pupils, and classrooms: International studies of schooling from a multilevel perspective* (pp. 25–36). San Diego, CA: Academic Press.

Manuscript received August 1, 1997
Accepted December 31, 1997

# Chapter 6

# On the Effectiveness and Limitations of Tutoring in Reading

TIMOTHY SHANAHAN
University of Illinois at Chicago

In my office, there is a print, "Su Primer Libro," by Edward Gonzales. It shows an older man in overalls sitting with a child and a book. The man is pointing something out on the page to the little girl, who sits in rapt attention. Few images are more compelling than that of a teacher teaching a single child. American education has been attracted hopefully to such images. President Bill Clinton (1996) has called for the mobilization of "a million volunteer reading tutors all across America" and for unleashing the energy and enthusiasm of [college students] to help every eight-year-old learn to read." The president believes he can increase elementary reading achievement through the use of tutors supported by college work-study programs. "We *know* [italics added] that individualized tutoring works," President Clinton said.

Recently, Rebecca Barr and I published an analysis of Reading Recovery, an early educational tutorial for low-achieving first graders (Shanahan & Barr, 1995). We found it to be an effective approach, although not as effective as its proponents have claimed. Since that publication appeared, we have been challenged occasionally by detractors of Reading Recovery who apparently share the president's conviction about tutoring. "Of course it works. They teach only one child at a time. Anything would work that way," we have been told by teachers and researchers alike.

But does tutoring actually work, and under what circumstances does it work? This chapter reviews empirical studies of the use of tutoring to teach reading in order to offer appropriate guidance in terms of practice, policy, and research. Tutoring is an example of "active social mediation of individual learning," to use the Salomon and Perkins (Chapter 1) terminology. They describe this type of instructional arrangement as being among "the most fundamentally social forms of learning" because of the close relationship between the facilitating social agent or tutor and the learner. And it should be somewhat easier to understand teacher-student relationships or the function or meaning of specific interactions in a tutoring context than in a classroom one where each event is subject to the multiple interpretations of the various participants. Thus, tutoring presents an almost ideal locus for understanding the social aspects of teaching.

Unfortunately, most analyses of tutoring have considered the cognitive aspects of tutor-student interactions with little regard for the social dimensions. Consequently, this review must emphasize cognitive issues such as difficulty, attention,

217

and time on task more than social ones such as identification, affiliation, and status. The studies reviewed here thus provide essential context for the conduct of future studies of social issues in teaching and learning. If social research is to provide a greater understanding of learning, it will need to consider the connections between cognitive processes and social relations.

This is not to say that there have been no investigations of social aspects of tutoring. Several studies, for example, have found that peer tutoring arrangements lead to more positive interpersonal relationships or greater social acceptance among the participants (Bowermaster, 1978; Eiserman, 1988; Jason, Erone, & Soucy, 1979; Larnen & Ehly, 1976). That taking part in peer tutoring improves social status, at least under some circumstances, appears to be more true for girls (Pillen, Jason, & Olson, 1988) and for younger students (Eiserman, 1988). Possibly some students, particularly older boys, are more self-conscious or shy within tutoring sessions, or tutoring itself might carry a social stigma under certain conditions. Various studies have reported on the importance of tutor empathy (Colligan, 1974), same-sex tutoring (Galen & Mavrogenes, 1979), and perceptions of caring (Kaiden, 1994) in tutoring effectiveness. Juel (1991) has suggested the power of close personal identification between tutors and students, although she did not actually vary this condition within her research. It seems apparent that tutoring works best when students have a clear feeling that the tutors are trying to help. How this actually plays out in determining the choices made by tutors or the engagement of tutees awaits future investigations.

The *American Heritage Dictionary* defines tutor as a "private instructor," or "one who gives additional, special, or remedial instruction." Initially, the notion of private instruction referred to the idea that the tutor was hired to teach in a private setting, such as a household. Increasingly, however, tutors are employed by public schools, and the privacy notion has been transformed into the concept of one-to-one teaching (i.e., one teacher working with one student at a time). Given that definition, tutoring is, perhaps, the oldest form of instruction. In most cultures, the earliest teaching was provided to children individually in the home, and more formal arrangements—usually reserved for nobles—placed a strong emphasis on one-to-one teaching and mentoring. Schools and other forms of group teaching emerged later, but tutoring continued to have significance in basic education within the home and in the instruction of the privileged few. By the 17th century, for instance, the universities at Oxford, Cambridge, and Dublin were routinely assigning tutors to their elite students. Similar arrangements for the education of gentlemen were evident in other countries as well and continue today in the widely used *juku* or after-hours tutoring schools that specialize in examination preparation in Japan.

Within the United States in the 1990s, the tutoring concept has become quite specific. Tutoring increasingly refers to remedial instruction that is delivered by one teacher to one student, and this teacher is usually not the student's classroom teacher. He or she might be another professional educator, a paraprofessional, a parent or other volunteer, or even another student. In instances in which the classroom teacher is the tutor, as in some variations of Reading Recovery or in many after-school and summer programs supported by Title I, the instructional setting is outside the regular classroom.

The emphasis on one-to-one teaching for remedial purposes has been evident in most American tutoring programs over the past few decades, as revealed by an analysis of published research. Marked historic differences have been evident, however, as to who is the tutor in these studies. The preponderance of research on tutoring published in the United States from 1970–1985 focused on peer or cross-age tutoring among children. These studies assumed that tutoring was an effective form of instruction, and they were conducted to determine whether children could act as effective tutors and to determine what the effects of such tutoring would be on the tutors themselves. In fact, the efficacy of tutoring apparently was so self-evident to many researchers investigating such programs that, in some cases, they did not even bother to report on the effects of the programs on the children being tutored. During the 1980s, research attention began to shift from peer tutoring to specialized interventions for the lowest achieving children. These studies usually examined the use of professional teachers as tutors, and the studies were undertaken more to evaluate ambitious programs of intervention (only one part of which was tutoring) than to evaluate the effectiveness of the tutoring itself. Throughout, there has been attention to the use of parents as tutors, especially in European studies and those emphasizing special education populations. These studies, like those on peer tutoring, assume that tutoring works but want to know if a specific population of tutors can be effective. Only a few studies have considered the benefits of college tutors of the type envisioned in current public policy (Juel, 1996), although these have generally produced positive results.

Although studies of tutoring have been conducted in several academic areas, major public policy initiatives and educational innovations have been emphasizing the use of tutors within reading instruction. Consequently, this review considers only studies that have emphasized the use of tutors (whoever these tutors may be) for teaching reading.

Several research syntheses of the tutoring literature already exist, and this chapter relies heavily on the combined findings of those reviews. In addition, I used PsychInfo to identify recently published studies (1990–1997) on tutors or tutoring that focused on reading education with elementary-aged children. Eighty articles were identified in this way; however, a large number of these articles were not useful. Some focused solely on the learning of the tutors, some were about computerized tutors, and many were about side issues such as oral reading accuracy.

## IS TUTORING REALLY EFFECTIVE?

The effectiveness of tutoring is widely accepted, and this belief has garnered consistent support from research. Cohen, Kulik, and Kulik (1982) cited four major reviews of tutoring from the educational literature published between 1969 and 1982 (Devin-Sheehan, Feldman, & Allen, 1976; Ellson, 1976; Fitz-Gibbon, 1977; Rosenshine & Furst, 1969). All of these reviews indicated that peer tutoring led to significant academic learning gains in reading, math, and other areas. Cohen and his colleagues used these reviews as the basis of their own review, a meta-analysis of the achievement outcomes of 52 tutoring studies, mostly studies of peer tutoring or tutoring by paraprofessionals. They found an average effect size of .40 with regard to the academic achievement gains of the tutored students. This means that students who were tutored gained an additional 40% of a standard deviation in reading achievement over control group students who had not received tutoring. These gains were both statistically significant and educationally meaningful. As the authors put it, "These programs have definite and positive effects on the academic performance and attitudes of those who receive tutoring" (p. 244).

Two literature reviews (Scruggs & Richter, 1985a, 1985b), one analyzing 17 studies of peer tutoring with students who suffered from behavioral disorders and another considering 24 studies of peer tutoring with students with learning disabilities, also revealed positive results. The review of learning disabilities studies found that "all investigators reported that tutoring had successfully increased academic performance" (p. 295), and some of the studies also found social and emotional benefits for the students being tutored. The tutees who had behavioral disorders also were found to make more academic gains with tutoring than without.

Cook, Scruggs, Mastropieri, and Casto (1985–1986) used meta-analysis to evaluate the effects of 19 tutoring studies in which children with disabilities served as the tutors. The mean effect size across all academic areas was .53 for the tutees. Results were similarly positive in a more recent review of the effects of tutoring that focused on nonpeer arrangements. Wasik and Slavin (1993) analyzed 16 studies of first-grade tutorials for children at risk of reading failure. They considered studies of Reading Recovery, Success for All, Prevention of Learning Disabilities, the Wallach Tutoring Program, and Programmed Tutorial Reading. An average effect size of .51 was evident in the various comparisons that they tabulated, suggesting that the tutored children gained substantially more than control comparisons. In another review, Mathes and Fuchs (1994), considering only the effects of peer tutoring on students with mild learning disabilities, examined 11 studies and found an effect size of .36. Finally, Shanahan and Barr (1995, p. 973) examined studies of Reading Recovery and found that

from all of this it seems reasonable to conclude that children who receive Reading Recovery instruction make sizable gains in reading achievement during the first-grade year. These gains compare favorably with those of higher achieving first graders who receive only regular classroom instruction, or such instruction along with compensatory support.

Thus, research clearly supports the use of many forms of tutoring with a wide range of students. These eight literature reviews, summarizing more than 100 studies, found a rather consistent pattern of tutored children doing better than students who were not tutored. These results can be amplified as well. Many tutoring studies have used research methodologies—such as single-subject designs—that do not allow their results to be combined easily with the results of other studies. However, such studies have usually found tutoring to be beneficial to academic achievement. Similarly, many studies were excluded from the various reviews because of their failure to report key statistics such as means and standard deviations, although they had reported significant achievement gains due to tutoring.

Given that many laypersons and professionals assume that tutoring works, these results should not be surprising. What is more interesting, however, is that tutoring does not always work, and in some circumstances it works better than others. The remainder of this chapter considers specific research findings that have implications for educational policies and practices.

## DOES TUTORING ALWAYS WORK?

Despite the overwhelming evidence that tutoring works, it should be apparent that tutoring is not a panacea. In the 11 studies that they examined, Mathes and Fuchs found a wide range of effect sizes associated with tutoring, ranging from as low as .07 (essentially no meaningful gain over that made by a control group) to as high as .75 (a substantial and educationally valuable advantage). In their review, Cohen et al. (1982) did not report on the effect sizes associated with tutoring in particular studies, but they did provide mean effect sizes for various groupings of 2–42 studies. One collection of 14 studies that they summarized had a mean effect size of .16, and another grouping of 2 studies had an effect size of only .06. In other words, several studies showed little or no gain attributable to tutoring beyond that accomplished by the control students. Only one study, this one reviewed by Cohen and his colleagues, found regular classroom instruction without tutoring to be superior to regular instruction with it, and in the majority of studies the benefits of tutoring were modest at best. In only 16 of the 45 studies reviewed did tutoring lead to appreciable gains. "The other studies reported small or trivial effects of tutoring on tutees" (Cohen et al., 1982, p. 243).

Wasik and Slavin (1993), in their review, concluded that one-to-one instruction alone was not sufficient to explain the effectiveness of various tutorials. Some tutorials (e.g., Direct Instruction Skills Plan) taught by experienced teachers did not result in impressive short- or long-term learning gains for the children. This particular approach provided tutoring by the classroom teachers themselves.

Moreover, the occasional study—such as the one cited by Cohen et al.—has found that tutoring not only fails to lead to superior gains over regular instruction but actually produces significantly lower achievement than that accomplished by students without tutors. How can this be? Cunningham and Allington (1994) have documented how children can lose considerable amounts of instructional time moving between classroom and compensatory instruction. With a loss of 10–15 minutes of instructional time each day to allow movement from classroom to tutor and back again, it might be difficult for tutoring—no matter how well designed and delivered—to outbalance the time loss.

Of course, tutoring also might represent an unfortunate alteration of curriculum. Tutored children could be receiving less appropriate, less achievement-supportive teaching than that offered in the regular classroom. Trading sound instruction for weak or inappropriate instruction, even when the replacement teaching is offered on a one-to-one basis, is obviously a poor deal. For example, in one recent study (Mantzicopoulos, Morrison, Stone, & Setrakian, 1992), two tutoring interventions for at-risk first graders were compared with regular first-grade instruction. Neither tutoring arrangement led to higher achievement than that of at-risk children in the regular program, although one of the efforts did lead to higher word attack and phonetic analysis scores; these scores were not accompanied by gains in reading comprehension or overall reading achievement, however. According to the authors, "One-to-one tutoring is not likely to result in comprehensive achievement gains if its focus is on narrow and isolated instructional activities" (Mantzicopoulos et al., 1992, p. 582). Neither of these programs of tutoring were sufficient to support a rate of learning equivalent to that accomplished by the average children who were not at risk.

Tutoring can, of course, be undermined by poor teaching. In a study of tutoring, 55 professional teachers were observed during their interactions with young readers (Wheldall, Colmar, Wenban-Smith, Morgan, & Quance, 1995). It was found that the teachers had a tendency to use inappropriate materials and to use interaction patterns (such as immediate interruption when the children made oral reading errors and lack of praise) that have been associated with low learning gains in past studies. Tutoring is usually effective, but the availability of tutoring does not guarantee learning. "The differences that were obtained among the tutorial programs may reflect differences in teaching expertise in addition to differences in professional development and instructional program characteristics" (Shanahan & Barr, 1995, p. 977).

Finally, it is important to note that many of these studies may be overrating the gains actually made by the tutored children. Since most of the tutored subjects in these studies were low achieving, one would expect their test scores to have a tendency to rise on repeated assessment because of unreliability of measurement. This "regression to the mean" effect is a problem whenever subjects are selected because of their low place in the achievement distribution and whenever comparison groups are nonequivalent. Several studies assigned the lowest achieving students to the tutoring condition on the basis of test scores or teacher evaluation; they then used either a somewhat higher achieving at-risk group or the rest of the distribution as a control. This design increases the possibility of finding gains that do not exist by placing the effects of the standard error of measurement on one side of the equation, favoring the tutored groups over the controls. None of the earlier reviews used comparability of control group as a quality selection factor (although most did require that there be a control group). It is, consequently, impossible to estimate from these reviews the extent to which the overall gains might be due to regression. In an analysis of this problem with Reading Recovery research that compared studies with equivalent control groups and studies without such groups, it was found that the effect sizes were inflated substantially by regression effects (Shanahan & Barr, 1995). The overall effects of Reading Recovery were sufficiently large to maintain the conclusion that the approach was effective, although this analysis suggested the method to be much less beneficial than claimed in the original studies. The vast majority of tutoring studies reported significant gains due to tutoring, but most studies reported small to moderate effect sizes, much lower estimates than those commonly associated with Reading Recovery. Interventions that were evaluated with nonequivalent control groups and that found only small to moderate effect sizes might not actually be helping students much. Again, the conclusion is clear. Tutoring programs usually lead to at least small residual gains in achievement beyond that accomplished through regular classroom instruction, but tutoring in no way guarantees improved learning. In establishing tutoring programs, care must be taken to ensure adequate time on task for students, high quality of instruction, and appropriateness of curriculum. Otherwise, tutoring can actually lead to lower rather than higher achievement.

## DOES TUTORING WORK FOR ALL STUDENTS?

Tutoring is often proposed as the means to help low-achieving or at-risk students catch up, but research indicates that tutoring is not especially effective with many low-achieving readers. Mathes and Fuchs (1994), in their meta-analysis of tutoring studies, reported that tutoring is more effective with disabled students who are mainstreamed in the regular classroom than with those assigned to special education classes. Tutoring delivered to disabled readers placed in regular classes had an effect size of .42, while tutoring of those in special education settings had an effect size of only .27. It was not possible to determine, from Mathes and Fuchs's analysis, whether this was attributable to differences in instructional setting or differences in the students themselves; it seems possible that those who were mainstreamed might have somewhat different cognitive, linguistic, or experiential profiles from those placed in special education settings.

And it is not just peer tutoring that results in such varied outcomes for individual children. Reading Recovery, certainly one of the most ambitious of the tutoring programs, employs successful classroom teachers as instructors, and these teachers receive an extensive amount of training. Daily instruction is provided to the children in a program found to be among the most effective educational interventions (Shanahan & Barr, 1995). Even so, Reading Recovery fails to help a large number of students. Not surprisingly, many students are dropped from the program because of poor attendance or mobility problems that prevent their full participation. However, Hiebert (1994) has documented that a large number of referrals are made by Reading Recovery to special education simply because the students fail to make adequate progress even with this intensive instruction. In one analysis, it was found that about 20% of the children who received Reading Recovery instruction went on to special education (Lyons & Beaver, 1995), which indicates the ineffectiveness of even this program with certain low-achieving students. Unfortunately, Reading Recovery has not provided sufficient data about the students who are dropped from the program or who complete the program but do not make adequate gains.

Morris, Shaw, and Perney (1990) developed an after-school tutoring program for low-achieving readers in Grades 2 and 3. Their carefully designed program used adult volunteers and focused heavily on appropriate responsiveness to student needs. It was successful with approximately 60% of the children served. About half of those with whom it was successful increased their reading scores to average classroom levels, and the other half made a year's progress on a standardized test of reading, although they did not catch up with the class averages. The other 40% of the participants "progressed in reading but at a slower rate than their peers" (Morris et al., 1990, p. 146). Morris and his colleagues did not speculate on the reasons for these differences in outcomes.

Vellutino and his colleagues (1996) offer some insights as to why children may fail to benefit from tutoring. In one of the most thorough analyses of tutoring conducted in recent years, they found substantial differences in the success of various groups of first graders who were receiving daily tutoring assistance. They were less interested in how the tutored children performed when compared with other groups of poor readers who did not receive tutoring than they were in the differences that existed between those who benefitted from tutoring and those who did not. All children ($N = 74$) tutored in this study were identified by teachers as having great difficulty in reading; they scored in the bottom 15th percentile of a standardized beginning reading test, and they had average IQs. An extensive battery of tests was administered to the participants before and after tutoring in order to determine the differences between the groups. This battery of tests included measures of phoneme segmentation; rapid automatized naming; rapid articulation; syntactic and semantic processing; sentence, word, and visual memory; paired-associate learning; letter and word identification; word attack; print awareness; print conventions; and various other measures of cognitive processing, world knowledge, math ability, and attentional and organizational processes. Professional teachers with at least 2 years of teaching experience provided the tutoring, and they received 30 hours of training.

Individual linear regression analysis was conducted for each child to calculate an estimated slope for his or her growth in terms of reading ability. The individual slopes were rank ordered, and students were divided into four separate groups for the purposes of analysis. These groups were labeled very limited growth, limited growth, good growth, and very good growth, and the groups were compared with each other and with normal-achieving first graders. Vellutino et al. found no distinctions among the groups on the cognitive measures that evaluated semantic, syntactic, visual, and attentional abilities. However, the measures that evaluated phoneme segmentation, name encoding, name retrieval, and working memory were reliable discriminators. Students who were low in these phonologically based skills did not make significant progress when tutored. Vellutino and his colleagues indicate that early tutoring is useful because of its ability to raise the reading achievement of many students who are having difficulty, but also because of its diagnostic value in separating out those suffering from specific cognitive limitations—as opposed to experiential ones—that will require more rigorous educational support.

Juel (1996) took a very different approach to trying to understand failure within tutoring. She documented the tutoring behaviors and choices of college athletes who were tutoring beginning readers. In Juel's (1996) study, "the most successful tutors seemed (with minimum training from their instructor) to engage in scaffolded interactions" (p. 284). The most effective tutors provided children with just enough information to figure out how to spell or read unknown words. Unlike Vellutino and his colleagues, Juel attributed the differences in learning outcomes to differences in tutoring rather than to variance in the children's abilities. Her analysis of covariance design, which controlled for initial differences in various achievement measures, did not allow prediction of who would be most likely to benefit from tutoring. On the other hand, Vellutino et al. assumed that the quality of tutoring would be equivalent across all of their groups, and, thus, no instructional protocols were analyzed, a major uncontrolled factor given the purpose of the study. Although it is certain that tutoring works better for some students than others, these provocative studies do not allow us to reliably attribute these differences to characteristics of the children, qualities of the tutoring, or some interaction of these traits.

## IS TUTORING THE BEST INTERVENTION?

Marston, Deno, Kim, Diment, and Rogers (1995) compared several teaching strategies for use with students with learning disabilities. They evaluated the effectiveness of reciprocal teaching, effective teaching, computer-aided instruction, various forms of direct instruction, and peer tutoring. They found achievement gains comparable to those accomplished by normal learning peers after 10 weeks of instruction only for the computer-aided and direct instruction groups, although reciprocal teaching also was associated with substantial learning gains. Although peer tutoring resulted in some learning, it was not as effective as the alternatives. "Clearly, peer tutoring—as conducted by our teachers—is not an approach that we could recommend" (Marston et al., 1995, p. 34).

Similarly, when tutoring was compared with various forms of enriched classroom teaching, it did substantially less well than when it was compared with no special or improved teaching. Mathes and Fuchs (1994) report that tutoring had an average effect size of .36 in comparison with no treatment control groups but that this effect size dropped to a negligible .14 in comparisons with various improvements attempted by the classroom teacher. Tutoring works well, but not necessarily any better than other interventions.

These findings indicate that tutoring can have great value but that the quality of classroom instruction needs to receive adequate attention in educational reform as well. Simmons, Fuchs, Fuchs, Mathes, and Hodge (1995) conducted an experiment comparing a no-intervention control with direct instruction and direct instruction with tutoring. They found that the combined program of intervention led to substantially greater reading gains than would have occurred as a result of peer tutoring or direct instruction alone. Similarly, efforts such as Success for All (Ross, Smith, Casey, & Slavin, 1995) have been successful presumably because they have combined tutoring for those who need it with more extensive programmatic and curricular reforms that address the learning needs of the other children as well. Hiebert (1994) has shown how tutoring programs, even when effective, can fall short of raising average achievement in a school by focusing too narrowly on the needs of a few low-achieving students. Tutoring makes greater sense in the context of improvements designed to raise average achievement than solely as a method for helping just the lowest readers to attain average, but possibly mediocre, outcomes.

## IS TUTORING MORE EFFECTIVE FOR YOUNGER OR FOR OLDER STUDENTS?

America Reads and several state educational initiatives, as well as many early educational interventions such as those reviewed by Wasik and Slavin (1993), emphasize the use of tutors within the primary grades. However, it is important to remember that tutoring has been found to be effective for students at a variety of grade levels. Cohen et al. (1982), consistent with current policy efforts, did report that tutoring was most effective in the primary grades; they found that programs serving tutees in Grades 1–3 accomplished an effect size of .45, much higher than that for tutoring programs for older students (.28). However, many of the studies reviewed by Mathes and Fuchs (1994) focused on students in the upper grades, and the pattern was reversed. I compared the average effect sizes from their review for studies of upper grade programs with those for programs that served primary grade students or primary grade students in combination with upper grade students. Average effect sizes were .46 for programs for older students and .22 for those that emphasized primary grades. In addition, it should be noted that only one of the recent studies reporting no benefits from tutoring was conducted entirely in kindergarten and first grade (Mantzicopoulos et al., 1992).

Morris, Ervin, and Conrad (1995), in an attempt to challenge the notion that remedial reading gains could be accomplished only by young readers, reported a case study of effective tutoring with an older nonreader. Certainly, tutors can be very effective with primary grade children, but their ability to engender learning gains is not limited by the ages of the students taught. Policymakers might want to emphasize particular grade levels over others because of unbalanced achievement patterns or political expediency, but there appears to be no pedagogical justification for such an emphasis with regard to the use of tutors. On the contrary, given the nation's achievement patterns, as revealed by the National Assessment of Educational Progress (Campbell, Reese, O'Sullivan, & Dossey, 1996) and the International Education Assessment (Elley, 1994), it is clear that schools are having the greatest difficulty responding to the reading education needs of older students, and tutoring could be beneficial in responding to those needs.

Given all of the attention to the use of tutors to help raise reading achievement, it is worth noting that tutoring has usually been found to be more productive in other areas of the curriculum. Cohen et al. found that tutoring was substantially more effective in the area of math (effect size of .60) than in reading (.29), although they were able to identify more studies of tutoring in reading than in all other subject areas combined. Similarly, Greenwood, Terry, Utley, Montagna, and Walker (1993) found an effect size of .57 for tutoring in math and only .39 for tutoring in reading. This is not to say that tutors cannot be helpful in reading, only that the progress in reading is not likely to be as consistent as that achieved in mathematics.

Why tutoring is more effective in math than reading is not clear, nor did these reviewers speculate on explanations. One possibility might be that math tutoring has a tendency to emphasize computation, a relatively easy-to-learn basic skill, while reading tutoring might include harder-to-teach reasoning processes underlying comprehension and interpretation. Under such circumstances, math would be easier to teach, and progress in reading would be more gradual. However, this hypothesis is not consistent with the actual conditions of the various studies. Most tutoring studies in reading have emphasized low-level skills, such as word recognition and oral reading, as opposed to reading comprehension. This has been true even of many of the interventions for older students, as the tutees have tended to be remedial students. (Even many of the studies that report tutoring as effective in raising reading comprehension have tended to have this impact by improving students' abilities to read words more effectively.)

Moreover, it is not entirely clear whether tutoring is actually more successful with lower level skills than higher level ones. Mathes and Fuchs (1994) concluded that programs that emphasized decoding did neither better nor worse than those with a broader focus. Unfortunately, they combined programs that guided oral reading and those that taught reading comprehension. Also, several tutoring programs that claimed to be providing broad-based instruction often did no more than add a few comprehension questions to a lesson that was largely skills oriented. Under these circumstances, no differences are likely.

## DO TUTORS NEED TRAINING?

Not surprisingly, interventions that employed professional teachers as tutors reported more substantial gains than did peer tutoring, parent tutoring, or various volunteer models, although these were all successful (Cohen et al., 1982; Mathes & Fuchs, 1994; Shanahan & Barr, 1995; Wasik & Slavin, 1993). Several of the programs that used teachers as tutors, most notably Reading Recovery, also provided extensive tutor training. An exception to this is the Direct Instruction Skills Plan reviewed by Wasik and Slavin (1993). This model provided certified teachers with only 3 days of training and was among the least effective tutoring programs considered in the authors' comparisons.

Cohen et al. (1982) compared studies that provided tutor training with those that did not, and they found only a modest advantage for those with such training. However, they mixed math and reading studies in this comparison, and even a cursory examination of various tutoring studies reveals substantial variance in the nature of the training that was provided, variance that would not be captured in a simple dichotomous comparison. Sometimes the tutor training reported in these studies has been less than 1 hour in duration, and no qualitative information is provided by the investigators.

There have been few direct studies of tutor training for reading instruction, but those that have been conducted support its value. Various studies of Reading Recovery have shown that its tutor training program alters teaching behaviors and changes teachers' basic instructional conceptions (Pinnell & McCarrier, 1990; Smith-Burke, 1991; Stephens, Gaffney, Weinzierl, Shelton, & Clark, 1991). Studies of less ambitious training programs for parent, teen, and teacher tutors have also shown clear changes in tutoring behavior due to the training (Wheldall, Coleman, Wenban-Smith, Morgan, & Quance, 1995; Wheldall & Mettem, 1985). Only two studies were found that attempted to evaluate the impact of tutor training on the learning gains of the tutees, both with positive results. One of these studies evaluated the effects of a Reading Recovery–style tutoring intervention that employed teachers without Reading Recovery training and found it to be less effective in improving reading achievement, as measured by a standardized test, than the program with well-trained tutors (Pinnell, Lyons, DeFord, Bryck, & Seltzer, 1994).

Also, Leach and Siddall (1990) were able to generate faster learning progress in reading accuracy and comprehension for a group of young children by providing parent tutors with a 1.5-hour training program. Children taught by tutors who did not receive the training were not as successful.

Thorough training is not always possible, of course, as a result of costs and other logistics. Tutor training might not be as necessary in situations in which the tutors are carefully supervised and instructional decisions are actually made by knowledgeable, professional teachers (Duvall, Delquadri, Elliott, & Hall, 1992; Morris, Shaw, & Perney, 1990). Duvall (with parent tutors) and Morris (with volunteer adult tutors) were both able to demonstrate solid reading improvement for tutees using closely supervised but minimally trained tutors.

## HOW MUCH TUTORING IS BENEFICIAL?

Educators often assume that greater amounts of instruction will lead to greater amounts of learning (Carroll, 1963). This, of course, is usually true. However, tutoring research raises some problems concerning time use. Some previous literature reviews have indicated that tutoring programs of longer duration are less effective than those that are short term, and some programs have rigid rules about when tutoring begins and ends, affecting the amount of tutoring that can be provided.

Cohen et al. (1982) reported that tutoring programs that lasted for up to 4 weeks resulted in an average effect size estimate of .95; those of 5–18 weeks averaged .42, and those of 19–36 weeks averaged .16. These differences, reported in the single most-cited review on tutoring, are striking and clearly suggest that it would be best to limit the amount of tutoring provided to children. The claim that amount of tutoring is negatively correlated with educational gains is especially troubling given that many studies have shown that gains from tutoring are not well maintained after the tutors are withdrawn.

Ross, Smith, Casey, and Slavin (1995) showed that the rather substantial Reading Recovery effect sizes of .80–.90 for students completing the tutorial program in first grade had diminished to .29 by third grade if no additional intervention was provided. This decline in the relative value of Reading Recovery appears to continue into fourth grade as well (Shanahan & Barr, 1995). This evidently is not due to any real regression in reading but is simply the result of the initial advantages from the tutoring become submerged in the eventually even greater effects of regular instruction and experience. It is a relative drop in value rather than any substantive loss in what is learned. This decline is evident in other tutoring programs as well (Greenwood et al., 1993). Greenwood et al. tracked 3 years of student learning for children in Grades 1–6 and found that the advantages of the peer-tutored groups declined markedly over time. They indicated the need for additional intervention to help these children maintain their gains from tutoring.

How can we explain the "less is more" effect? One possibility is that tutoring programs limit the duration of their program on the basis of student progress. For example, students are discontinued in Reading Recovery and Success for All once they make satisfactory progress. Students who make the most rapid gains, and possibly the greatest amount of gain, receive less tutoring than their peers who make slower progress. However, few of the early studies involved such a design, so it is unlikely that the time effect can be explained satisfactorily in this way.

Another possibility has to do with the nature of the interventions themselves. Most of the works included in the Cohen analysis were peer tutoring studies, and there are various reasons why peer tutoring might be better if limited. The student tutors are likely to possess less knowledge than adult tutors, and this could impose a ceiling effect on progress. Also, peer tutoring arrangements require greater management efforts on the part of teachers, since the teacher is less directly in control of the children's attention, and this might be more difficult to maintain after Hawthorne effects have dissipated.

Whatever the explanation, recent studies contradict this finding. The impressive gains attributable to Reading Recovery are usually accomplished after approximately 12 weeks of tutoring. Juel (1996) found that many children who received tutoring only through first grade failed to show adequate improvement in reading. She extended her program to these students in second grade and was able to demonstrate clear and substantial learning gains due to the additional tutoring. Likewise, Jason and his colleagues (1995) were able to show clear benefits of 3 years of tutoring for the primary grade high-risk children in their study. Measurable gains were evident each year that the students received help. These studies provided substantial training and supervision to tutors, and the tutors were carefully supervised. Amount of tutoring evidently matters, but the actual benefits are likely to be conditional with regard to amount of knowledge of the tutors and the supervision and management structures that are in place. With well-trained tutors working with a well-structured curriculum, it is possible to make longer tutoring programs effective even with nonprofessionals such as college students.

## WHY DOES TUTORING WORK?

We could use tutoring more effectively if we had a more complete idea as to why it works. Unfortunately, there have been few studies that have attempted to determine how tutoring influences learning. It appears that individual instruction may be superior to group instruction overall, at least with low achievers (Pinnell et al., 1994), but whether this is due to greater amounts of instructional time or the nature of the specific teaching interactions that take place is unknown (Rasinski, 1995).

We simply do not know why tutoring programs work, although there are many hypotheses and a few empirical clues. Several explanations of tutoring have been proposed, including greater individual involvement, improved attention, increased time on task, teacher explanations that are more likely to match the prior knowledge of the student, greater match of curricular demands to student needs, more appropriate individual pacing, more immediate and relevant feedback to student attempts, and greater opportunity for student identification with the tutor. To sort out such possibilities will require a very different type of research that does more than simply document that tutoring works or that tutoring works better or less well than some other intervention. I suspect that findings from such studies could be useful not only in helping us to construct better tutoring programs but in helping us to better understand what works in classrooms.

Several of the reviews maintained that well-structured tutoring programs work best (Cohen et al., 1982; Ellson, 1969; Rosenshine & Furst, 1969; Wasik & Slavin, 1993), but how this structuring alters students' instructional experiences was not evident from the reviews. Cohen et al. maintained that tutoring that replaced class lessons was modestly more effective than that which supplemented teaching. This is counterintuitive, because replacement models do not increase the amount of instruction that students receive. A basic criticism of so-called pull-out instructional programs, such as those sponsored by Chapter/Title 1, has been that they do not increase the amount of teaching (Allington & Cunningham, 1996). The slight superiority of replacement tutoring over supplementary tutoring in the Cohen et al. analysis is probably due both to the predominance of peer tutoring in the replacement studies and to the emphasis on the learning of regular students as opposed to remedial ones in such programs.[1]

Examinations of more recent studies revealed how difficult it is to ascertain whether tutoring replaces or supplements classroom teaching. The supplemental nature of after-school, summer, and home-based programs is easy to recognize, of course. Unfortunately, many studies that claim to be supplemental take place within the school day, and it is unclear whether the same amount of classroom-based reading instruction is actually available to the tutored children as to those who are not tutored. Something has to be reduced if something is added within the school day, but what is dropped or reduced is rarely explained in these studies.

By far the most helpful attempts to determine why tutoring works were those that examined specific tutoring interactions and linked these interactions to student learning. I found three such studies. Juel (1996), for instance, carefully documented the instructional choices made by the tutors in her program and correlated these choices with student learning gains. She found that the amount of scaffolding and modeling, as well as the number of minutes spent on certain aspects of the curriculum (letter-sound relationships, controlled vocabulary materials), were associated with student learning. The individual nature of this instruction made it possible for tutors to construct sufficiently supportive situations in which the children could successfully participate in the various reading tasks. Other interaction studies, in peer tutoring situations, have shown that tutoring increased academic engagement on the part of the tutees and that it increased the use of certain academic materials (Greenwood, 1991; Greenwood, Delquadri, & Hall, 1989). These changes were both related to achievement gains in reading. Beyond these hints, however, we have little clear evidence as to why tutoring works, and none of these studies attempted to experiment with the variables of interest.

## CONCLUSIONS

On the basis of this review of the literature, it seems clear that tutoring can be an effective strategy for improving student achievement. Although it appears that tutors with more training and experience do best, even programs that employed young children as tutors were sometimes effective. Certainly, there is good reason to believe that college tutors in the elementary schools can be effective. While tutoring can help, educators should not expect it to automatically lead to gains in school achievement or student learning, nor should it impede or distract from efforts to reform schools or improve classroom teaching; tutoring will have a greater impact within the context of sound instruction. Often tutoring programs had only a small influence on reading achievement, and some had none at all. A more complete determination of the value of tutoring and a more thorough specification of quality criteria await future research examining in greater depth the social dimensions of the tutor-student relationship. Barnes (1996–1997) recently indicted Reading Recovery for its inattention to such issues in its tutoring plan. She claimed that an overemphasis on time on task severely limited opportunities for sound interactions between tutors and students, and she suggested that this may convey a lack of respect for the learner. While Reading Recovery has been a successful instructional approach, a more optimal balance between cognitive and social interactions might be accomplished without any loss of achievement. In a similar vein, Johnston (1984) has speculated that tutoring, because of the close social connection that it allows, may actually foster student dependence and that this probably would be counterproductive. While he provided various case studies showing this lack of autonomy, no studies were found that systematically considered how tutors could prevent such an occurrence.

Future research needs to take a more theoretical approach to tutoring in order to determine why it works in various situations. Particularly important will be considerations of the importance of tutor-student social relationships and how these relationships shape the learning environment. Initial efforts in this regard have been very informative and suggest the importance of time on task, quality of explanations, use of appropriate modeling or demonstration, emphasis on specific student learning needs, responsiveness to errors, and an empathetic or caring relationship between tutor and student. Research should try to determine the relative value of such variables while considering the interactions of the social and cognitive processes inherent in tutoring. Although tutoring programs have placed the greatest emphasis on cognitive processing, it is difficult to imagine maximum progress being made without similar attention to the social dimensions within which these cognitive interactions must take place.

## NOTE

[1]The issue of relative effects calls for an important aside. Effect sizes are useful because they allow standard comparisons across studies. However, interpretation of effect sizes should be tempered by an understanding of the relative value and cost of particular interventions. Generally, large gains are easier to obtain with average populations than with remedial ones, at least if regression effects are controlled. Similarly, the costs of accomplishing various effect sizes can differ substantially across programs. A tutoring program for low-achieving students might require greater amounts of time and other resources to be as effective as one for a more average population. It is important to remember this, or on the basis of effect sizes alone it would be possible to conclude that peer tutors are more effective than volunteer tutors (e.g., minimally trained college work study students) and that volunteers are nearly as effective as certified teacher-tutors. However, most peer tutoring studies have emphasized students without learning problems, and most of the teacher-based studies include only students with severe learning problems.

# REFERENCES

Allington, R. L., & Cunningham, P. M. (1996). *Schools that work.* New York: HarperCollins.

Barnes, B. (1996–1997). But teacher you went right on: A perspective on Reading Recovery. *The Reading Teacher, 50,* 294–301.

Bowermaster, M. (1978). Peer tutoring. *The Clearing House, 52,* 59–60.

Campbell, J. R., Reese, C. M., O'Sullivan, C., & Dossey, J. A. (1996). *NAEP 1994 trends in academic progress.* Princeton, NJ: Educational Testing Service.

Carroll, J. B. (1963). A model of school learning. *Teachers College Record, 64,* 723–733.

Clinton, B. (1996, December 21). *Radio address of the president to the nation.* Washington, DC: The White House.

Cohen, P. A., Kulik, J. A., & Kulik, C. C. (1982). Educational outcomes of tutoring: A meta-analysis of findings. *American Educational Research Journal, 19,* 237–248.

Colligan, J. T. (1974). *Achievement and personality characteristics as predictors of observed tutor behavior.* Unpublished doctoral dissertation, Arizona State University.

Cook, S. B., Scruggs, T. E., Mastropieri, M. A., & Casto, G. C. (1985–1986). Handicapped students as tutors. *Journal of Special Education, 19,* 155–164.

Cunningham, P. M., & Allington, R. L. (1994). *Classrooms that work: They can all read and write.* New York: HarperCollins.

Devin-Sheehan, L., Feldman, R. S., & Allen, V. L. (1976). Research on children tutoring children: A critical review. *Review of Educational Research, 46,* 355–385.

Duvall, S. F., Delquadri, J. C., Elliott, M., & Hall, R. V. (1992). Parent-tutoring procedures: Experimental analysis and validation of generalization in oral reading across passages, settings, and time. *Journal of Behavioral Education, 2,* 281–303.

Eiserman, W. D. (1988). Three types of peer tutoring: Effects on the attitudes of students with learning disabilities and their regular class peers. *Journal of Learning Disabilities, 21,* 249–252.

Elley, W. B. (1994). *The IEA study of reading literacy: Achievement and instruction in thirty-two school systems.* Oxford, England: Pergamon Press.

Ellson, D. G. (1976). Tutoring. In N. Gage (Ed.), *The psychology of teaching methods.* Chicago: University of Chicago Press.

Fitz-Gibbon, C. T. (1977). *An analysis of cross-age tutoring.* Washington, DC: National Institute of Education. (ERIC Document Reproduction Service No. ED 148 807)

Galen, N. D., & Mavrogenes, N. A. (1979). Cross-age tutoring: Why and how. *Journal of Reading, 44,* 17–20.

Greenwood, C. R. (1991). Longitudinal analysis of time, engagement, and achievement in at-risk versus non-risk students. *Exceptional Children, 57,* 521–535.

Greenwood, C. R., Delquadri, J. C., & Hall, R. V. (1989). Longitudinal effects of classwide peer tutoring. *Journal of Educational Psychology, 81,* 371–383.

Greenwood, C. R., Terry, B., Utley, C. A., Montagna, D., & Walker, D. (1993). Achievement, placement, and services: Middle school benefits of classwide peer tutoring used at the elementary school. *School Psychology Review, 22,* 497–516.

Hiebert, E. H. (1994). Reading Recovery in the United States: What difference does it make to an age cohort? *Educational Researcher, 23*(9), 15–25.

Jason, L. A., Danner, K. E., Weine, A. M., Kurasaki, K. S., Johnson, J. H., Warren-Sohlberg, L., & Reyes, O. (1995). Academic follow-up data on two cohorts of high-risk transfer children. *Early Education and Development, 5,* 277–288.

Jason, L. A., Erone, L., & Soucy, G. (1979). Teaching peer tutoring behaviors in first- and third-grade classrooms. *Psychology in the Schools, 16,* 261–269.

Johnston, P. (1984). Instruction and student independence. *Elementary School Journal, 84,* 338–344.

Juel, C. (1991). Cross-age tutoring between student athletes and at-risk children. *The Reading Teacher, 45,* 178–186.

Juel, C. (1996). What makes literacy tutoring effective? *Reading Research Quarterly, 31,* 268–289.

Kaiden, E. (1994). Repeat attendance at a college tutoring center: The students' perspectives. *Research and Teaching in Developmental Education, 11*, 49–62.

Larnen, S. C., & Ehly, S. (1976). Peer tutoring: An aid to individual instruction. *The Clearing House, 49*, 273–277.

Leach, D. J., & Siddall, S. W. (1990). Parental involvement in the teaching of reading: A comparison of hearing reading, paired reading, pause, prompt, praise, and direct instruction methods. *British Journal of Educational Psychology, 60*, 349–355.

Lyons, C. A., & Beaver, J. (1995). Reducing retention and learning disability placement through Reading Recovery: An educationally sound cost-effectiveness choice. In R. L. Allington & S. A. Walmsley (Eds.), *No quick fix: Redesigning literacy programs in America's elementary schools* (pp. 16–36). New York: Teachers College Press.

Mantzicopoulos, P., Morrison, D., Stone, E., & Setrakian, W. (1992). Use of the SEARCH/TEACH tutoring approach with middle-class students at risk for reading failure. *Elementary School Journal, 92*, 573–586.

Marston, D., Deno, S. L., Kim, D., Diment, K., & Rogers, D. (1995). Comparison of reading intervention approaches for students with mild disabilities. *Exceptional Children, 62*, 20–37.

Mathes, P. G., & Fuchs, L. S. (1994). The efficacy of peer tutoring in reading for students with mild disabilities: A best-evidence synthesis. *School Psychology Review, 23*, 59–80.

Morris, D., Ervin, C., & Conrad, K. (1995). A case study of middle school reading disability. *The Reading Teacher, 49*, 368–377.

Morris, D., Shaw, B., & Perney, J. (1990). Helping low readers in Grades 2 and 3: An after-school volunteer tutoring program. *Elementary School Journal, 91*, 133–150.

Pillen, B. L., Jason, L. A., & Olson, T. (1988). The effects of gender on the transition of transfer students into a new school. *Psychology in the Schools, 25*, 187–194.

Pinnell, G. S., Lyons, C. A., DeFord, D. E., Bryck, A., & Selzer, M. (1994). Comparing instructional models for the literacy education of high-risk first graders. *Reading Research Quarterly, 29,* 8–39.

Pinnell, G. S., & McCarrier, A. (1990). *Teachers' applications of theoretical concepts to new instructional settings* (Arthur Anderson Foundation Research Report No. 8). Columbus: Ohio State University.

Rasinski, T. (1995). On the effects of Reading Recovery. *Reading Research Quarterly, 30,* 264–270.

Rosenshine, B., & Furst, N. (1969). *The effects of tutoring upon pupil achievement: A research review.* Washington, DC: Office of Education. (ERIC Document Reproduction Service No. ED 064 462)

Ross, S. M., Smith, L. J., Casey, J., & Slavin, R. E. (1995). Increasing the academic success of disadvantaged children: An examination of alternative early intervention programs. *American Educational Research Journal, 32*, 773–800.

Scruggs, T. E., Mastropieri, M. A., & Richter, L. (1985). Peer tutoring with behaviorally disordered students: Social and academic benefits. *Behavioral Disorders, 10*, 283–294.

Scruggs, T. E., & Richter, L. (1985). Tutoring learning disabled students: A critical review. *Learning Disabilities Quarterly, 8,* 286–298.

Shanahan, T., & Barr, R. (1995). Reading Recovery: An independent evaluation of the effects of an early instructional intervention for at-risk learners. *Reading Research Quarterly, 30*, 958–997.

Simmons, D. C., Fuchs, L. S., Fuchs, D., Mathes, P., & Hodge, J. P. (1995). Effects of explicit teaching and peer tutoring on the reading achievement of learning-disabled and low-performing students in regular classrooms. *Elementary School Journal, 95*, 387–408.

Smith-Burke, M. T. (1991, December). *Meeting the needs of young at-risk children in urban schools.* Paper presented at the annual meeting of the National Reading Conference, Palm Springs, CA.

Stephens, D., Gaffney, J., Weinzierl, J., Shelton, J., & Clark, C. (1991). *Five teachers teaching: Beliefs and practices of Reading Recovery teachers-in-training.* Urbana-Champaign, IL: Center for the Study of Reading.

Vellutino, F., Scanlon, D. M., Sipay, E. R., Small, S. G., Pratt, A., Chen, R., & Denckla, M. B. (1996). Cognitive profiles of difficult-to-remediate and readily remediated poor readers: Intervention as a vehicle for distinguishing between cognitive and experiential deficits as basic cause of specific reading disability. *Journal of Educational Psychology, 88,* 601–638.

Wasik, B. A., & Slavin, R. E. (1993). Preventing early reading failure with one-to-one tutoring: A review of five programs. *Reading Research Quarterly, 28,* 179–200.

Wheldall, K., Coleman, S., Wenban-Smith, J., Morgan, A., & Quance, B. (1995). Teacher-child oral reading interactions: How do teachers typically tutor? *Educational Psychology, 12,* 177–194.

Wheldall, K., & Mettem, P. (1985). Behavioural peer tutoring: Training 16-year-old tutors to employee the pause, prompt, and praise method with 12-year-old remedial readers. *Educational Psychology, 5,* 27–44.

Manuscript received September 15, 1997
Accepted December 24, 1997

# Chapter 7

# Telecommunications and Teacher Education: A Social Constructivist Review

WILLIAM E. BLANTON, GARY MOORMAN, AND WOODROW TRATHEN
Laboratory on Technology and Learning, Appalachian State University

In the opening chapter of this volume, Salomon and Perkins articulated the importance of viewing social entities as learners and of the critical role that tools play in the learning and development of both individuals and groups. Combined with the revolution in technology, this theory provides educators and educational researchers a unique opportunity to chronicle how the most powerful set of tools in history affects culture, its social systems, and its individuals. Today, personal computers are capable of storing 300 pages of text per megabyte of memory, and the storage capacity of computers is ever-increasing. Many university departments have file servers with the capacity to store the equivalent of 4,000 books. The Internet affords the creation of an expanding multitude of cultural artifacts. For example: Project Gutenberg (http://www.promo.net/pg/) aims to have 10,000 books available on the Internet; the Library of Congress' American Memory page (http://rs6.loc.gov/ammem/ndlpedu/) provides an American history and culture resource; the Coalition for Networked Information (http://www.cni.org/docs/humartiway/humartiway.rept.txt) is a project of the Association for Research Libraries that explores the use of high performance networks for the advancement of scholarship; and the Complete Works of William Shakespeare (http://the-tech.mit.edu/Shakespeare) includes a searchable index. We also have at our disposal a phalanx of tools to lead the journey through the World Wide Web and its infinite space and structure: browser search engines, bookmarks, "listservs," bulletin boards, Simeon mail, Eudora mail, CuSeeMe, and other computer-mediated and video-mediated conferencing systems.

These new computer technologies have changed the way we engage in common activities. One can now browse a virtual bookstore and order from Amazon Books (http://www.amazon.com), access more than 3,600 newspapers worldwide at the American Journalism Review Web site (http://www.newslink.org/), or search more than 25,000 multidisciplinary journals at Information Express (http://www.express.com) or UnCover (http://uncweb.carl.org/) and have articles delivered by fax or mail. In addition, the Internet affects social relations and practices, as people are provided opportunities to engage in both synchronous and asynchronous conversation. Participants may follow the topic of conversation, change it, create another, reflect on it, or lurk, emerging as a spontaneous voice at any time. Chat systems enable real time e-mail, and multi-user dungeons (MUDs) enable users to develop personas and interact with others in "chat" rooms (Danet, Rudenburg, & Rosenbaum-Tamari, in press). Multi-user object oriented (MOO) systems incorporate choices and levels of mediated telecommunications activity (Curtis & Nichols, 1993). Thus, Chat systems, MUDs, and MOOs transform cyberspace into imaginary areas where participants can congregate around virtual coffeehouses, cafes, and other settings.

The social systems of teaching and learning also are affected by computer-based technologies. There seems to be general agreement that the classrooms of the next century must function differently than classrooms of today (e.g., Hawkins & Collins, in press). Vision statements for future classrooms usually include the use of telecommunications and multimedia. These tools allow access to multiple representations of information, collaboration, and communication with others (often beyond classroom walls) and the generation and public display of knowledge. The mandate for public schooling could not be clearer: We have entered an era when computer-based technology and telecommunications have affected virtually every institution in our culture and connected us with other cultures across the globe. To send young adults into a global community without the knowledge of when, how, and why to use these emerging technologies is unthinkable. Furthermore, the mandate stresses the development of higher order thinking and problem-solving skills necessary for the appropriate use of these new computer technologies.

The integration of computer technology and telecommunications into mainstream public education has been, to say the least, slow and difficult. Consider Papert's (1993) parable of the time traveling professionals, a group of surgeons and a group of elementary teachers from a century ago. Imagine the confusion on the part of the surgeons as they enter the modern operating room. Yet, aside from some minor changes, today's classrooms would seem a familiar place to most of the teachers. For the time traveling surgeon to perform modern surgery would require years of additional training, if indeed it would be possible at all. In contrast, it is not hard to imagine the time traveling teacher taking over a classroom after only a few days of observation.

Public schools lag behind in the infusion of telecommunications technology. Although the ratio of computers per student dropped from 125 in 1984 to 10.5 in 1995, the Panel on Educational Technology (1997), in their *Report to the President*, paints a grim picture of problems with access and usage. Most school computers lack adequate hard drives, are not networked locally or to the Internet, and are located in isolated labs rather than classrooms. There is little technical support; fewer than 5% of schools have a full-time computer coordinator. In a workplace already marked by lack of time for planning and professional development, teachers are confronted with implementing computerized instruction that, at least initially, requires more time. The lack of effective staff development and initial teacher education in computer technology compounds the problem.

Effective schools in the next millennium will require a teaching force that has acquired knowledge of computer and telecommunications technologies as well as the necessary accompanying changes in pedagogical activity. Unfortunately, as reported by the Office of Technology Assessment (OTA), there seems to be a gap between knowledge in the existing teaching workforce and that required by the schools in the next century. Institutions preparing teachers have been one source of the problem:

Technology is not central to the teacher preparation experience in most colleges of education. Consequently, most new teachers graduate from teacher preparation institutions with limited knowledge of the ways technology can be used in their professional practice. Most technology instruction in colleges of education is teaching about technology as a separate subject, not teaching with technology across the curriculum. (OTA, 1995, p. 165)

The Panel on Educational Technology (1997) concurs with this indictment, noting that preservice educational requirements often are met by taking classes that teach only how to operate a computer (devoid of actual use) or methods courses that only talk about how to implement computer-based instruction. The panel concludes that teacher education has not successfully prepared future teachers to use these technologies as pedagogical tools.

According to both OTA and the Panel on Educational Technology, traditional transmission approaches to computer training, characterized by prepackaged content and skills delivered in decontextualized settings, are inadequate. What is needed instead is the integration of computer technology into university classrooms and clinical teaching settings where opportunities to use multimedia and telecommunications technologies exist. We argue that, in the absence of fundamental changes in the predominant instructional paradigm, the implementation of computer-based technology will be ineffective. From a social contructivist perspective, this paradigm shift will require two fundamental changes in public schooling. First, the community of practice of education must change to include the ongoing integration of computer-based technology and telecommunications into all classrooms. Second, teachers and other educators must acquire the knowledge and skills necessary for full participation in this fundamentally different community.

The focus of this chapter is on the second of these two changes and is based on a growing realization that telecommunications technology is a powerful tool that may be used to solve many of the problems facing the preparation of teachers. Tools such as microcomputers, telecommunication networks, and multimedia platforms have the potential to transform schools of education. These tools can constitute new social arrangements, promote different learning interactions and joint activity, and encourage critical reflection.

## TELECOMMUNICATIONS IN EDUCATION

From our view, there is little doubt that colleges and universities should be the sites where a significant effort to integrate computer technology into public education is initiated. We are also persuaded that this effort has already begun. *The Sixth National Survey of Desktop Computing in Higher Education* (Green, 1995) sampled more than 650 two- and four-year colleges and universities on the use of technology and multimedia. Among the findings: The percentage of courses using e-mail and multimedia doubled in a single year; 7 million students and faculty use the Internet regularly; 6% of all courses access Web-based resources to support instruction; more than half of the reporting institutions have a Web site; and three fourths indicate that Internet training is a computing priority.

The broad application of telecommunications technology in education is the result of research and development efforts begun in the 1980s. Examples include "The Computer Chronicles," the Apple Global Education Project, the AT&T Learning Network, the National Geographic Kids Network, the Earth Lab, and the Global Lab (Laboratory of Comparative Human Cognition, 1992). The development of "virtual school" systems represents a transformative side effect of the expansion of the Internet and telecommunications into the public school system (e.g., the Wired-for-Learning project) (Clark, 1997). Tennessee State University's "Explorers of the Universe" (http://coe2.tsuniv.edu/explorers) uses telecommunications to apprentice public school students in a community of astronomers. Students access raw astronomical data, perform actual research and data analysis, and publish results on the Internet. In this apprenticeship, the Internet is used as a research tool to gather basic information, disseminate research results, and facilitate communication among scientists, teachers, and students.

Although not abundant, there are innovative demonstration projects that explore the application of computer-based technologies to teacher preparation. The Peabody College of Vanderbilt University (Pellegrino & Altman, 1997) has developed interactive video-based case studies that "anchor" pedagogical knowledge in richly contextualized scenarios. Harris (1994) designed a virtual teacher education course in which students use Internet resources as they research, draft, and publish projects, all electronically. "StudentJournal" at the University of Nebraska at Lincoln is an electronic tool students and supervising teachers use for journal writing, record keeping, and critical analysis of teaching (Anders & Brooks, 1994). Others use video- and computer-mediated conferences among university supervisors, cooperating teachers, and student teachers (Bednar, Ryan, & Sweeder, 1993; Clawson & Weiner, 1993; Hakes, 1991; Swift & Coxford, 1988). The University of Wyoming's compressed video system connects student teachers, cooperating teachers, and university faculty in discussions of problems and instructional issues (OTA, 1995). Miami University has developed EDTNet for student teachers and supervisors (Perry & Brooks, 1987). The MICH: EdCorps network at the University of Michigan connects colleges of education throughout the state (Swift & Coxford, 1988). Teacher-LINK at the University of Virginia (Bull, Harris, Lloyd, & Short, 1989) and the Beginning Teacher Computer Network at Harvard University (Merseth, 1988) support communication between public schools and universities.

At this point, it seems possible to develop comprehensive programs for the preparation of teachers that integrate computer-based telecommunications across teacher education. Computer- and video-mediated conferences are tools especially suited for constituting social arrangements that enable the joint construction of knowledge. Discourse created by these tools provides an opportunity for prospective teachers to relate everyday classroom teaching experiences to theoretical knowledge acquired in university courses and, conversely, to use theoretical knowledge to make sense out of everyday classroom events.

The introduction of any tool into a social context has the potential to do harm as well as good. The infusion of telecommunications technology into teacher education should be thoughtfully considered and buttressed by a strong research base. This is particularly important in light of proposed funding levels for telecommunications. The Panel on Educational Technology (1997) notes that current research and development efforts in education are significantly underfunded: Only about 0.1% of the nation's $300 billion education budget is spent on research and development. Parenthetically, this compares with approximately 23% of the total expenditure for pharmaceutical research. The committee recommends an investment of $1.5 billion a year, a fivefold increase in current spending. The possibility of large increases in available funds for research necessitates clear understanding of existing research and a clear vision of future research directions. Thus, the focus of this review is on research concerned with how the applications of telecommunications affect the preparation of teachers. We use the existing research, coupled with a social constructivist theoretical perspective, to provide a framework and direction for future research.

Two problems with the literature in this area became evident to us in writing this review. First, the research lacks theoretical and methodological rigor. Second, only a few studies have specified a link among social constructivist philosophy, conceptual models, and research questions and methods. Consequently, we have organized this chapter to present strengths and weaknesses of the research and to provide future directions. These directions include a social constructivist theoretical philosophy, a conceptual model consistent with the philosophy, and resulting research questions and methods.

## REVIEW OF THE LITERATURE

Our charge in writing this chapter was to review the research on the application of computer-based telecommunications to teacher preparation from the perspective of social constructivism. In Chapter 1, Salomon and Perkins offered four defining concepts that shape this theoretical perspective's view of learning and development. First, individual learning is embedded in social processes; other individuals and groups are always involved in such learning. Next, learning is mediated by participation in a social process of knowledge construction; knowledge and outcomes are jointly constructed and distributed across the social system. Third, social artifacts or "tools" provide the scaffolding for learning; these tools are the vehicles for transporting cultural knowledge among members of the social group and from one generation to the next. Finally, the collective group itself is a learning system; as a learner, the group functions better or worse depending on how its structures are able to address conditions for learning. In summary, from a social constructivist perspective, psychological processes and social structures originate and reside in social interactions, with social groups taking on the identity of learners. Our overarching goals were to review the research literature within the context of these ideas, determine the strengths and weaknesses of the research, interpret trends in the kinds of research questions posed, and identify patterns of results across the corpus of research reviewed.

## Method

We focused our search on computer-based telecommunications via the Internet (including e-mail, "listservs," bulletin boards, chat groups, and video-mediated conferencing). We were interested in these tools not as delivery mechanisms but, rather, as mediators of learning interactions in educational settings. In beginning our search of the literature, it became immediately evident that we had to narrow our search. Invoking editorial license, we made the decision to limit our review to telecommunications in undergraduate and graduate teacher education. Our reasoning was that teacher education would be a cornerstone for the implementation and diffusion of telecommunication technology; university faculty use telecommunications with preservice and graduate-level students, who in turn use it with their students, who in turn begin to incorporate telecommunications into their lives and communities. We also limited our search to research articles.

We searched the ERIC system using the following terms in various combinations: *preservice teacher education, preservice training, preservice teachers, in-service teachers, in-service teacher education, in-service training, electronic mail, computer uses in education, computer utilization, Internet, constructivism, learning, education majors, interpersonal communications, learning, educational technology, instructional systems, performance technology, telecommunications, teleconferencing, distance education, student teaching, teacher educator education, student teaching, teacher education programs, teacher certification in distance education, teacher educators in distance education,* and *teacher qualifications in distance education.* This initial search provided abstracts of almost 800 articles.

We reviewed the abstracts to identify articles that appeared relevant to our review. We read these articles carefully to determine whether they met the criteria for inclusion and to identify additional relevant articles cited as references. We also noted journals that consistently published relevant articles, and we reviewed their tables of contents for the previous 10 years to capture additional articles. This search resulted in a final body of literature that included 52 articles.

A word of caution is in order about this body of articles. In our effort, we discovered an enormous amount of writing about telecommunications and teacher education. We feel comfortable in saying that telecommunications applications are being widely used in teacher education and that many teacher educators are writing about their experiences. The quality of this literature ranges from excellent to strikingly poor, with the majority falling closer to the latter point on the continuum. For example, the 1997 *Technology and Teacher Education Annual* contained nearly 350 papers presented at the annual conference of the Society for Information Technology and Teacher Education, but only 13 of these papers met both our criteria for selection and a reasonable standard of quality.[1] Therefore, we found that part of our activity, out of necessity, was to eliminate articles that were poorly written, described poorly designed or methodologically flawed research, and/or were incomplete. Despite limitations, we are confident that we have captured a representative, if not absolutely comprehensive, body of literature related to telecommunications and teacher education.

We organize our review around three broad categories of studies. The first category includes studies that have telecommunications technology as the primary concern of the research. These studies generally are interested in how telecommunications projects are implemented, a broad measure of their success (e.g., number of messages or student satisfaction), and problems that arise. The second category involves studies that look at the effects of telecommunications on individuals and groups. These studies focus on changes in learning and patterns of participation. Studies in the final category of our review examined the introduction of telecommunications in a social setting and the resulting changes in community discourse as evidenced in dialogue among members. Throughout the review, we have selected "prototypical" studies to explore in more depth. This allows us to capture the theoretical perspective, important questions, methods, and interpretations representative of the studies.

## FOCUS ON TELECOMMUNICATIONS

Studies in our first category are descriptive of efforts to implement telecommunications technology into teacher education classes or programs and represent the most prevalent form of study. They tend to be atheoretical, although there are notable exceptions, which we focus on at the end of this section. Despite this limitation, many practical insights emerge from this literature.

Studies within this category focus on three topics. First, there are studies that explored the use of distance learning. Second, there are studies that analyzed the use of telecommunications as part of on-campus graduate and undergraduate course work. The final group of studies focused on the use of telecommunications in the supervision of early field experiences and student teaching.

### Use of Telecommunications in Distance Learning

In our first pass through the literature, we found a large number of articles that dealt with how various telecommunications technologies, particularly e-mail and audio/video conferencing, were being used. Unfortunately, the bulk of these articles were not research reports or did not meet the quality standards we imposed. Four studies did meet our criteria: Burge and Howard's (1990) report on the use of audio-only conference courses taught through the graduate programs of the Ontario Institute for Studies in Education; Platten and Barker's (1987) study on the Texas Interactive Instructional Network, a one-way video and two-way audio satellite system; Hill's (1997) research on interactive audio-video conferencing in the Georgia Statewide Academic and Medical System distance learning project; and Schrum's (1992) development and analysis of an online professional development course on telecommunications.

Funding is a major concern in writings on distance learning. In three of the four studies just mentioned, financial considerations were a major reason for the research. The potential for reaching large numbers of students at relatively low costs was cited by Platten and Barker as a primary reason for establishing the interactive network and conducting the study. Hill included a cost-benefit analysis as part of her study, concluding that economic gains for the courses were greater than costs. According to Burge and Howard, funding limitations were the reason for implementing the low-cost audio conferencing system in Ontario.

All four reports were consistent in their findings about distance learning telecommunications technology. Students were generally positive about their experiences. Hill (1997) and Platten and Barker (1987) found that a majority of students were willing to take another similar course. Convenience was the most frequently cited reason for taking courses. Older students and students living at the greatest distance from the university were the most positive. Problems related to the technology were common. More than half of the sites in the Platten and Barker study missed at least one broadcast as a result of technical problems. Some students found the technology intimidating, although consistently they grew more comfortable as well as more adept in its use across time. Lack of an opportunity to interact with the instructor and with other students was a common complaint, although Schrum reported that at least one student enjoyed the anonymity of the experience.

As is the case throughout this review, we look in more detail at prototypical studies. Both Hill's (1997) study, representing interactive video conferencing, and Schrum's (1992) study, representing a course taught via the Internet, are worth a closer look.

Hill (1997) surveyed 129 students and 21 faculty members involved in the Georgia Statewide Academic and Medical System distance learning project. This project uses two-way teleconferencing at 370 sites. No theoretical rationale was provided, but two specific research questions framed the study: Is distance learning equal in quality to traditional learning? and Are the benefits worth the cost? In regard to the first question, Hill found that students generally had positive experiences; 89% reported they were glad they took a course and would take another. Students farther from the main campus and older students were generally more satisfied with their experience. Despite finding the logistical problems burdensome, faculty were positive, 90% reporting that they would teach in the project again. Both student and faculty satisfaction increased with usage. Intimidation by the technology was noted as a problem; 35.6% of the students were reluctant to ask questions during the teleconference. In regard to the second research question, a separate cost-benefit analysis determined that the economic benefits of the courses were greater than the costs.

Schrum's (1992) article is interesting particularly in that it reported on the use of telecommunications to teach a course on telecommunications (Telecommunications and Information Access for Educators). Her case study of the first year of implementation included data from e-mail, personal correspondences, field notes on telephone calls, informal interviews, and surveys. Principles from adult learning theory were used in designing the course, but the study itself was atheoretical. The 40 participants in the course represented a range of telecommunications expertise from novice to expert. A common reason for taking the course was convenience. Most students liked the immediate feedback provided via e-mail or phone, and few expressed concerns about the lack of face-to-face contact; some even cited this as a benefit. While technical problems and financial concerns regarding tele-communications charges were cited, they were not seen as major impediments. Overall, the course was seen as a success. Three recommendations were included: Educators should explore emerging technologies in relevant and meaningful ways; further development of appropriate courses is needed; and further research is needed.

## Use of Telecommunications in On-Campus Courses

Our second group of studies focuses on telecommunications in undergraduate and graduate teacher education courses. In our initial search, it became evident to us that the use of e-mail in courses is extensive. In comparison with the literature on distance education, we found a large number of studies to review; as was the case with distance education, however, we also eliminated large numbers of re-ports as lacking in quality. We are convinced, however, that there are consistent and worthwhile findings in this body of studies.

The majority of these studies are atheoretical. Russett (1994), for example, provided an overview of the Internet and reviewed the literature on telecommuni-cations in teacher education but failed to provide any theoretical rationale for teach-ing and/or learning or for the relationship between telecommunications and anxi-ety, a variable in the study. Similarly, studies by Anderson (1995), Baines (1997), Francis-Pelton and Pelton (1996), Powers and Dutt-Doner (1997), Sumrall and Sumrall (1995), and Waugh (1994) involved little or no theoretical perspective; their rationale is captured by Lowry, Koneman, Osman-Jouchoux, and Wilson's (1994) explanation: "We wondered how e-mail could be used as an instructional strategy."

For the most part, these studies contained descriptive analyses of e-mail mes-sages. Powers and Dutt-Doner (1997) analyzed 800 messages from one group of 66 students and 680 from a second group of 56 students. They found that five themes emerged in both data sets: peer support, sharing information, reflecting on a required field experience component, debating controversial issues, and discuss-ing the course. In Waugh's (1994) electronic network, the majority of 634 mes-sages were from students, and approximately half of these messages contained questions that fell into four categories: personal, technical, network strategies, and course requirements. Baines (1997) compared responses to articles available on the World Wide Web, 59 responses posted on an interactive bulletin board, and 57 handwritten or word-processed responses. Responses posted on the bulletin board were more brief, had shorter sentences, and were generally more informal and conversational in tone.

Results, discussions, and conclusions in these studies focused on recommenda-tions for implementing similar projects. Lowry et al. (1994), for example, studied a graduate seminar that used "electronic discussion groups." Results of a survey and analysis of e-mail logs led to "four important issues to be considered in the use of electronic discussion groups": the need to front end technical support and logis-tics, the insight that e-mail discussants form work groups in the same way as in face-to-face situations, the fact that participants enjoy and value e-mail discus-sions, and the need for more research. The finding of positive student response to e-mail was consistent, but it was noted that students complained about the number of messages they received, particularly those who failed to regularly check their e-mail. Baines (1997) found that his students complained about access to networked computers (despite wide campus availability), the problems in revising written responses on their e-mail system (despite being taught a simple method to copy word-processed documents onto the e-mail system), and the inconvenience of reading articles on the screen (despite being able to easily print articles free of charge). Waugh (1994) found similar drawbacks, yet he concluded that the e-mail in his study was not an electronic lecture and resulted in higher levels of interaction and individualization of instruction. Sumrall and Sumrall (1995) used limited data to argue specifically for the integration of computer-based technology into teacher education, as opposed to isolated technology classes. Virtually all of the articles described in this section endorsed telecommunications on the basis of little or no evidence.

Two of the studies we reviewed provided at least limited theoretical rationale. The literature on educators' resistance to change framed a study that paired in-service teachers in a graduate program at the University of New Mexico with both in-service and undergraduate students at George Mason University (Norton & Sprague, 1996). Pairs collaborated via e-mail to create lessons that integrated databases into the curriculum. Results of a survey of beliefs and attitudes about telecommunications found significant changes only among undergraduate subjects. There were no differences in the quality of lesson plans on any of five criteria. Williams and Merideth (1995) based their study on both a social and a cognitive construction of knowledge perspective. They argued for the need to create more complex thinking through classroom discussion, noting the literature reports that most "discussions" in classrooms are merely recitations relying on lower order thinking. They hypothesized that the use of computer-mediated communications would enhance "undominated dialogue." Four categories emerged from 248 professor and student messages: initial testing of the "listserv" system, chatting, technology related, and course content related. A survey revealed wide use of e-mail, along with high levels of satisfaction and a slight increase in sense of professional competence. A list of advantages and disadvantages was generated, and the results mirrored those just described.

The two studies that provided the most theoretically grounded rationales also offered the strongest insights into the use of telecommunications. We examine these two investigations as the prototypical studies for this section. The literature on staff development framed Slough and McGrew-Zoubi's (1996) study. During a workshop, science teachers posted final projects, which incorporated concepts, processes, and principles about chemistry and environment, on a collaborative homepage. A survey and interviews showed an increase in use of e-mail and the Internet, along with improved attitudes toward telecommunications. The researchers argued that the Internet has the potential to promote constructivist views of knowledge by engaging students in the construction of homepages and moving teachers away from their role as the sole source of knowledge. They noted that extended time, support for the change process, and modeling are needed if lasting change is to take place. The concept of portfolios and other alternative assessment tools was developed. Although not well supported, they reach the conclusion that "the World Wide Web Home Page meets the requirements of an alternative assessment tool" (p. 11).

Anderson and Lee (1995) framed their study around the theoretical concept of multiple literacies. Through their description of the study and explanations of sample e-mail messages, they suggested that developing literacy in telecommunications is important for membership in the educational community. They found that e-mail can provide a means for requesting support, building concepts, taking risks, supporting and affirming membership in the class, and building a more democratic environment. The permanent and asynchronous quality of e-mail networks is thought to lead to more recursive and reflective dialogue, particularly when the dialogue is brought back into the class. The authors cited problems in terms of students failing to see the purposes of e-mail, time spent on e-mail detracting from other learning activities, the frustration accompanying the technology, and the level of technical support and accessibility. Despite these drawbacks, Anderson and Lee were enthusiastic about the potential of e-mail networks to support instruction and learning in teacher education classes. They provided an extensive list of suggestions for implementing e-mail instruction and organizing activities prior to, during, and upon completion of the course.

## Use of Telecommunications in Field Experiences

Our last topic in this first category of studies is research on telecommunications in field experiences, such as student teaching and practica. In our judgment, these studies are the strongest of the three topics, and this strength is a reflection of the greater use of theory to frame the studies. For example, Hoover (1994) used as a rationale the movement of the teaching profession from an applied science to professional inquiry. Similarly, McIntyre and Tlusty (1992, 1993) discussed the importance of reflection and dialogue in learning to teach. Larson and Clift (1996) cited both cognitive and social constructivist perspectives, noting how telecommunications technology has the potential to mediate and transform the experiences of student teachers. Loiselle, Dupruy-Walker, Gingras, and Gagnon (1996) and Thomas, Larson, Clift, and Levin (1996) addressed issues related to collaborative learning between experts and novices; Thomas et al. coined the term "teleapprenticeship" to describe their project. This use of theory to organize the research and explain results is a clear strength of these studies.

A common strategy in these studies was to archive e-mail messages, count them, and then develop analytic categories. Hoover (1994), for example, found that her group of 19 secondary student teachers averaged 7 messages a week (3 were required) that fell into three general categories: combating frustration through camaraderie and support, promoting a focus on content-specific pedagogy, and forging the way toward critical inquiry. McIntyre and Tlusty (1992, 1993) categorized 294 messages from 11 student teachers (an average of 1.6 per week) into five categories: technological literacy, supervision, reflectivity, moral support, and collegiality. Loiselle et al. (1996) looked at "critical incidents," those messages (108 out of a total of 444 from 10 interns) that described problems arising during teaching. They adopted a framework that categorized messages according to relationships among teacher, student, subject matter, and context.

Typically, this set of articles provides descriptions of insights gained through the implementation of projects using telecommunications. Reports of the number of messages, as just cited, are typical. Coupled with survey or observational data, these studies make observations on students' perceptions or attitudes toward tele-communications. Similar to the studies related to telecommunications in on-campus courses, consistent findings are that large amounts of e-mail lead to frustration on the part of students (Hoover, 1994; McIntyre & Tlusty, 1992; 1993), limiting access to telecommunications tools reduces participation (Durham & Sunal, 1991; Sunal, Sunal, Helfeldt, & Durham, 1991), and technical assistance is important to project success (Larson & Clift, 1996; McIntyre & Tlusty, 1992, 1993; Thomas et al., 1996). However, once the technology is in place, students are able to use e-mail in professionally valuable ways, including posing questions to their peers, seeking advice, and responding to queries (LaMaster & Tannehill, 1997). Students find that increased contact with university supervisors is an important aspect of tele-communications systems (McIntyre & Tlusty, 1992, 1993) but not a replacement for face-to-face interactions (Larson & Clift, 1996). Nor does telecommunications reduce student teachers' focus on the immediate demands of the classroom (Loiselle et al., 1996; McIntyre & Tlusty, 1992, 1993). A consistent recommendation in these studies is that telecommunications technology should be learned contextually rather than in isolated course work (Hoover, 1994; Larson & Clift, 1996; Loiselle et al., 1996; McIntyre & Tlusty, 1992, 1993; Thomas et al., 1996).

These studies often make unsubstantiated or undersupported claims for telecommunciations technology. McIntyre and Tlusty (1993) noted that the number of responses (a mean of only 1.6 per week, when 1 was required) did not support a claim of increased reflectivity but went on to assert that "it is clear to these readers of thousands of mail messages from student teachers that indeed student teachers are reflecting as they use the electronic dialogue journal" (p. 16). LaMaster and Tannehill (1997) found that students' responses occurred almost exclusively as a result of a course requirement, and they found no significant change in attitudes toward technology; however, they still reported that students valued e-mail. On the basis of e-mail from 19 secondary-level student teachers, Hoover (1994) concluded that "within a telecommunications network lies the potential for self-supervision necessary to empower teachers with a voice in shaping the future of education" (p. 656). These conclusions seem to be typical of much of the literature we reviewed; there is a commitment to telecommunications on the part of researchers that results in conclusions unwarranted by the data.

An exception is the prototypical study by Larson and Clift (1996). An important strength of their study was the use of cognitive and social constructivist perspectives as a basis for their study and, consequently, in reporting their findings. From this view, teacher education must provide experiences and knowledge that can be used by preservice teachers to construct knowledge and attitudes. The authors noted that technology can mediate and transform the experiences of student teachers.

This view is in contrast to currently popular competency-based teacher education, which views technology as best taught in isolation as a set of skills. Larson and Clift argued that constructivism supports an infusion model in which technology is integrated into all or most education classes. Their study reported on the Year-Long Project, part of the Teaching Teleapprenticeships project in the College of Education at the University of Illinois (we continue to report on this project later in the review). The focus was on how students view technology: as a tool, as a resource, as an influence on their perspective of teaching and learning, or some combination of these views. Data sources included multiple open-ended question-naires, in-depth biographical interviews with 2 participants, and field notes from 45 students. Larson and Clift found that students' definitions of technology were superficial and lacked personal, contextual, and social applications. Students were enthusiastic about learning about technology but resented the time commitment, particularly in decontextualized settings where there were no immediate applica-tions. Students were unable to articulate how technology might affect teaching and learning and reported needing more than to be shown or told about telecommuni-cations. Applications and the contextualization of technology (in both setting and content) were seen as important. There was strong evidence of learning through e-mail, but students did not see it as a replacement for face-to-face contact. These results, viewed through a social constructivist perspective, led the authors to argue for an infusion model of technology instruction.

## FOCUS ON INDIVIDUAL AND GROUP EFFECTS
## OF TELECOMMUNICATIONS

The studies we review in this second section differ from those in the first in their attempt to go beyond descriptions of telecommunications projects to an examina-tion of project effects on individuals and groups. These studies were interested in how telecommunications changed individuals and their patterns of participation and attempted to uncover the role of telecommunications in achieving educational goals. In particular, telecommunications in these studies was a tool used to mediate subjects' learning and thinking.

A common use of telecommunications is to link participants who ordinarily would have little contact. Nason (1996) used e-mail conferencing to link preservice sci-ence teachers with practicing scientists in order to move students from a "science as fact-based" perspective to a "science as process" perspective. Similarly, Kolloff and Ogden (1996) used e-mail to link preservice teachers with middle-grade stu-dents to talk about books the students were reading and reading workshop activi-ties that were occurring in the classroom. In both studies, the researchers con-cluded that interactions through e-mail fostered the construction of richer, more powerful pedagogical understandings. Nason suggested that communicating with practicing scientists about the constructivist nature of knowledge had an impact on preservice science teachers' views of science and their perceived roles as science teachers. Kolloff and Ogden found that e-mail discussion enabled preservice teachers to infer the attitudes adolescents held about reading and writing in general, particu-lar books and authors, and specific instructional activities. As a result, preservice teachers expanded their knowledge of adolescent literature and developed instructional strategies for implementing reading workshops in the middle grades.

The most common use of telecommunications as a tool for creating or increasing communication can be found in field placement situations. We review additional field placement studies later, but two studies are interesting in the way they linked students, teachers, and university supervisors in facilitative ways. Tannehill and LaMaster (1996) used e-mail to create two peer discussion groups: student peers in field experiences who used e-mail to communicate about and reflect on their teaching episodes and cooperating teacher peers who were supervising student teachers and who used e-mail to communicate about and reflect on issues that arose from their roles as supervisors. Yan, Anderson, and Nelson (1994) used e-mail to link student teachers with each other and with university supervisors. The rationale in both studies was that e-mail communication would enhance student teachers' reflective thinking; however, e-mail messages revealed little in the way of critical thinking, although student teachers were willing to openly participate in telecommunications discussions. The teacher peers in the Tannehill and LaMaster study, on the other hand, were willing and able to respond to one another with appropriate guidance and suggestions.

Nason's (1996) study is prototypical of the use of computer-based communication in field placement settings. She required students in a secondary science methods course to join online science lists and then identify a "practicing" scientist on the list with whom to correspond. Her intent was to enrich students' understanding of the nature of science and the effectiveness of science education. The students developed an Internet interview, querying scientists about their personal histories, views of science and science education, and work lives. Students collaboratively compiled and analyzed the data, a process, Nason argued, that led to a paradigm shift in their thinking about science as a process rather than a fact-based endeavor. Nason concluded that the practicing scientist made an impact on students that was in evidence during their student teaching, but she offered no data to support this claim.

These examples are typical of much of the research in this area and mirror the results reported in the previous section. Presumably, telecommunications is used as a tool to enhance some other aspect of teacher education, such as reflective thinking. Often, discourse is examined as the indicator that educational goals have been reached. Yet, results are not always evident in these reports, and often are contradictory to the goals of the study.

A major criticism of these studies is that investigators make causal claims based on inappropriate or inadequate evidence. It is not unusual to find claims made that students constructed meaning about their experiences or reflected on their teaching. As an illustration, Yan et al. (1994) sorted e-mail messages into six reflective thinking categories but failed to establish how the e-mail discussions were causally related to reflective thinking. The evidence used for making such claims is limited to the simple fact that students "sent e-mail messages" and the messages could be categorized. To provide evidence for such claims requires an analysis of discourse supporting the inference that meaning was constructed. In other words, there must be evidence of both individual and collective construction of meaning. Studies of this type would benefit from a clear description and understanding of how telecommunications tools are used to facilitate subject matter acquisition, cognitive activity, and social interaction.

Gallego's (1997) study attempted to explore how students' discourse on a computer network reflected individual knowledge acquisition as well as contributions to the shared knowledge of the group. Gallego created an e-mail discussion list (students only) that linked preservice teachers in a literacy course at one university with communication/psychology students in a child development course at another university. At both sites, students interacted with children whose backgrounds were linguistically and culturally different from their own. The discussion served as a "virtual" cross-cultural collaboration space where students could explore connections among course content, experiences with children, personal knowledge, and different points of view in order to co-construct knowledge about literacy and diversity. Dialogue was analyzed for evidence of "double voiced discourse" (Bakhtin, 1984, 1986), that is, the use of others' discourse to understand one's own thinking and, in some cases, echo another point of view in transforming one's knowledge. Gallego noted initial "setbacks" as students struggled to construct discourse norms for the new community. Data demonstrated that, in some instances, university students participated in such discourses. However, data also indicated that students still held faulty and narrow perspectives of the scope and value of cross-cultural experiences and multiculturalism, a perspective the discussion activity sought to change.

The failure of telecommunications to produce an expected outcome is common, especially when the outcome is linguistic evidence of change in thinking. McEwan (1996) used e-mail and videotaped assessments to enhance the implementation of democratic classroom management techniques. She found that students used e-mail out of a sense of requirement rather than truly being engaged in the process, and she found that responding to students' questions with more questions frustrated students, unless balanced with direct answers and suggestions. Data revealed no correlation between students' demonstration of management proficiency and their use of e-mail and no difference between attitudes of students who used e-mail and those who did not toward the videotape evaluation. Zhao and Campbell (1995) attempted to use e-mail as a tool for reflective thinking. Their data showed a clear change from the first of three required case studies to the last, a shift from experience-based to theory-based beliefs and from behavioral approaches to cognitive-humanistic approaches to teaching. Their data, however, failed to demonstrate that e-mail was the source of the change. Initially, they found that preservice teachers' use of e-mail was only as a bulletin board for posting required case studies. After a change in the assignment, students increased their use of e-mail prior to the posting of the final case study; however, the content of messages sent to this discussion list revealed that 87% were more confirming of than challenging to ideas posted.

A factor to consider when telecommunications is used as a tool to transform teacher education is the level of structure imposed on use and participation. Overly structured conditions seem to restrict the free exchange of ideas among e-mail correspondents. Thomas, Clift, and Sugimoto (1996) structured the use of e-mail communications between two university methods instructors and students in a field placement who were also taking methods courses. Their goal was to create an e-mail environment that would facilitate preservice teachers' learning of course-related concepts and encourage learning from and with one another. Telecommunications assignments were highly structured:

> As part of course assignments, students completed a two-paragraph response to assigned articles and shared their responses by e-mail with the class, raised one question on the chapter or article to be discussed in future classroom discussions, and sent three written lesson plans, two weekly reflective journals (1–2 pages long), classroom observations, and a personal statement on the literacy process to the two instructors by e-mail. (Thomas et al., 1996, p. 167)

Electronic mail data indicated that half of the messages were course related and that reflection occurred, but only between individual students and the instructors, not between students. The researchers suggested that the structure of the activity (heavily assignment oriented) influenced the students' use of the tool; students used the tool primarily to meet course demands, because the activity was not structured to allow for a spontaneous free flow of ideas.

In contrast, preservice teachers' use of telecommunications in unstructured conditions seems to lead to socioemotional correspondence rather than informational, professionally oriented exchanges. Roddy (1997) created a (completely unstructured) e-mail discussion list for preservice teachers, faculty members, and other ancillary participants to discuss issues that were of interest to students. Little direction was provided by university personnel. Analysis of e-mail data suggested that the open format provided a forum for the discussion of different points of view, related experiences, and reasoned judgments, although this was only one of many response categories.

Attempting to balance unstructured and structured activity, Schlagal, Trathen, and Blanton (1996) hoped to create conditions for the use of telecommunications as a mediating tool for the exchange of ideas about teaching. Preservice teachers were placed in an experimental year-long program in which they took methods courses alongside early field experiences during the first semester and then moved into student teaching in the second semester. Preservice teachers (placed in four different schools) communicated on e-mail discussion lists with each other and with university faculty. The e-mail discussions were open but structured by instructors' queries and observations about themes. Students were encouraged to ask questions about things that puzzled them and to look for connections between course concepts and what they were seeing and experiencing in their placements. Analysis revealed four message categories: responses to class assignments, socioemotional exchanges, housekeeping queries and bulletins, and spontaneous, sustained exchanges of ideas. Within the final category, several substantive strands of reflective dialogue emerged, as well as inquiry into issues of observed practice (e.g., "Why does she...?"), classroom application (e.g., "How do I...?" or "Why should I...?"), and model building (e.g., "Shouldn't we think about things this way?"). These sustained exchanges—the longest strand continued for 6 months—revealed the creation of a community of discourse about teaching through "the joint construction of meaning, as students and professors engage in public discussion over issues of teaching, application, and knowledge" (Schlagal et al., 1996, p. 181). Three structural factors were identified as contributing to the reflective dialogue: open, thematic prompts; focus and direction of messages; and time to think and write. However, reflection generally occurred in dialogue between preservice teachers and professors and rarely in dialogue among preservice teachers, the same finding as in Thomas et al. (1996) and Tannehill and LaMaster (1996). In addition, even with the structured activity, a large proportion of e-mail exchanges were uninspired summations of experiences and socioemotional exchanges.

To summarize this point, telecommunications may mediate the joint construction of meaning and critical analysis. But evidence that telecommunications mediates reflective thinking seems to be dependent on the structure of the activity that students are engaged in and a clear understanding of the object and desired outcome of the activity. In *How We Think*, Dewey (1933) characterized reflection as "active persistent, and careful consideration of any belief or supposed form of knowledge in the light of the grounds that support it and the further conclusions to which it tends" (p. 9). It is doubtful that simply sending e-mail messages achieves the reflection described by Dewey. The demonstration of reflection begins with the selection of an object (content) of reflection, followed by the application of reflective processes. Therefore, to examine how telecommunications and computers mediate reflective activity requires objects of reflection and processes for reflection, and these elements must be made salient for students.

Research conducted by Helen Harrington and her colleagues at the University of Michigan serves as a good example of how telecommunications can be used as a tool to promote reflective thinking, and it is the prototypical example of research for this section of our review. Harrington created the Dialogical Community Exercise (DCE) and structured it to encourage students' free exchange of ideas about moral issues in education (Harrington & Quinn-Leering, 1994) and to stimulate reflective thinking (Harrington, 1997; Harrington & Hathaway, 1994; Harrington & Quinn-Leering, 1996a, 1996b). In Harrington and colleagues' studies, preservice teachers were involved in computer conferencing activities that were open but structured around educational themes and dilemmas. As a means of avoiding dialogue dominated by instructors, only students participated, and they did so anonymously. The focus (object) of the DCE activity was students' thinking and beliefs about moral issues in education. Harrington and Quinn-Leering (1994) provided the following description of the DCE:

Students were provided with a comprehensive rationale of the activity, participated anonymously, were free to enter into the conversation at their convenience, and were encouraged to address taken for granted assumptions they and other participants brought to the discussion. In this way, we attempted to exchange norm-referenced expectations, share equally and reciprocally in the communicative process, and question the validity claims of statements—all components of an ideal speech community. (p. 662)

The expected outcome was an evidenced change in students' thinking and critical reflection, as revealed in the dialogue. The computer served as a primary tool, complemented by the use of language.

To examine whether or not DCE activity could provide scaffolding to support moral discourse, Harrington and Quinn-Leering (1994) analyzed two dialogues that occurred among 26 students during one semester. Both dialogues were initiated by an "item" that described a teaching dilemma. Messages were analyzed via two separate analytic frames. One analysis looked for "transactive features," that is, reasoning that builds on prior reasoning. Both higher order (operational) and lower order (representational) transactions were found. Interestingly, twice as many transactions were categorized as higher order. The second analysis sought evidence in the dialogues of moral development as reflected in attempts to coordinate care, justice, and truthfulness. This analysis revealed that students did attempt to make this coordination, but in many different ways. The researchers argued that a benefit of the DCE was that students had the opportunity to see how others balance care, justice, and truthfulness. They concluded that the DCE and other forms of computer conferencing can facilitate an understanding of how students think about moral issues.

In Harrington's work, Dewey's (1933) concept of reflective thinking is used to operationally define reflection as having three components: a consideration of beliefs or forms of knowledge, grounds that support them, and conclusions to which they lead (or consequences). Analyzing conference dialogue, Harrington (1997) found that the DCE activities generated both shared values and perspectives and contact with different values and perspectives. Generally, the discussion began with commonly shared values; as it progressed, however, participants discussed other sides of the issues. This satisfied the first criterion of reflection. However, data indicated that as students became aware of other points of view, they did so uncritically, adopting a belief that any opinion was as good as any other, a relativistic stance.

In another study, Harrington and Hathaway (1994) engaged preservice teachers in the DCE to facilitate discussion about educational themes with a focus on the second criterion, expressing reasons and grounds for perspectives. Conference dialogue revealed that students' stated reasons for beliefs fell into three categories of "taken-for-granted" assumptions: sociocultural assumptions, epistemic assumptions, and psychological assumptions. In addition, the data revealed differences in students' awareness of their own and others' taken-for-granted assumptions; these differences were consistent with differences in the nature of participation in the conference. Students who were more aware of their grounds for beliefs addressed other participants more directly in the conference, asking specific questions and holding their fellow participants accountable for their perspectives. Yet, not all students became aware of grounded assumptions for their stated positions, even when others pointed them out. This study suggested that some, but not all, of the participants in the DCE activity satisfied the second criterion of reflection.

Considering the third criterion, recognizing the consequences of beliefs, Harrington and Quinn-Leering (1996a, 1996b) found that students engaged in the DCE considered both positive and negative consequences of their perspectives in the dialogue. In addition, the dialogues revealed that considerations of consequences moved from statements about classroom students to teachers, school-level concerns, and broader societal issues. The nature of the topics served to restrict the movement of consideration of consequences; instructional issues seemed to focus discussion on consequences only for students and teachers, while other issues involved all four levels. Again, the data revealed a reluctance on the part of preservice teachers to challenge each other's positions.

From a social constructivist viewpoint, the strength of Harrington's work is revealed in her understanding that reflection is a thinking activity aimed at an object. In her studies, the object was beliefs about moral issues in education. Activity toward the object was mediated through the tools of the DCE, computers, telecommunications, and, perhaps most important, language. The intended outcome was a more thoughtful and reflective teacher.

## FOCUS ON TELECOMMUNICATIONS
## AND COMMUNITY DISCOURSE

Using telecommunications in an attempt to promote dialogue that transforms thinking is now common practice. However, only a few studies have considered the impact of such activity on the patterns of discourse in a community. There is some evidence that telecommunications is ill suited for sustaining dialogue momentum, the continuance of a dialogue about an idea or issue through several rounds of responses (Farquhar, McGinty, & Kotcho, 1996).

Trathen and Moorman (1996), however, found evidence of dialogue momentum as they explored how telecommunications dialogue was structured and used to enhance and extend course concepts. Preservice teachers from seven different universities participated in an e-mail discussion list; all students were enrolled in a local version of a methods course on content area reading. Discussion was completely open, and topics were controlled by students as much as by professors. In using Burbules's (1993) conceptualization of dialogue to analyze e-mail, the researchers argued that

there is the distinction between "convergent" situations, these are situations that assume the potential existence of a single correct answer, and "divergent" situations, which assume multiple possible interpretations.... The other distinction in the Dialogical situation involves attitudes that dialogue partners have about one another. Some situations are "critical"; that is dialogue partners assume skeptical or questioning attitudes. In such situations, value is given to expertise and objective accuracy.... In contrast, dialogue situations can be "inclusive"; in such situations dialogue partners adopt attitudes of equality toward one another. (Trathen & Moorman, p. 10)

These distinctions create four dialogue prototypes: conversation (inclusive-divergent), inquiry (inclusive-convergent), instruction (critical-convergent), and debate (critical-divergent). Results indicated that patterns of discourse mediated through e-mail were created and sustained across time. Data instantiated three of Burbules's four prototypes: conversation (predominant prototype), inquiry, and instruction. However, no evidence of debate was located in the discussion data. Evidence of negative or "antidialogical" elements in the discourse (i.e., deference to authority, name calling, shouting down, and nonresponsiveness) was revealed, but these exchanges were few. The researchers also found that participation structures varied as the topics changed. In addition, as activities shifted from more structured and task oriented to spontaneous and open, dialogue structure was affected. This research represents a consideration of the activity of a collective group as revealed in its dialogue.

Similarly, Marttunen (1997) used computer-mediated communication as a tool to promote the development of argumentation structures in discourse. Marttunen's research focused on the level and development of argumentation and counterargumentation observed in preservice teachers' e-mail exchanges across a semester. The effectiveness of two different e-mail modes in developing argumentation structures was compared. Argumentation was operationally defined as a claim grounded in stated reasons; counterargumentation refers to a grounded claim targeted against someone else's claim or opinion (e.g., a critique of or attack on another's arguments). Marttunen reasoned that e-mail discussion might serve as a useful activity for students to practice and develop argumentation for three reasons: Students can consider and construct their ideas and arguments carefully, students are exposed to various points of view and approaches to reasoning, and students become actively involved in the discourse structures through their writing. Students participated in either a discussion mode or a seminar mode of telecommunications activity. The discussion mode "was based on the students' self-direction: they had the freedom to select the discussion themes from the study contents by themselves, and thus, they could write texts on those topics they found interesting and worth discussing" (Marttunen, 1997, p. 348). Conversely, in the seminar mode, a tutor selected the discussion topics and gave the students content-related feedback. In the former, the tutor's role was that of a facilitator of learning; in the latter, the tutor served as a director of learning.

Marttunen examined the set of e-mail exchanges and coded the quality of both argumentation and counterargumentation. Log-linear models were used to analyze the multidimensional associations of the categorical variables that were created. Results revealed that the general level of argumentation in the students' messages was quite poor, but the level improved over time. In addition, evidence of counterargumentation in students' messages was rare; when it occurred, however, its level was very good. Comparing across the two activity modes, Marttunen found that the discussion mode produced more and better counterargumentation structures. These results were interpreted as indicating that interaction, including critique and debate between students, should be encouraged and that e-mail environments in which students are self-directive are more suitable for developing argumentation and counterargumentation structures.

As can be seen, there is a suggestion that open, self-directed structures may facilitate participation in telecommunications activity. Nonetheless, the difficulty in obtaining results demonstrating that reflection may be mediated through telecommunications still persists. One explanation is that undergraduates have participated in institutions where the practice is not to treat knowledge as an object that can be compared, criticized, modified, and viewed from multiple perspectives (Zhao & Campbell, 1995). Students transport the discourse from those institutional settings to other institutional settings. To overcome this problem requires social arrangements and tools that mediate new practices. In addition to creating the new social arrangements, institutions must provide "safe places" where students can participate in the practice.

Poole (1996) reported results from a study that used e-mail to create authentic learning activities in preservice mathematics methods instruction. Preservice teachers were paired with elementary student groups. Each week for 10 weeks, the elementary student groups were given appropriate, nonroutine mathematics problems; worked on solutions; and sent both the solution and a description of the process back to their preservice partner via e-mail. Preservice teachers then sent students feedback about their solutions and the processes used. The researcher examined the quality of the problems sent and compared across time, preservice teachers' perceptions about the authenticity of the learning activity, and the effect of mathematical anxiety levels on preservice teachers' success in writing quality problems and perceiving the activity as authentic. Analyses revealed that preservice teachers wrote better problems toward the end of the activity than at the beginning. Teachers with low math anxiety were better able to create mathematical problems that were appropriate for the abilities of the students. Teachers with high anxiety in math had a more difficult time deciphering what their students could do, making adjustment more difficult. They found the activity to be less authentic and useful, although no specific analyses of data were reported. Thus, the findings pointed to a difference in how groups of subjects participated in the activity. However, the activity did not affect the types of problems either group wrote. Preservice teachers did not choose to challenge their student groups with nonroutine, conceptual problem-solving situations, opting instead for more computation-based problem situations.

Another example of research focused on subjects' changing patterns of participation in an activity system was provided by Brett, Woodruff, and Nason (1997). Preservice teachers' engagement in computer-mediated conferences on mathematics ideas, theories, interpretations, and pedagogical applications was examined across three semesters. Data sources consisted of qualitative and quantitative analyses of contributions to the electronic conversations, tests of mathematical subject matter knowledge, and questionnaires and interviews. Results revealed that preservice teachers increased participation in the electronic conferences, even as their requirements increased in other parts of the program. In addition, a subgroup of 11 female participants who had performed low on math content exams and had indicated a concern about their ability to learn math were selected for focused case analyses on activity participation patterns.

From these data, the researchers created three groups of participation patterns: high active, gaining active, and low active. High active participants contributed to the electronic dialogue from the beginning and continued at a high level throughout. They seemed to be the most active knowledge builders, reflecting on their understanding through cycles of dialogue and showing the most insight about the origins of their own difficulties with mathematics and the nature of mathematics teaching. All high active subjects had some kind of computer access from home, so home access to a computer may have been a critical factor in determining how often and how well students used the conference for reflection on mathematical concepts. Gaining active participants changed the most, from little participation early to high activity levels by the end of the study. However, their contributions

were consistently fewer, shorter, and less critical than those of high active participants. Low active participants' contributions remained few throughout the project
and seemed rarely to move above the level of sharing information and building
support, providing little evidence of reflecting and substantively elaborating ideas.

These findings were interpreted through the metaphor of a learning community.
Such a community was identified as being composed of function, identity, discourse, and shared values. Function is the force that articulates the goals or objec-
tives of the community. The electronic community provided a framework for reflecting in such a way that understanding mathematical concepts and procedures
became one of the objects cementing the community together. Identity is constructed
through participation in the community and is necessary for establishing an emotional bond to maintain group cohesion. Electronic dialogue revealed changes in
high active participants' identity as they began to think of and refer to themselves
as mathematicians. Discourse is a tool that enables the development of the other
factors and leads to the articulation of shared values. Examination of the themes
and language used in discourse revealed a set of shared values and distinct discourse patterns for each participant group. Brett et al. (1997) explained their findings as follows:

> The electronic commentary allowed the Discourses to be both made explicit, and become objects for
> reflection, questioning and revision. The working out of participants' identities—such as "being math-
> ematicians"—enabled the establishment of Shared Values and the defining of the community's Func-
> tion. Additionally, discourse allowed participants to develop new ways of thinking about mathematics
> as well as how to teach it. We see from the patterns of contributions an increase in the amount of
> involvement in the database with time, an indicator of growing community. (p. 28)

In another study, Warner (1996) explored preservice teachers' existing beliefs
about teaching, learning, and pupils and how these beliefs are affected by participation with elementary students in a computer-mediated learning environment. In
partial fulfillment of requirements for an introduction to teaching course, 19
preservice teachers served as interns in the Fifth Dimension (5D), an after-school
program based on cultural-historical activity theory (see Blanton, Moorman, Hayes,
& Warner, 1997, for a full description of the 5D activity setting). This clinical
experience, along with course activities, was intended to assist interns in viewing
learning through the theoretical perspectives on which 5D is constructed. These
perspectives include the following: Learning leads the cognitive development of
pupils, teaching is often more facilitative than instructive, and altering traditional
power relationships between pupils and adult is necessary if learning is to occur.
Four data sources were used: a 10-item instrument given prior to and after the
course to measure changes in attitudes and beliefs toward teaching, learning, and
pupils; interns' field notes about their involvement in 5D submitted via e-mail; an
electronic discussion using "notes conference" software that organizes a discussion around the topic; and transcripts of class discussions. Analysis of pretest and
posttest results and the various electronic and face-to-face dialogues revealed shifts
in preservice interns' beliefs. Initially, students expressed beliefs that teaching is
telling, learning is passive receptivity, and pupils succeed in classrooms if they can

master the recitation script. Over the course of the study, students came to view teaching as guided assistance, learning as a socially constructed process, and pupils as succeeding in classrooms in which contexts are created for assisted learning. Warner interpreted his findings as evidence that an activity system mixing an array of tools to mediate class activity and clinical teaching activity promoted changes in the beliefs possessed by the interns.

Researchers are beginning to think and talk about the need to study the culture and contexts in which preservice teachers' learning of and with telecommunications occurs. However, few studies of this type exist in the literature. One example is provided by the work of Clift, Levin, and colleagues (Clift, Thomas, Levin, & Larson, 1996; Levin, Waugh, Brown, & Clift, 1994; Thomas, Clift, & Sugimoto, 1996) in the teaching teleapprenticeships project. We use their body of research as the prototype for this section. Their research, which spanned several years, explored the use of telecommunications tools in university course work and student field placements, with a focus on the interactions among the different contexts of teacher education. Part of their analysis focused on the expanding and changing nature of their research model, from a simplistic linear exploration of relationships among prospective teachers and their use of telecommunications technology to a complex, multidimensional conceptualization of these relationships as they occur in individual and social contexts.

Clift et al. (1996) provided an evolutionary history of the project, describing the formation and transformation of both theory and practice. Elementary and secondary science, English, and math preservice teachers were studied as they encountered telecommunications technology, first in university contexts and then again in public school settings. Survey, interview, observational, and e-mail data revealed a complex interaction among variables. One important finding was that preservice teachers' uses of telecommunications technology were more strongly affected by the type and frequency of its uses in field placement context than by the level of involvement preservice teachers experienced in the university context. In settings where telecommunications was already in use, prospective teachers readily incorporated it into their teaching, even serving as models and mentors for the established faculty. Conversely, preservice teachers without on-site support in public school settings did not use or value telecommunications applications that they had learned in university methods courses. Data also revealed that prospective elementary teachers were more inclined to use and value telecommunications technology for social and professional exchanges than were prospective secondary teachers. In contrast, preservice secondary teachers were more likely to use the Internet to gather professional resources, although these were primarily the math and science teachers. Overall, secondary schools were less likely to encourage preservice teachers' use of telecommunications technology.

The researchers found similar dynamics in the university context. For example, university professors offered preservice teachers different levels of support when asking them to use telecommunications applications, and this had an impact on their attitudes and levels of use; low levels of support led to poor attitudes and low levels of use. Data also revealed that, as preservice teachers used telecommunications tools, groups evolved their own norms and rules for what was and was not useful practice related to telecommunications. Analyses of e-mail use indicated that even though many students and teachers used telecommunications applications to increase communication, some busy students and professors used e-mail to distance themselves from communicating with others. Another variable that seemed to affect telecommunications use was the nature of the task demands that the university context placed on preservice students. A related finding was that the status-power imbalance between university instructors and students influenced the activity patterns of telecommunications exchanges: Communication between university instructors and students was valued and responded to more often than communication between students. The researchers suggested that this might explain why student groups did not engage in professional reflective activity with one another. In support of this claim, many of the preservice teachers indicated that reading e-mail was not seen as an important professional exchange of information, but writing e-mail was viewed as an aid to reflection. Data also suggested that when sustained dialogue was deemed important or in times of emotional distress, telecommunications was not valued as a communication tool. In general, the prospective teachers viewed e-mail as simply another form of communication rather than as a replacement for the sometimes preferable face-to-face interaction.

Clift et al. concluded that universities can support continued use of telecommunications by providing preservice teachers with a purpose for its use, as long as the university is willing to support and assist those students in their school contexts. Likewise, the structure of telecommunications tasks, as well as the structure of the entire system (its goals and principles), has an impact on the use of telecommunications in that system and the ability of the participants to acquire knowledge for its use. This has implications for the role of telecommunications use in the training of preservice teachers:

We find that our data support the features of purpose and task demands as powerful forces that not only encourage technology use, but actively discourage its absence. If students perceive that technology will help them accomplish goals they wish to (or are required to) accomplish, they will use this technology. This has led us to conclude that course work in technology and telecommunications is not nearly as important as embedding technology and telecommunications use throughout the university curriculum. (Clift et al., 1996, p. 19)

The research on teleapprenticeship also demonstrates the need for developing more complex and context-sensitive models for researching the impact of telecommunications in teacher training.

## SUMMARY

At this point, we summarize the research into five main findings. First, much of the research targets how computer and telecommunications tools affect classrooms and students. A disturbing characteristic of this research is that the quest for funding or reducing the cost of instruction shapes the design and influences the interpretation of results. Unfortunately, this quest offsets theoretical concerns, resulting in the formulation of trivial questions leading to obvious conclusions. For example, a consistent finding is that students are positive about using computers and telecommunications but become frustrated when they encounter problems such as limited access to equipment, lack of instructional and technical support, and large numbers of e-mail messages. Attitudes toward using computers and telecommunications are also correlated with relevant prior knowledge and experience.

Second, the failure to ground studies in theory limits the sophistication of research methods. A clear example is analysis of e-mail messages. A common tactic is to fit messages into emergent categories that seldom reflect a theoretical perspective. In the entire body of research we reviewed, no two categorization methods or supporting literature sources were the same. This finding should not be too surprising, since research in this area is in a nascent state. As the research evolves, we should expect clearer grounding in theory, better questions, and more sophisticated methods. Suggestions for possible directions are provided in the final section of this chapter.

Third, integration of computer and telecommunications technology into teacher education appears to increase and perhaps improve communication among users, suggesting the power of technology to change the system of social relations in a learning community. Based on the research evidence, we know that the structure of learning systems affects the pattern, frequency, and intensity of participation. How specific elements of the learning community affect the nature and quality of participation remains to be specified.

Fourth, researchers often make claims that are not supported by data. Numerous studies assert that participants engage in critical reflection. However, evidence of reflection is scant and appears to be restricted to exchanges between professors and students. The evidence suggests that students are not critical in their reflection but, rather, develop a relativistic stance to alternative points of view. Most important, the limited instances of reflection reported were the result of embedding reflection in meaningful activity, not simply "reflecting." To document reflection, researchers must first clearly define reflection and then design research that engages students in the consideration of meaningful concepts. Other unsupported claims include that telecommunications fosters democratic relationships and environments and sharpens analytic and verbal skills through writing.

Finally, after completing this review, we have reached the conclusion that the research is philosophically and theoretically barren. With regard to the focus of this chapter, only a few studies were grounded in a theory of social constructivism. This grounding is critical for the design of research that can successfully evaluate the effects of telecommunications on learning systems. In the final section, we suggest a theoretical perspective and analytic framework for future research.

## DISCUSSION AND RECOMMENDATIONS

Our initial expectation was that researchers would see telecommunications as a tool with the potential to bridge theory and practice, but we failed to find any investigations on how telecommunications might be used as a tool to connect the scientific knowledge of teacher preparation with everyday teaching practices. The majority of studies focus on the technological tools rather than the learning system as the critical variable. As Salomon and Perkins articulated so well in Chapter 1, social contructivist theory views the social system itself as a learning entity and, therefore, as the unit of analysis. The research literature currently does not contain a single study on how a teacher preparation system using computers and telecommunications learns and changes over time, how it affects other systems, and how it is affected by other systems. As Bodker (1997) reminds us:

Activities do not take place in isolation but instead are interwoven with other activities...and in particular, computer-based artifacts often contribute to several activities.... In a similar way, an activity does not make use of a single artifact—rather, a number of artifacts are juxtaposed in their mediation of a particular activity. (p. 150)

A philosophically based theoretical approach that enables the creation or application of models that instantiate principles of social constructivism is clearly needed. Others in this volume, particularly Salomon and Perkins and O'Connor, have done an excellent job of outlining the basic tenets of social constructivist theory. In this section, we offer cultural-historical activity theory (CHAT) as a conceptual tool to guide reseach on telecommunications in teacher education. As the theory dictates, we begin with a brief historical background.

## Cultural-Historical Activity Theory

CHAT views human consciousness as emerging from object-oriented activity. Its philosophical roots are found in the works of Kant, Fichte, Schelling, and Hegel, along with their antagonists, Feuerbach and Marx (Raeithel, 1991). Against Hegel and Feuerbach, Marx framed the principle that praxis, everyday activity, produces and transforms the material and social world. Marx (1909, 1964, 1971, 1973, 1988) also put forward the claim that the interaction between human beings and the material world is dynamic, cumulative, and transformative. Thus, "thinking" has a history (Y. Engestrom, 1987; Margolis, 1988). The basic principles of CHAT, practical activity, social activity, and tool mediation are anchored in these ideas.

A line of thinking similar to CHAT emerged in both sociology and science. The modern "sociology of knowledge" (Mannheim, 1936) substitutes multiple perspectives and dialogues for the dominant single perspective and monologue. In 1935, Fleck presented his exposition that the interpretation of a scientific fact is the outgrowth of social construction mediated by discourse and theoretical perspective (Fleck, 1979). A pivotal shift occurred with the publication of Berger and Luckmann's (1966) *Social Construction of Reality*, stimulating inquiry on the connection between cognitive and social structures (e.g., Cicourel, 1964, 1973; Garfinkel, 1967; Goffman, 1959, 1961, 1963). More recently, Latour (e.g., Latour, 1988; Latour & Woolgar, 1979) has presented a convincing argument that the production and meaning of scientific facts are the products of discourse and an ensemble of social and material processes; for example, laboratory equipment, computers, and other artifacts (Latour, 1994, 1996).

In the field of psychology, CHAT is associated with the writings of the Russian "troika," L. S. Vygotsky (Vygotsky, 1962, 1978; Rieber, 1997; Rieber & Carton, 1987, 1993; Rieber & Wollock, 1997), A. N. Leont'ev (1978, 1981a, 1981b), and A. R. Luria (1961, 1966, 1976, 1979, 1982), who were influenced by Spinozistic monism, Hegelian dialectics, classical German idealism, and Marxism (Bronckart,

1996; Raeithel, 1991; van der Veer, 1984). Although Dewey (1894, 1920) had developed a similar theoretical viewpoint, Western interest in CHAT began with the English translations of Vygotsky's *Thought and Language* (1962), *The Psychology of Art* (1971), and *Mind in Society* (1978). Beginning in 1965, the journal *Soviet Psychology* made English translations of other important Russian work available. *The Concept of Activity in Soviet Psychology* (Wertsch, 1981) introduced many Western scholars to seminal concepts.[2] Together, this body of Russian work suggests four principles.

The first principle of CHAT is that consciousness emerges out of socially organized practical activity (labor), the intentional goal-directed activity of humans who possess the ability to reflect on their progress toward the attainment of their goals. Labor includes play, work, education, governance, family life, distribution of cultural resources, and much more. Engaging in the labor of practical activity, human beings use instrumental and psychological tools to transform material objects, such as lumber and stone, and ideal objects, such as plans, into socially valued outcomes. In doing so, they transform their own physical characteristics and thinking processes. A key question, then, is the following: In what kinds of learning activity central to the preparation of teachers should computers and telecommunications be applied?

The second principle is that social processes give rise to individual processes. Rather than emerging from within the individual, cognitive activity has a cultural and social origin. In the beginning stages of development, the purposeful acts of the individual are accomplished through the joint activity of the learner and another person performing together as a working social system (Luria, 1932). Vygotsky's (1978) "general law of cultural development" poses that higher order thinking processes appear on two planes, first between people on the interpsychological plane and then within the individual on the intrapsychological plane.

The zone of proximal development (ZPD) accounts for movement between the interpsychological and intrapsychological planes. This is the distance between learning and development as a result of independent problem solving and potential learning and development as a result of problem solving under adult or more capable peer guidance (Vygotsky, 1978). Newman and his colleagues (Newman, Griffin, & Cole, 1989) described ZPD as "the construction zone," the activity space where interlocutors, culture, and cognition create each other. The mechanism for activity in the ZPD is *internalization/externalization* (Leont'ev, 1981b; Vygotsky, 1978): For individuals and groups, moments of external activity transform internal cognitive processes and knowledge structures, and moments of internal activity organize and regulate external social processes. Given these ideas, a central issue for teacher preparation is how computers and telecommunications can be used to co-construct individual and group ZPDs and mediate internalization/externalization processes.

The third principle is that consciousness evolves through tool-mediated activity that unites the mind with the real world of objects and events (Cole, 1995b, 1995c, 1996; Ilyenkov, 1977). Vygotsky (1978) appropriated Marx's idea of "material tools," adding a "psychological tool." Material tools or instruments are directed outward and bring about "external" effects on material objects. In Salomon and Perkins's terms (see Chapter 1), this idea represents "effects with" technology. Psychological tools (e.g., language, number systems, plans, and concepts), on the other hand, are aimed inward and outward, producing "internal" effects on both individuals and social groups. For individuals, the effects are self-regulation and the regulation of others; for social groups, the effects are shared thinking, negotiated meaning, and practices. This idea is similar to Salomon and Perkins's notion of "effects of" technology. Cole adds that tools carry the reified social practices, cognitive activities, and codes for how they were used by their creators, mediating a connection between the user and the culture of prior generations. From the perspective of teacher preparation, a vital question is how computers and telecommunications mediate learning activity and affect thinking processes of individuals and social processes of groups.

The fourth principle is the distinction between scientific and spontaneous concepts (Vygotsky, 1978). Each kind of concept has different origins and courses of acquisition. Scientific concepts, such as the scientific knowledge of teaching, are systemically organized bodies of knowledge, are flexible, and can be generalized to contexts other than the one in which they are acquired. Concepts of this kind are embedded in cultural systems and transmitted through formal schooling. We are consciously aware of the scientific concepts we possess; we think with and apply them intentionally. Because scientific concepts are linguistic entities, they are acquired through verbal explanation and become contextualized as they move "downward" and are applied to spontaneous objects and events. Salomon and Perkins (Chapter 1) refer to "high road" to describe learning of scientific concepts. Spontaneous concepts are acquired in the course of participation in the activities in which they are typically used. Spontaneous concepts are less flexible and are limited in their application to the situated context in which they are acquired. Spontaneous concepts begin with a grasp of concrete events and phenomena and develop as they move "upward" and are integrated into formal knowledge systems. Salomon and Perkins describe the acquisition of spontaneous concepts as "low road" learning. This distinction provides a structure for thinking about the movement of scientific concepts of learning, development, and teaching down to the level of meaningful practice and the movement of spontaneous concepts acquired in clinical settings up to the level of knowledge systems. Research is needed to determine how computers and telecommunications affect the relationship between scientific concepts (theoretical knowledge) and spontaneous concepts (everyday knowledge) associated with teacher preparation.

To summarize, the major function of the activity of human beings is to transform material and ideal objects into desired outcomes. In doing so, both individuals and communities create and accumulate knowledge and acquire identity. Anchoring consciousness in practical activity is founded on the principle that psychological functions cannot be transformed and social identities cannot be acquired by socially isolated individuals. Similar to Salomon and Perkins's continuum of individual to collective activity, CHAT proposes that an individual is always *in* activity, remaining in contact with a community and its system of social relations through tools and objects of activity. If changes in psychological functions of individuals and groups are to be expected, the mediating components of both learning and institutional systems must be continuously transformed.

Building on the tradition of Vygotsky, Leont'ev, and Luria, the current generation of cultural-historical activity theorists and researchers proposes that activity is the appropriate unit of analysis for observing and explaining learning and development. Activity is defined by the cultural-historical interpretations of roles, goals, tools, and other means of participating in institutional contexts (Wertsch, 1985a, 1985b). Among the different units of analysis that have been presented are mediated action (Wertsch, 1991, 1994), activity or event (Rogoff, 1990, 1995), activity system (Cole & Engestrom, 1993), and activity setting (Tharp & Gallimore, 1988). Although these researchers define units differently, there is commonality in their use of the term *activity,* which they agree is the point for inquiry and simultaneously the basic context in which learning and development occur.

CHAT forces a critical change in the view teacher educators must take on learning systems mediated through computers and telecommunications. Based on the theory, we have derived a set of questions to guide research:

1. What principles should be used in designing learning systems mediated through computers and telecommunications to promote desired learning interactions?

2. How does a learning system transform, expand, and sustain itself over time?

3. What effects on neighboring systems does a learning system mediated through computers and telecommunications have?

4. What learning activities should be mediated through computers and telecommunications?

5. How can computers and telecommunications mediate the co-construction of individual and group ZPDs?

6. What are the effects of computer- and telecommunications-mediated learning activities on individual thinking processes (e.g., reflection) and social processes of groups (e.g., negotiation of shared meaning)?

7. How can computers and telecommunications mediate the relationship between theoretical and everyday knowledge?

The answers to these and other questions may best be found in research that explores the complex social relations constituting learning systems mediated through tools.

## Learning by Expanding

Y. Engestrom's (1987) model of collective activity, learning by expanding, is ideal for examining the introduction of computer and telecommunications technologies into teacher education. In Engestrom's view, the unit of analysis must be the collective subject, such as a telecommunications network. The goal is to analyze and account for changes resulting from the joint activity of the community and individuals engaged in activity. To demonstrate the collective nature of human activity and the distributed nature of human cognition, Engestrom (1993) conceptually expanded Vygotsky's (1978) and Leont'ev's (1981a) models of mediated activity. The elements of the new model are explained as follows:

The *subject* refers to the individual or subgroup whose agency is chosen as the point of view...the *object* refers to the "raw material" or "problem space" at which the activity is directed and which is molded or transformed into *outcomes* with the help of physical and symbolic, external and internal *tools* (mediating instruments and signs). The *community* comprises multiple individuals and/or subgroups who share the same general object. The *division of labor* refers to both the horizontal division of tasks between the members of the community and to the vertical division of power and status. Finally the *rules* refer to the explicit and implicit regulations, norms and conventions that constrain actions and interactions within the activity system. Between the components of an activity system, continuous construction is going on. The human beings not only use instruments, they also continuously renew and develop them, whether consciously or not. They not only obey rules, they also mold and reformulate them—and so on. (Y. Engestrom, 1993, p. 67)

Figure 1 imposes the model on a teacher preparation program applying computer technology and telecommunications. The community is composed of university faculty, students, and administrators, along with members of participating local education agencies. The activity system may be viewed from the perspective of any member of the community. Members of the community also come from social groups who have social languages. The program produces a beginning teacher who possesses the characteristics of a professional decision maker. This outcome involves a change in the attitudes, beliefs, and values of prospective teachers entering the program, along with the acquisition of the identity of a teacher, literacies, and knowledge. The objects to be transformed into the outcome include students, texts of various kinds, theoretical and everyday knowledge, and reflection. The tools used to mediate activity aimed at transforming the objects into the outcome are course syllabi, textbooks and readings, instructional strategies, clinical experiences, computers, telecommunications, e-mail journals, and protocols mediating meaning construction and reflection. Discourse is a central tool, mediating cognitive activity and dialogue and complementing the use of other tools. Traditional university rules and procedures mediate the activity system. Of particular importance are discourse rules. The division of labor involves joint activity and interlocutors. Ideally, this activity system, along with mediating neighboring activity systems in the college of education, university, local education agencies, and other social institutions, will achieve the desired outcome.

Similar to an individual, an activity system learns, expands, and transforms itself. Y. Engestrom (1993) used Marx's idea of contradiction (misfit between the components of the activity system) as the apparatus stimulating change. Contradictions create disturbances, discoordinations, and ruptures in the flow of activity. Movement of the system through expansive cycles is energized by contradictions and their resulting turbulence. Solutions and innovations are invented or transported from other systems to solve problems and move the system toward equilibrium.

A learning system is always confronted by at least four contradictions. The first is the contradiction of "educative" and "miseducative experiences" (Dewey, 1938). The issue of whether or not telecommunications provides desirable educational experiences must be resolved. A second contradiction is the mismatch between the constituent components of an activity system. Tools such as telecommunications

**FIGURE 1**
**Teacher Preparation Activity System**

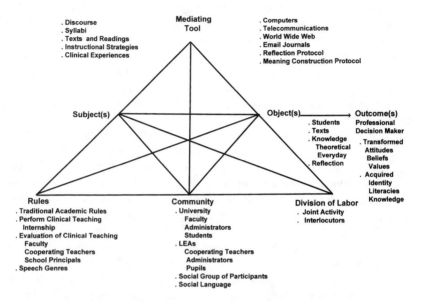

and computers may not be sufficient for constituting the kinds of social interactions necessary for the joint construction of meaning and reflection on teaching. A third contradiction is discord between the activity and a more culturally advanced form of the activity. For example, a conflict may exist between the usual way of preparing teachers and a proposed way that uses computers and telecommunications. For a number of reasons, some faculty may prefer the old way. A fourth contradiction is conflict between the object of the activity system and the object of a nearby system. The view of a teacher preparation program may be that using telecommunications to assist in supervision of student teachers will increase the number of undergraduates the program can place in its local school system. As a result, however, parents complain that their children are spending an unreasonable amount of time with student teachers instead of accomplished and certified teachers. They assail the school board, arguing that the system helps the college of education at the expense of their children's learning. The teacher preparation program responds that the local system should assume a fair share of the responsibility for teacher preparation.

The collective activity system creates and imports innovations to solve problems and to stabilize the system. Three innovations appear to be most important in leading to modifications and transformations (Y. Engestrom, 1995). A *solution innovation* is created to "fix" problems related to a component of the activity system. That is, a problem may appear when an inappropriate tool is used, rules and procedures fail to coordinate activity, or the division of labor needs to be changed. The solution is the selection or creation of a more appropriate tool, rule, or division of labor. For example, rather than straightforward e-mail discussions and e-mail journals, students may need a tool such as a structured protocol to mediate reflection on their teaching experiences. A *trajectory solution* is directed toward changing the path of the activity system. The object (e.g., individual e-mail journals sent to an instructor for comments) may not yield a desired outcome (e.g., the objectification of ethical teaching practices). The collective refocuses on the object and selects a new object: e-mail journal entries posted to the community for public discussion. Finally, a *systems innovation* occurs when members of the activity system generate a new model for their activity. In this case, each mediating component of the activity system is analyzed and evaluated, leading to the creation of a new activity system.

In summary, the collective subject, engaging in cycles of expansive transformation, is analogous to an individual moving through Vygotsky's (1978) zone of proximal development (Y. Engestrom, 1986, 1991). Learning and development within the activity system occur when the collective subject creates a tool to solve a problem. Learning and development by the individual subject occur when a previously unknown concept or skill is acquired and used in a socially meaningful way within the activity system.

A wide range of research tools is applicable to researching learning systems, such as the appropriation of learning by expanding presented in Figure 1. For example, the "formative experiment" (Newman, 1990), the "design experiment" (Brown, 1992; Hawkins & Collins, in press; Reinking & Watkins, 1996), the "romantic method" (Cole, 1995a), "situated evaluation" (Bruce & Rubin, 1993), and "rapid prototyping" (Tripp & Bichelmeyer, 1990) are all applicable. Coupled with observation over cycles of transformation and expansion, this methodology can provide useful data for understanding the ontogeny of learning systems (Cole, 1996).

Discursive techniques describe episodes, milestones, disruptions, and representations of the learning system. Shuttling ethnographic data among theories and levels of analysis (microgenesis, meseogenesis, and macrogenesis) can inform the researcher of the extent to which the model instantiates CHAT and whether or not theoretical principles promote desired learning interactions for both participants and the system. Since discourse is the primary tool used to mediate activity, it facilitates the transformation of actions into cultural practices and provides information about other tools being used (e.g., Wertsch, 1985b, 1991, 1994). Drawing on Lotman (1988a, 1988b, 1990), Wertsch argues that discourse has two functions. On one hand, the univocal function is to transport information and the given meaning residing in discourse. On the other hand, the dialogic function is to serve as a "thinking device" mediating the construction of new meanings. In this sense, discourse is more than simply a "means of transport" or "container" of a given meaning. Wertsch views discourse from a Bakhtinian perspective (1981, 1984), as a mediational tool requiring both borrowing meaning from a common store of cultural meanings and creating new meanings for personal use. An individual's utterances are intimately linked with the cultural-historical settings from which they are appropriated. Similarly, R. Engestrom (1995) demonstrates how participants package utterances to mediate the production of meaning during joint activity.

Wertsch and R. Engestrom's thinking leads to replacing "thick" with dialogic ethnography (Rip, Hess, & Layne, 1992). A number of discourse analysis methods are applicable (e.g., Drew & Heritage, 1992; Edwards, 1997; Jefferson, 1992; Lukes, 1995; Schlegoff, 1992). Additional techniques have been developed, including participant structure analysis (e.g., Goffman, 1981; Philips, 1973), semantic trace analysis (Waugh, Miyake, Cohen, & Levin, 1988), message thread analysis (Ruopp, Gall, Drayton, & Pfister, 1993), and message act analysis (Quinn, Mehan, Levin, & Black, 1983). These analyses provide an understanding of the acquisition of theoretical and everyday knowledge, the construction of meaning, the coordination of joint activity, and the invention and application of new tools. Traditional methods of investigating cognitive strategies can also be used to understand the nature and use of psychological tools. These methods gain strength when embedded in a CHAT framework.

In summary, CHAT and the model of learning by expanding are robust tools for researching the application of computers and telecommunications to teacher preparation. The strength of the theory is its potential to unify philosophical and methodological orientations aimed at understanding the learning and development of both individuals and communities. The model seeks to account for learning and development by including both human participants and tools in the analysis of individual and collective activity. If educators are to take full advantage of the power of telecommunications and other emerging technologies, a deep understanding of their impact on both individuals and learning systems is crucial. As we have pointed out, current research efforts are far from adequate in providing such an understanding. We believe that CHAT, along with the model of learning by expanding, provides needed direction for educational researchers.

## NOTES

[1] A problem that we encountered, and one we believe will continue to plague the profession, is space limitations in professional journals. The kinds of research that are needed to explore telecommunications are complex and require lengthy reports. This is especially true with research using a social constructivist paradigm. One possible solution to this problem is for journal editors to coordinate the publication of a volume with a Web site. The journal could devote its current space to articles, make an expanded version available on the Web site, and constitute a discussion based on both readings. This is currently done, with great success, with the journal *Mind, Culture and Activity*. Further information on this project may be obtained from Mike Cole, Laboratory of Comparative Human Cognition, University of California at San Diego (e-mail: mcole@weber.ucsd.edu).

[2] Nationally and internationally, cultural-historical activity theory is represented in the work of a diverse group (e.g., Bakhurst, 1991; Bakhurst & Syponwich, 1995; Cole, 1996; Y. Engestrom, 1987; Lave, 1988a, 1988b; Rogoff, 1990, 1995; Tryphon & Voneche, 1996; van der Veer & Valsiner, 1991, 1994; Wertsch, 1985b, 1991; Wertsch, Del Rio, & Alvarez, 1995). Cultural-historical activity theory has been applied to education (Davydov, 1990; Forman, Minick, & Stone, 1993; Hedegaard, Hakkarainen, & Engestrom, 1984; Hicks, 1995; Lukes, 1995; Moll, 1990; Newman, Griffin, & Cole, 1989), instructional design (Duffy & Cunningham, in press), how institutions think (Douglas, 1986), how societies remember (Connerton, 1989), collective remembering (Middleton & Edwards, 1990), learning and development (Rogoff, 1990, 1995), work and practice (Chaiklin & Lave, 1993; Engestrom & Middleton, 1996; Martin, Nelson, & Tobach, 1995), verbal thinking (Tulviste, 1991), computer technology (Nardi, 1996), and cognition (Resnick, Levine, & Teasley, 1991).

## REFERENCES

Anders, D., & Brooks, D. W. (1994). Electronic journal writing for student teachers. *Journal of Computing in Teacher Education, 10*(4), 6–11.

Anderson, J., & Lee, A. (1995). Literacy teachers learning a new literacy: A study of the use of electronic mail in a reading education class. *Reading, Research, and Instruction, 34*, 222–238.

Anderson, R. (1995). Using the Internet in graduate language teacher education. In D. Willis, J. Robin, & J. Willis (Eds.), *Technology and teacher education annual, 1995* (pp. 102–106). Charlottesville, VA: Association for the Advancement of Computing in Education.

Baines, L. (1997). Plainspeak or technomorph? Communication in a web-enriched teacher education course. In J. Willis, J. Price, S. McNeil, B. Robin, & D. Willis (Eds.), *Technology and teacher education annual, 1997* (pp. 788–791). Charlottesville, VA: Association for the Advancement of Computing in Education.

Bakhtin, M. M. (1981). *The dialogic imagination: Four essays by M. M. Bakhtin.* Austin: University of Texas Press.

Bakhtin, M. M. (1984). *Problems of Dostoevsky's poetics.* Minneapolis: University of Minnesota Press.

Bakhtin, M. M. (1986). *Speech genres and other late essays.* Austin: University of Texas Press.

Bakhurst, D. (1991). *Consciousness and revolution in Soviet philosophy.* Cambridge, England: Cambridge University Press.

Bakhurst, D., & Syponwich, C. (Eds.). (1995). *The societal self.* Thousand Oaks, CA: Sage.

Bednar, M. R., Ryan, F. J., & Sweeder, J. J. (1993). Fostering effective communication during the student teaching experience: The video connection. *Technology and Teacher Education Review, 4*, 196–199.

Berger, P. L., & Luckmann, T. (1966). *The sociology of knowledge: A treatise in the sociology of knowledge.* Garden City, NY: Anchor Books.

Blanton, W. E., Moorman, G. B., Hayes, B. A., & Warner, M. W. (1997). Effects of participation in the fifth dimension on far transfer. *Journal of Educational Computing Research, 16*, 371–396.

Bodker, S. (1997). Computers in mediated human activity. *Mind, Culture, and Activity, 4*, 149–158.

Brett, C., Woodruff, E., & Nason, R. (1997, March). *Communities of inquiry among preservice teachers investigating mathematics.* Paper presented at the annual meeting of the American Educational Research Association, Chicago, IL.

Bronckart, J. (1996). Units of analysis in psychology and their interpretation: Social interactionism. In A. Tryphon & J. Voneche (Eds.), *Piaget-Vygotsky: The social genesis of thought* (pp. 85–106). East Sussex, England: Psychology Press.

Brown, A. L. (1992). Design experiments: Theoretical and methodological challenges to creating complex interventions in classroom settings. *Journal of Learning Sciences, 2,* 141–178.

Bruce, B. C., & Rubin, A. (1993). *Electronic quills: A situated evaluation of using computers for classroom writing.* Hillsdale, NJ: Erlbaum.

Bull, G., Harris, J., Lloyd, J. & Short, L. (1989). The electronic academical village. *Journal of Teacher Education, 18,* 27–33.

Burbules, N. (1993). *Dialogue in teaching: Theory and practice.* New York: Teachers College Press.

Burge, E., & Howard, J. (1990). Audio-conferencing in graduate education: A case study. *American Journal of Distance Education, 4*(2), 3–13.

Chaiklin, S., & Lave, J. (Eds.). (1993). *Understanding practice: Perspectives on activity and context.* Cambridge, England: Cambridge University Press.

Cicourel, A. V. (1964). *Method and measurement in sociology.* New York: The Free Press.

Cicourel, A. V. (1973). *Cognitive sociology: Language and meaning in social interaction.* London: Penguin.

Clark, A. (1997). *Charlotte-Mecklenburg: A community wired-for-learning.* T.H.E. ONLINE. http://www.thejournal.com/past/OCT/1997/exclu1/html

Clawson, B. N., & Weiner, A. M. (1993). Two-way, interactive A/V applied to the supervision of student teachers. *T. H. E. Journal, 20*(11), 67–69.

Clift, R. T., Thomas, L., Levin, J., & Larson, A. (1996, April). *Learning in two contexts: Field and university influences on the role of telecommunications in teacher education.* Paper presented at the annual meeting of the American Educational Research Association, New York City.

Cole, M. (1995a, April). *Utopian methodology for cultural-historical psychology.* Paper presented the Third International Congress on Activity Theory, Moscow.

Cole, M. (1995b). Cultural-historical psychology: A meseo-genetic approach. In L. M. W. Martin, K. Nelson, & E. Tobach (Eds.), *Sociocultural psychology: Theory and practice of doing and knowing* (pp. 168–204). Cambridge, England: Cambridge University Press.

Cole, M. (1995c). Socio-cultural-historical psychology: Some general remarks and a proposal about a meseo-genetic methodology. In J. V. Wertsch, P. Del Rio, & A. Alvarez (Eds.), *Sociocultural studies of mind* (pp. 187–214). Cambridge, England: Cambridge University Press.

Cole, M. (1996). *Cultural psychology: A once and future discipline.* Cambridge, MA: Belknap Press.

Cole, M., & Engestrom, Y. (1993). A cultural-historical approach to distributed cognition. In G. Salomon (Ed.), *Distributed cognitions* (pp. 1–46). Cambridge, England: Cambridge University Press.

Connerton, P. (1989). *How societies remember.* Cambridge, England: Cambridge University Press.

Curtis, P., & Nichols, D. A. (1993, May). *MUDS grow up: Social virtual reality in the real world.* Paper presented at the Third International Conference on Cyberspace at Austin, TX.

Danet, B., Rudenberg, L., & rosenbaum-Tamari, Y. (in press). "Hmmmm...where's that smoke coming from?" Writing, play, and performance on the internet relay chat. In S. Raphaeli, P. Sudweek, & M. McLaughlin (Eds.), *Network and net play: Virtual groups on the internet.* Cambridge, MA: AAI Press/The MIT Press.

Davydov, V. V. (1990). *Types of generalizations in instruction.* Reston, VA: National Council of Teachers of Mathematics.

Dewey, J. (1894). The new psychology. *Andover Review, 11*, 281–285.

Dewey, J. (1920). *Reconstruction in philosophy.* New York: Henry Holt.

Dewey, J. (1933). *How we think.* Chicago: Henry Regency.

Dewey, J. (1938). *Experience and education.* New York: Macmillan.

Douglas, M. (1986). *How institutions think.* Syracuse, NY: Syracuse University Press.

Drew, P., & Heritage, J. (Eds.). (1992). *Talk at work: Interaction in institutional settings.* Cambridge, U.K.: Cambridge University Press.

Duffy, T. M., & Cunningham, D. J. (in press). Constructivism: Implications for the design and delivery of instruction. In D. H. Jonassen (Ed.), *Handbook of research on educational communication and technology.* New York: Scholastic.

Durham, R., & Sunal, D. (1991, February). *The enhancement of teacher education through the use of communication technology.* Paper presented at the meeting of the Association of Teacher Educators, New Orleans, LA.

Edwards, D. (1997). *Discourse and cognition.* Thousand Oaks, CA: Sage.

Engestrom, R. (1995). Voice as communicative action. *Mind, Culture, and Activity, 2,* 192–214.

Engestrom, Y. (1986). The zone of proximal development as the basic category of educational research. *Quarterly Newsletter of the Laboratory of Comparative Human Cognition, 8*(1), 23–47.

Engestrom, Y. (1987). *Learning by expanding: An activity-theoretical approach to developmental research.* Helsinki: Orienta-Konsultit.

Engestrom, Y. (1991). Activity theory and individual and social transformation. *Activity Theory, 7/8,* 6-17.

Engestrom, Y. (1993). Developmental studies of work as a testbench of activity theory: The case of primary care medical practice. In S. Chaiklin & J. Lave (Eds.), *Understanding practice: Perspectives on activity and context* (pp. 64–103). Cambridge, England: Cambridge University Press.

Engestrom, Y. (1995). Innovative organizational learning in medical and legal settings. In L. M. W. Martin, K. Nelson, & E. Tobach (Eds.), *Sociocultural psychology: Theory and practice of doing and knowing* (pp. 326–389). Cambridge, England: Cambridge University Press.

Engestrom, Y., & Middleton, D. (1996). *Cognition and communication at work*. Cambridge, England: Cambridge University Press.

Farquhar, J., McGinty, B., & Kotcho, C. (1996). *The Internet as a tool for the social construction of knowledge*. Indianapolis, IN: Association for Educational Communications and Technology. (ERIC Document Reproduction Service No. ED 397 793)

Forman, E. A., Minick, N., & Stone, C. A. (Eds.). (1993). *Contexts for learning*. New York: Oxford University Press.

Fleck, L. (1979). *Genesis and the development of a scientific fact*. Chicago: University of Chicago Press.

Francis-Pelton, L., & Pelton, T. (1996). Teaching by example: Using WWW, usenets, and e-mail in a pre-service course. In D. Willis, J. Price, & J. Willis (Eds.), *Technology and teacher education annual, 1996* (pp. 401–405). Charlottesville, VA: Association for the Advancement of Computing in Education.

Garfinkel, H. (1967). *Studies in ethnomethodology*. New York: Prentice-Hall.

Gallego, M. (1997). *Creating cross-cultural space: On-line learning in pre-service education*. Manuscript submitted for publication.

Goffman, E. (1959). *The presentation of self in everyday life*. New York: Doubleday.

Goffman, E. (1961). Asylums: Essays in the social situation of mental patients and inmates. Garden City, NY: Anchor Books.

Goffman, E. (1963). *Stigma*. Englewood Cliffs, NJ: Prentice-Hall.

Goffman, E. (1981). *Forms of talk*. Philadelphia: University of Philadelphia Press.

Goodwin, C., & Heritage, J. (1990). *Conversion analysis. Annual Review of Anthropology, 19,* 283–307.

Green, K. C. (1995). *Campus computing, 1995: The sixth national survey of desktop computing in higher education*. Encino, CA: Campus Computing.

Hakes, B. T. (1991). Two-way video and audio: Removing the walls of schools and teacher preparation institutions. In D. Carey, R. Carey, D. Willis, & J. Willis (Eds.), *Technology and teacher education annual, 1991* (pp. 152–154). Charlottesville, VA: Association for the Advancement of Teacher Education.

Harrington, H. (1997). Technology's second level effects: Fostering democratic communities. *Journal of Technology and Teacher Education, 5,* 203–222.

Harrington, H., & Hathaway, R. (1994). Computer conferencing, critical reflection, and teacher development: Aligning means and ends. *Teaching and Teacher Education, 10,* 543–554.

Harrington, H., & Quinn-Leering, K. (1994). Computer conferencing, moral discussion and teacher development. In J. Willis, B. Robin, & D. Willis (Eds.), *Technology and teacher education annual, 1994* (pp. 661–665). Charlottesville, VA: Association for the Advancement of Computing in Education.

Harrington, H., & Quinn-Leering, K. (1996a). Computer conferencing and moral discourse. *Journal of Technology and Teacher Education, 4,* 49–68.

Harrington, H., & Quinn-Leering, K. (1996b). Considering teaching's consequences. *Teaching and Teacher Education, 12,* 591–607.

Harris, J. (1994). Telecommunications training by immersion: University courses online. *Machine-Mediated Learning, 4,* 177–185.

Hawkins, J., & Collins, A. (Eds.). (in press). *Design experiments: Integrating technologies into schools*. Cambridge, England: Cambridge University Press.

Hedegaard, M., Hakkarainen, P., & Engestrom, Y. (Eds.). (1984). *Learning and teaching on a scientific basis*. Aarhus, Sweden: Psykologisk Institut, Aarhus Universitet.

Hicks, D. (1995). Discourse, learning, and teaching. In M. W. Apple (Ed.), *Review of research in education* (Vol. 21, pp. 49–95). Washington, DC: American Educational Research Association.

Hill, M. (1997). Teacher education through distance learning: Cost effectiveness and quality analysis. In J. Willis, J. Price, S. McNeil, B. Robin, & D. Willis (Eds.), *Technology and teacher education annual, 1997* (pp. 82–85). Charlottesville, VA: Association for the Advancement of Computing in Education.

Hoover, L. (1994). Use of telecomputing to support group-oriented inquiry during student teaching. In J. Willis, B. Robin, & D. Willis (Eds.), *Technology and teacher education annual, 1994* (pp. 652–656). Charlottesville, VA: Association for the Advancement of Computing in Education.

Ilyenkov, E. V. (1977). *Dialectical logic: Essays on its history and theory*. Moscow: Progress.

Jefferson, G. (Ed.). (1992). *Lectures on conversation: Vols. 1 & 2. Harvey Sacks*. Oxford, England: Basil Blackwell.

Kolloff, M., & Ogden, D. (1996). Electronic conversations between middle grade students and preservice/inservice teachers. In D. Willis, J. Price, & J. Willis (Eds.), *Technology and teacher education annual, 1996* (pp. 152–154). Charlottesville, VA: Association for the Advancement of Computing in Education.

Laboratory of Comparative Human Cognition. (1992). *SGER: Enabling wide-area network research in the science classroom*. La Jolla: University of California at San Diego.

LaMaster, K., & Tannehill, D. (1997). Preservice teachers as mentors during an early field experience through electronic communication (e-mail). In J. Willis, J. Price, S. McNeil, B. Robin, & D. Willis (Eds.), *Technology and teacher education annual, 1997* (pp. 753–775). Charlottesville, VA: Association for the Advancement of Computing in Education.

Larson, A. E., & Clift, R. T. (1996). Technology education in teacher preparation: Perspectives from a year-long elementary teacher education program. *Educational Foundations, 10*(4), 33–49.

Latour, B. (1988). *The pasteurization of France*. Cambridge, MA: Harvard University Press.

Latour, B. (1994). On technical mediation—Philosophy, sociology, genealogy. *Common Knowledge, 3*, 29–64.

Latour, B. (1996). *Arimis or the love of technology*. Cambridge, MA: Harvard University Press.

Latour, B., & Woolgar, S. (1979). *Laboratory life: The construction of scientific facts*. Princeton, NJ: Princeton University Press.

Lave, J. (1988a). *Cognition in practice*. New York: Cambridge University Press.

Lave, J. (1988b). *Cognition and practice: Mind, mathematics, and culture in everyday life*. Cambridge, England: Cambridge University Press.

Leont'ev, A. N. (1978). *Activity, consciousness, and personality*. Englewood Cliffs, NJ: Prentice Hall.

Leont'ev, A. N. (1981a). *Problems in the development of mind*. Moscow: Progress.

Leont'ev, A. N. (1981b). The problem of activity in psychology. In J. V. Wertsch (Ed.), *The concept of activity in Soviet psychology* (pp. 37–71). Armonk, NY: M. E. Sharpe.

Levin, J., Waugh, M., Brown, D., & Clift, R. (1994). Teaching teleapprenticeships: A new organizational framework for improving teacher education using electronic networks. *Machine-Mediated Learning, 4*, 149–161.

Loiselle, J., Dupruy-Walker, L., Gingras, J., & Gagnon, M. (1996). Analyzing and supporting preservice teachers' practice using computer mediated communication. In D. Willis, J. Price, & J. Willis (Eds.), *Technology and teacher education annual, 1996* (pp. 836–840). Charlottesville, VA: Association for the Advancement of Computing in Education.

Lotman, Y. (1988a). Text within a text. *Soviet Psychology, 26*, 32–51.

Lotman, Y. (1988b). The semiotics of culture and the concept of a text. *Soviet Psychology, 26*, 52–58.

Lotman, Y. M. (1990). *Universes of the mind.* Bloomington: Indiana University Press.

Lowry, M., Koneman, P., Osman-Jouchoux, R., & Wilson, B. (1994). Electronic discussion groups: Using e-mail as an instructional strategy. *Tech Trends, 39*(2), 22–24.

Lukes, A. (1995). Text and discourse in education: An introduction to critical discourse analysis. In M. W. Apple (Ed.), *Review of research in education* (Vol. 21, pp. 3–48). Washington, DC: American Educational Research Association.

Luria, A. R. (1932). *The nature of human conflicts: On emotion, conflict, and will.* New York: Liverite.

Luria, A. R. (1961). *The role of speech in the regulation of normal and abnormal behavior.* London: Pergamon Press.

Luria, A. R. (1966). *Higher cortical functions in man.* New York: Basic Books.

Luria, A. R. (1976). *Cognitive development.* Cambridge, MA: Harvard University Press.

Luria, A. R. (1979). *The making of mind.* Cambridge, MA: Harvard University Press.

Luria, A. R. (1982). *Language and cognition.* New York: Interscience.

Mannheim, K. (1936). *Ideology and utopia: An introduction to the sociology of knowledge.* New York: Harcout, Brace.

Margolis, J. (1988). The novelty of Marx's theory of praxis. *Journal for the Theory of Social Behavior, 19,* 367–388.

Martin, L. M. W., Nelson, K., & Tobach, E. (Eds.). (1995). *Sociocultural psychology: Theory and practice of doing and knowing.* Cambridge, England: Cambridge University Press.

Marttunen, M. (1997). Electronic mail as a pedagogical delivery system: An analysis of the learning of argumentation. *Research in Higher Education, 38,* 345–363.

Marx, K. (1909). *Capital* (Vol. 1). London: William Glaisher.

Marx, K. (1964). *Selected writings in sociology and social philosophy.* New York: McGraw-Hill.

Marx, K. (1971). *Capital* (Vol. 3). Moscow: Progress.

Marx, K. (1973). *Grundrisse: Foundations of the critique of political economy.* London: Penguin Books.

Marx, K. (1988). *Economic and philosophical manuscripts of 1844.* Buffalo, NY: Prometheus Books.

McEwan, B. (1996, April). *It is as much the how as the what: Examining my own practices for teaching classroom management.* Paper presented at the annual meeting of the American Educational Research Association, New York City.

McIntyre, S., & Tlusty, R. (1992, April). *Computer-mediated discourse: Electronic dialogue journaling and reflective practice.* Paper presented at the annual meeting of the American Educational Research Association, San Francisco, CA.

McIntyre, S., & Tlusty, R. (1993, April). *Electronic dialogue journaling and its effect on reflective practice with preservice teachers.* Paper presented at the annual meeting of the American Educational Research Association, Atlanta, GA.

Merseth, K. (1988). Project at Harvard Graduate School of Education. *Education Week, 7,* 1.

Middleton, D., & Edwards, D. (Eds.). (1990). *Collective remembering.* London: Sage.

Moll, L. C. (Ed.). (1990). *Vygotsky and education.* Cambridge, England: Cambridge University Press.

Nardi, B. A. (Ed.). (1996). *Context and consciousness.* Cambridge, MA: MIT Press.

Nason, P. (1996). Practicing scientists mentor pre-service science teachers via Internet. In D. Willis, J. Prince, & J. Willis (Eds.), *Technology and teacher education annual, 1996* (pp. 296–299). Charlottesville, VA: Association for the Advancement of Computing in Education.

Newman, D. (1990). Opportunities for research on the organizational impact of school computers. *Educational Researcher, 19*(3), 8–13.

Newman, D., Griffin, P., & Cole, M. (1989). *The construction zone.* Cambridge, England: Cambridge University Press.

Norton, P., & Sprague, D. (1996). *On-line collaborative lesson planning: An experiment in teacher education.* In D. Willis, J. Price, & J. Willis (Eds.), *Technology in teacher education annual 1996* (pp. 885–889). Charlottesville, VA: Association for the Advancement of Computing in Education.

Office of Technology Assessment. (1995). *Teachers and technology: Making the connection.* Washington, DC: U.S. Government Printing Office.

Panel on Educational Technology. (1997). *Report to the president on the use of technology to strengthen K–12 education in the United States.* Washington, DC: U.S. Government Printing Office.

Papert, S. (1993). *The children's machine: Rethinking schools in the age of the computer.* New York: Basic Books.

Pellegrino, J. W., & Altman, J. E. (1997). Information technology and teacher preparation: Some critical issues and illustrative solutions. *Peabody Journal of Education, 72,* 89–121.

Perry, B., & Brooks, D. (1987). *EDTNet department of teacher education computer network grant.* Miami, OH: Miami University Graduate School.

Philips, S. (1993). *The invisible culture: Communicatication in classroom and community on the Warm Springs Indian Reservation.* Prospect Heights, IL: Waveland Press.

Platten, M., & Barker, B. (1987). *Texas Tech University's "Models of Teaching" over satellite: A description and evaluation of college credit coursework delivered via the TI-IN interactive satellite network.* Lubbock: College of Education, Texas Tech University. (ERIC Document Reproduction Service No. ED 288 491)

Poole, D. (1996). Telecommunications as a link between preservice teachers, students, and mathematics. In D. Willis, J. Price, & J. Willis (Eds.), *Technology and teacher education annual, 1996* (pp. 248–251). Charlottesville, VA: Association for the Advancement of Computing in Education.

Powers, S., & Dutt-Doner, K. (1997). Enhancing the preservice teacher experience through electronic discussions. In J. Willis, J. Price, S. McNeil, B. Robin, & D. Willis (Eds.), *Technology and teacher education annual, 1997* (pp. 1213–1217). Charlottesville, VA: Association for the Advancement of Computing in Education.

Quinn, C. N., Mehan, H., Levin, J. A., & Black, S. D. (1983). Real education in nonreal time: The use of electronic message systems for instruction. *Instructional Science, 11*(4), 313–327.

Raeithel, A. (1991). Activity theory as a foundation for design. In C. Floyd, H. Zulighoven, R. Budde, & R. Keil-Slawik (Eds.), *Software development and reality construction* (pp. 391–415). Berlin: Springer.

Reinking, D., & Watkins, J. (1996). *A formative experiment investigating the use of multimedia book reviews to increase elementary students' independent reading* (Reading Research Report No. 55). Athens: National Reading Research Center, University of Georgia.

Resnick, L. B., Levine, J. M., & Teasley, S. D. (Eds.). (1991). *Perspectives on socially shared cognition.* Washington, DC: American Psychological Association.

Rieber, R. W. (Ed.). (1997). *The collected works of L. S. Vygotsky: Vol. 4. The history of the development of higher mental functions.* New York: Plenum.

Rieber, R. W., & Carton, A. S. (Eds.). (1987). *The collected works of L. S. Vygotsky: Vol. 1. Problems of general psychology.* New York: Plenum.

Rieber, R. W., & Carton, A. S. (Eds.). (1993). *The collected works of L. S. Vygotsky: Vol. 2. The fundamentals of defectology.* New York: Plenum.

Rieber, R. W., & Wollock, J. (Eds.). (1997). *The collected works of L. S. Vygotsky: Vol. 3. Problems of the theory and history of psychology.* New York: Plenum.

Rip, A., Hess, D. J., & Layne, L. L. (Eds.). (1992). *Knowledge and society: The anthropology of science and technology (Vol. 9).* Greenwich, CT: JAI Press.

Roddy, M. (1997). Using the Internet to unite student teaching and teacher education. In J. Willis, J. Price, S. McNeil, B. Robin, & D. Willis (Eds.), *Technology and teacher education annual, 1997* (pp. 1218–1221). Charlottesville, VA: Association for the Advancement of Computing in Education.

Rogoff, B. (1990). *Cognitive apprenticeship: Cognitive development in social context.* New York: Oxford University Press.

Rogoff, B. (1995). Observing sociocultural activity on three planes: Participatory appropriation, guided participation, apprenticeship. In J. V. Wertsch, P. Del Rio, & A. Alvarez (Eds.), *Sociocultural studies of mind* (pp. 139–164). Cambridge, England: Cambridge University Press.

Ruopp, R., Gall, S., Drayton, B., & Pfister, M. (1993). *LabNet: Toward a community of practice*. Hillsdale, NJ: Erlbaum.

Russett, J. (1994, March). *Telecommunications and pre-service science teachers: The effects of using electronic mail and a directed exploration of Internet on attitudes*. Paper presented at the meeting of the National Association for Research in Science Teaching, Anaheim, CA.

Schlagal, B., Trathen, W., & Blanton, W. (1996). Structuring telecommunications to create instructional conversations about student teaching. *Journal of Teacher Education, 47*, 175–183.

Schlegoff, E. A. (1992). Conversation analysis and socially shared cognition. In L. Resnick, J. M. Levine, & S. D. Teasley (Eds.), *Perspectives on socially shared cognition* (pp. 150–171). Washington, DC: American Psychology Association.

Schrum, L. (1992). Professional development in the information age: An online experience. *Educational Technology, 32*(12), 49–53.

Slough, S., & McGrew-Zoubi, R. (1996, March–April). *Area under constructivism: A pilot study using a World Wide Web home page to assess professional development*. Paper presented at the meeting of the National Association for Research in Science Teaching, St. Louis, MO.

Sumrall, W., & Sumrall, C. (1995). Introducing electronic mail applications within preservice elemetary science method courses. *Journal of Computing in Teacher Education, 11*(4), 23–30.

Sunal, D., Sunal, C., Helfeldt, J., & Durham, J. (1991, April). *Use of LAN technology to enhance the quality of field-based teacher education programs*. Paper presented at the meeting of the American Educational Research Association, Chicago, IL.

Swift, K., & Coxford, A. (1988). Computer networking for student teachers. *The Innovator, 19*(1), 5.

Tannehill, D., & LaMaster, K. (1996). Mentoring in teacher education through electronic mail. In D. Willis, J. Price, & J. Willis (Eds.), *Technology and teacher education annual, 1996* (pp. 707–710). Charlottesville, VA: Association for the Advancement of Computing in Education.

Tharp, R. G., & Gallimore, R. (1988). *Rousing minds to life*. Cambridge, England: Cambridge University Press.

Thomas, L., Clift, R., & Sugimoto, T. (1996). Telecommunication, student teaching, and methods instruction: An exploratory investigation. *Journal of Teacher Education, 46*, 165–174.

Thomas, L., Larson, A., Clift, R., & Levin, J. (1996). Integrating technology in teacher education programs: Lessons from the Teaching Teleapprenticeship project. *Action in Teacher Education, 17*(4), 1–8.

Trathen, W., & Moorman, G. (1996, April). *Using e-mail to create pedagogical dialogue among teachers and students*. Paper presented at the annual meeting of the American Educational Research Association, New York City.

Tripp, S. D., & Bichelmeyer, B. (1990). Rapid prototyping: An alternative instructional design strategy. *Education Technology Research and Development, 38*, 31–44.

Tryphon, A., & Voneche, J. (Eds.). (1996). *Piaget-Vygotsky: The social genesis of thought*. East Sussex, England: Psychology Press.

Tulviste, P. (1991). *The cultural-historical development of verbal thinking*. Commack, NY: Nova.

van der Veer, R. (1984). Early periods in the work of L. S. Vygotsky: The influence of Spinoza. In M. Hedegaard, P. Hakkarainen, & Y. Engestrom (Eds.), *Learning and teaching on a scientific basis* (pp. 87–98). Aarhus, Sweden: Psykologisk Institut, Aarhus Universitet.

van der Veer, R., & Valsiner, J. (1991). *Understanding Vygotsky*. Oxford, England: Basil Blackwell.

van der Veer, R., & Valsiner, J. (Eds.). (1994). *The Vygotsky reader*. Oxford, England: Basil Blackwell.

Vygotsky, L. S. (1962). *Thought and language*. Cambridge, MA: MIT Press.

Vygotsky, L. S. (1971). *The psychology of art*. Cambridge, MA: MIT Press.

Vygotsky, L. S. (1978). *Mind in society*. Cambridge, MA: Harvard University Press.

Warner, M. W. (1996). *The effects of participation in two activity systems on changing preservice teachers' beliefs about teaching, learning, and pupils*. Unpublished doctoral dissertation, Boone, NC: Appalachian State University.

Waugh, M. (1994, April). *On-line questioning patterns in an instructional telecommunications course for teachers*. Paper presented at the annual meeting of the American Educational Research Association, New Orleans, LA.

Waugh, M., Miyake, N., Cohen, M., & Levin, J. (1988, April). *Analysis of problem-solving interactions on electronic networks*. Paper presented at the annual meeting of the American Educational Research Association, New Orleans, LA.

Wertsch, J. V. (Ed.). (1981). *The concept of activity in Soviet psychology*. Armonk, NY: M. E. Sharpe.

Wertsch, J. V. (Ed.). (1985a). *Culture, communication, and cognition*. Cambridge, England: Cambridge University Press.

Wertsch, J. V. (1985b). *Vygotsky and the social formation of mind*. Cambridge, MA: Harvard University Press.

Wertsch, J. V. (1991). *Voices of the mind: A sociocultural approach to mediated action*. Cambridge, MA: Harvard University Press.

Wertsch, J. V. (1994). The primacy of mediated action in sociocultural studies. *Mind, Culture, and Activity, 1*, 202–208.

Wertsch, J. V., Del Rio, P., & Alvarez, A. (Eds.). (1995). *Sociocultural studies of mind*. Cambridge, England: Cambridge University Press.

Williams, H., & Merideth, E. (1995). Internet outposts: Communication patterns in computer-mediated classrooms. In D. Willis, J. Robin, & J. Willis (Eds.), *Technology and teacher education annual, 1995* (pp. 638–642). Charlottesville, VA: Association for the Advancement of Computing in Education.

Yan, W., Anderson, M., & Nelson, J. (1994). Facilitating reflective thinking in student teaching through electronic mail. In J. Willis, B. Robin, & D. Willis (Eds.), *Technology and teacher education annual, 1994* (pp. 657–660). Charlottesville, VA: Association for the Advancement of Computing in Education.

Zhao, Y., & Campbell, K. (1995, October). *Refining knowledge in a virtual community: A case-based collaborative project for preservice teachers*. Paper presented at the Computer Support of Collaborative Learning Conference, Bloomington, IN.

Manuscript received September 25, 1997
Accepted December 12, 1997

# Chapter 8

# From Deficit Thinking to Social Constructivism: A Review of Theory, Research, and Practice in Special Education

STANLEY C. TRENT
University of Virginia

ALFREDO J. ARTILES
University of California, Los Angeles

CAROL SUE ENGLERT
Michigan State University

Currently special education is in poor health. Plagued by criticisms about program efficacy, many educators, policymakers, and researchers now argue for changes in how students with disabilities are educated. In the midst of heated debates about redefining current practices, social constructivism has emerged as a theory that has the potential to make instruction in special education more holistic and relevant and emphasize more the strengths and knowledge that children bring to the classroom setting. While we do not elevate social constructivism as a cure for the complex problems now facing the field, we do believe that instruction emanating from social constructivist theory can inform instructional practices and can contribute to improved learning outcomes for children with disabilities.

Thus, the purpose of this chapter is to outline the emerging contributions that social constructivism has made to the field of special education, specifically in the area of literacy instruction for students with mild disabilities. We focus on literacy because of its central importance in the education of students, particularly those with disabilities. In addition, we limit the discussion to the mild disabilities group because it is the largest segment of the special education population in the United States. In the first section, we contextualize the significance of social constructivism by offering a historical sketch of the evolution of special education social organization. We emphasize that this summary is not an exhaustive account of historical periods or events, nor is it an indictment against instructional approaches derived from a deficit perspective. Rather, our goal is to illustrate how special education has relied too heavily on deficit thinking and must now enhance existing practices with alternative approaches that consider the sociocultural contexts in which children with disabilities learn. We next summarize some basic theoretical principles

We extend thanks to consulting editors Candace Bos and Michael Gerber, and Daniel P. Hallahan, James M. Kauffman, and P. David Pearson for their feedback on prior versions of this chapter.

of social constructivism and present components of exemplary literacy programs derived from a social constructivist perspective.

We conclude with a cautionary note. As special educators develop a knowledge base grounded in social constructivism, they must face at least four critical challenges. First, special education must transcend polarized views about instruction and what constitutes "best practice." Second, practitioners and researchers must develop clear definitions of constructs to facilitate communication among colleagues and to enhance the generalizability of empirical findings. Third, social constructivist theory compels us to understand the interplay between human development and learning from a more complex perspective. Thus, special educators must use this theory not only to develop alternative instructional models but to reformulate their understandings of the notions of competence and disability. Fourth, we must transcend the overemphasis on instructional strategies that has characterized our field. Indeed, a social constructivist perspective challenges us to be mindful of the contexts in which instruction takes place. For this purpose, we reflect on the need to conduct research on instructional approaches that includes a view of teachers as learners within the context of school-wide reforms. We hope that this reflective look at special education will lead to increased dialogue among disparate camps in the field. In addition, we hope that this chapter will contribute to the emergence of special education practices that focus more on teaching, learning, and improved academic outcomes for children with disabilities.

## THE SOCIAL ORGANIZATION OF EARLY SPECIAL EDUCATION FOR CHILDREN WITH MILD DISABILITIES IN THE UNITED STATES: THE PREEMINENCE OF DEFICIT THINKING

MacMillan and Hendrick (1993) contend that multiple theories working simultaneously contributed to the development of programs for children with mild disabilities, particularly mental retardation. Two of these theories are the "child saving" theory and the "social control" theory. Child saving theory advocates argue that special education for individuals with mental retardation emerged from a need for differentiated curricula for an increasingly diverse school-aged population composed of children with impairments and immigrants from central and eastern Europe. Proponents of this theory also contend that well-intentioned educators developed special programs designed to increase the number of self-sufficient, self-supporting citizens along all levels of socioeconomic strata. Conversely, social control theory advocates argue that separate programs for the mildly retarded in public schools were created to separate immigrants, African American children, Native American children, and poor children from middle-class and wealthy White children.

Indeed, we agree with MacMillan and Hendrick (1993) that a number of forces contributed to the establishment of special programs in public schools. Moreover, we contend that both of the theories just outlined were guided to some degree by an overreliance on a model that attributed learning and behavior problems to deficits that reside within children. We believe this overemphasis on a deficit model has contributed to many of the problems we currently face in the special education field. With this in mind, we now provide information about the origins of special education in the United States based on the child saving and social control theories. Our intent is not to provide a comprehensive analysis of special education history and theories. Instead, we identify the circumstances that led to special education program development and illustrate how a preeminent focus on deficit thinking has guided beliefs and practices in the field.

## Deficit Thinking From a Child Saving Perspective

At one level, the evolution of deficit thinking in special education stemmed from beliefs that, although some individuals functioned in ways considered "subnormal," they were still humans and deserved to be educated. A review of the history of the development of programs for children with mild disabilities reveals that, in the early 1800s, advocates of the child saving theory attempted to determine the etiology of students' symptoms that resulted in learning and behavior problems. These psychologists, physicians, and educators developed therapies and instructional interventions designed to improve the educational outcomes and quality of life of individuals with disabilities. For example, during the mid-1800s, Edouard Seguin became a leading figure in the move to establish institutions for individuals who were "feebleminded" (i.e., mentally retarded). According to Robinson and Robinson (1976), Seguin advocated sensory training to serve as remediation for two types of problems related to this disability: "a superficial type in which the peripheral nervous system has been damaged or weakened and [a] profound type in which the central nervous system has always been defective" (p. 34).

Seguin advocated a "moral treatment" model to remediate the problems experienced by individuals who were mentally retarded. This treatment was based on manipulation of the environment versus medical (e.g., purging) or religious interventions (exorcism). According to Rothman (1971), moral therapy consisted of "constructive activity, kindness, minimum restraint, structure, routine, and consistency in treatment. Furthermore, obedience to authority and conformity to rules were primary features of child-care institutions and child-rearing dogma in mid-nineteenth century America" (p. 54). Seguin and his colleagues believed that, with this type of therapy, individuals with mental retardation could reenter the community and lead somewhat productive and self-sufficient lives. Influenced by European movements to achieve social justice and humane treatment for the middle class and the poor, his ideas became very popular in the mid- to late 1800s, and many advocacy groups pushed to develop institutions across the country in which personnel could replicate his work (Blatt, 1987).

As was the case with mental retardation, the behaviors exhibited by individuals labeled mentally ill (e.g., emotionally and behaviorally disordered) in the early 1800s were attributed to a host of factors, most of which were linked to the individual. According to Kauffman (1997), possible causes for this disability included masturbation and other such superstitions as "'idleness and ennui,' 'pecuniary embarrassment,' 'sedentary and studious habits,' 'inhaling tobacco fumes,' 'gold fever,' [and] 'indulgence of tempers'" (Stribling, 1842) (p. 69). However, Kauffman reported that, during the mid-19th century, other factors emerged to explain the etiology of behavior disorders. This shift in thinking prompted educators to consider the effect of the environment on the development of behavior problems (e.g., children's interactions with parents, parent child rearing practices). Similar to what occurred with mental retardation, the belief that behaviorally deviant individuals could learn appropriate behaviors resulted in implementation of a moral treatment approach in many institutions and residential programs.

In contrast to mental retardation and behavioral disorders, research and theory about learning disabilities did not emerge until the 20th century. Still, researchers continued to link symptoms (e.g., inability to read) to deficits that resided within children. Alfred Strauss, considered one of the founding fathers of contemporary learning disability theory, was influenced significantly by Kurt Goldstein, who studied the effects of head wounds on the functioning of World War I veterans (Hallahan & Cruickshank, 1973). Also, Strauss's work with children with mental retardation at the Wayne County Training School in Michigan led him to believe that some children's inability to read could be linked to brain damage and consequent processing difficulties. Eventually, Heinz Werner joined Strauss at the training school, and the two men became even more interested in "whether the psychological manifestations of brain injury found in adults by Goldstein would also be observable in children" (Hallahan & Cruickshank, 1973, p. 60). Findings from their research pointed to the existence of two types of children with mental retardation: exogenous (i.e., retardation due to neurological defects) and endogenous (i.e., retardation due to familial factors). Specifically, they found that exogenous children's IQs declined during their stay at the training school, while the IQs of endogenous children increased significantly. In 1947, on the basis of these findings, they "recommended without elaboration the attenuation of inessential stimuli and the accentuation of essential stimuli in the environment of such a child (exogenous)" (Hallahan & Cruickshank, 1973, p. 64).

William Cruickshank and several of his students and colleagues were responsible for extending the work of Strauss and Werner to children who appeared to be intellectually normal. Based on studies of children with normal or near-normal intelligence, he, along with a host of other learning disability theorists, came to believe that "motor development precedes and is necessary for perceptual development" (Hallahan & Cruickshank, 1973, p. 90). In addition, they concluded that control of the environment and perceptual-motor training were needed to remediate deficits in children with learning disabilities.

## Deficit Thinking From a Social Control Perspective

While researchers developed theories and interventions designed to improve learning outcomes for children with disabilities, certain sociocultural and sociopolitical forces blurred visions of meeting the needs of these children in an effective, equitable, and democratic manner. These forces included economics, systemic constraints, and negative beliefs about the educability and worth of people with disabilities that emerged shortly after the Civil War (Blatt, 1987; Kauffman, 1997; Rizzo & Zabel, 1988). For instance, Seguin developed a model that was comprehensive in scope and that honored—to some degree—the need for a fluid, contextual interpretation of the manifestation of disabilities. Unfortunately, however, his ideas took a back seat to the aspects of his model that focused on deficits within the individual and to the predominant societal belief that individuals who were retarded were not educable. As implementation of interventions deteriorated; as more and more persons with severe disabilities were placed in institutional settings; as fiscal, material, and human resources became more and more inadequate; and as beliefs about the insignificance of "idiots" gained prominence, individuals with mental retardation were institutionalized for life and were treated harshly (Blatt, 1987).

Beliefs about race and ethnicity also influenced the development of constructs designed to define and deal with differences. Menchaca (1997) asserted that beliefs emanating from deficit thinking contributed to beliefs about race and intelligence and eventually, we would argue, to the push for separate, special education programs in public schools. In tracing the emergence of deficit thinking in the United States, she concluded that the quest for wealth coupled with racist discourse contributed to the displacement of Native Americans and the enslavement of Blacks. As this quest persisted, scientists began to publish work about the craniology and facial features of Native Americans and Blacks that lent credibility to a theory claiming that people of color originated from species below that of Caucasians. In the mid-1800s, social Darwinism contributed to negative attitudes about individuals with disabilities (MacMillan & Hendrick, 1993) and also reinforced the belief that people of color were intellectually inferior and needed to be governed by Whites (Menchaca, 1997).

Although many scientists and researchers refuted the work of hereditarianists, these deficit theories influenced educational policies and practices significantly. For example, in 1896 the U.S. Supreme Court "passed Plessy v. Ferguson and officially gave the states the right to segregate racial minorities in separate schools" (Menchaca, 1997, p. 17). As public schools were faced with educating increased numbers of immigrant children and former slaves, the introduction of the intelligence test in the United States provided further justification for segregation based on race and ethnicity. Furthermore, these tests afforded school systems the opportunity to legitimize their efforts to identify children for special education services primarily in classes for the mildly mentally retarded. Specifically, intelligence tests (e.g., the new Binet-Simon scales) were used to identify mental deficits within children that precluded their successful functioning in school. As Menchaca relates (1997):

Racial differences in intelligence, it was contended, are most validly explained by racial differences in innate, genetically determined abilities. What emerged from these findings, regarding schooling, were curricular recommendations that the "intellectually inferior" and the social order would best be served by providing these students concrete, low-level, segregated instruction commensurate with their alleged diminished intellectual abilities. (p. 38)

In more recent times, overreliance on deficit thinking resulted in incompatible policies designed to meet the needs of children who previously had not experienced appropriate and equitable treatment in public schools. During the 1950s, for example, African Americans, along with supporters, fought for legislation to end public school segregation on the basis of race. This advocacy resulted in a Supreme Court ruling that ended "separate but equal" schooling in the United States (i.e., Brown v. The Board of Education of Topeka, Kansas, 1954). During the 1960s and 1970s, parent advocates sought access and equity for their children who had been denied enrollment in public school settings as a result of physical, mental, or emotional disabilities. This advocacy and subsequent litigation led to the enactment of several pieces of legislation, one of the most important being the Education for All Handicapped Children Act (EHCA) of 1975 (now reauthorized as the Individuals with Disabilities Education Act [1997]). Some of the safeguards of EHCA included "an active search to locate all handicapped children excluded from public education, nondiscriminatory diagnostic procedures, individualized education programs, adequate due process procedures for handicapped children, and placement in the least restrictive environment for learning (Lazerson, 1983, p. 42). (Least restrictive environment stipulates that, to the fullest extent possible, students with disabilities will be educated in classrooms with their nondisabled peers.) Despite these safeguards, many policy analysts argue that the incompatibility of these two federal actions contributed to the overrepresentation of children of color in special education programs (Lazerson, 1983; Mercer, 1973; Richardson, 1979; Sarason & Doris, 1979; Trent & Artiles, 1995). This resulted in advocacy on the part of non-White parents who believed that the practice was an attempt to maintain segregation within integrated schools. As stated by Lazerson (1983):

Nonwhite and non-English-speaking parents joined the coalition, in part with the same ends in mind as the whites, but more often under a different incentive: too many of their children were being classified as handicapped and were being channeled into special education programs with little pretense that they would be educated. (p. 41)

Note also that, while EHCA provided many safeguards for parents and their children with disabilities, school systems primarily made special education placements based on a norm-referenced, deficit-based diagnostic model. Even when attempts were made to address disproportionate representation of minority children in special education, norm-referenced data remained the major tool for identification and placement. For example, Sleeter (1996) argued that the learning disability diagnosis was used to differentiate the learning problems of middle-class White children from those of children of color. The emergence of learning disabilities, then, allowed educators to systematically separate children within special education by race. However, when parents protested this practice, subsequent litigation resulted in decreased enrollment of minority children in programs for the mentally retarded and increased enrollment of these children in programs for the learning disabled (Tucker, 1980).

In summary, it appears that the individuals who established special education in the United States were motivated by opposing forces. Some advocates of special education programs believed that the country was morally obligated to educate, to the fullest extent possible, children with impairments. These advocates, including physicians, psychologists, and educators, worked diligently to identify causes for disabilities that might lead to ameliorative instructional interventions and therapies. In some instances, however, special education programs were used as a means to segregate children on the basis of race, ethnicity, and socioeconomic status (Lazerson, 1983; Mercer, 1973; Richardson, 1979). This overreliance on a deficit perspective coupled with cultural, sociopolitical, and economic forces characterized early special education efforts. Because of these persistent problems, many special education researchers and practitioners began to advocate for a paradigmatic shift that would transcend deficit thinking and promote a more fluid, contextual framework for examining disability, teaching, and learning in special education.

## Emergence of a Paradigmatic Shift

The special education field made impressive gains in the development of an empirical knowledge base after World War II. For example, after 1950 the field witnessed the emergence of the psychological process model, the behavioral model, and the cognitive strategy model. Although this progression did not occur in a linear, mutually exclusive fashion, many educators argue that the emergence of these models represents advancement in special education theory and practice. However, some special educators did not see these changes in special education theory as advancement. For example, Poplin asserted that "the transition from one mode to the other represents little more than methodological change" (Poplin, 1988, p. 389). This deficit perspective, she purported, resulted in commonalities that run across the four models related to emphasis, etiology, diagnosis, assessment, instruction/treatment, and goals. In addition, Poplin asserted that these commonalities continue to emphasize deficits over strengths and focus on the teaching of discrete, task-analyzed skills in the absence of context, meaning, and relevance (see Table 1 for a presentation of Poplin's critique).

Poplin (1985, 1988) acknowledged that reductionism served as a beginning in educators' attempts to meet the needs of children who experienced failure in school. However, she argued that the progression of the field—based largely on a deficit perspective—had not resulted in the accomplishment of this goal. Instead of focusing on a deficit model, Poplin and a growing number of special education theorists and researchers focused on the strengths of learners as a basis for remediation. In addition, they concluded that holistic/constructivist theories about teaching and learning will, if put into practice, improve learning outcomes for children with disabilities (Coles, 1987; Denti & Katz, 1995; Dudley-Marling & Dippo, 1995; Englert & Palincsar, 1991; Heshusius, 1989). Based largely on the work of Vygotsky (1978) and neo-Vygotskian scholars, these advocates of social constructivism have initiated a new line of research in special education. We next present some of the theoretical principles undergirding this work.

## Theoretical Principles of Social Constructivism

Vygotsky (1978), the architect of sociocultural theory, called for the "intellectualization of mental functions," whereby mental functions are brought under conscious and voluntary control. Notably, the work of Vygotsky (1978) has provided

**TABLE 1**
**Overview of Theoretical Models of LD, 1950–Present**

| | Medical Model (1950s) | Psychological Process Model (1960s) | Behavioral Model (1970s) | Cognitive/Learning Strategies (1980s) |
|---|---|---|---|---|
| Emphasis | Neurological pathways | Prerequisite skills for academic success | Academic product of consequent behavior | Information processing and meta-cognition necessary for academic success |
| Etiology | Brain damage or dysfunction | Minimal neurological dysfunction | Lack of learned behaviors or learned nonadaptive behaviors | Insufficient strategies or study skills with which to process information necessary for school success |
| Diagnosis | Largely neurological | Soft neurological signs psychological process testing | Discrepancy between IQ and academic achievement, criterion-referenced tests and observation of specific academic and social school tasks | Discrepancy between IQ and academic achievement, with cognitive skills tests and/or observation of specific strategies |
| Assessment | Academic assessment, largely anecdotal case studies | Psychological process; some basic academic skills | Testing of student behavior against task analysis of skills, examination of reinforcement contingencies | Testing of student behavior and processing against known cognitive and/or learning strategies used by successful learners, often task analyzed |
| Instruction/ Treatment | Extremely structured, clutter-free environment; motoric and other neuro-logical training; some basic skills emphasis; some medication | Psychological or psycho-linguistic training with less emphasis on actual aca-demic skills; medication, sensory integration, and/ or modality training | Direct instruction using task analysis of skills (behaviors) and application of reinforcement principles | Direct instruction in strategies used by successful school learners; also use of principles of reinforcement, particularly self-management and self talk |
| Goals | Function in community | Function in school; less community emphasis | Almost exclusively school-related goals, some social but primarily academic mainstream | Almost exclusively school-related goals; some social but primarily academic mainstream |
| Some major figures | Werner, Strauss, Lehtinen, Cruickshank | Kirk, Frostig, Minskoff, Kephart, Barsch, Wepman | Lovitt, Carnine, Jenkins, Haring, Bateman | Torgesen, Hallahan, Deshler, Schumaker, Alley, Meichenbaum, Feuerstein, Wong |

From Poplin, M. S. (1988). The reductionistic fallacy in learning disabilities: Replicating the past by reducing the present. *Journal of Learning Disabilities,* 389–400. Copyright 1988 by PRO-ED, Inc. Reprinted by permission.

a conceptual framework involving four principles that might guide the redesign of educational contexts so that learners are initiated into the cognitive practices of the broader society and community. These principles are as follows: (a) apprenticeship in applied settings, (b) access to empowering modes of discourse, (c) guided instruction that leads to self-regulated learning, and (d) learning in cultural historical contexts.

### Apprenticeship in Applied Settings

First, Vygotsky's work suggests that cognitive practices are acquired through apprenticeships in applied settings. Together with more knowledgeable members, children are acculturated into the cognitive practices and strategies of skilled problem solvers in the content areas in which the strategies are used. Although this tradition suggests that knowledge-about-action is constructed in contextualized settings, the education of special education students has typically emphasized memorization and rote learning of skills and strategies in settings detached from the functional and authentic contexts in which they are to be used. However, the separation of knowledge from goal-embedded contexts leaves children with disabilities in a passive role complicated by the demands on the learner to amass the discrete parts of knowledge into a meaningful whole. This is akin to restricting one's study of a dynamic sport such as baseball to a study of bodies, bats, and balls and expecting that the learner will fathom how to play baseball and be motivated to play (Gee, 1992). Literate thinking and actions must be grounded in the social purposes of the cognitive practice in authentic problem-solving activities (Flowers, 1994). Children acquire complex skills through social interactions in situated contexts, which allows them to see how the various parts of the process fit together.

### Access to Empowering Modes of Discourse

Second, through cognitive apprenticeships, children are given access to modes of discourse not available "naturally." "Education in general is fundamentally a process of mastering new traditions of discourse" (Applebee, 1996, p. 9). Schools provide access to the secondary discourses that are not part of children's home environment. These discourses include particular ways-of-talking (language) and ways-of-acting (strategies, procedures, conventions) that are known and practiced by members of a sociocultural group (Gee, 1992). Potentially, knowledge of these discourses can inform the members regarding the intellectual activities related to "what it means to do" reading, writing, mathematics, science, or social studies. Access to these discourses is especially important for students with mild disabilities because they do not automatically recognize strategies for problem solving, and they often fail to develop adequate metacognitive knowledge related to the control of cognitive processes. It is even likely that many of the students who fail in school may not be simply those who do not learn enough facts but those who do not gain access to school-based discourses (Michaels & O'Connor, 1990). Thus, teachers must explicitly teach children with disabilities at a higher cognitive level that makes visible the meta-level strategies that are valued and privileged in schools and other spheres of life (Michaels & O'Connor, 1990).

## Guided Instruction That Leads to Self-Regulated Learning

Third, Vygotsky's work suggests that an apprenticeship model entails a process of guided instruction, with a gradual transfer of regulation to the learners themselves of the cognitive actions and processes supported in social interactions with others (Stone, 1989). Vygotsky maintained that strategic patterns of reasoning reflected on an interpsychological plane (between or among individuals) are exercised by individuals on an intrapsychological plane (within an individual) (see Palincsar & Brown, 1989). There are several component features of a guided apprenticeship. One feature involves the gradual transfer of the cognitive process to the learner. This means that a more knowledgeable or expert person provides more support, but gradually the learner participates to an increasing degree while the expert hands over control of the various parts of the process. This suggests a complex instructional role for teachers that requires that they constantly adapt their behavior as the learner progresses, adding or removing support in relation to the emergent goals and the learner's performance in the academic context.

A second feature of a guided apprenticeship involves instruction in a cognitive process in advance of learners' independent performance. Vygotsky's (1978) work suggests that good teaching awakens to life those cognitive functions that are in a state of maturing. Teachers must lead students to adopt more sophisticated cognitive approaches and tactics for solving complex problems than students are capable of devising on their own (Stone, 1989). Inherent in this principle is the assumption that mistakes are inevitable and that errors can provide the occasion for the restructuring of knowledge, leading to the potential development of more sophisticated mental functions. Thus, rather than reducing tasks to discrete analytical components to promote errorless learning, Vygotsky's work suggests that teachers should mediate performance in ways that enable a child to solve a problem or achieve a goal that would be beyond his or her unassisted efforts. Such scaffolds make it possible for the learner to participate in a complex process from the very beginning. Various types of verbal mediational tools can scaffold and transform cognitive performance, including teacher modeling, instructing, and questioning (Tharp, 1993) as well as sign-based systems such as schematics, diagrams, or maps (Wertsch, Tulviste, & Hagstrom, 1993). Vygotsky defined this type of instruction as honoring the child's zone of proximal development (ZPD). He defined ZPD as the distance between what children can do without assistance and what they can accomplish with the assistance of a capable other.

A third feature of a guided apprenticeship is the gradual appropriation and transformation by learners of the scaffolds and intellectual tools available in the sociocultural context. Higher mental functions are internalized through social and dialogic interactions with other members of a sociocultural group. These collaborative ways-of-thinking and ways-of-acting are first experienced in interactions with peers and teachers but, over time, are gradually internalized by learners to guide, determine, and mediate their own mental activity. Collaborative discourse and conversations about cognitive practices become the genetic precursors to the inner dialogues that the learner constructs to mediate his or her own thoughts and actions. Hicks (1996) warns, however, that there is not a direct transfer of knowledge from a teacher or expert to a novice. There is a reciprocal effect of the learner on the context: Learners are not only shaped by and transformed by the discourse in the situated contexts of the academic subject; they transform the discourse through their own cognitive actions. The construction of knowledge is interactive, social, and jointly mediated (Wertsch, 1994). Within this social context, language and discourse have a prominent position in the learning process.

A fourth feature of the guided apprenticeship is the importance of the social collective in learning. According to Vygotsky (1993), higher processes

arise during the process of a child's social development by means of the transferal to himself of those forms of cooperation which the child absorbs in the process of interaction with the surrounding social environment. We see that collective forms of cooperative work precede individual forms of behavior, grow out of their foundation, and act as the direct roots and sources of their appearance.... Thus, the higher functions of intellectual activity arise out of collective behavior, out of cooperation with the surrounding people, and from social experience. (p. 196)

Vygotsky proceeds to make the case that, in heterogeneous collectives and groups, children with disabilities are lifted to higher levels. In collaboration with teachers and peers, for example, children have an opportunity to practice advanced forms of academic discourse while receiving support from the group to carry out mental processes. Collaboration provides the social context for conversations that allows children to "grow into the intellectual life of those around them" (Wells & Chang-Wells, 1992; Newman, Griffin, & Cole, 1989). Children with disabilities are especially likely to benefit from collaborative interactions in a social context.

### Learning in Cultural Historical Contexts

The fourth major principle of social constructivist theory stems from the fourth feature of the guided apprenticeship. Through this principle, Vygotsky emphasized that learning and development are cultural historical phenomena that unfold in holistic, practical activity (Englert & Palincsar, 1991). In this vein, social constructivist theory assumes that individuals are active learners who craft knowledge based on their prior experiences. It is further assumed that individuals use cultural tools to function in their social milieus. These tools have been appropriated and transformed from previous generations and can be ideational (symbols, constructs) or material (Cole, 1996). Vygotsky's view of cultural tools was based on three assumptions: "(a) the use of tools introduces new possibilities for human action; (b) language is a tool used both to represent the environment and to direct behavior; and (c) human tools...are best thought of as culturally constituted systems of rules of use" (Stone & Reid, 1994, p. 74). Stone and Reid (1994) explained that as we obtain cultural tools, we also learn about implicit ways to use tools to transform our behavior; thus, what is of interest is not the symbol system per se but how people make use of it.

Within the sociocultural milieu of the classroom, students' schoolwork is a reflection of the appropriation and transformation of tools. In other words, students' academic and cognitive work is embedded in their past cultural heritage, at the same time that their cognitions and practices are situated in the mutually constructed meanings of the present classroom setting. Students are members of classroom communities that develop their own routines, forge shared understandings about rules and rights, and organize participation and interactional structures. For this reason, it is necessary to understand learning and developmental processes as situated in rich sociocultural contexts that should lead children to think about rules, rights, and justice within the larger society.

## A CASE IN POINT: SPECIAL EDUCATION LITERACY PROGRAMS BASED ON THE PRINCIPLES OF SOCIAL CONSTRUCTIVISM

Several research programs based on the principles of social constructivism are now prominent in the special education literature. Many of these programs have been highly successful in enhancing the academic learning and achievement of students with mild disabilities. In this section, we review these programs in order to highlight components of alternative approaches that might inform the design of effective instructional programs for children with special needs. Because literacy represents one of the major content areas in which many children with disabilities require specialized instruction, we provide descriptions of programs in this area.

### Reciprocal Teaching

One program of research that illustrates the nature of sociocultural theory in applied settings is reciprocal teaching (Palincsar, 1984, 1986). Reciprocal teaching was designed by Palincsar and Brown to support students with poor comprehension of expository text. The premise of reciprocal teaching is that, through repeated and shared social dialogues, the learner comes to discover the form and meaning of the more experienced readers' strategies and utterances (Palincsar & Brown, 1989). Having participated in a social dialogue about printed or oral texts, the learner presupposes and transforms the dialogue in the form of inner self-guiding speech to direct cognitive activity during independent comprehension activities (Wertsch, 1991).

In reciprocal teaching, discussions about texts are not open-ended, given the importance of specific ways-of-thinking and ways-of-responding to texts basic to effective comprehension. Four strategies provide a discursive framework for talking about informational texts: questioning, summarizing, clarifying, and predicting. These strategies provide teachers and students with a language and communicative mechanisms for engaging in the literate practices of good comprehenders. In essence, these strategies constitute a secondary discourse that informs participants about the particular reading practices of the community (the unique ways of interacting with texts) and serves to mediate the cognitive actions of the social group as they work to perceive, interpret, respond to, and evaluate texts.

Palincsar and Brown's (1989) prototype for the participation of learners in the literacy discourse is also highly consonant with the principles of an apprenticeship model. Ordinarily, teachers do not have teaching frameworks that invite children to take leadership in directing and initiating discursive moves in school lessons. However, in the reciprocal teaching lessons, students and their teachers take turns leading discussions about particular portions of the text. The discussion leader, for example, may ask questions pertinent to the text, summarize the same segment of text, clarify points in the text that are unclear, and predict what information will follow in the text. Interactively, other members of the group participate in the discussion by answering questions or asking additional questions, commenting or elaborating on the summary, clarifying and seeking clarification about confusing points, and generating additional predictions. Together, the group carries out the reading processes as the various comprehension activities are socially distributed and shared by the members.

What may be particularly advantageous for poor comprehenders and students with mild disabilities is the flexible nature of support available in the reciprocal teaching dialogue. Teachers and peers in the reading group provide various levels of support to participants based on ongoing student needs. At the same time that teachers are consciously attempting to turn over more responsibility for leading and sustaining the dialogue to student participants, they can intervene to assist individual students on a moment-to-moment basis by providing further explanations, modeling strategies, reinforcing or "revoicing" students' ideas, or prompting students to self-regulate. Classroom dialogues provide teachers with unique sources of data about the cognitive states of students, permitting them to successfully support members of a group who need to be coached in higher mental functions or who lack specific ways of responding to texts.

Several studies on reciprocal teaching have produced the following outcomes: (a) marked improvement in students' abilities to summarize, generate questions, clarify, and predict; (b) improvement on comprehension measures that were large, reliable, and durable; and (c) increased generalization of strategies to other settings (Palincsar & Brown, 1984). Furthermore, the researchers who conducted those studies concluded that the instruction of students in isolated strategies (e.g., instruction in questioning alone, followed by instruction in summarizing alone) did not produce the same effects as the full reciprocal teaching procedure (Brown & Palincsar, 1987). It was the combination of strategies that afforded students the greatest levels of comprehension (see also Campione et al., 1994).

There was also evidence that students began to self-regulate and direct their own comprehension performance. Students' scores increased on privately read assessment passages, indicating that what was learned in social interactions was transformed into a "self-imposed, intrapsychological process" (Wertsch, 1991). Finally, analyses of the discussions showed that lesson discourse became less teacher directed and spontaneous over time as children began to monitor their own understanding and began to use the strategies independently (Palincsar & Brown, 1989).

## The Early Literacy Project

A second literacy project based on a sociocultural perspective is the Early Literacy Project. Five principles figured prominently in the design of the curricular approach used in the Early Literacy Project, including assumptions that teachers should (a) embed instruction in meaningful and contextualized activities, (b) emphasize students' membership in communities, (c) provide social and dialogic interactions that support students' performance in their zones of proximal development, and (d) teach strategies for self-regulated learning in order to apprentice students to participate in knowledge-creating communities. The project was designed to promote literacy achievement among students with mild disabilities in the early grades (Grades 1–4) in resource room and basic classroom (e.g., noncategorical self-contained) settings.

The activities of the curriculum included choral reading, partner reading, journal writing, chair sharing, morning news, and story discussion or literature response (Englert, Raphael, & Mariage, 1994). All activities were related through the use of thematic units that engaged students in studying a variety of topics (e.g., whales, bats). Students read both expository and narrative texts as part of the thematic units and engaged in a process of inquiry as they used the strategies related to gathering, integrating, synthesizing, and constructing information as part of a process of building and communicating new meanings (for further information about the curricular approach, see Englert et al., 1994, in press). Skill and strategy instruction occurred within and across the language domains associated with the authentic contexts of reading, writing, speaking, or listening. Furthermore, there was an interrelationship among the domains in that what students read or heard, they wrote about, and vice-versa. Students were involved in listening, reading, writing, and speaking activities related to literacy the entire school day.

The Early Literacy Project exemplified sociocultural principles in several ways (Englert et al., 1994; Englert & Mariage, 1996). First, cognitive processes were taught and practiced in contextualized, holistic activities. All students, regardless of reading and writing skills, were perceived as readers and writers. From the first day of school to the end of the year, students involved in the project were expected to read and write whole texts.

Second, scaffolds were used to support the participation of students in advance of independent performance. Students who lacked conventional reading skills were given predictable books to read and participated chorally in reading texts while they were taught the specific reading skills they lacked. Similarly, students were taught various spelling and writing strategies to support their writing performance while teachers developed conventional writing skills in the context of modeling and guiding student talk related to personal experience stories in a group composition activity known as morning news. Scaffolds were used throughout the curriculum to mediate performance, including word banks, question words (to support the composition of personal experience stories), verbal prompts, cognitive strategies, story maps, and social collaborations among pairs or groups of students engaged in literacy activities. Englert and Mariage (1996) give an example of how a child's written 15-word story—"I was goge to go fish ing. Wito [with] my grdad. We wit (went) ovre [over] my. Cusit [cousin's] hese"—occasioned a large number of questions from his peers related to the story, such as "When did you go fishing?" "What fish did you catch?" and "Where did you go fishing?" At an interpsychological level, these questions provided scaffolds that mediated the author's ability to retrieve and relate a more expanded oral text. By the end of the year, this author had begun to internalize—at an intrapsychological level—the mental functioning enacted in prior interactions with the peer audience. His journal entries were nearly four times as long, and the written content of the entries suggested that the author was enacting an implicit dialogue with his audience as he explained when the event happened, where it took place, and what happened. The scaffolds provided by other people in prior social interactions came to mediate his performance in the form of internalized thought and action.

Third, Early Literacy Project teachers used an apprenticeship model of guided instruction. Using think alouds and interactive conversations with students about reading and writing texts, teachers sought to make cognitive strategies visible to students by modeling particular ways-of-talking (language) and ways-of-acting (strategies, procedures, conventions) in situated literacy contexts. For example, teachers might think aloud about how to read or write a particular text genre. Over time, however, the teachers prompted students to assume increasing control of the cognitive functions that were first experienced on the public and social plane (Vygotsky, 1978) by progressing from interacting with students in whole-class or large-group discussions to involving students in collaborative reading and writing activities and asking them to read or compose texts independently. Within these various participation structures, teachers sought to transfer control of the social discourse related to self-regulation and problem solving to students. As the teacher stepped back from the traditional role of leading the lesson, new roles were created that required students to demonstrate, challenge, convince, interpret, evaluate, or explain to others (Englert & Mariage, 1996). When students were unable to perform particular facets of a cognitive process, teachers and peers served as cognitive resources to support learners through questions, prompts, or models in a flexible way. Thus, cognition was distributed and shared by the various members of the classrooms in a flexible way.

Fourth, teachers provided access to modes of discourse related to reading, writing, and learning-to-learn processes. As part of the goal of apprenticing students in secondary discourses related to literacy, teachers provided students with access to a variety of text genres. These genres were experienced on a recurring basis across the school year as part of the thematic units. For example, teachers might have students with mild disabilities read and write narrative stories, read or write an explanation related to a particular object associated with the thematic unit, write personal experience stories on the topic, or develop a compare-contrast paper contrasting the elements within or across the various units of study.

Especially important discourses that were modeled in the Early Literacy Project classrooms were the learning-to-learn processes related to the reading and writing of informational text involving superordinate and subordinate ideas. This process entailed several cognitive processes involving brainstorming, organizing, reading for information, and drafting (see Englert, Berry, Bright, & Thornhill, 1997). This process is described in greater detail subsequently to highlight the nature of the apprenticeship of students in more formal models of cognitive thought and action (see further examples in Bos & Anders, 1990; Scanlon, Duran, Reyes, & Gallego, 1992).

Typically, teachers in the Early Literacy Project initiated the learning-to-learn process by asking students to brainstorm ideas related to the topic of a thematic unit. (Halliday & Martin, 1993). In the brainstorming process, the class started with a collective or common knowledge of a given topic. Within this process, students were positioned as informants who could share their personal experience and knowledge about the world. Their experiences and knowledge were then connected to scientific concepts.

In a second phase, following the recommendation of Vygotsky (1978), teachers used everyday knowledge arising from brainstorming activities as fertile ground for the construction of scientific thought and understanding. Vygotsky describes spontaneous, or everyday, concepts as arising from and embedded in everyday experiences. Scientific concepts, on the other hand, have elements abstracted out from concrete everyday experiences. A purpose of schooling is to systematically organize these elements into taxonomic structures that can then be applied to a number of concrete situations (Halliday & Martin, 1993). Accordingly, students in the project reflected on the brainstormed ideas in an organizing stage as they began to transform everyday knowledge into taxonomic or scientific knowledge consisting of categories of subtopics and related details. Teachers and students made this process explicit by developing a semantic map or web of ideas as they formed classes of related superordinate and subordinate ideas (Scanlon, Duran, Reyes, & Gallego, 1992). The web also became the means for teachers to "intellectualize" cognitive activity by helping students organize thought and activity in ways very similar to the classification processes that are a fundamental part of science and constitutive of "writing science" (Halliday & Martin, 1993). Through the mediational potentials afforded them by the webs, students were participating in the construction and classification of classes and subclasses of ideas, as well as seeing relations between parts and wholes (Englert, Berry, Bright, & Thornhill, [1996).

In a third phase, the webs served as an anchor or linchpin as teachers and students began to do research related to the reading and comprehension of information from expository texts. Expository texts often present complex cognitive demands because of their lexical density and grammatical ambiguity, and students had great difficulty in identifying and summarizing relevant information. The result was that many students simply copied text verbatim because of the difficulty in deciding what information was relevant and how it could be extracted from the larger context. However, with the use of the webs, students on the project were able to anticipate and recognize categories of information in texts, as well as use that knowledge to generate oral or written summaries that contained the central information. In the research classrooms, teachers used the web as a basis for taking students on "walks" through reference texts to identify relevant information. Teachers drew attention to boldface information in printed informational texts and guided students in considering what text information was important and unimportant as they (a) reviewed the categories of information in the web, (b) read short sections of informational text, (c) determined what text information should be added to the web and where it should be added, and (d) expanded or revised the web to correspond to the knowledge in the text in an iterative and bidirectional set of interactive activities (the text affected the construction of the webs, and the webs affected how texts were read and summarized). In effect, cognitive activity was off-loaded onto the webs until the point at which students could perform the cognitive actions of summarizing and organizing ideas without visible or symbolic representations of the process. Thus, the webs served as a scaffold to mediate cognitive performance (Englert, Tarrant, Mariage, & Oxer, 1994).

Finally, teachers used the maps to guide writing processes as they transformed the mapped ideas into written drafts of expository reports about the topic. At first, teachers modeled how to transform webs into scientific texts by making ways-of-talking and ways-of-acting visible to students in think alouds. However, teachers gradually shifted responsibility to students as they began to pair students with other writers in writing teams and dyads. Teachers and students transformed the subclasses of ideas into scientific texts with introductions, main idea and detail sentences, and conclusions. These were constructed in a manner similar to the structures of scientific texts described by Halliday and Martin (1993).

Several studies of the Early Literacy Project classrooms across a number of years revealed that students with mild disabilities seemed to be acquiring a knowledge of reading and writing scientific texts. Their texts became longer and more organized. These improvements were noted within the supported, interactive, and social contexts afforded students during the thematic units, as well as within the independent conditions associated with end-of-year posttesting (Englert et al., 1995). Significant improvements in the ability to write a number of different text structure genres set Early Literacy Project students apart from their control counterparts, suggesting that the apprenticeship of students in the language and discourse of authors, readers, and learners was a critical aspect of independent and successful performance. Moreover, Early Literacy Project students were significantly superior to the control students in reading achievement and writing fluency (Englert, Mariage, Garmon, & Tarrant, in press). Nevertheless, some of the analyses indicated that there were differences among teachers in their ability to construct a lesson discourse that provided access to control of the ways-of-thinking and ways-of-talking that undergirded literacy success (Englert et al., 1995). The authors concluded that descriptive and evaluative studies need to be conducted "that inform educators about the potential value of the various ways of orchestrating the social and dialogic interactions in classrooms in order to develop an understanding of the ways-of-talking and ways-of-thinking that are related to literacy independence and proficiency" (Englert & Mariage, 1996, p. 167).

## Related Literacy Research

There are many other examples of discursive-based approaches to literacy instruction that have been guided by a sociocultural perspective. There are several notable special education researchers whose work has been described within this tradition. Wong (1996), for example, examined the use of interactive models of instruction in teaching revision skills (Wong, Wong, Darlington, & Jones, 1991) and compare-contrast essay writing (Wong, Butler, Ficzere, & Kuperis, 1997). Graham and MacArthur (1988) and Graham and Harris (1989a, 1989b) have also undertaken a highly productive line of research, spanning a decade, that has focused on the effectiveness of strategy instruction in writing. The contributions of these two highly respected lines of work suggest that strategy instruction is effective in mediating the cognitive performance of writers with mild disabilities. Strategy instruction significantly improves the ability of students with disabilities to compose well-organized essays. This research provides evidence that what has been externalized in the social discourse can become internalized by students to direct cognitive performance.

Similarly, in reading, several researchers have made significant progress in contributing to a literature that shows educational applications of a sociocultural approach in special education contexts. Bos and Anders (1990; Bos, Anders, Filip, & Jaffe, 1989) developed interactive discussions and content-enhancing activities to facilitate students' construction of content knowledge and text comprehension. In the interactive teaching and learning strategies models, teachers and students used mediated discussions that entailed the following: (a) activation of prior knowledge using a map or chart, (b) tying new knowledge to old knowledge, (c) reading to confirm and integrate one's understanding and relationships, (d) reviewing and revising the map or chart, and (e) using the map or chart to study what has been learned. The results across four studies revealed substantial effect sizes for the interactive teaching strategies in comparison with vocabulary definition instruction (Bos et al., 1989). This work was extended by Scanlon, Duran, Reyes, and Gallego (1992) in their examination of an interactive semantic mapping model used with students with learning disabilities in Grades 4–6, middle school, and high school. Their study suggested that students who had participated in the interactive semantic mapping condition demonstrated greater recall and comprehension of content area concepts than did students who participated in control conditions. Taken together, this set of studies in the area of expository and narrative comprehension (Idol & Croll, 1987) indicates that semantic maps combined with interactive discourse can mediate reading comprehension and recall by helping teachers and students intellectualize mental functions in such a way that cognitive performance is improved and cognitive processes come under the control of students with disabilities.

Finally, a study by Echevarria and McDonough (1995) focused on a sociocultural approach to the development of instructional conversations in a bilingual special education setting. In contrast to reductionistic approaches to literacy instruction, the instructional conversation model was designed to present reading material in a holistic manner. Reading language was expressed in a natural fashion within a meaningful context as the teacher introduced the story theme or idea, related the theme to students' background experience, guided the generation of prediction questions, read and discussed sections of the text, and related the theme and background knowledge to the ongoing text-based discussions. Rather than dividing the group into a variety of reading levels, the teachers used peers to scaffold the performance of lower readers so that all students could follow the story and participate in the discussion. Over time, the learners came to understand reading as a process of meaning making, as opposed to prior conceptions of reading as a process of sounding out words or working on skills in isolation. Echevarria and McDonough concluded that one of the most important elements of the instructional conversations was the development of themes that provided a cognitive link between the story and the prior knowledge of the bilingual readers with disabilities. The instructional conversations capitalized on what students brought to the situation, rather than solely focusing on remediation of deficit areas, to support learners in the areas of language development, reading comprehension, and the understanding of important concepts (for additional studies with limited English proficient and special education students, see Campione et al., 1994; Klingner & Vaughn, 1996).

In summary, it appears that recent literacy instruction research based on social constructivist theory has enormous potential to enrich the special education knowledge base. Moreover, a growing body of research focusing on constructivistic math and science instruction has started to emerge in the literature (Mercer, Jordan, & Miller, 1996; Scruggs & Mastropieri, 1994). However, considerable disagreement exists among special educators as to how they can best serve children with disabilities. More specifically, special educators are still in conflict over which paradigm should guide instruction in special education. We believe this current state of affairs warrants attention and must be addressed if the field is to move forward. Hence, we conclude the chapter with a discussion about this problem and provide recommendations that might help us transcend current conflicts among individuals who share the common desire to improve educational services and life chances for individuals with disabilities. Specifically, we focus on four areas we consider worthy of greater attention among special education practitioners, teacher educators, and researchers: (a) the need to transcend polarized views, (b) the need for conceptual clarity, (c) the need for refinement of the notions of competence and disability, and (d) the need to view teachers as learners within the context of school-wide reform.

## THE ROAD AHEAD: FUTURE CHALLENGES FOR SPECIAL EDUCATION PRACTICE AND RESEARCH

### Transcending the Paradigm Wars

From our vantage point, we believe that special educators are unable to resolve conflicts related to instruction because we continue to be preoccupied with extreme views that leave no room for integration. This is apparent in the current debates about instruction. It seems that those who oppose social constructivism do so because of extremists who provide only vague descriptions about instruction based on social constructivist principles. Without detailed descriptions, they find it difficult to comprehend how children with disabilities, through student-centered activities facilitated by a teacher, can construct knowledge that will lead to skill mastery. On the other hand, many social constructivists can see only flaws in procedures espoused by extremists at the reductionist end. They are unable to fathom how direct instruction and approaches emanating from behaviorist theory can represent the only ways to teach students with disabilities effectively. Thus, in our preoccupation with extreme views, we fail to see that commonalities exist between the two paradigms. For example, many researchers have documented the effectiveness of approaches deemed by Poplin and others to be ineffective (Engelman, 1997; Engelman, Becker, Carnine, & Gersten, 1988; Lloyd, Epstein, & Cullinan, 1981).

Moreover, components from instructional models deemed by Poplin to be reductionist are included as important components in the work of constructivists.

For instance, when providing students "access to empowering modes of discourse," constructivist teachers expose students to learning strategies and metacognitive skills (although not in a highly scripted, direct instruction format). Scruggs and Mastropieri (1994) found that effective constructivist science teachers still provide students with "carefully structured and sequenced, teacher-led presentations, as well as systematic and effective classroom and behavior management" (p. 307). Mercer, Jordan, and Miller (1996) reported that effective constructivist math teachers provide "a continuum of explicit-to-implicit instruction that accommodates a diversity of learners" (p. 147). Hence, it appears that our inability to transcend extreme views has precluded widespread understanding of how common threads run across various instructional models and paradigms. In a similar fashion, our myopic views have precluded the conduct of research designed to determine the efficacy of integrated models in special education. A growing body of research suggests that effective teachers may not be purists but learn to integrate strategically instructional models based on the needs of their students (Teddlie, Kirby, & Stringfield, 1989). This way of thinking must become the norm rather than the exception among special education theorists and researchers.

## Conceptual Clarity

A problem mentioned consistently in analyses of social constructivism in general and special education is conceptual confusion. For example, Marshall (1996a) stated that there are alternative understandings and formulations of social constructivist approaches. Marshall also alluded to cognitive constructivism and sociocultural theory to illustrate the diversity of understandings among theorists within the same intellectual community. This variety of interpretations has created confusion about certain aspects of social constructivism, including the notion of "construction of knowledge" (e.g., How does it occur?) and the use of the same terms or metaphors to communicate different or changing constructs (e.g., information processing) (Marshall, 1996b). Furthermore, social constructivist research often draws from an interdisciplinary knowledge base in which distinct intellectual communities bring their "ontological, epistemological, and methodological constructs and commitments" to the study of a particular phenomenon (Green et al., 1996, p. 233). This practice has an enormous potential to offer important insights into the education of children with disabilities; however, researchers must clarify the basic constructs, terminology, and definitions used in these studies to minimize conceptual confusion.

Hence, in order to capitalize on notions borrowed from other disciplines, special educators must first understand the intellectual communities from which the constructs were imported. As Green et al. (1996) argued, "To understand the emic, or insider's, point of view, it is necessary to become initiated into the discourse within the community, and to the historical understanding of the development of the ideas within that intellectual ecology" (p. 232). Next, we must be mindful of the need for conceptual clarity in the discourse about and application of social constructivist approaches. In this vein, we must make explicit the underlying theoretical assumptions of the constructs and metaphors used in our research. For example, in our overview of social constructivist research in literacy, we provided descriptions of the underlying principles that guided the research, the activities that teachers used to facilitate/mediate learning, and the resulting outcomes for students. A positive consequence of this practice is a more substantive understanding about the disciplinary roots of the constructs used to develop this research. In addition, operationalization of constructs will promote generalizability, provide examples of effective practice for educators, and pave the way for the development of more assessment tools that can be used to document efficacy (e.g., student and teacher learning, transfer of knowledge).

On the other hand, if we fail to provide explicit rationales and descriptions of practices that are guided by social constructivist theory, and if we fail to document how these practices affect academic outcomes for students, then we will have done little to advance the value of this paradigm, the credibility of our findings, and the emergence of widespread improved learning outcomes for children with disabilities.

## Refinement of a Social Constructivist Theory of Competence and Disability

At this point, we reiterate the fact that many educators who focused on the etiology of learning problems from a deficit perspective did so with the hope of developing interventions to ameliorate or minimize these problems. Moreover, we acknowledge that many children come to school with problems that preclude their ability to progress at a rate—without assistance—commensurate with that of their peers. These problems, deficits, or differences—whatever one wishes to call them—may be genetic (e.g., chromosomal abnormalities, metabolic problems, poor nutrition, neurological difficulties) or behavioral in nature (e.g., "[injurious] activities or maternal substance abuse" [AAMR Ad Hoc Committee, 1992, p. 71]). Even when some of these students receive research-based interventions with a high degree of treatment fidelity, they still may not be able to achieve at a "normal" rate. We cannot deny this reality (Hallahan, in press). However, as we established at the outset of this chapter, it is also known that, for many children labeled with a mild disability, causality is not readily apparent but is still linked, sometimes inappropriately, to deficits that reside within children, their families, and their communities (Artiles & Trent, 1994; Darling-Hammond, 1997; Hardman, Drew, & Egan, 1996; Valencia & Solorzano, 1997).

Keogh, Gallimore, and Weisner (1997) provide us with information about the shortsightedness of this practice. These authors reviewed the cross-cultural literature about reading achievement and found similarities across groups that accounted for some of the difficulty these children experienced in reading. Their review also uncovered beliefs among teachers that, in comparison with students in predominantly Anglo schools, students who attend predominantly African American and Hispanic schools do not receive appropriate reading instruction. Keogh et al. speculated "that inappropriate instructional programs, not just processing deficits in children, account for at least some of the high numbers of problem learners in selected cultural groups" (p. 111). They also found that

in the studies reported, a small number of students continued to be identified as problem learners even under optimal instruction. These may well be children with processing deficits characteristic of the traditional definition of learning disabilities. These children clearly require differentiated remedial instructional programs. (p. 111)

Thus, it is imperative that we develop a more fluid, culturally situated definition of disability that not only identifies deficits but focuses explicitly on student strengths and instructional contexts (Gindis, 1995). Also, this refined definition of disability must focus on factors outside the school setting that may be manipulated to influence student learning. We argue that the tenets of social constructivist theory can help in reaching this goal. For example, a fundamental notion of social constructivism is that development has social origins. As we discussed earlier, Vygotsky (1978) argued that developmental functions first appear on the interpsychological plane through participation in culturally valued activities with more knowledgeable others. Subsequently, children appropriate these functions in the intrapsychological plane. Although Vygotsky did not disregard the biological origin of certain disabilities, he stressed that some impairments are not noticed until they are situated in particular sociocultural contexts; that is, he argued that we must be cognizant of the social psychological consequences of and reactions to impairments (Das, 1995).

Since development has social origins, it stands to reason that human development is semiotically mediated. Specifically, people's social and individual functioning can be mediated by cultural artifacts, including language, values, beliefs, writing, schemes, inner speech, mnemonic strategies, and other symbol systems (Gutierrez, Baquedano-López, & Turner, 1997). Knowledge of the child's ZPD allows teachers to use these cultural artifacts to guide the child toward self-regulated learning. Unfortunately, many discussions about the ZPD have been limited in that they do not acknowledge the multiple levels of an activity embodied in the ZPD and have not recognized the temporal dimension of the ZPD (i.e., the role of teachers' and students' future expectations/goals has been ignored) (Griffin & Cole, 1984). As the definitions of competence and disability are refined, we must remember that a ZPD comprises bidirectional processes in which both the child and the more capable other stretch their understandings, learn, and develop. We contend that the social origin of development view will benefit practice and research in the area of mild disabilities because it will expand our understanding of these individuals' developmental processes and will force us to focus on the mediating role that teachers and peers play in promoting learning and development. In addition, Gindis (1995) explained that the use of the ZPD in assessment (with its emphasis on the ability to benefit from an adult's help) offers the possibility of making qualitative distinctions between groups of students (e.g., students with mental retardation, bilingual learners, and so-called "deprived" children) that might otherwise be indistinguishable by traditional assessment tools (e.g., IQ tests).

Based on this discussion, we contend that, in order to be mediators of learning, teachers must possess accurate cultural historical knowledge. The work of several researchers has shown that this knowledge can be acquired through nontraditional assessment approaches. For example, some researchers have used the Ecocultural Family Interview to glean information from parents that could be used to assist educators in planning for students. According to Keogh et al. (1997):

> This interview is focused on family life, covering aspects of how everyday living is organized, the daily routines, and what is problematic about the routines. Thus, it provides information about domestic workloads, childcare tasks, the use of services, sources of support, roles of spouse, and so forth, as well as information about the parents' perceptions and their short- and long-term goals for their children. (p. 110)

The Ecocultural Family Inventory has been adopted for use with several cultural groups. Preliminary results indicate that this is a useful tool for supplementing traditional assessment measures as well as for informing curricular and instructional decisions. In the future, knowledge about and use of such tools must be incorporated into teacher education programs that prepare preservice and in-service teachers in the areas of assessment and instruction. In addition, teachers must be prepared to take seriously the concerns and goals that parents have for their children with disabilities. As Harry, Allen, and McLaughlin (1996) suggest, teachers should begin dialogue with parents "by discussing parental goals for the child and proceed to discussing how best these goals can be attained. It is important also for teachers to explain the goals they are trying to attain and to clarify for parents how different goals require different methods" (p. 200). In the process, teachers must learn to use the cultural artifacts obtained through discourse with parents to guide their instruction. Finally, teacher educators must prepare teachers to make use of cross-cultural studies that illustrate how the interactions between children's learning styles and instructional programs may differentially affect learning. Several researchers, for example, have determined that sociolinguistic features within a culture may be in conflict with expected modes of communication in classrooms. Failure to consider such differences may influence student learning negatively. On the other hand, researchers have discovered that incorporating culturally specific communicative styles into the classroom setting may contribute to improved learning outcomes for students (Au & Carrol, 1996; Tharp, 1989).

In sum, a social constructivist view of competence and disability has enormous implications for special educators. As suggested in the first section of this chapter, the prevalent view in the special education field has been that disability is located within the individual. Social constructivist theory affords us the possibility to also view "competence," "ability," and "disability" as situated in sociocultural contexts; that is, this theory enables us to develop a more fluid and culturally mediated understanding of difference and competence. Even if these practices do not help us minimize the need for special education, they have the potential to help us provide more powerful interventions that will yield more efficacious outcomes for students with disabilities.

## A View of Teachers as Learners Within the Context of School-Wide Reform

As special educators strive to improve learning for students with disabilities, it is necessary that a view of teachers as learners be established among practitioners, teacher educators, and researchers. As we have noted, a basic tenet of social constructivism is that development is a social phenomenon, yet most inquiries in general and special education have focused on children's learning and developmental processes as if the teachers working with them were invisible. Hence, we contend that our understanding of teaching and learning processes with students with disabilities will be greatly enhanced by conducting investigations of teacher learning within the larger context of school-wide reform. Interestingly, our assertion is consistent with the work of researchers outside the special education field who study how educators implement reform efforts. For example, Elmore, Peterson, and McCarthey (1996), based on their longitudinal study of three school districts engaged in extensive reform efforts, concluded that "the transformation of teaching practice is fundamentally a problem of enhancing individual knowledge and skill, not a problem of organizational structure; getting the structure right depends on first understanding that problem of knowledge and skill" (p. 240).

These and other researchers have also reported that change is difficult to achieve when new skills are required on the part of teachers (e.g., McDiarmid, 1995; Sarason, 1990; Schumm & Vaughn, 1995; Sykes, 1996; Tyack & Cuban, 1995; Wilson, Peterson, Ball, & Cohen, 1996). Hence, just as do children, adults need scaffolds and guidance as they engage in actions designed to accomplish mutually constructed purposes. Unfortunately, there is a paucity of research in the special education literature based on the principles of constructivism that provides rich descriptions of the discourses and actions that lead to teacher learning and development and improved student performance (Dudley-Marling & Dippo, 1995; Hargreaves, 1994; Huberman, 1993). Englert and Tarrant (1995), however, provide us with an exemplar that paves the way for future research.

Through an action research study, these researchers identified a process that led to teacher growth and improved student outcomes. Specifically, teachers needed ongoing assistance from knowledgeable others (e.g., university faculty, other teachers) as they established common visions and engaged in the implementation of reform efforts through study group discourse. Teachers then engaged in discourse with knowledgeable others about the language and acts (e.g., research-based strategies, procedures, and conventions in study groups) that might help them meet the needs of learners with disabilities more appropriately. However, within this framework, Englert and Tarrant (1995) cautioned that teachers must also be allowed to contribute individual goals and choices. In their study, they found that dialogue around constructivist principles of teaching and learning gave teachers the freedom to share stories about the implementation (including revisions and modifications) of research-based interventions. In addition, they found that "within these stories, abstract knowledge was communicated in a language form that could be examined, borrowed, and transformed" (p. 331). Hence, discourse within an interpsychological plane was internalized at the intrapsychological level. Finally, this iterative, discursive process led to self-regulated learning among teachers and resulted in refined practices. For instance, Englert and Tarrant (1995) found that "the content of what teachers had to say at meetings altered, and not just added to, what constituted the Early Literacy Project" (p. 331).

Englert and Tarrant provide us with a framework for studying and facilitating special education reform efforts from a constructivist perspective. Future investigations must continue this line of research, seeking answers to questions such as the following:

1. How might practitioners and researchers construct common purposes as they participate in the implementation of structural and instructional special education reforms?

2. What kinds of assistance and guided participation processes facilitate practitioners' appropriation of tools and practices?

3. How might changes in the sociocultural organization of learning influence learning and development among teachers and students with and without disabilities?

An action research study that aims to answer these questions might proceed as follows. First, members of the study group or learning community will share views about teaching and learning and identify how cumulative teaching experiences, beliefs, knowledge, and skills can be integrated and translated into mutually constructed visions, goals, and actions. Next, mutually constructed hypotheses can be tested through implementation of action plans. Because team members may find it difficult to translate new learning into practice, group members who possess certain skills and expertise must provide scaffolds (e.g., modeling, coaching, feedback) as materials, instructional approaches, and strategies are identified, implemented, and refined. Finally, team members must design ways to assess student and teacher learning based on their "trying out" of integrated approaches. We hypothesize that this action-oriented approach will encourage continual reflection, editing, revising, and refinement of discourse and actions (Osterman & Kottkamp, 1993).

## Data Collection

As Cazden (1986, 1988) recommends, multiple tools to collect data will be required. Sources might include (a) discourse during study group sessions, (b) classroom discourse and actions, and (c) student products and outcomes. Evolving conceptions about teaching and learning can be documented through audiotaped study group sessions, written action plans, videotapes of action plan implementation, observation summaries, and reflexive journals. Student interviews (targeted students with learning disabilities and their nonlabeled peers), videotapes of action plan implementation, observation summaries, and student performance on assessment tools can be used to document changes in student learning.

## Data Analysis

As indicated earlier, the primary focus of such studies will be to document how changes in discourse influence changes in teacher practices and student performance. Hence, the unit of analysis will be not an individual but individuals in context (e.g., the language, objects, persons, and events that interact within the environment) (Gilbert, 1992; Thomas, 1992). In analyzing the data, researchers must search for patterns or rules that emerge in talk and actions and document how these patterns change over time (Cazden, 1986; Lincoln & Guba, 1985).

To establish and maintain trustworthiness and credibility of findings, researchers can use the quasi-judicial approach outlined by Bromley (1986). Major components of this approach include (a) careful and constant scrutiny of data sources, (b) triangulation of the data (Guba & Lincoln, 1994), (c) respondent corroboration of evidence and interpretations, (d) prolonged engagement, and (e) delineation of final interpretations and implications based on ongoing data analysis and member checking procedures.

From a longitudinal standpoint, such studies will document to what extent the actions that emerge from collaborative discourse can result in improved learning for teachers and students with disabilities. Similar to what has occurred in the past, attempts to change the social organization of schools will not be easy. Like Seguin, our efforts will be thwarted by fiscal and systemic constraints, tradition, and incompatible philosophies about teaching and learning. Yet, such inquiry is crucial in helping practitioners and researchers identify patterns in thinking, communication, and actions that improve teaching and learning and contexts wherein these efforts can be created and sustained over time. In addition, studies of this nature should help educators and policymakers identify the types of education and support "enactors" will need in order to provide instruction for an increasingly diverse student population. Finally, in-depth case study research will help us elucidate the messiness and complexity of implementation efforts in special education, providing anchors that will eventually lead to generalizable findings (Walton, 1992).

## Summary and Conclusions

In this chapter, we have examined the theories, research, and instructional practices that have guided the special education field. Specifically, we have discussed how deficit thinking has influenced special education policy, service delivery options, and models of instruction for children with disabilities. In addition, we have summarized emerging practices emanating from social constructivist theory and identified how elements of this theory might contribute to the development of alternative approaches that extend current notions about disability, teaching, and learning. We also have presented challenges that must be tackled by special education researchers and practitioners as they attempt to refine approaches based on social constructivist principles.

As these approaches continue to be refined, we encourage our colleagues to focus less on extreme views and determine—among those of us who hold less extreme views—where our paths cross, where commonalities exist, and where we can integrate the practices emanating from our collective research. Next, we need to embark upon a reform of hope that seeks, as a major goal, to help practitioners bridge the gap between research and practice in a sustained capacity and on a larger scale. Such efforts, which will require increased collaboration among practitioners and researchers, should result in improved outcomes for significantly larger numbers of children with disabilities. To us, this clearly represents the next step for the field of special education. At this point, if we fail to develop reforms and research agendas that bridge the gap between research and practice, then we will have done nothing; as history illustrates, our efforts will result only in continued cosmetic reforms with no significant, widespread benefits for teachers or students. Children who have always learned despite our paradigmatic shifts, structural reforms, and policy changes will continue to learn, and children who have always failed will continue to fail. We must strive to do better.

## REFERENCES

AAMR Ad Hoc Committee on Terminology and Classification. (1992). *Classification in mental retardation* (9th ed.). Washington, DC: American Association on Mental Retardation.

Applebee, A. N. (1996). *Curriculum as conversation.* Chicago: University of Chicago Press.

Artiles, A. J., & Trent, S. C. (1994). Overrepresentation of minority students in special education: A continuing debate. *Journal of Special Education, 27,* 410–437.

Au, K. H., & Carrol, J. H. (1996). Current research on classroom instruction: Goals, teachers' actions and assessment. In D. L. Speece & G. K. Keogh (Eds.), *Research on classroom ecologies: Implications for inclusion of children with learning disabilities* (pp. 17–37). Mahwah, NJ: Erlbaum.

Blatt, B. (1987). *The conquest of mental retardation.* Austin, TX: Proed.

Bos, C. S., & Anders, P. L. (Eds.). (1990). *Interactive teaching and learning: Instructional practices for teaching content and strategic knowledge.* New York: Springer-Verlag.

Bos, C. S., Anders, P. L., Filip, D., & Jaffe, L. E. (1989). The effects of an interactive instructional strategy for enhancing reading comprehension and content area learning for students with learning disabilities. *Journal of Learning Disabilities, 22,* 384–390.

Bromley, D. (1986). *The case study in psychology and related disciplines.* London: Wiley.

Brown, A. L., & Palincsar, A. S. (1987). Reciprocal teaching of comprehension strategies. A natural history of one program for enhancing learning. In J. Borkowski & J. D. Day (Eds.), *Intelligence and cognition in special children* (pp. 81–132). New York: Ablex.

Campione, J. C., Gordon, A., Brown, A. L., Rutherford, M., & Walker, J. (1994). "Now I'm a *real* boy:" Zones of proximal development for those at risk. In N. C. Jordan & J. Goldsmith-Phillips (Eds.), *Learning disabilities: New directions for assessment and intervention* (pp. 245–274). Boston: Allyn and Bacon.

Cazden, C. B. (1986). Classroom discourse. In M. E. Wittrock (Ed.), *Handbook of research on teaching* (3rd ed.). New York: Macmillan.

Cazden, C. B. (1988). *Classroom discourse: The language of teaching and learning.* Portsmouth, NH: Heinemann.

Cole, M. (1996). *Cultural psychology: A once and future discipline.* Cambridge, MA: Harvard University Press.

Coles, G. (1987). *The learning mystique: A critical look at "learning disabilities."* New York: Pantheon.

Darling-Hammond, L. (1997). *The right to learn: A blueprint for creating schools that work.* San Francisco: Jossey-Bass.

Das, J. P. (1995). Some thoughts on two aspects of Vygotsky's work. *Educational Psychologist, 30,* 93–97.

Denti, L. G., & Katz, M. S. (1995). Escaping the cave to dream new dreams: A normative vision for learning disabilities. *Journal of Learning Disabilities, 28,* 415–424.

Dudley-Marling, C., & Dippo, D. (1995). What learning disability does: Sustaining the ideology of schooling. *Journal of Learning Disabilities, 28,* 408–414.

Echevarria, J., & McDonough, R. (1995). An alternative reading approach: Instructional conversations in a bilingual special education setting. *Learning Disabilities Research and Practice, 10,* 108–119.

Elmore, R. F., Peterson, P. L., & McCarthey, S. J. (1996). *Restructuring in the classroom: Teaching, learning, and school organization.* San Francisco: Jossey-Bass.

Engelman, S. (1997). Theory of mastery and acceleration. In J. W. Lloyd, E. J. Kameenui, & D. Chard (Eds.), *Issues in educating students with disabilities* (pp. 177–195). Mahwah, NJ: Erlbaum.

Engelman, S., Becker, W. C., Carnine, D., & Gersten, R. (1988). The direct instruction follow through model: Design and outcomes. *Education and Treatment of Children, 11,* 303–317.

Englert, C. S., Berry, R., Bright, T., & Thornhill, G. (1997, April). *Learning and reasoning: The intellectualization of knowledge in a discourse community.* Paper presented at the annual meeting of the American Educational Research Association, Chicago.

Englert, C. S., Garmon, A., Mariage, T., Rozendal, M., Tarrant, K., & Urba, J. (1995). The Early Literacy Project: Connecting across the literacy curriculum. *Remedial and Special Education, 18,* 253–275.

Englert, C. S., & Mariage, T. V. (1996). A sociocultural perspective: Teaching ways-of-thinking and ways-of-talking in a literacy community. *Learning Disabilities Research and Practice, 11,* 157–167.

Englert, C. S., Mariage, T. V., Garmon, A., & Tarrant, T. K. (in press). Accelerating reading progress in Early Literacy Project classrooms: The potential to return students to grade level. *Remedial and Special Education.*

Englert, C. S., & Palincsar, A. S. (1991). Reconsidering instructional research in literacy from a sociocultural perspective. *Learning Disabilities Research and Practice, 6,* 225–229.

Englert, C. S., Raphael, T. E., & Mariage, T. V. (1994). Developing a school-based discourse for literacy learning: A principled search for understanding. *Learning Disability Quarterly, 17,* 2–32.

Englert, C. S., & Tarrant, K. (1995). Creating collaborative cultures for educational change. *Remedial and Special Education, 16,* 323–336, 353.

Englert, C. S., Tarrant, K. L., Mariage, T. V., & Oxer, T. (1994). Lesson talk as the work of reading groups: The effectiveness of two interventions. *Journal of Learning Disabilities, 27,* 165–185.

Flowers, L. (1994). *The construction of negotiated meaning: A social cognitive theory of writing.* Carbondale: Southern Illinois University Press.

Gee, J. P. (1992). *The social mind: Language, ideology and social practice.* New York: Bergin & Garvey.

Gilbert, R. (1992). Text and context in qualitative educational research: Discourse analysis and the problem of contextual explanation. *Linguistics and Education, 4,* 37–57.

Gindis, B. (1995). The social/cultural implication of disability: Vygotsky's paradigm for special education. *Educational Psychologist, 30,* 77–81.

Graham, S., & Harris, K. R. (1989a). Components analysis of cognitive strategy instruction: Effects on learning disabled students' compositions and self-efficacy. *Journal of Educational Psychology, 81,* 353–361.

Graham, S., & Harris, K. R. (1989b). Improving learning disabled students' skills at composing essays: Self-instructional strategy training. *Exceptional Children, 56,* 201–216.

Graham, S., & MacArthur, C. (1988). Improving learning disabled students' skills at revising essays produced on a word processor: Self-instructional strategy training. *Journal of Special Education, 22,* 133–152.

Green, J. L., Kelly, G. J., Castanheira, L., Esch, J., Frank, C., Hodel, M., Putney, L., & Rodarte, M. (1996). Conceptualizing a basis for understanding: What differences do differences make? *Educational Psychologist, 31,* 227–234.

Griffin, P., & Cole, M. (1984). Current activity for the future: The Zo-ped. In B. Rogoff & J. Wertsch (Eds.), Children's learning in the "zone of proximal development" (*New Directions for Child Development, No. 23*, pp. 45–64). San Francisco: Jossey-Bass.

Guba, E. G., & Lincoln, Y. S. (1994). Competing paradigms in qualitative research. In N. K. Denzin & Y. S. Lincoln (Eds.), *Handbook of qualitative research* (pp. 105–117). Thousand Oaks, CA: Sage.

Gutierrez, K., Baquedano-López, P., & Turner, M. G. (1997). Putting language back into language arts: When the radical middle meets the third space. *Language Arts, 74*, 368–378.

Hallahan, D. P. (in press). Sound bytes from special education reform rhetoric. *Remedial and Special Education.*

Hallahan, D. P., & Cruickshank, W. M. (1973). *Psychoeducational foundations of learning disabilities.* Englewood Cliffs, NJ: Prentice Hall.

Halliday, M. A. K., & Martin, J. R. (1993). *Writing science: Literacy and discursive power.* Pittsburgh, PA: University of Pittsburgh.

Hardman, M. L., Drew, C. J., & Egan, M. W. (1996). *Human exceptionality: Society, school, and family.* Boston: Allyn & Bacon.

Hargreaves, A. (1994). *Changing teachers, changing times: Teachers' work and culture in the postmodern age.* New York: Teachers College Press.

Harry, B., Allen, N., & McLaughlin, M. (1996). "Old-fashioned, good teachers": African American Parents' views of effective early instruction. *Learning Disabilities Research and Practice, 11*, 193–201.

Heshusius, L. (1989). The Newtonian mechanistic paradigm, special education, and contours of alternatives: An overview. *Journal of Learning Disabilities, 22*, 403–415. [[AUTHOR: PLEASE CHECK PAGE NOS.]]

Hicks, D. (1996). Contextual inquiries: A discourse-oriented study of classroom learning. In D. Hicks (Ed.), *Discourse, learning, and schooling* (pp. 104–144). New York: Cambridge University Press.

Huberman, M. (1993). The model of the independent artisan in teachers' professional relations. In J. W. Little & M. W. McLaughlin (Eds.), *Teachers' work: Individuals, colleagues, and contexts* (pp. 11–50). New York: Teachers College Press.

Idol, L., & Croll, V. J. (1987). Story-mapping training as a means of improving reading comprehension. *Learning Disability Quarterly, 10*, 214–230.

Kauffman, J. M. (1997). *Characteristics of behavior disorders of children and youth* (6th ed.). Columbus, OH: Merrill.

Keogh, B. K., Gallimore, R., & Weisner, T. (1997). A sociocultural perspective on learning and learning disabilities. *Learning Disabilities Research and Practice, 12*, 107–113.

Klingner, J. K., & Vaughn, S. (1996). Reciprocal teaching of reading comprehension strategies for students with learning disabilities who use English as a second language. *The Elementary School Journal, 96*(3), 275–293.

Lazerson, M. (1983). The origins of special education. In J. G. Chambers & W. T. Hartman (Eds.), *Special education policies: Their history, implementation, and finance* (pp. 15–47). Philadelphia: Temple University Press.

Lincoln, Y. S., & Guba, E. G. (1985). *Naturalistic inquiry.* Beverly Hills, CA: Sage.

Lloyd, J., Epstein, M. H., & Cullinan, D. (1981). Direct teaching for learning disabilities. In J. Gottlieb & S. S. Strichart (Eds.), *Developmental theory and research in learning disabilities* (pp. 278–309). Baltimore: University Park Press.

MacMillan, D. L, & Hendrick, I. G. (1993). Evolution and legacies. In J. I. Goodlad & T. C. Lovitt (Eds.), *Integrating general and special education* (pp. 23–48). Columbus, OH: Merill/Macmillan.

Marshall, H. H. (1996a). Recent and emerging theoretical frameworks for research on classroom learning: Contributions and limitations [Special issue]. *Educational Psychologist, 31*, 147–240.

Marshall, H. H. (1996b). Guest editor's introduction. *Educational Psychologist, 31*, 147–149.

Marshall, H. H. (1996c). Implications of differentiating and understanding constructivist approaches. *Educational Psychologist, 31*, 235–240.

McDiarmid, G. W. (1995). *Realizing new learning for all students: A framework for the professional development of Kentucky teachers.* East Lansing: National Center for Research on Teacher Learning, Michigan State University.

Menchaca, M. (1997). Early racist discourses: The roots of deficit thinking. In R. Valencia (Ed.), *The evolution of deficit thinking* (pp. 13–40). New York: Falmer.

Mercer, C. D., Jordan, L., & Miller, S. P. (1996). Constructivistic math instruction for diverse learners. *Learning Disabilities Research and Practice, 11,* 147–156.

Mercer, J. R. (1973). *Labeling the mentally retarded: Clinical and social system perspectives on mental retardation.* Berkeley: University of California Press.

Michaels, S., & O'Connor, M. C. (1990). *Literacy as reasoning within multiple discourses: Implications for policy and education reform.* Paper presented at the Summer Institute for the Council of Chief State School Officers, Newton, MA.

Newman, D., Griffin, P., & Cole, M. (1989). *The construction zone: Working for cognitive change in school.* New York: Cambridge University Press.

Osterman, K. F., & Kottkamp, R. B. (1993). *Reflective practice for educators: Improving schooling through professional development.* Newbury Park, CA: Corwin Press.

Palincsar, A. S. (1984, April). *Reciprocal teaching: Working with the zone of proximal development.* Paper presented at the annual meeting of the American Educational Research Association, New Orleans, LA.

Palincsar, A. S. (1986). The role of dialogue in providing scaffolded instruction. *Educational Psychologist, 21,* 73–98.

Palincsar, A. S., & Brown, A. L. (1984). Reciprocal teaching of comprehension-fostering and comprehension-monitoring activities. *Cognition and Instruction, 1,* 117–175.

Palincsar, A. S., & Brown, A. L. (1989). Classroom dialogues to promote self-regulated comprehension. In *Advances in research on teaching* (Vol. 1, pp. 35–71). Greenwich, CT: JAI Press.

Poplin, M. S. (1985). Reductionism from the medical model to the classroom: The past, present and future of learning disabilities. *Research Communications in Psychology, Psychiatry and Behavior, 10*(1–2), 37–70.

Poplin, M. S. (1988). The reductionistic fallacy in learning disabilities: Replicating the past by reducing the present. *Journal of Learning Disabilities, 21,* 389–400.

Richardson, J. G. (1979). The case of special education and minority misclassification in California. *Educational Research Quarterly, 4,* 25–40.

Rizzo, J. V., & Zabel, R. H. (1988). *Educating children and adolescents with behavioral disorders: An integrative approach.* Boston: Allyn & Bacon.

Robinson, N. M., & Robinson, H. B. (1976). *The mentally retarded child: A psychological approach* (2nd ed.). New York: McGraw-Hill.

Rothman, D. (1971). *The discovery of the asylum: Social order and disorder in the new republic.* Boston: Little, Brown.

Sarason, S. B. (1990). *The predictable failure of educational reform: Can we change course before it's too late?* San Francisco: Jossey-Bass.

Sarason, S. B., & Doris, J. (1979). *Educational handicap, public policy, and social history: A broadened perspective on mental retardation.* New York: Free Press.

Scanlon, D., Duran, G. Z., Reyes, E., & Gallego, M. A. (1992). Interactive semantic mapping: An interactive approach to enhancing LD students' content area comprehension. *Learning Disabilities Research and Practice, 7,* 142–146.

Schumm, J. S., & Vaughn, S. (1995). Meaningful professional development in accommodating students with disabilities: Lessons learned. *Remedial and Special Education, 16,* 344–353.

Scruggs, T. E., & Mastropieri, M. S. (1994). The construction of scientific knowledge by students with mild disabilities. *Journal of Special Education, 28,* 307–321.

Sleeter, C. E. (1996). Radical structuralist perspectives on the creation and use of learning disabilities. In T. M. Skrtic (Ed.), *Disability and democracy: Reconstructing (special) education for postmodernity* (pp. 153–165). New York: Teachers College Press.

Stone, C. A. (1989). Improving the effectiveness of strategy training for learning disabled students: The role of communicational dynamics. *Remedial and Special Education, 10*(10), 35–42.

Stone, C. A., & Reid, D. K. (1994). Social and individual forces in learning: Implications for instruction of children with learning difficulties. *Learning Disability Quarterly, 17,* 72–86.

Stribling, R. T. (1842). Physician and superintendent's report. In *Annual reports of the court of directors of the Western Lunatic Asylum to the Legislature of Virginia.* Richmond, VA: Shepherd & Conlin.

Sykes, G. (1996). Reform of and as professional development. *Phi Delta Kappan, 77,* 464–467.

Teddlie, C., Kirby, P. G., & Stringfield, S. (1989). Effective versus ineffective schools: Observable differences in the classroom. *American Journal of Education, 97,* 221–236.

Tharp, R. G. (1989). Psychocultural variables and constants: Effects on teaching and learning in schools. *American Psychologist, 44,* 349–359.

Tharp, R. (1993). Institutional and social context of educational practice and reform. In E. A. Forman, N. Minick, & C. A. Stone (Eds.), *Contexts for learning: Sociocultural dynamics in children's development* (pp. 269–282). New York: Oxford University Press.

Thomas, D. (1992, April). *Putting nature to the rack: Narrative studies as research.* Paper presented at the Teachers' Stories of Life and Work Conference, Liverpool, England.

Trent, S. C., & Artiles, A. J. (1995). Serving culturally diverse students with behavior disorders: Broadening current perspectives. In J. M. Kauffman, J. W. Lloyd, T. A. Astuto, & D. P. Hallahan (Eds.), *Issues in the educational placements of pupils with emotional or behavioral disorders* (pp. 215–249). Hillsdale, NJ: Erlbaum.

Tucker, J. A. (1980). Ethnic proportions in classes for the learning disabled: Issues in nonbiased assessment. *Journal of Special Education, 14,* 94–105.

Tyack, D. B., & Cuban, L. (1995). *Tinkering toward Utopia: A century of public school reform.* Cambridge, MA: Harvard University Press.

Valencia, R. R., & Solorzano, D. G. (1997). Contemporary deficit thinking. In R. Valencia (Ed.), *The evolution of deficit thinking* (pp. 160–210). New York: Falmer.

Vygotsky, L. S. (1978). *Mind in society.* Cambridge, MA: Harvard University Press.

Vygotsky, L. S. (1993). The collective as a factor in the development of the abnormal child. In R. W. Rieber & A. S. Carton (Eds.), *The collected works of L. S. Vygotsky: The fundamentals of defectology (Abnormal psychology and learning disabilities), Vol. 2.* New York: Plenum.

Walton, J. (1992). Making the theoretical case. In C. Ragin & H. Becker (Eds.), *What is a case? The foundations of social inquiry* (pp. 121–137). Cambridge, England: Cambridge University Press.

Wells, G., & Chang-Wells, G. L. (1992). *Constructing knowledge together: Classrooms as centers of inquiry and literacy.* Portsmouth, NH: Heinemann.

Wertsch, J. V. (1991). *Voices of the mind: A sociocultural approach to mediated action.* Cambridge, MA: Harvard University Press.

Wertsch, J. V. (1994). Mediated action in sociocultural studies. *Mind, Culture, and Activity, 1,* 202–208.

Wertsch, J. V., Tulviste, P., & Hagstrom, F. (1993). A social approach to agency. In E. A. Forman, N. Minick, & C. A. Stone (Eds.), *Contexts for learning: Sociocultural dynamics in children's development* (pp. 336–356). New York: Oxford University Press.

Wilson, S. M., Peterson, P. L., Ball, D. L., & Cohen, D. K. (1996). Learning by all. *Phi Delta Kappan, 77,* 468–476.

Wong, B. Y. L. (1996). *The ABCs of learning disabilities.* New York: Academic Press.

Wong, B. Y. L., Butler, D. L., Ficzere, S. A., & Kuperis, S. (1997). Teaching adolescents with learning disabilities and low achievers to plan, write, and revise compare-and-contrast essays. *Learning Disabilities Research and Practice, 12,* 2–15.

Wong, B. Y. L., Wong, R., Darlington, D., & Jones, W. (1991). Interactive teaching: An effective way to teach revision skills to adolescents with learning disabilities. *Learning Disabilities Research and Practice, 6,* 117–127.

Manuscript received October 20, 1997
Accepted December 24, 1997